SHINOBU OHTAKA

It's Magi, volume 18!
Pay attention!!!

MAGI
Volume 18
Shonen Sunday Edition

Story and Art by
SHINOBU OHTAKA

MAGI Vol.18
by Shinobu OHTAKA
© 2009 Shinobu OHTAKA
All rights reserved.
Original Japanese edition published by SHOGAKUKAN.
English translation rights in the United States of America, Canada, the United Kingdom,
Ireland, Australia and New Zealand arranged with SHOGAKUKAN.

Translation & English Adaptation ◆ John Werry

Touch-up Art & Lettering ◆ Stephen Dutro

Editor ◆ Mike Montesa

Printed in the U.S.A.

Published by VIZ Media, LLC
P.O. Box 77010
San Francisco, CA 94107

10 9 8 7 6 5 4 3 2 1
First printing, June 2016

WWW.SHONENSUNDAY.COM

www.viz.com

MAGI

The labyrinth of magic

18

Story & Art by
SHINOBU OHTAKA

MAGI
The labyrinth of magic
18

CONTENTS

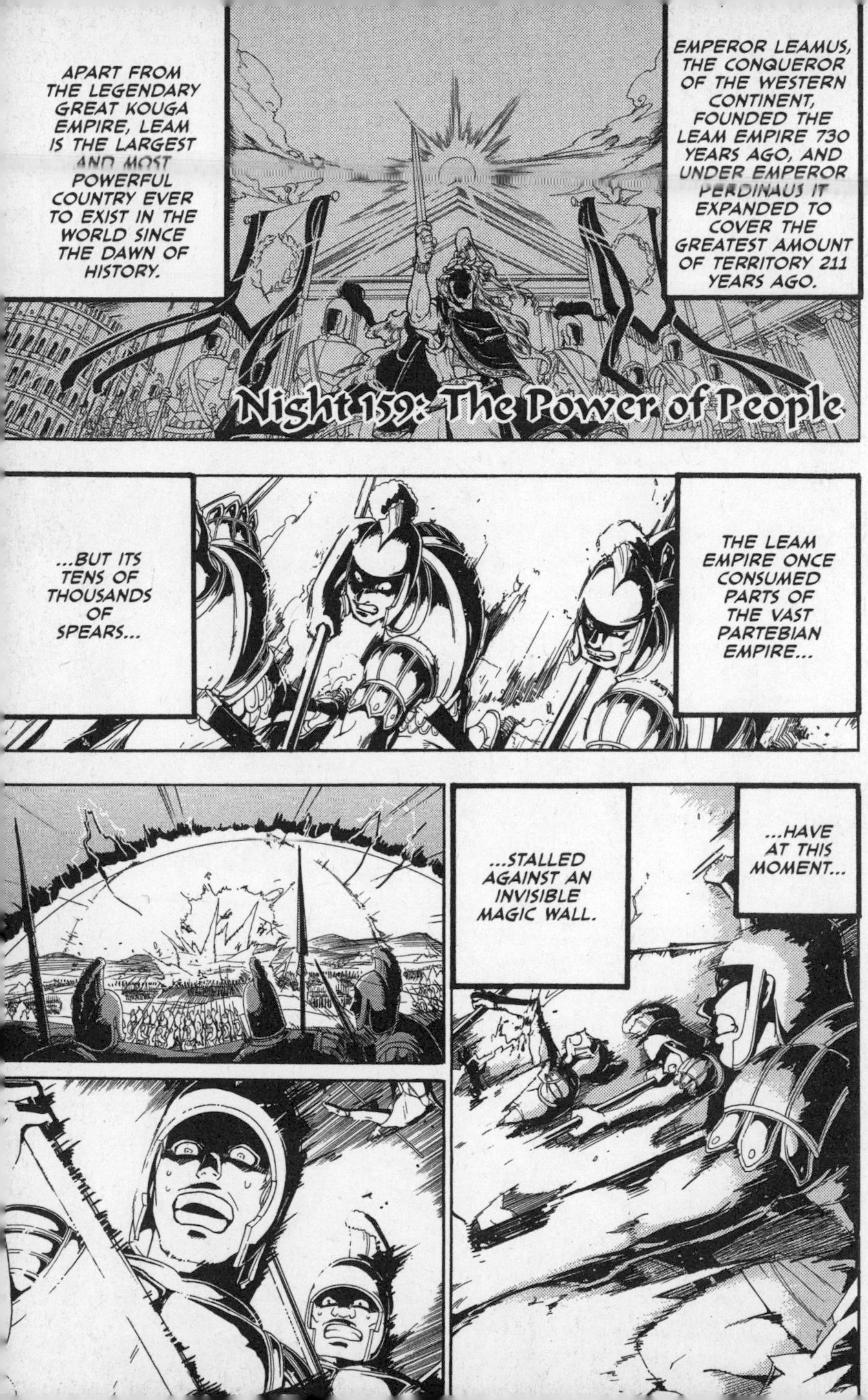
EMPEROR LEAMUS, THE CONQUEROR OF THE WESTERN CONTINENT, FOUNDED THE LEAM EMPIRE 730 YEARS AGO, AND UNDER EMPEROR PERDINAUS IT EXPANDED TO COVER THE GREATEST AMOUNT OF TERRITORY 211 YEARS AGO.
APART FROM THE LEGENDARY GREAT KOUGA EMPIRE, LEAM IS THE LARGEST AND MOST POWERFUL COUNTRY EVER TO EXIST IN THE WORLD SINCE THE DAWN OF HISTORY.
Night 159: The Power of People
THE LEAM EMPIRE ONCE CONSUMED PARTS OF THE VAST PARTEBIAN EMPIRE...
...BUT ITS TENS OF THOUSANDS OF SPEARS...
...HAVE AT THIS MOMENT...
...STALLED AGAINST AN INVISIBLE MAGIC WALL.

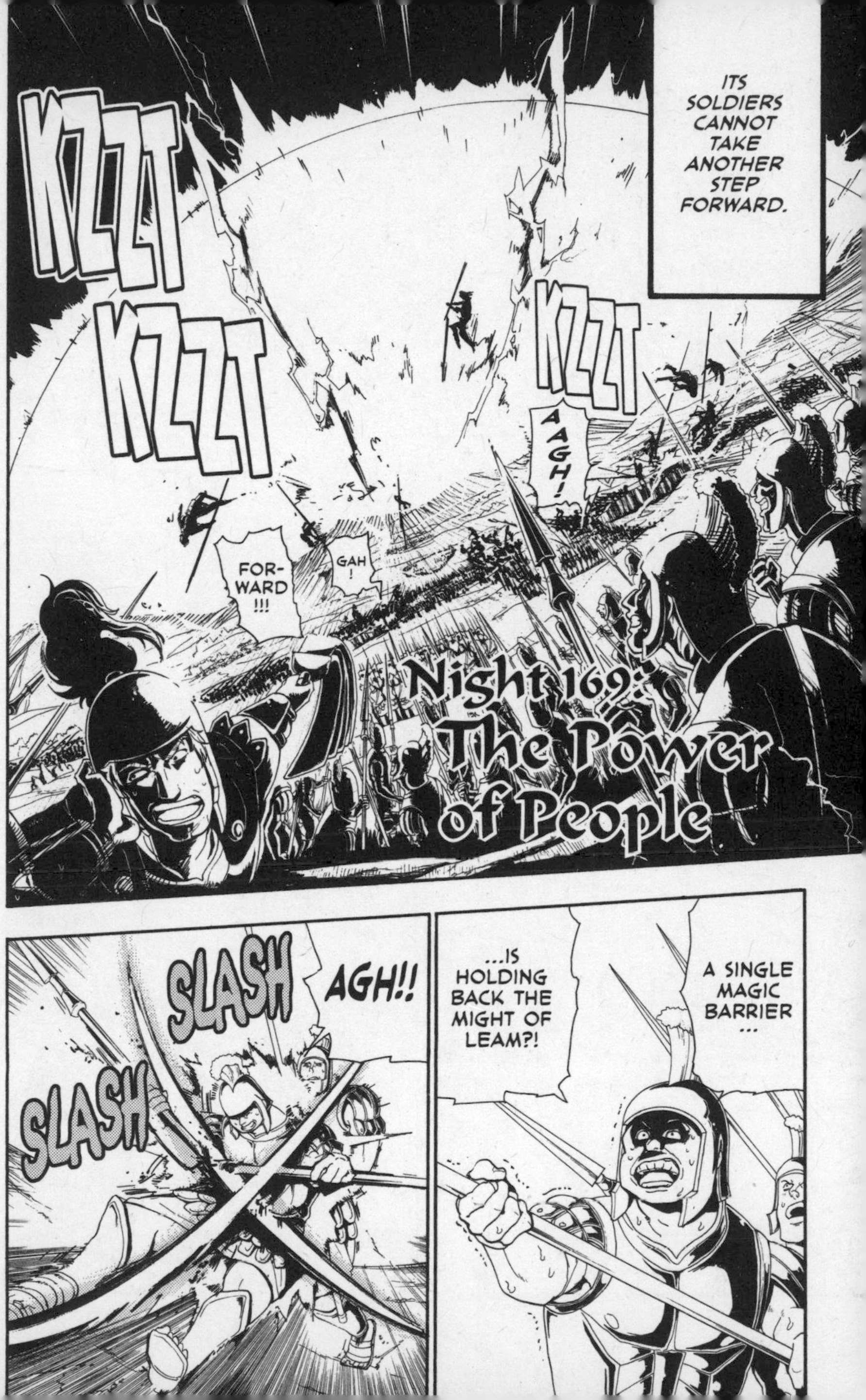
ITS SOLDIERS CANNOT TAKE ANOTHER STEP FORWARD.
KZZT
AAGH!
KZZZT
KZZZT
GAH!
FOR-WARD!!!
Night 169: The Power of People
A SINGLE MAGIC BARRIER ...
...IS HOLDING BACK THE MIGHT OF LEAM?!
AGH!!
SLASH
SLASH

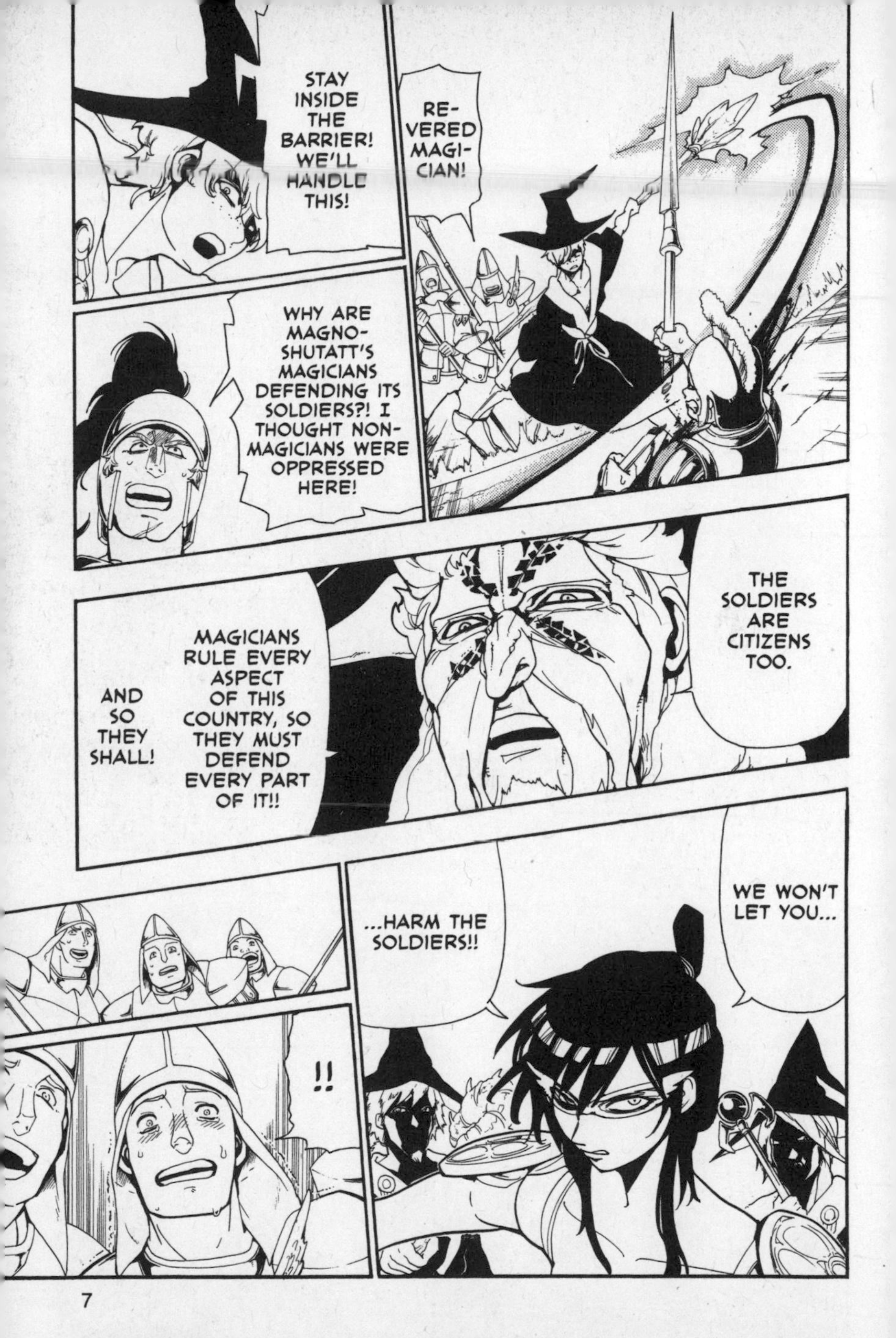
RE-VERED MAGI-CIAN!
STAY INSIDE THE BARRIER! WE'LL HANDLE THIS!
WHY ARE MAGNO-SHUTATT'S MAGICIANS DEFENDING ITS SOLDIERS?! I THOUGHT NON-MAGICIANS WERE OPPRESSED HERE!
THE SOLDIERS ARE CITIZENS TOO.
MAGICIANS RULE EVERY ASPECT OF THIS COUNTRY, SO THEY MUST DEFEND EVERY PART OF IT!!
AND SO THEY SHALL!
WE WON'T LET YOU...
...HARM THE SOLDIERS!!
!!

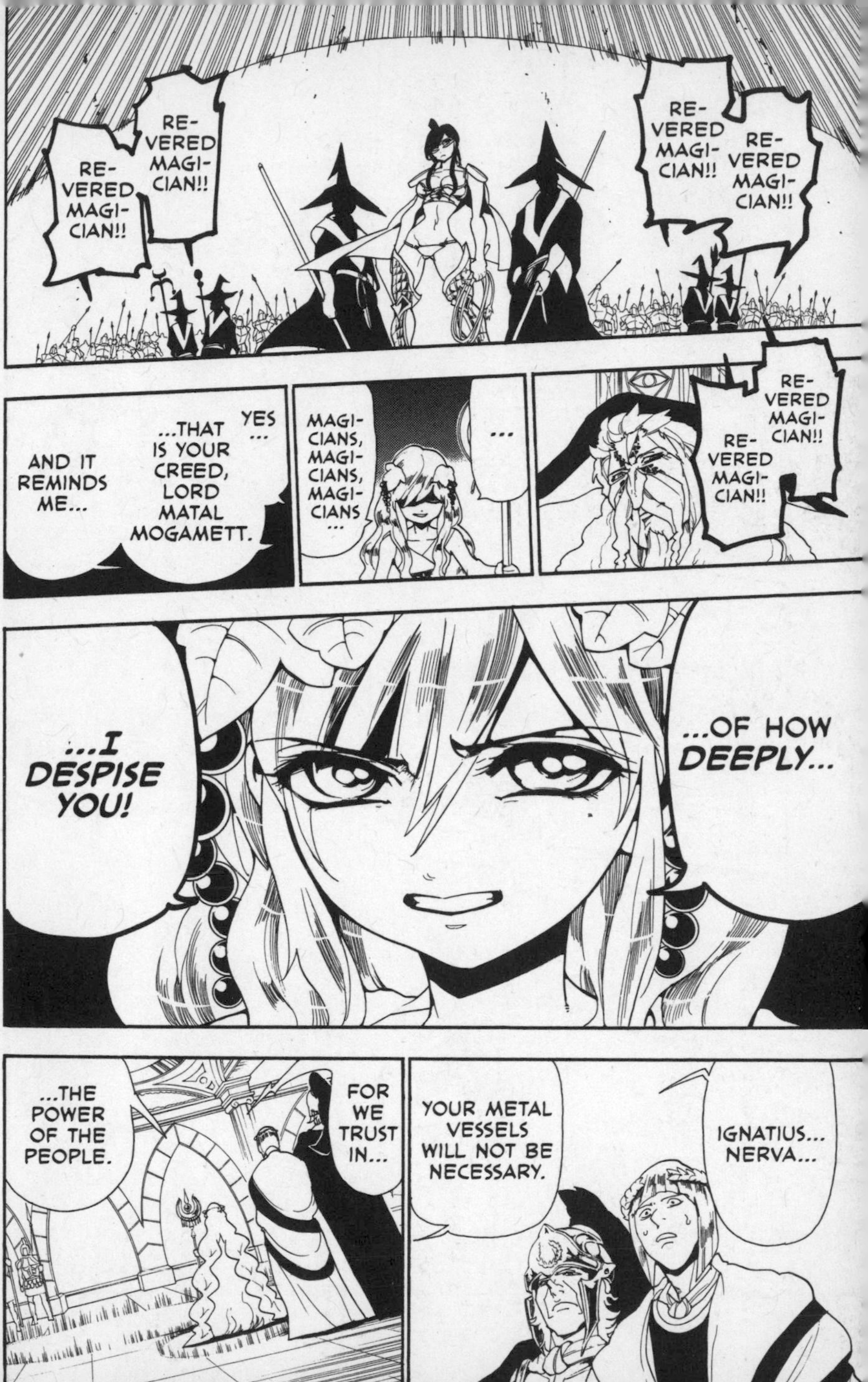
REVERED MAGICIAN!!
REVERED MAGICIAN!!
REVERED MAGICIAN!!
REVERED MAGICIAN!!
REVERED MAGICIAN!!
REVERED MAGICIAN!!
...
MAGICIANS, MAGICIANS, MAGICIANS...
YES...
...THAT IS YOUR CREED, LORD MATAL MOGAMETT.
AND IT REMINDS ME...
...OF HOW *DEEPLY*...
...I *DESPISE YOU!*
IGNATIUS... NERVA...
YOUR METAL VESSELS WILL NOT BE NECESSARY.
FOR WE TRUST IN...
...THE POWER OF THE PEOPLE.

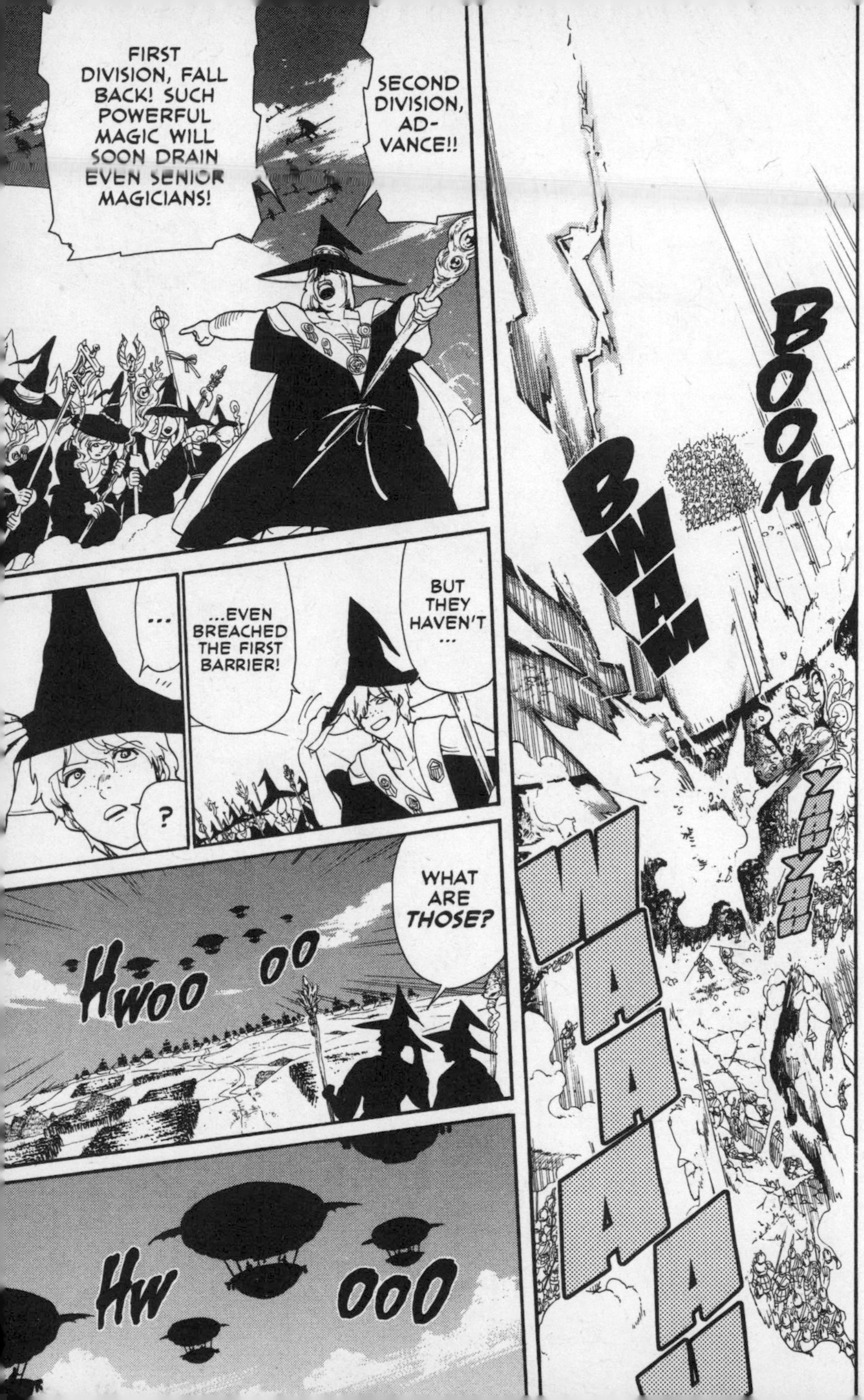

BOOM
BWAM
YAAAYAAA
WAAAA!!
SECOND DIVISION, ADVANCE!!
FIRST DIVISION, FALL BACK! SUCH POWERFUL MAGIC WILL SOON DRAIN EVEN SENIOR MAGICIANS!
BUT THEY HAVEN'T...
...EVEN BREACHED THE FIRST BARRIER!
...
?
WHAT ARE THOSE?
HWOO OO
HW OOO

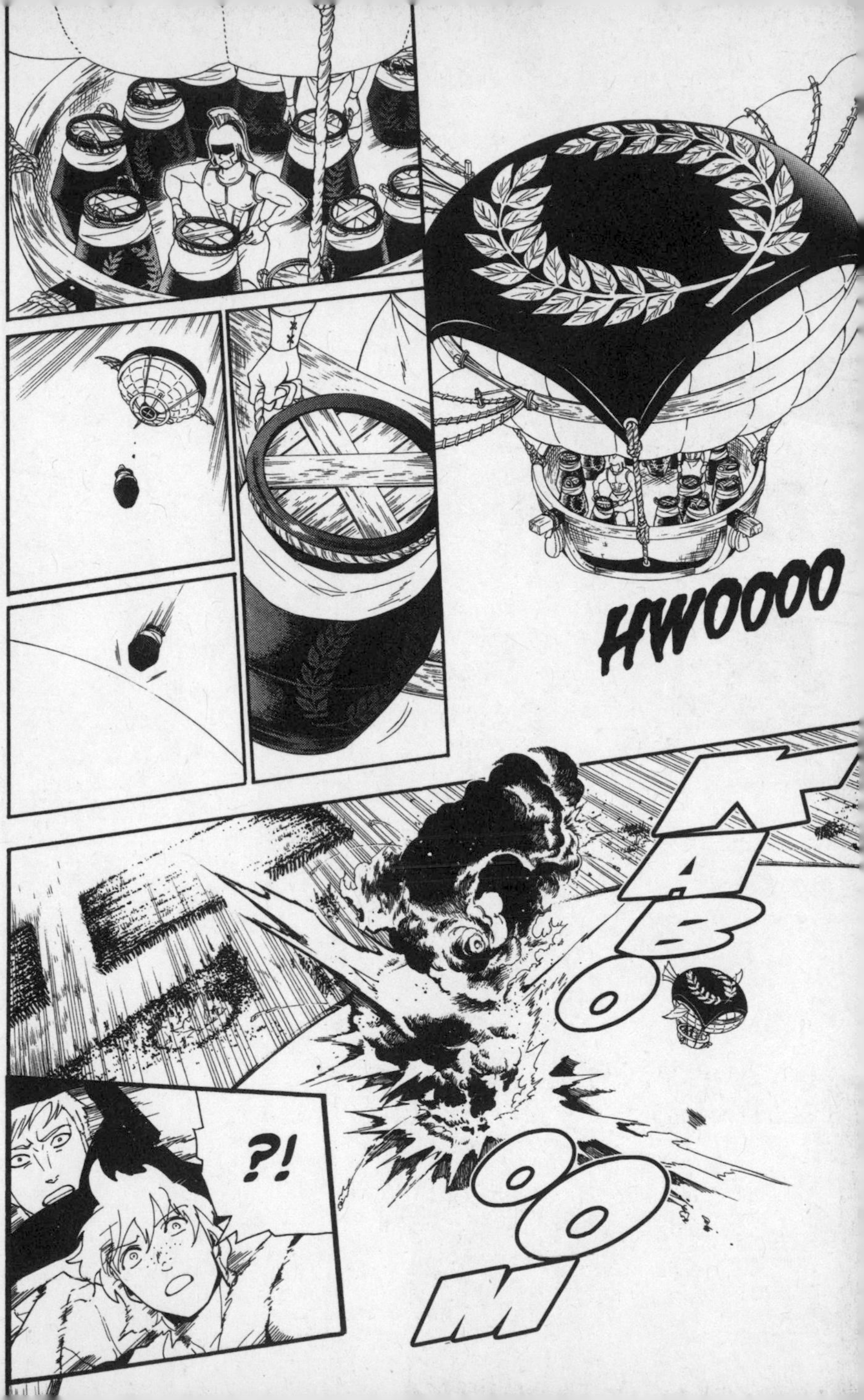
HWOOOO
KABOOOOM
?!

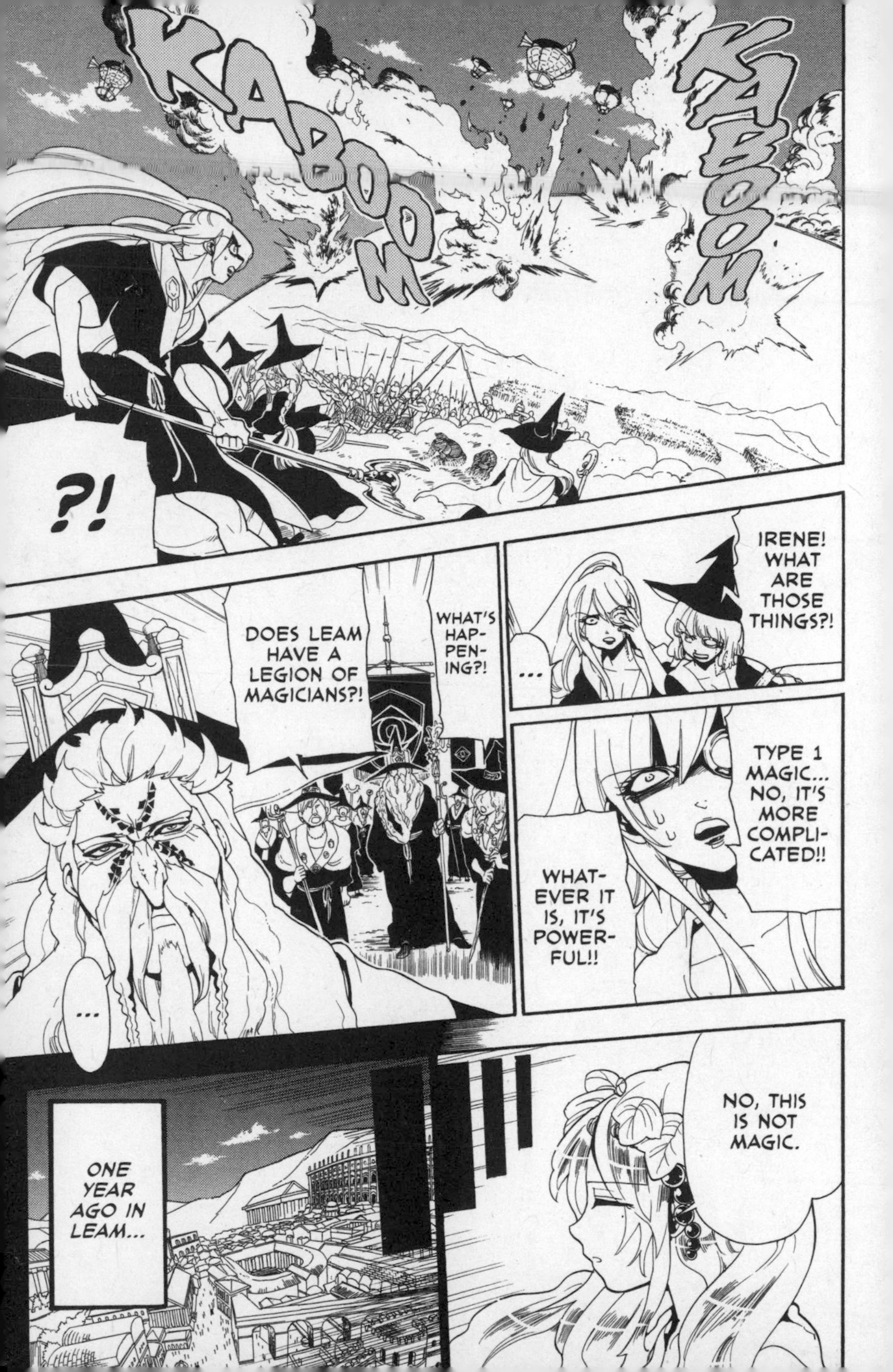
KABOOM
KABOOM
?!
IRENE! WHAT ARE THOSE THINGS?!
...
TYPE 1 MAGIC... NO, IT'S MORE COMPLICATED!!
WHATEVER IT IS, IT'S POWERFUL!!
WHAT'S HAPPENING?!
DOES LEAM HAVE A LEGION OF MAGICIANS?!
...
NO, THIS IS NOT MAGIC.
ONE YEAR AGO IN LEAM...

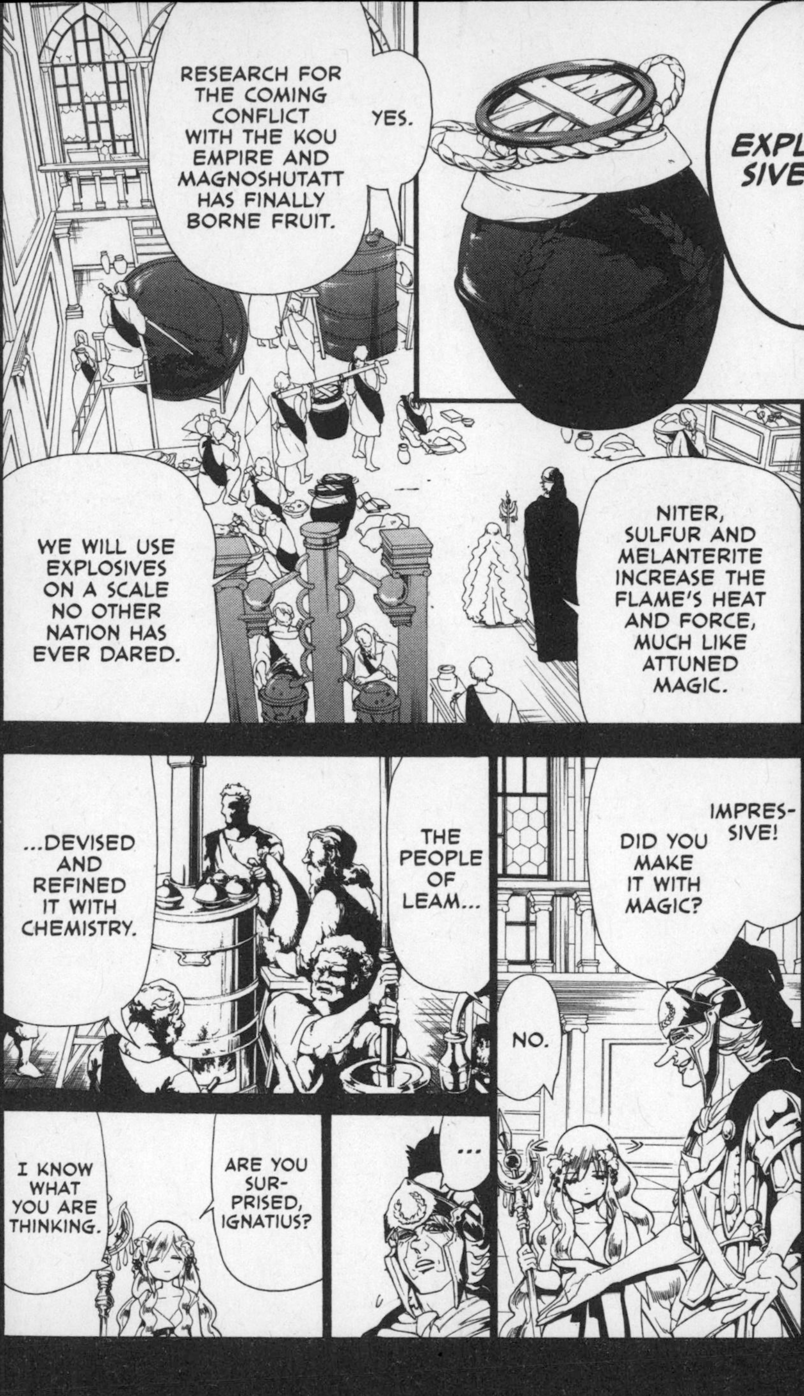
EXPLOSIVES?
YES.
RESEARCH FOR THE COMING CONFLICT WITH THE KOU EMPIRE AND MAGNOSHUTATT HAS FINALLY BORNE FRUIT.
NITER, SULFUR AND MELANTERITE INCREASE THE FLAME'S HEAT AND FORCE, MUCH LIKE ATTUNED MAGIC.
WE WILL USE EXPLOSIVES ON A SCALE NO OTHER NATION HAS EVER DARED.
IMPRESSIVE!
DID YOU MAKE IT WITH MAGIC?
NO.
THE PEOPLE OF LEAM...
...DEVISED AND REFINED IT WITH CHEMISTRY.
...
ARE YOU SURPRISED, IGNATIUS?
I KNOW WHAT YOU ARE THINKING.

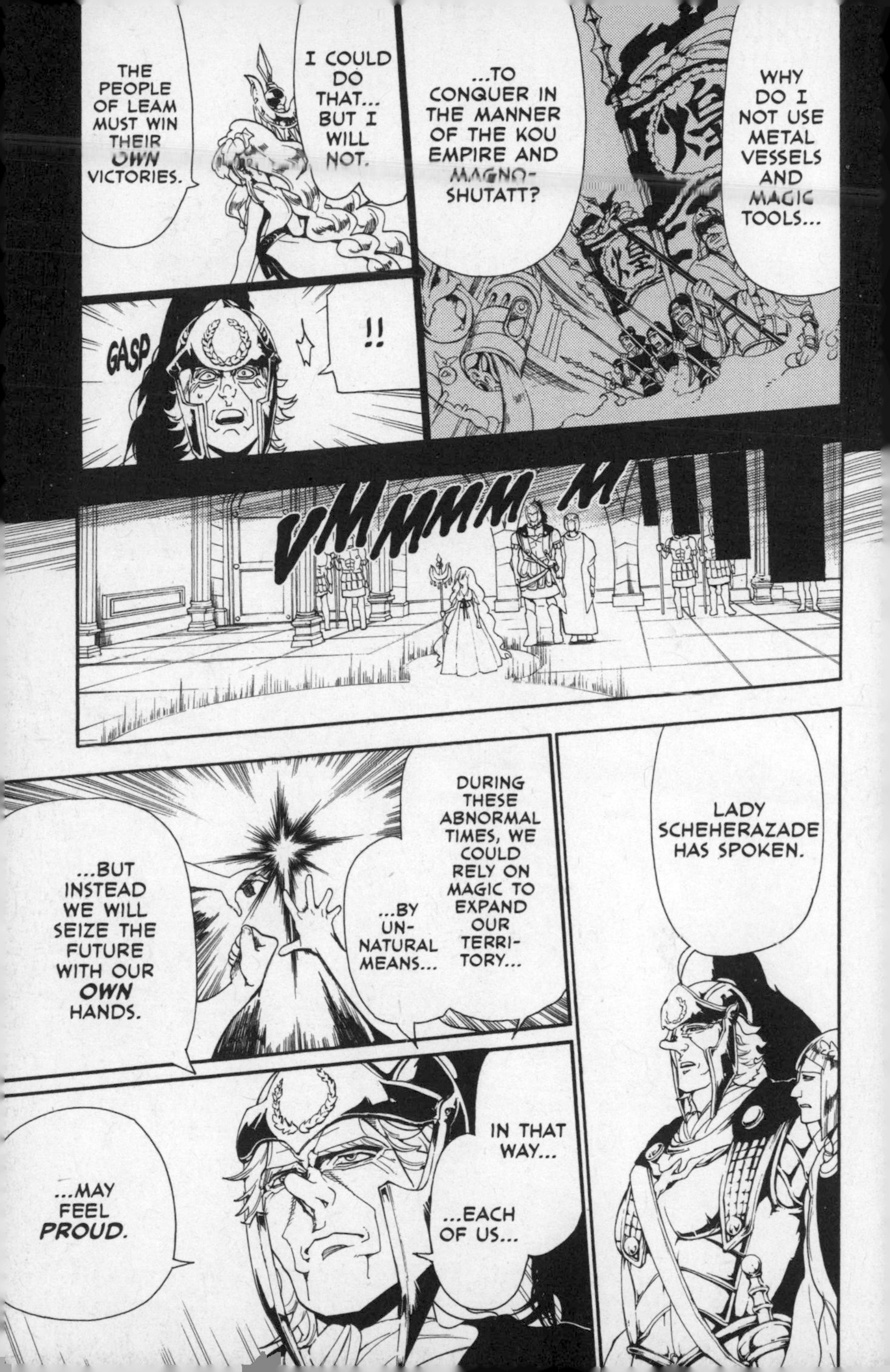
WHY DO I NOT USE METAL VESSELS AND MAGIC TOOLS...
...TO CONQUER IN THE MANNER OF THE KOU EMPIRE AND MAGNO-SHUTATT?
I COULD DO THAT... BUT I WILL NOT.
THE PEOPLE OF LEAM MUST WIN THEIR OWN VICTORIES.
GASP
!!
VMMMM M
LADY SCHEHERAZADE HAS SPOKEN.
DURING THESE ABNORMAL TIMES, WE COULD RELY ON MAGIC TO EXPAND OUR TERRITORY...
...BY UN-NATURAL MEANS...
...BUT INSTEAD WE WILL SEIZE THE FUTURE WITH OUR OWN HANDS.
IN THAT WAY...
...EACH OF US...
...MAY FEEL PROUD.

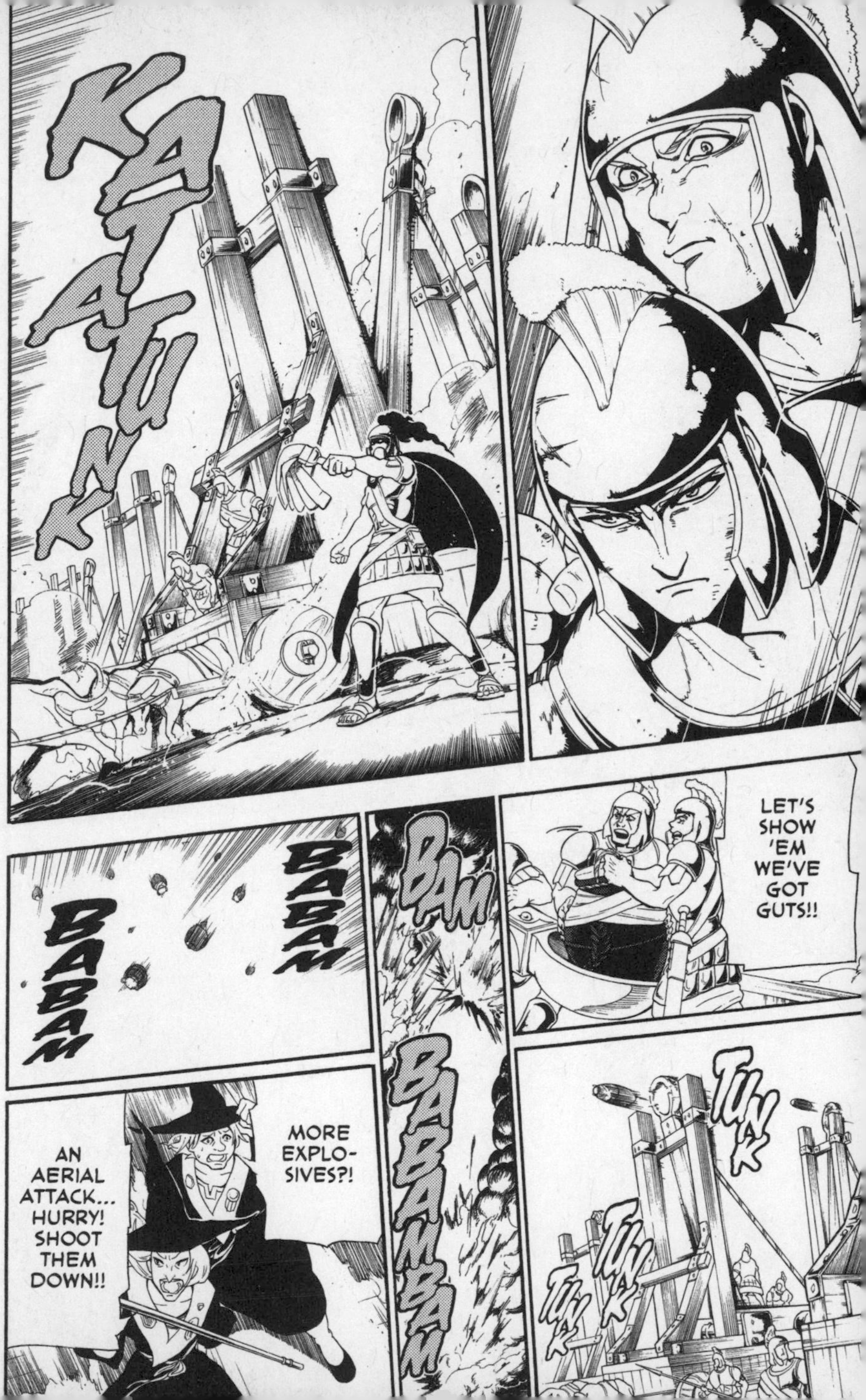
KATATUNK
LET'S SHOW 'EM WE'VE GOT GUTS!!
TUNAK
TUNAK
TUNAK
BAM
BABABAMBAM
BABAM
BABAM
MORE EXPLOSIVES?!
AN AERIAL ATTACK... HURRY! SHOOT THEM DOWN!!

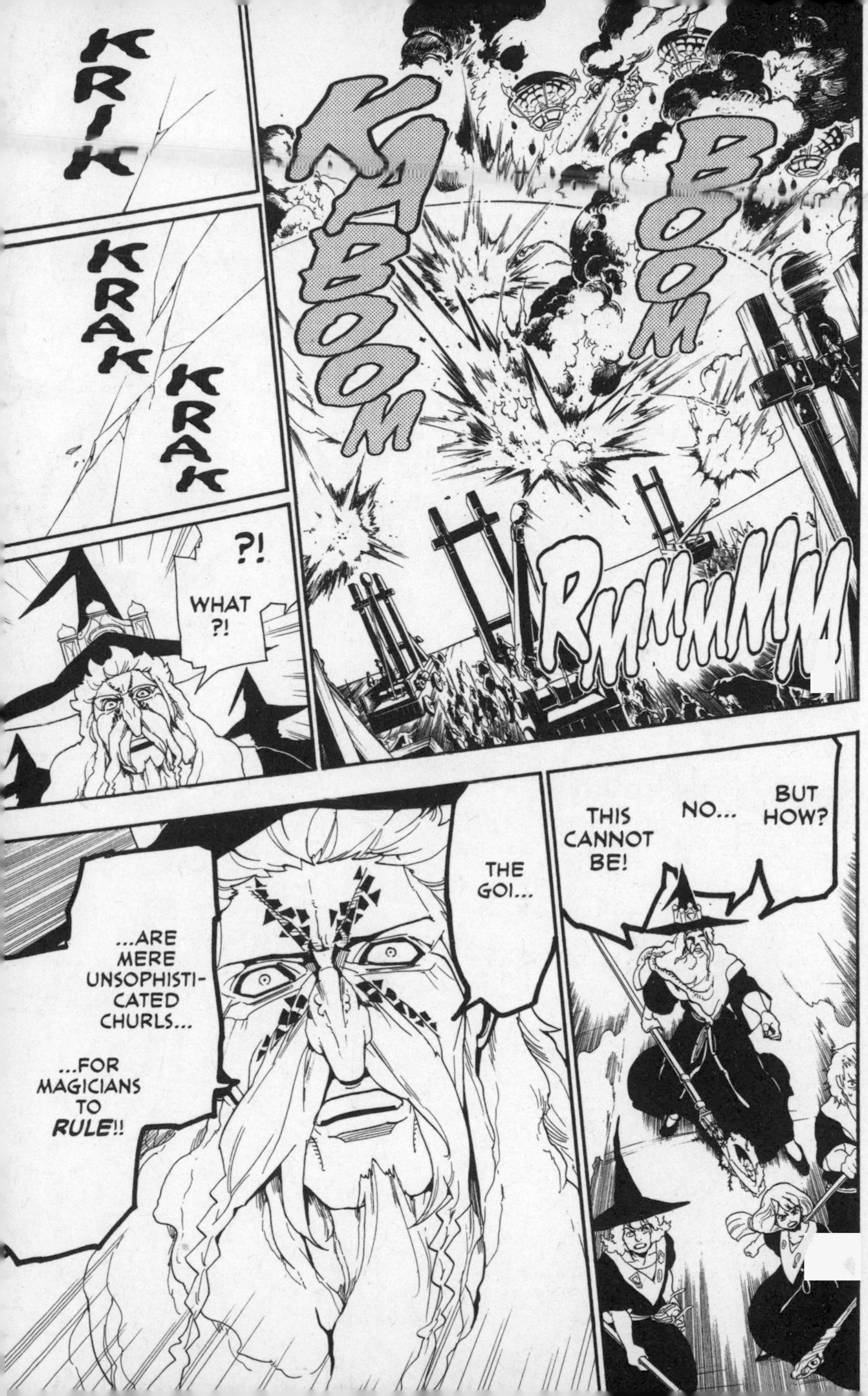

BOOM
KABOOM
RUMMMMM
KRIK
KRAK
KRAK
?!
WHAT?!
BUT HOW?
NO...
THIS CANNOT BE!
THE GOI...
...ARE MERE UNSOPHISTI-CATED CHURLS...
...FOR MAGICIANS TO *RULE*!!

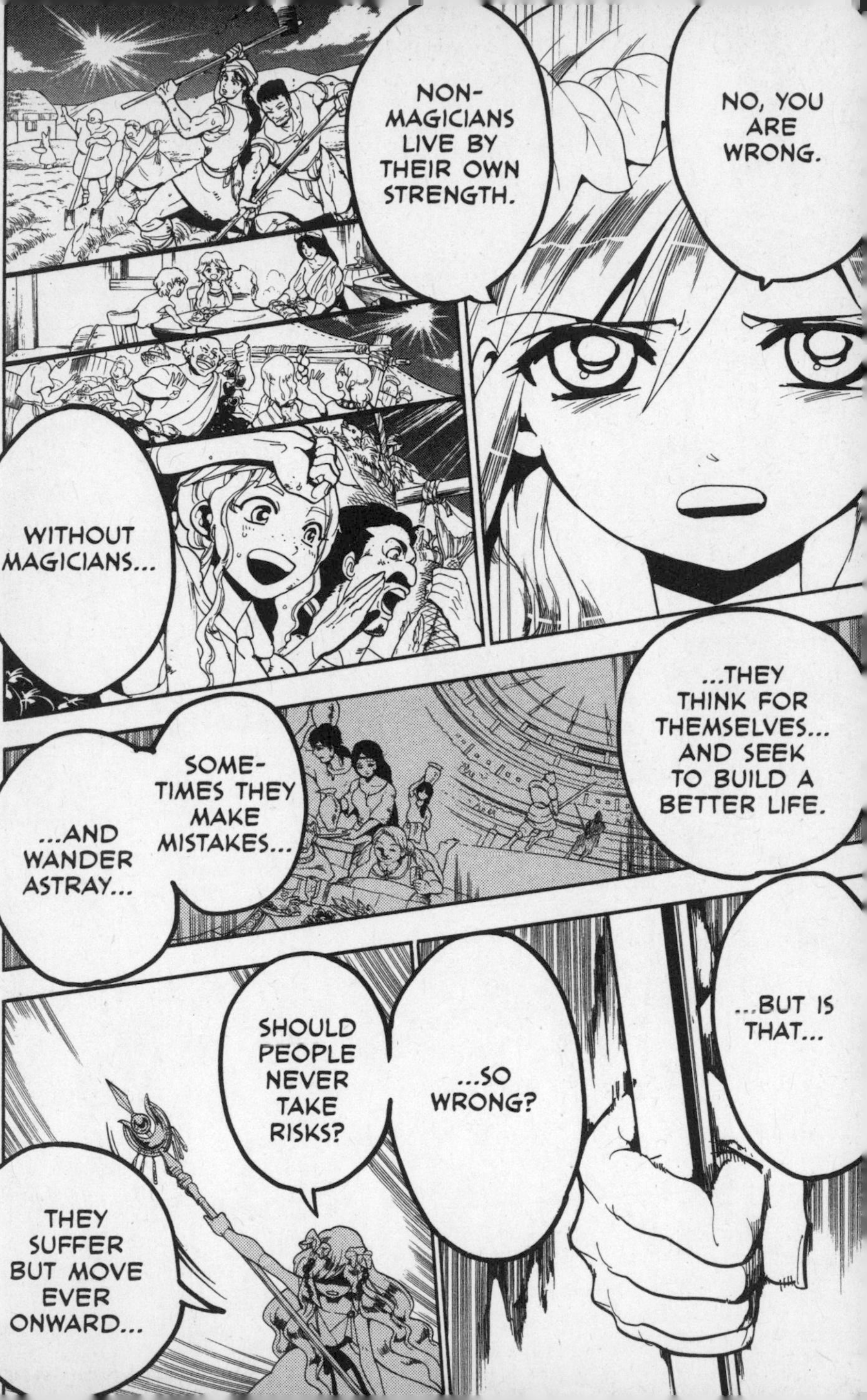
NO, YOU ARE WRONG.
NON-MAGICIANS LIVE BY THEIR OWN STRENGTH.
WITHOUT MAGICIANS...
...THEY THINK FOR THEMSELVES... AND SEEK TO BUILD A BETTER LIFE.
SOME-TIMES THEY MAKE MISTAKES...
...AND WANDER ASTRAY...
...BUT IS THAT...
...SO WRONG?
SHOULD PEOPLE NEVER TAKE RISKS?
THEY SUFFER BUT MOVE EVER ONWARD...

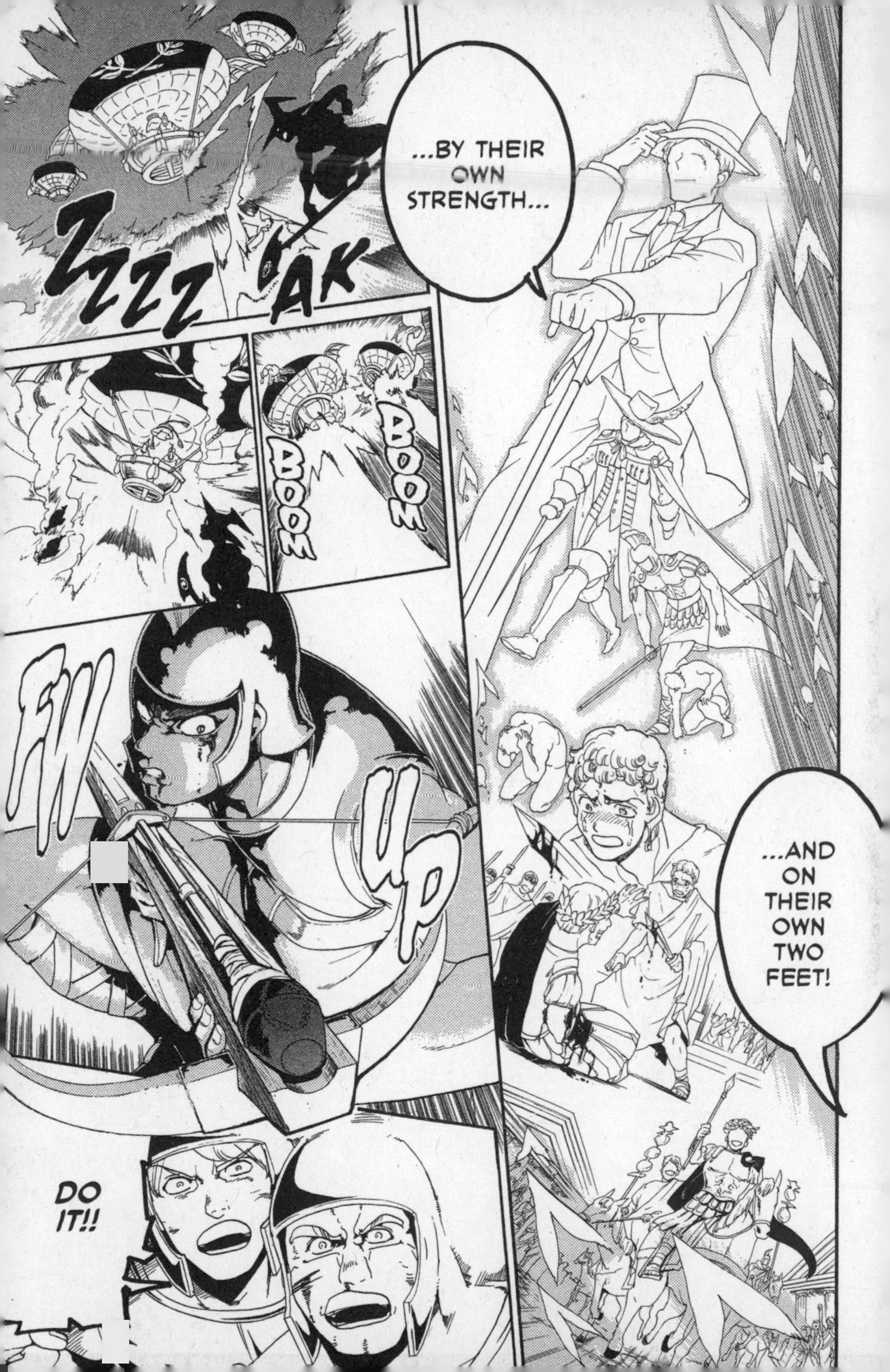
...BY THEIR OWN STRENGTH...
...AND ON THEIR OWN TWO FEET!
ZZZZAK
BOOM
BOOM
FWUP
DO IT!!

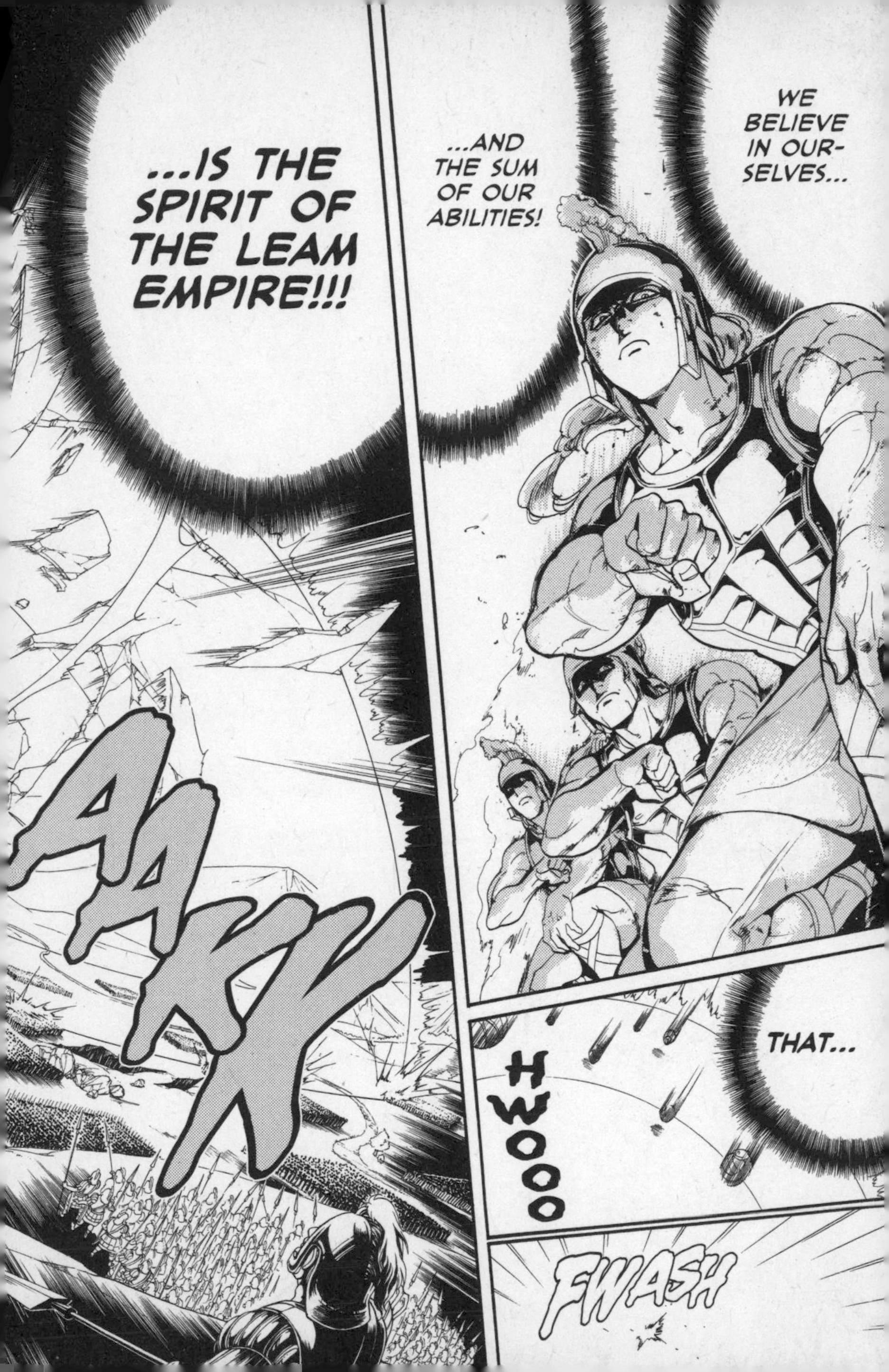
WE BELIEVE IN OUR-SELVES...
...AND THE SUM OF OUR ABILITIES!
THAT...
HWOOO
FWASH
...IS THE SPIRIT OF THE LEAM EMPIRE!!!
AAKK

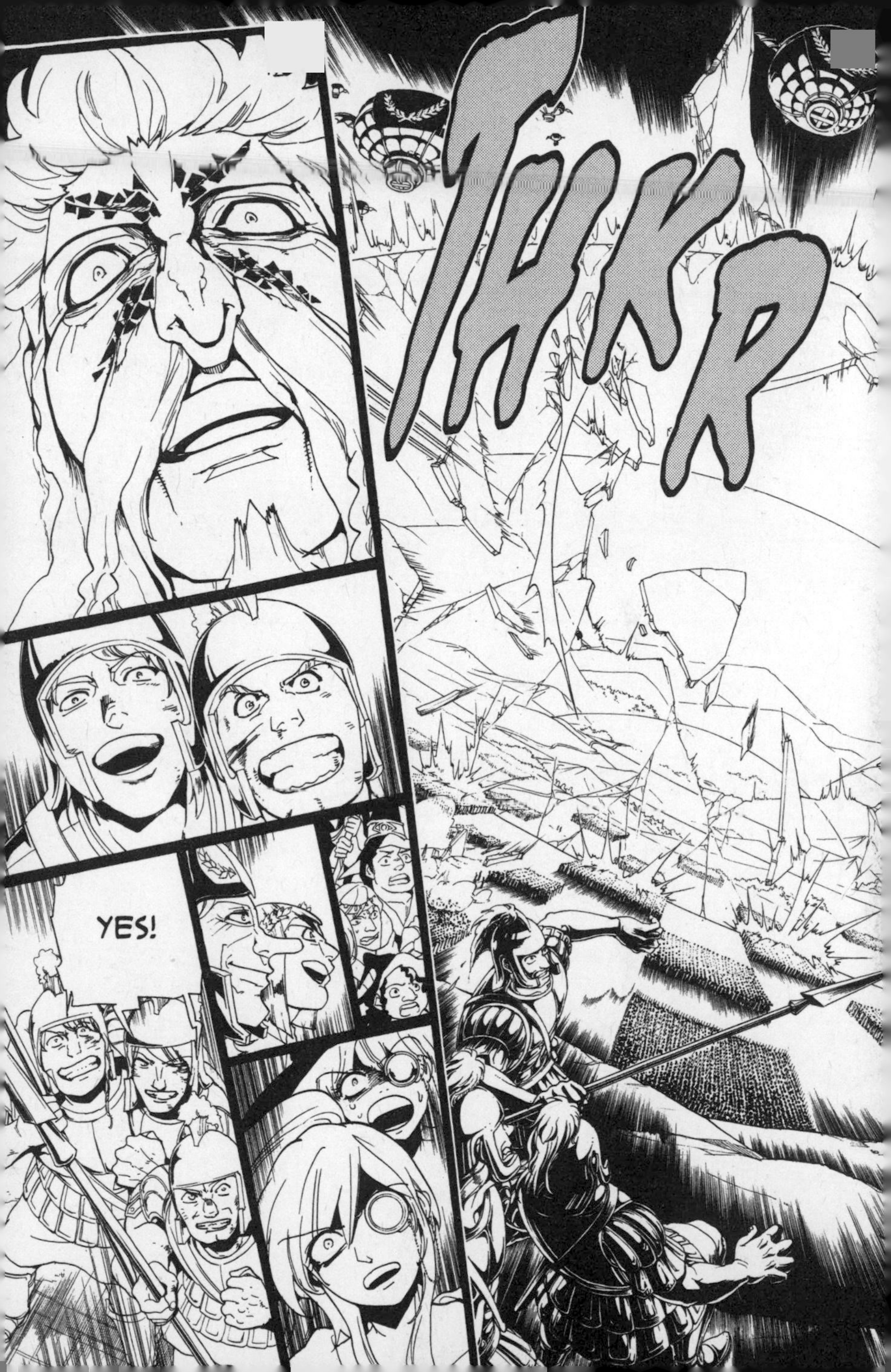
THKP
YES!

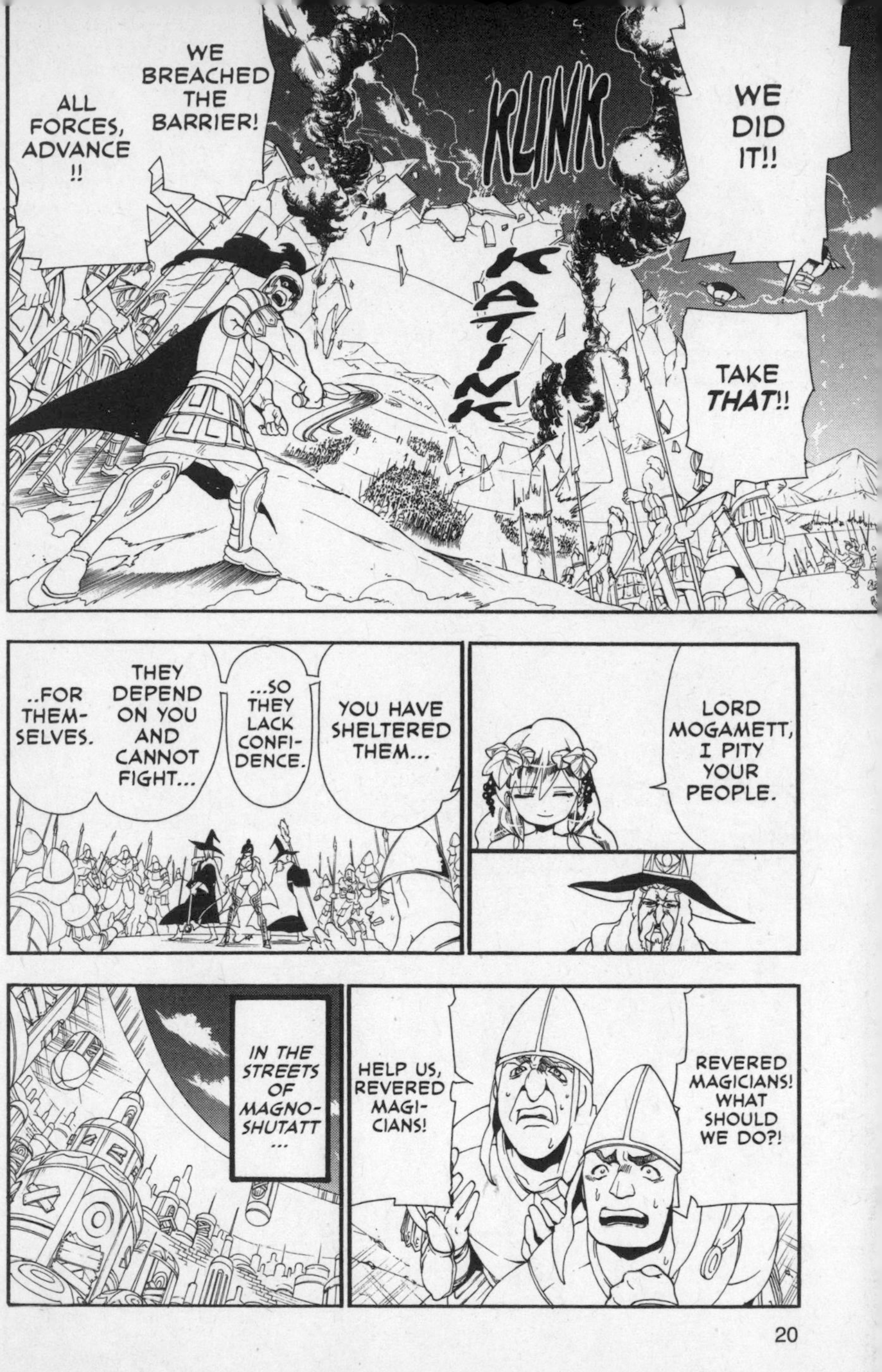
WE DID IT!!
KLINK
TAKE *THAT*!!
KATINK
WE BREACHED THE BARRIER!
ALL FORCES, ADVANCE!!
LORD MOGAMETT, I PITY YOUR PEOPLE.
YOU HAVE SHELTERED THEM...
...SO THEY LACK CONFIDENCE.
THEY DEPEND ON YOU AND CANNOT FIGHT...
..FOR THEMSELVES.
REVERED MAGICIANS! WHAT SHOULD WE DO?!
HELP US, REVERED MAGICIANS!
IN THE STREETS OF MAGNOSHUTATT...

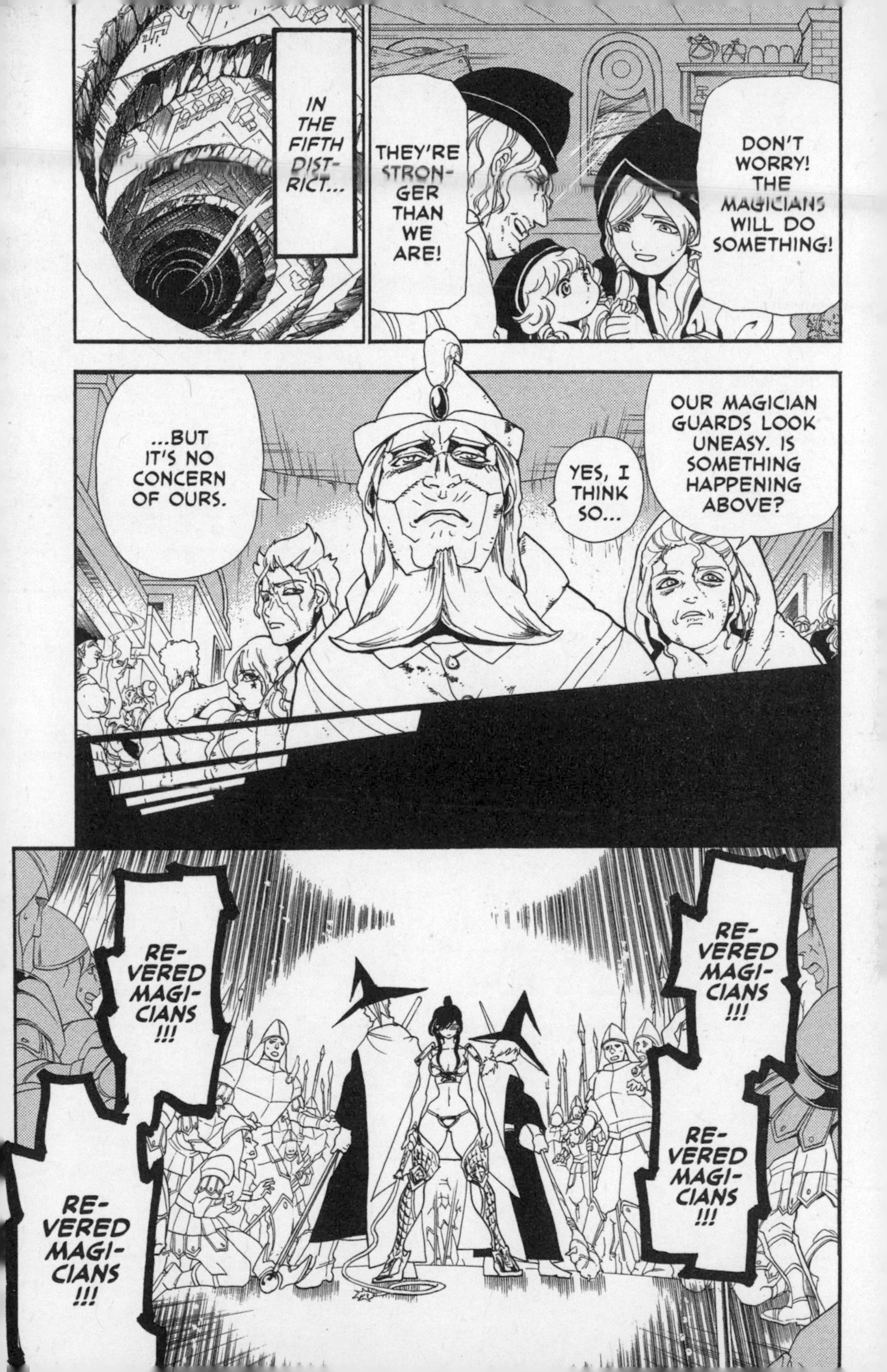
DON'T WORRY! THE MAGICIANS WILL DO SOMETHING!
THEY'RE STRONGER THAN WE ARE!
IN THE FIFTH DISTRICT...
OUR MAGICIAN GUARDS LOOK UNEASY. IS SOMETHING HAPPENING ABOVE?
YES, I THINK SO...
...BUT IT'S NO CONCERN OF OURS.
REVERED MAGICIANS!!!
REVERED MAGICIANS!!!
REVERED MAGICIANS!!!
REVERED MAGICIANS!!!

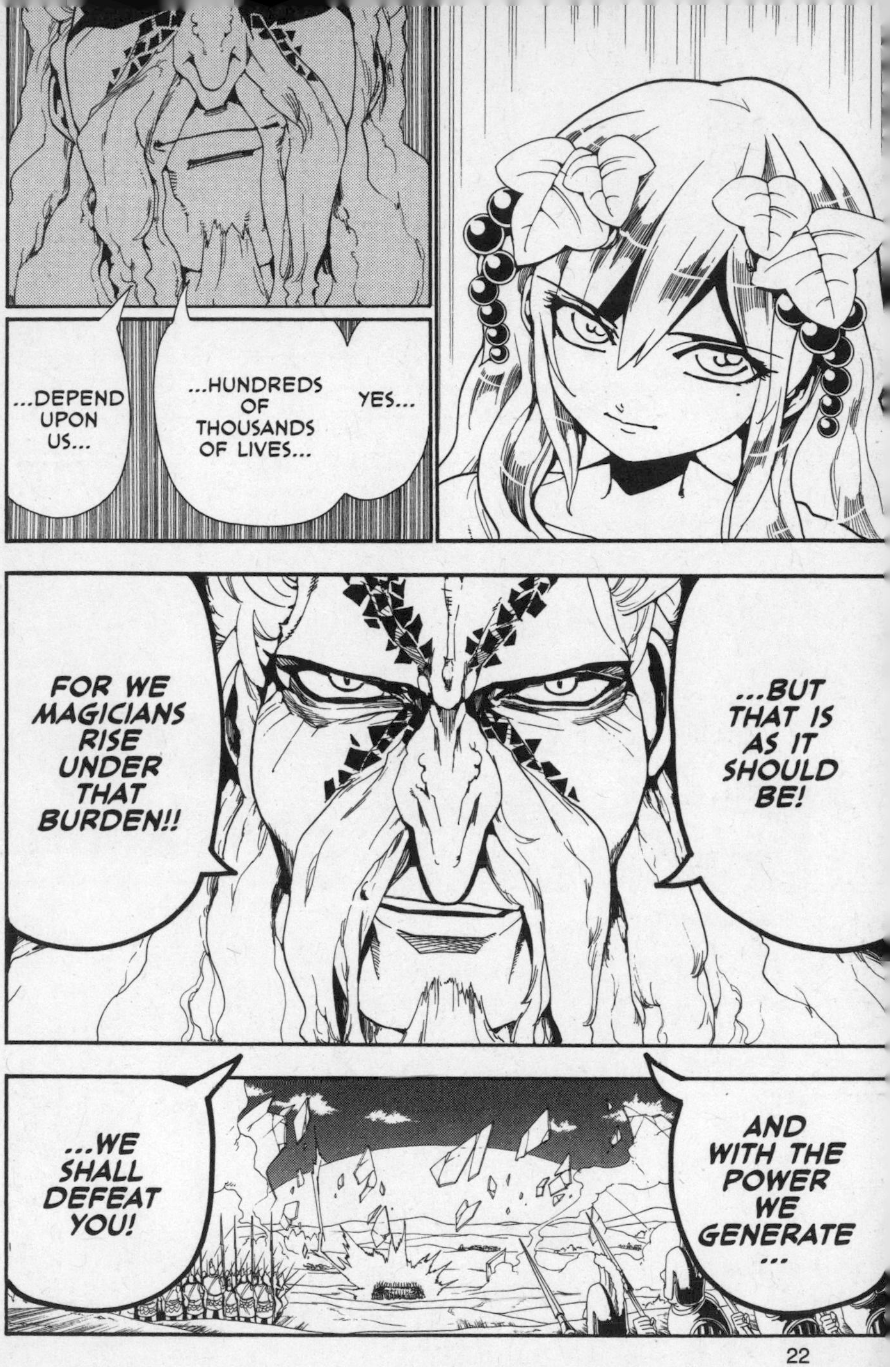
YES...
...HUNDREDS OF THOUSANDS OF LIVES...
...DEPEND UPON US...
...BUT THAT IS AS IT SHOULD BE!
FOR WE MAGICIANS RISE UNDER THAT BURDEN!!
AND WITH THE POWER WE GENERATE...
...WE SHALL DEFEAT YOU!

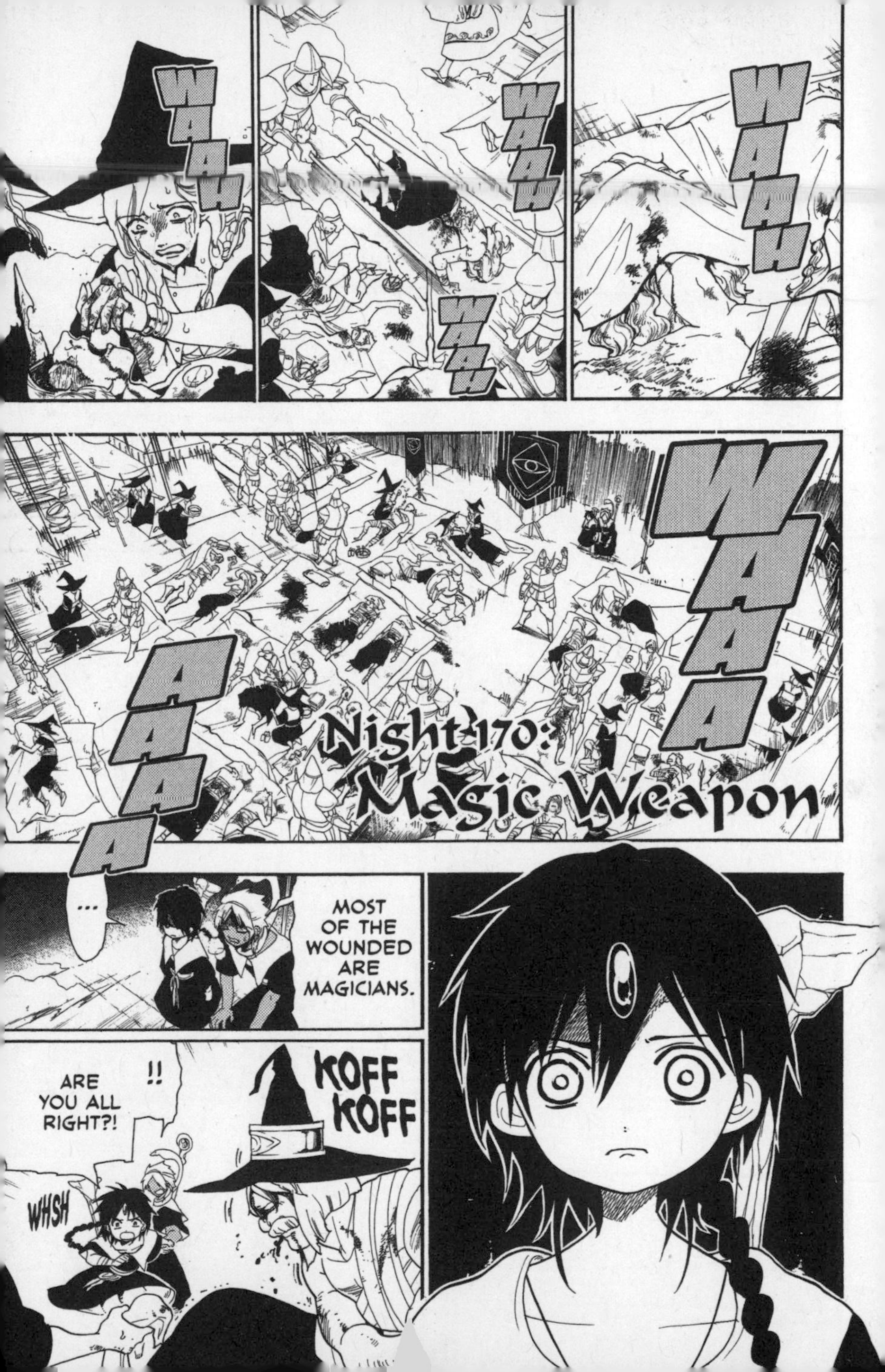
WAAH
WAAH
WAAH
WAAH
WAAAA
AAAA
Night 170: Magic Weapon
MOST OF THE WOUNDED ARE MAGICIANS.
...
KOFF KOFF
!!
ARE YOU ALL RIGHT?!
WHSH

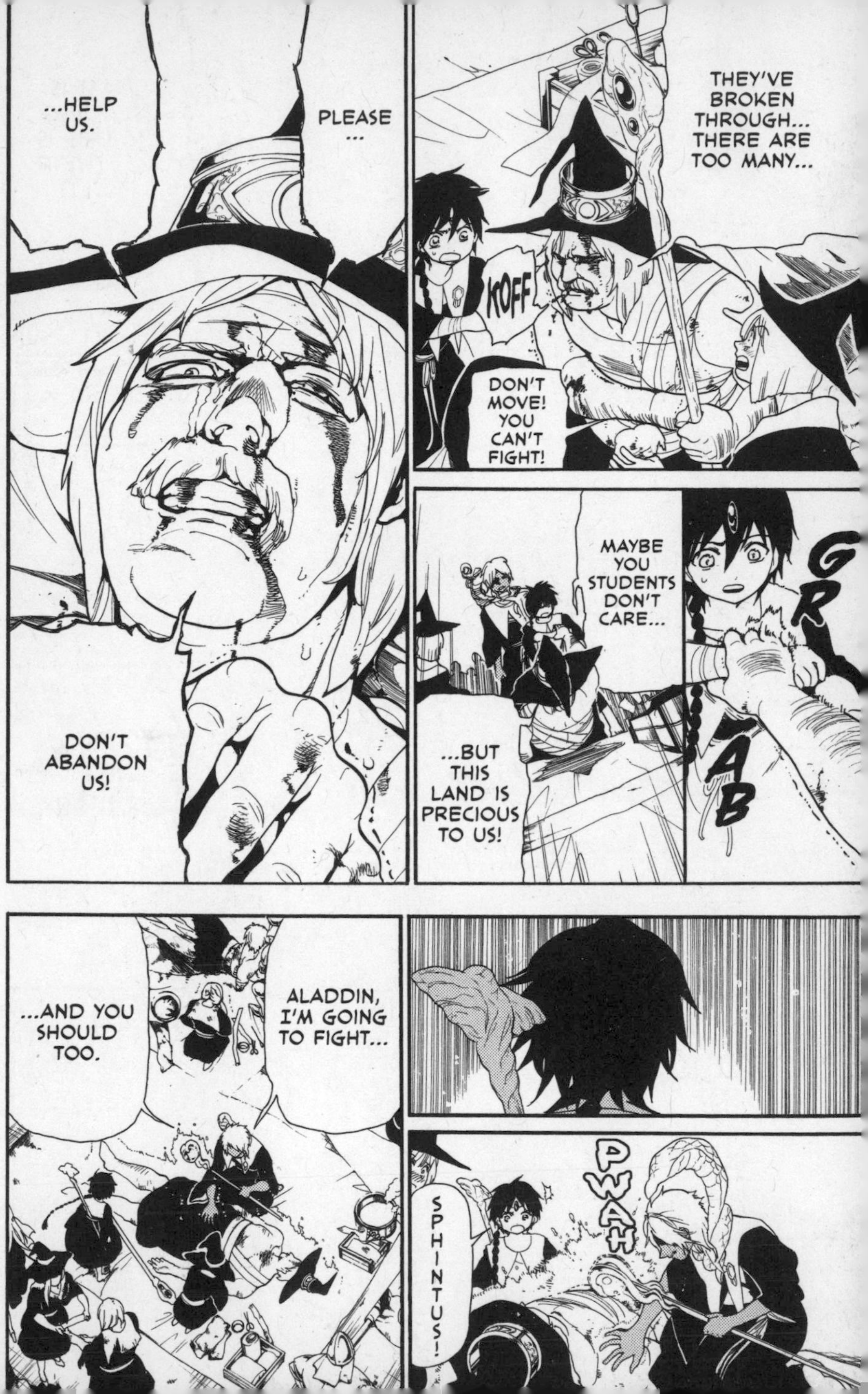
THEY'VE BROKEN THROUGH... THERE ARE TOO MANY...
KOFF
DON'T MOVE! YOU CAN'T FIGHT!
GRAB
MAYBE YOU STUDENTS DON'T CARE...
...BUT THIS LAND IS PRECIOUS TO US!
PLEASE...
...HELP US.
DON'T ABANDON US!
PWAH
SPHINTUS!
ALADDIN, I'M GOING TO FIGHT...
...AND YOU SHOULD TOO.

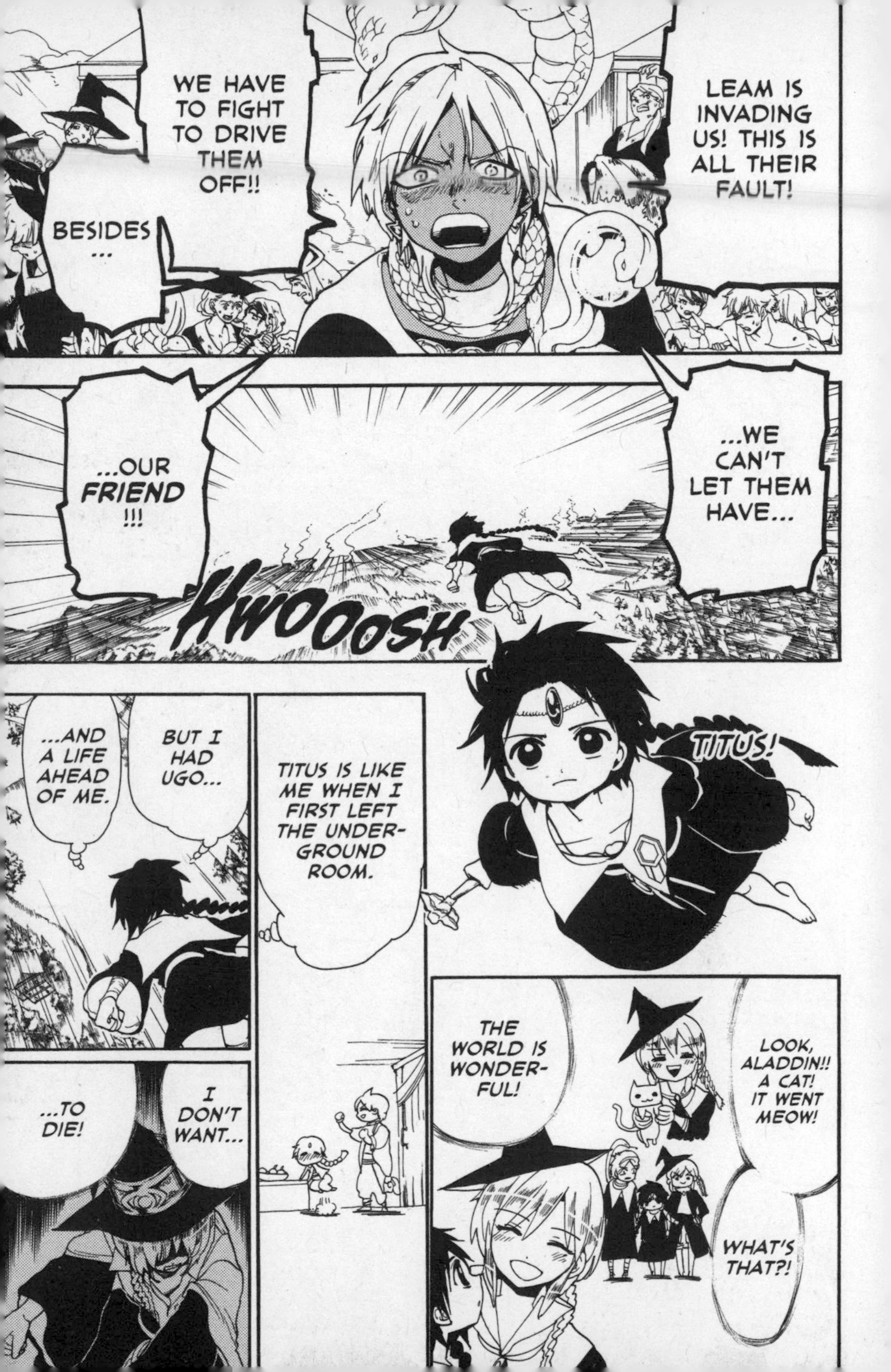

LEAM IS INVADING US! THIS IS ALL THEIR FAULT!
WE HAVE TO FIGHT TO DRIVE THEM OFF!!
BESIDES...
...WE CAN'T LET THEM HAVE...
...OUR FRIEND!!!
HWOOOSH
TITUS!
TITUS IS LIKE ME WHEN I FIRST LEFT THE UNDERGROUND ROOM.
BUT I HAD UGO...
...AND A LIFE AHEAD OF ME.
LOOK, ALADDIN!! A CAT! IT WENT MEOW!
WHAT'S THAT?!
THE WORLD IS WONDERFUL!
I DON'T WANT...
...TO DIE!

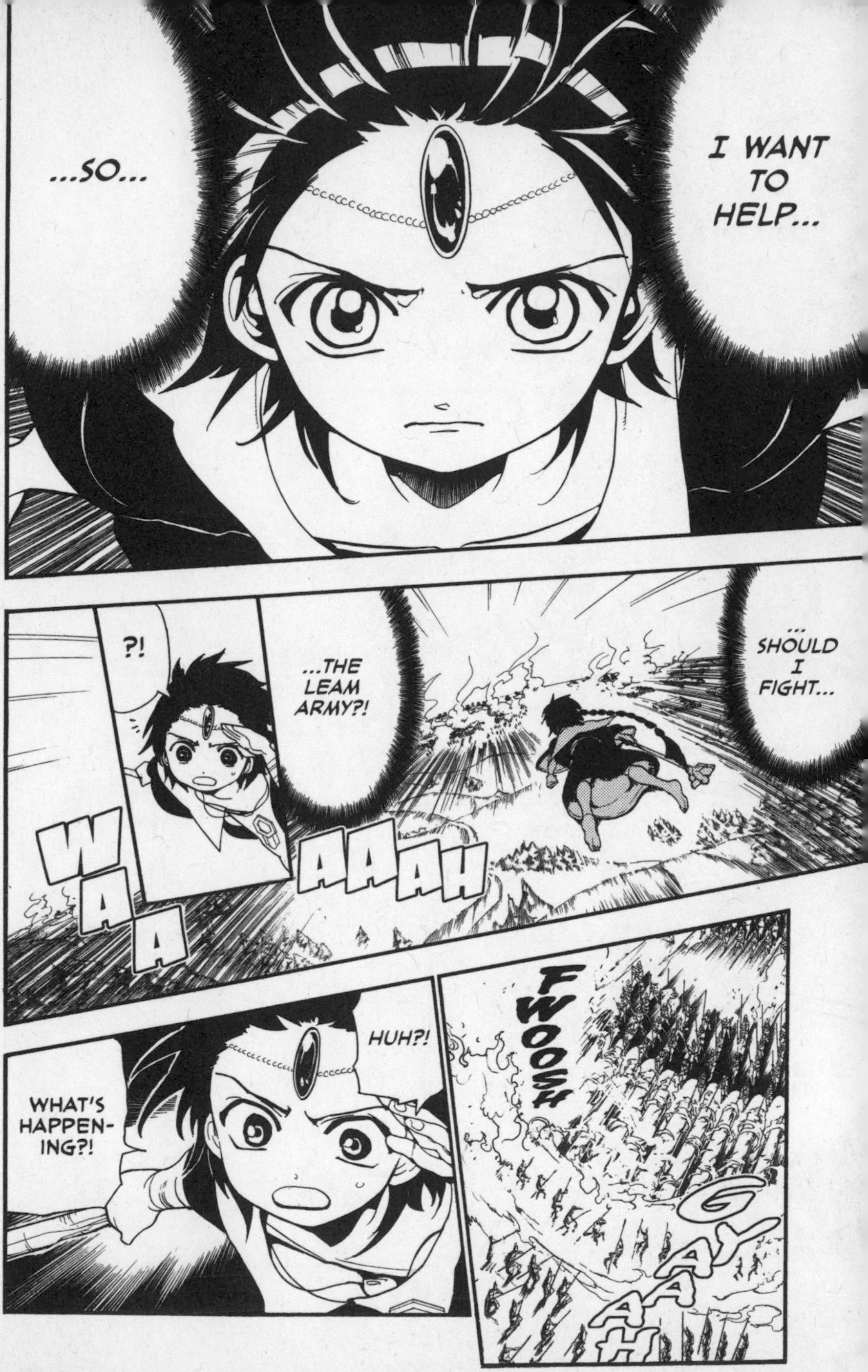
I WANT TO HELP...
...SO...
... SHOULD I FIGHT...
...THE LEAM ARMY?!
?!
WAAAAAAH
FWOOSH
GYAAAH
HUH?!
WHAT'S HAPPEN-ING?!

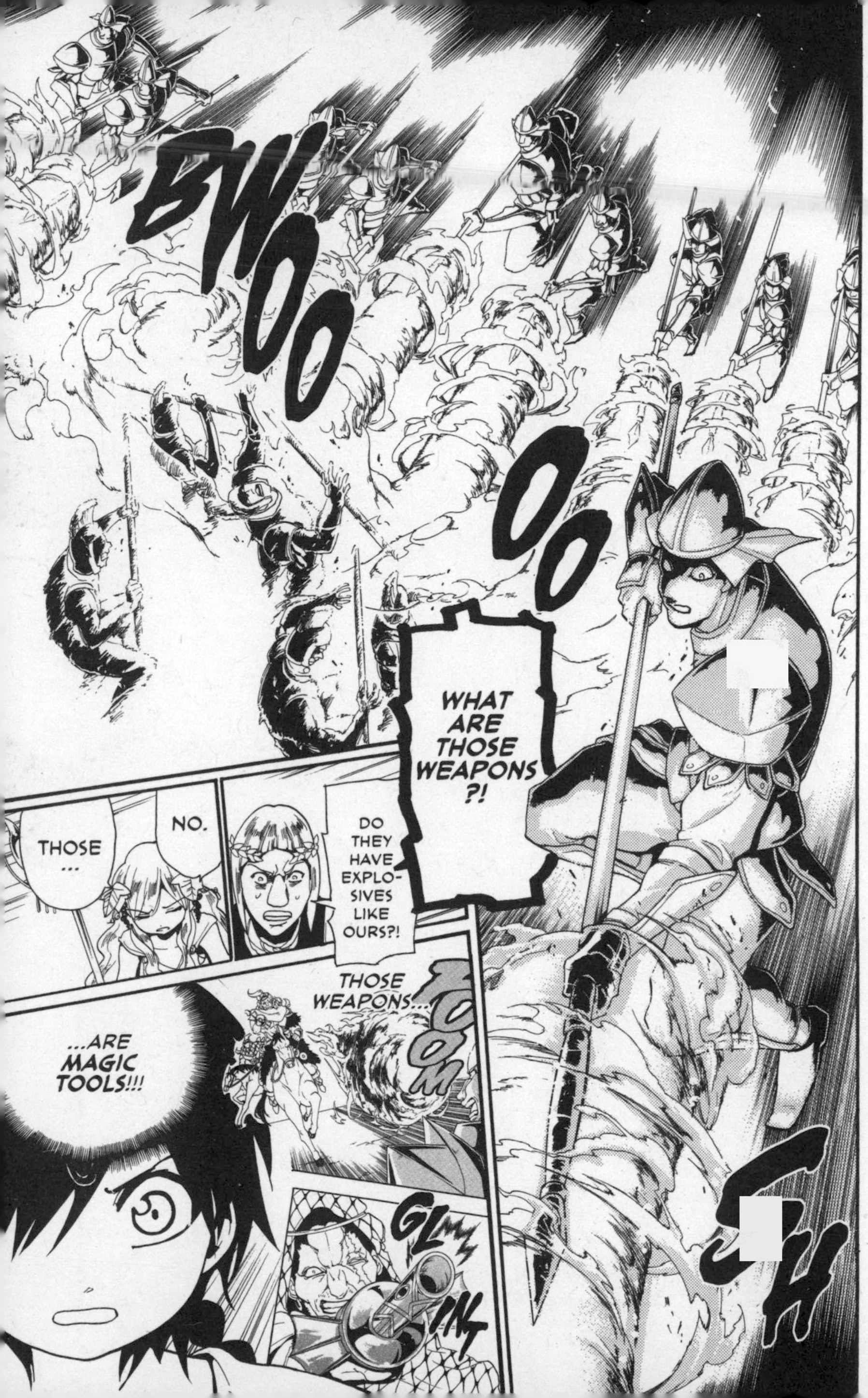
BWOOOOO
WHAT ARE THOSE WEAPONS?!
DO THEY HAVE EXPLOSIVES LIKE OURS?!
NO.
THOSE ...
THOSE WEAPONS...
...ARE MAGIC TOOLS!!!

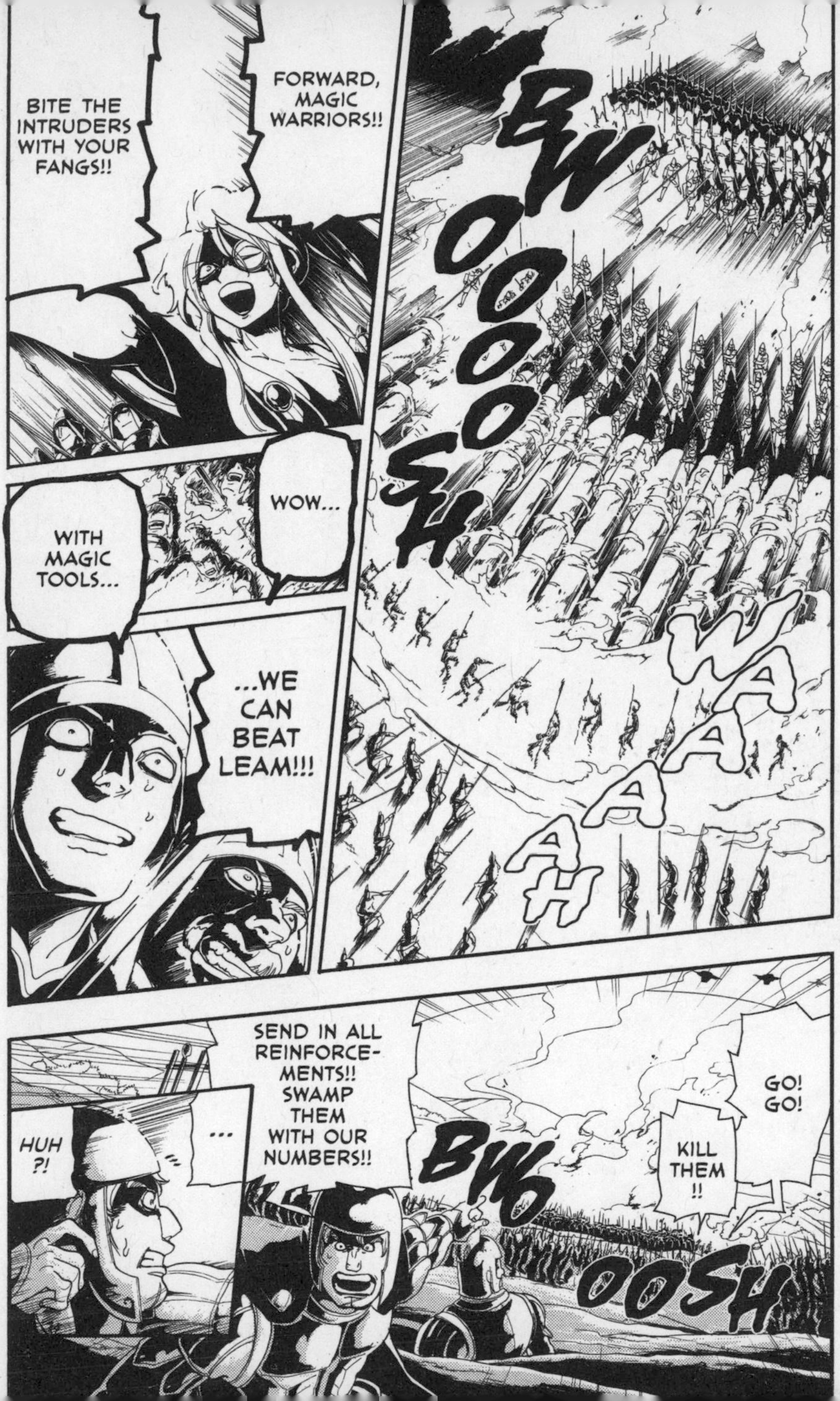
BWOOOOSH
WAAAAH
FORWARD, MAGIC WARRIORS!!
BITE THE INTRUDERS WITH YOUR FANGS!!
WOW...
WITH MAGIC TOOLS...
...WE CAN BEAT LEAM!!!
GO! GO!
KILL THEM!!
SEND IN ALL REINFORCE-MENTS!! SWAMP THEM WITH OUR NUMBERS!!
BWOOSH
...
HUH?!

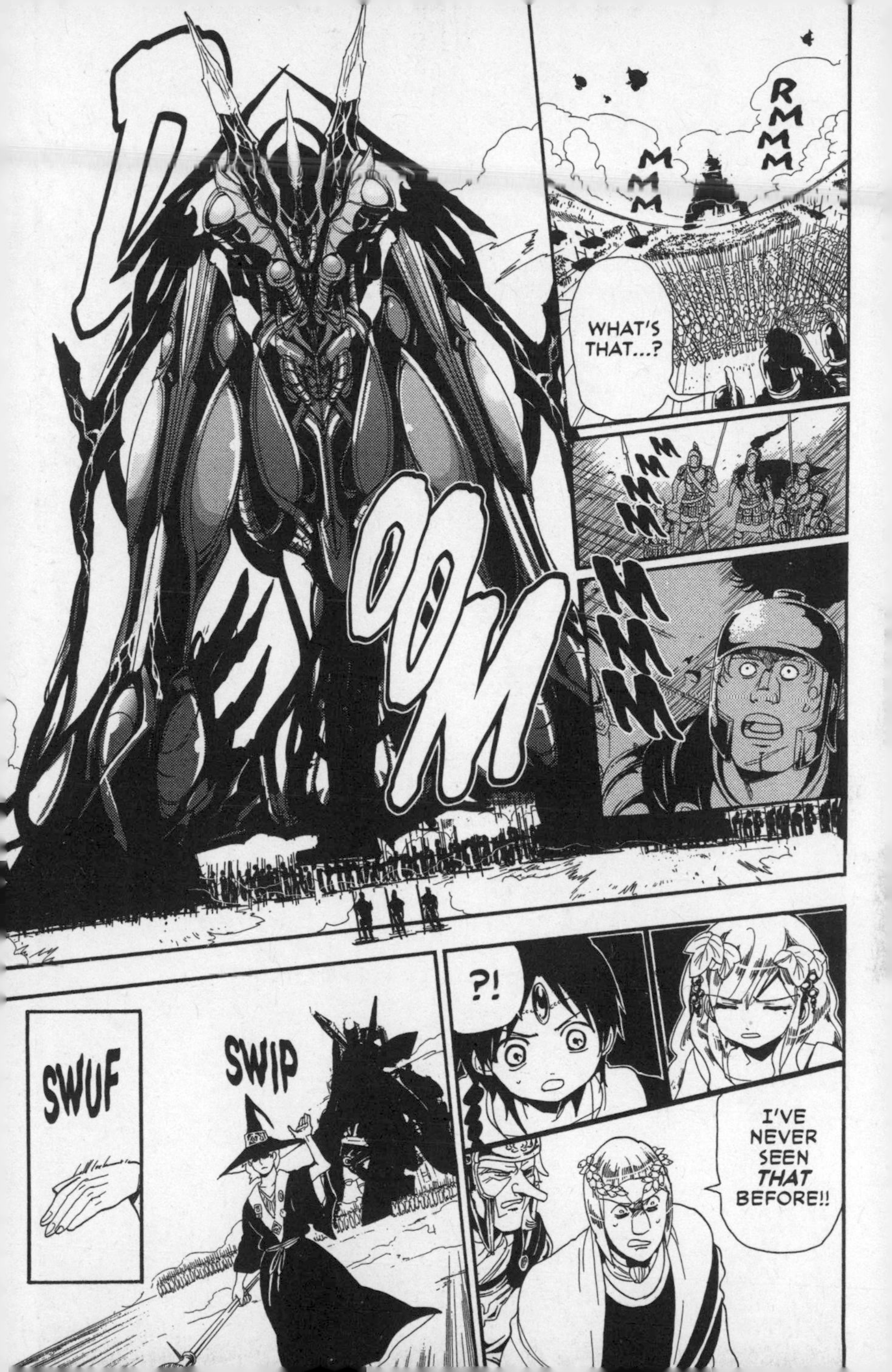

RMMM
MMM
WHAT'S THAT...?
MMMM
MMMM
DOOM
I'VE NEVER SEEN THAT BEFORE!!
?!
SWIP
SWUF

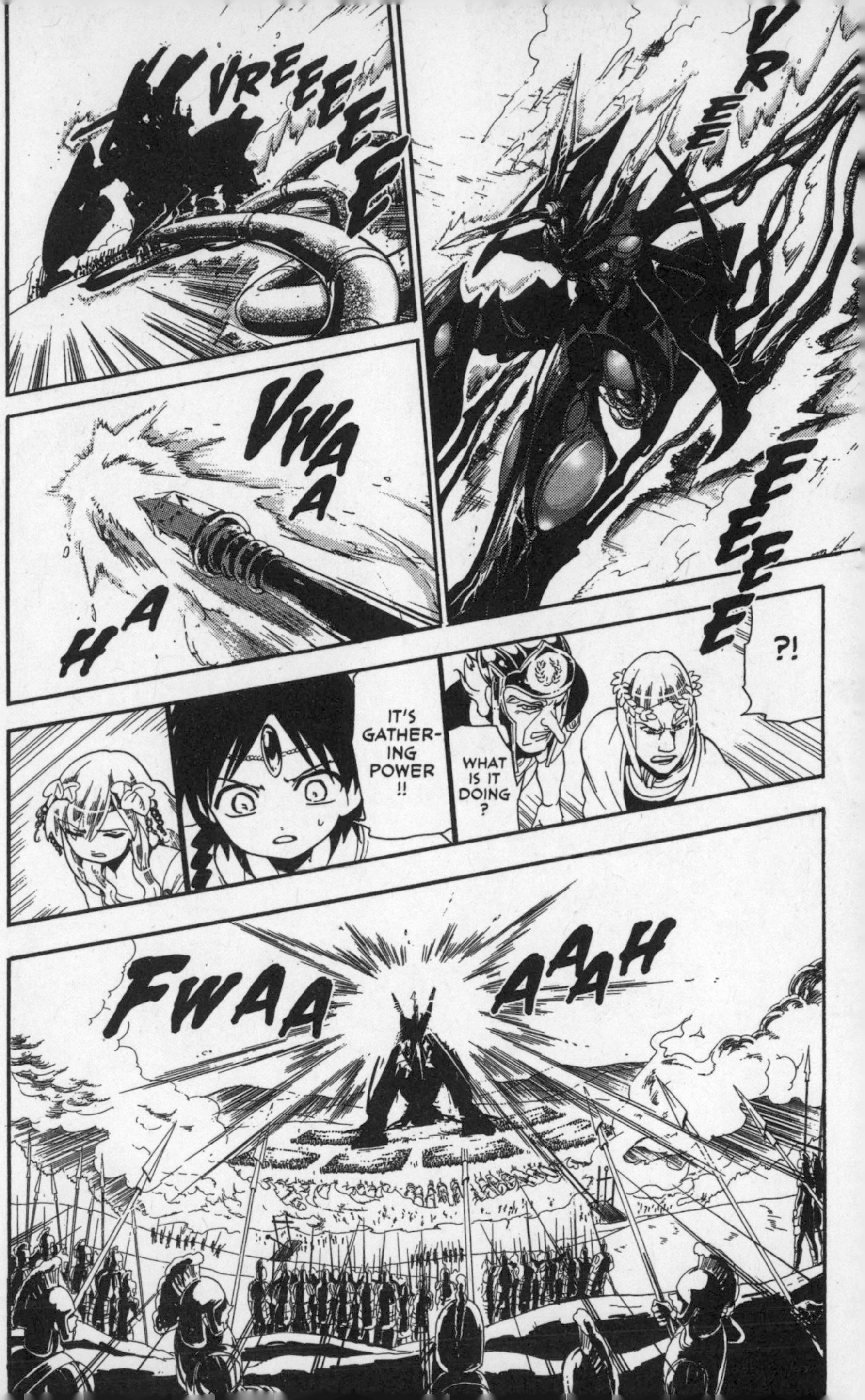
VREEEEEEEEEE
VREEEEE
VWAAAH
?!
WHAT IS IT DOING?
IT'S GATHERING POWER!!
FWAAAAAH

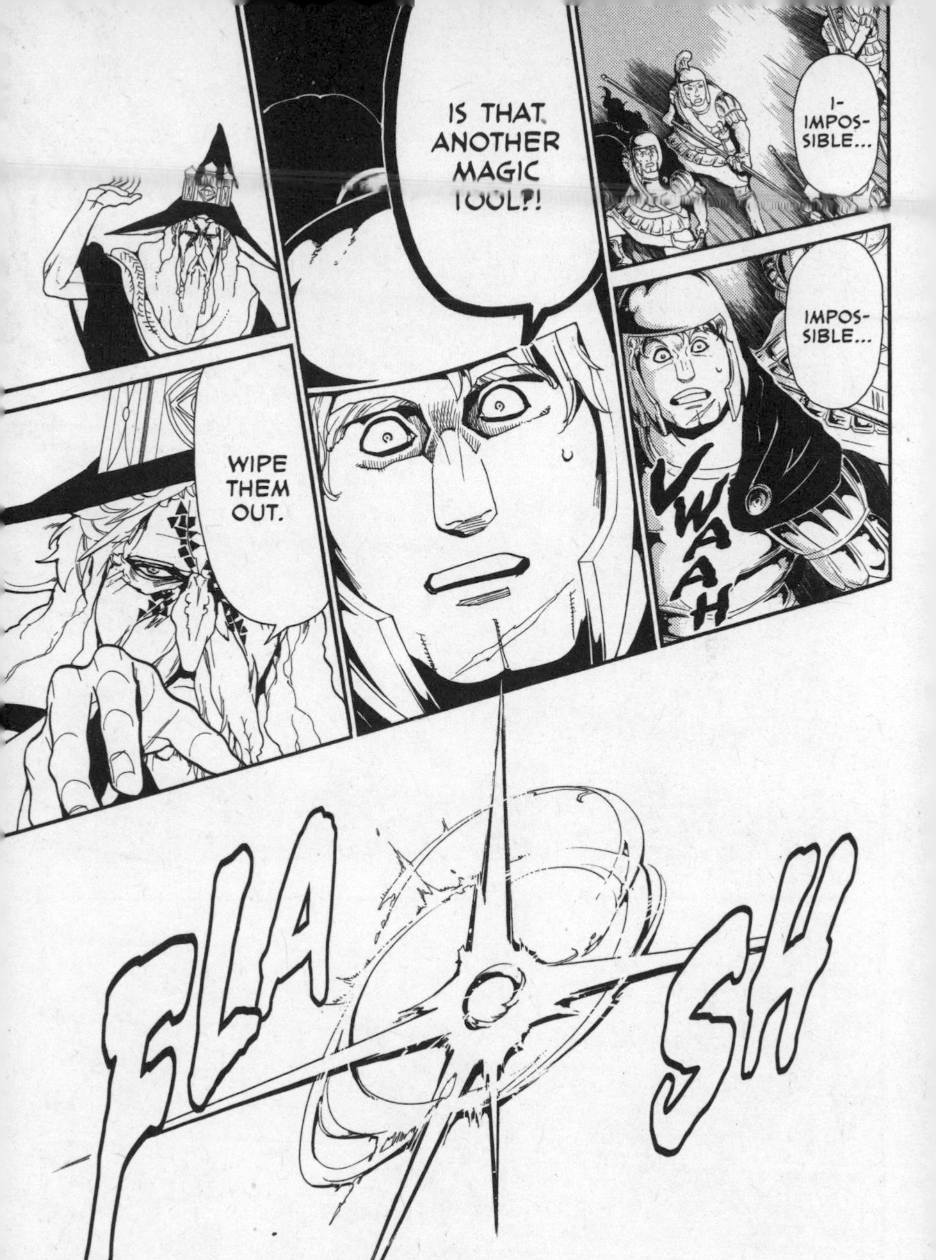
I- IMPOSSIBLE...
IMPOSSIBLE...
VWAAH
IS THAT ANOTHER MAGIC TOOL?!
WIPE THEM OUT.
FLASH

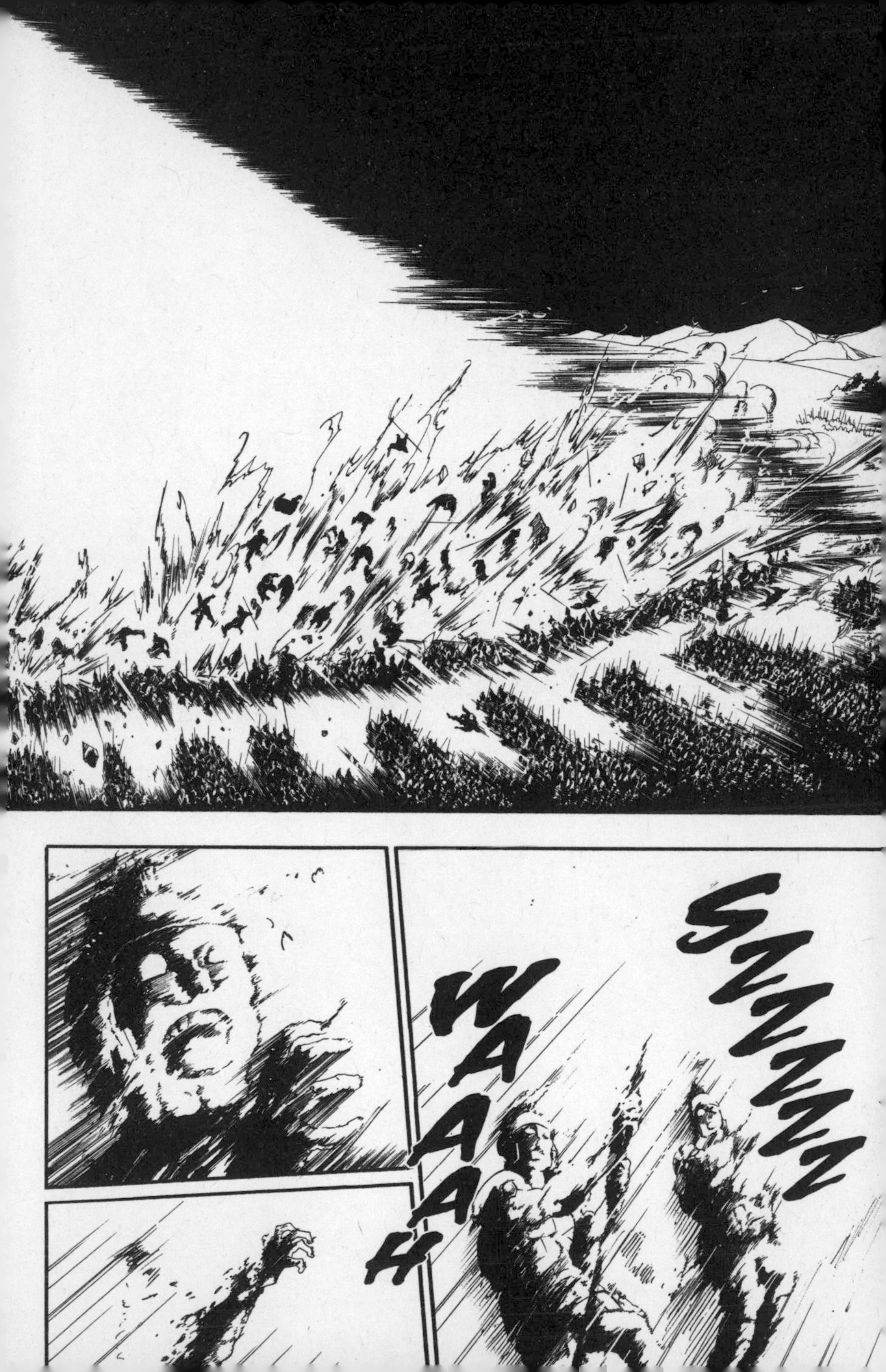
SZZZZZ
WAAAH

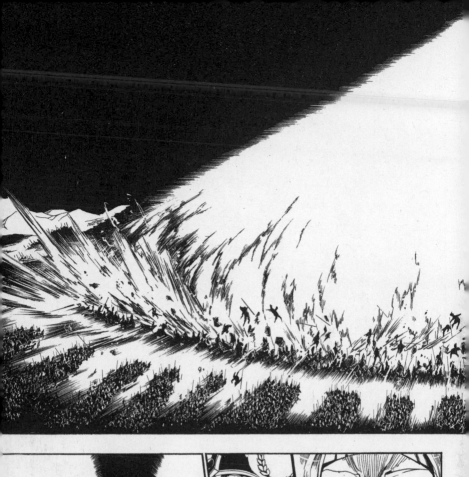

...THAT ISN'T MERELY DEFENSE!!

HEAD-MASTER...

SHUDDER

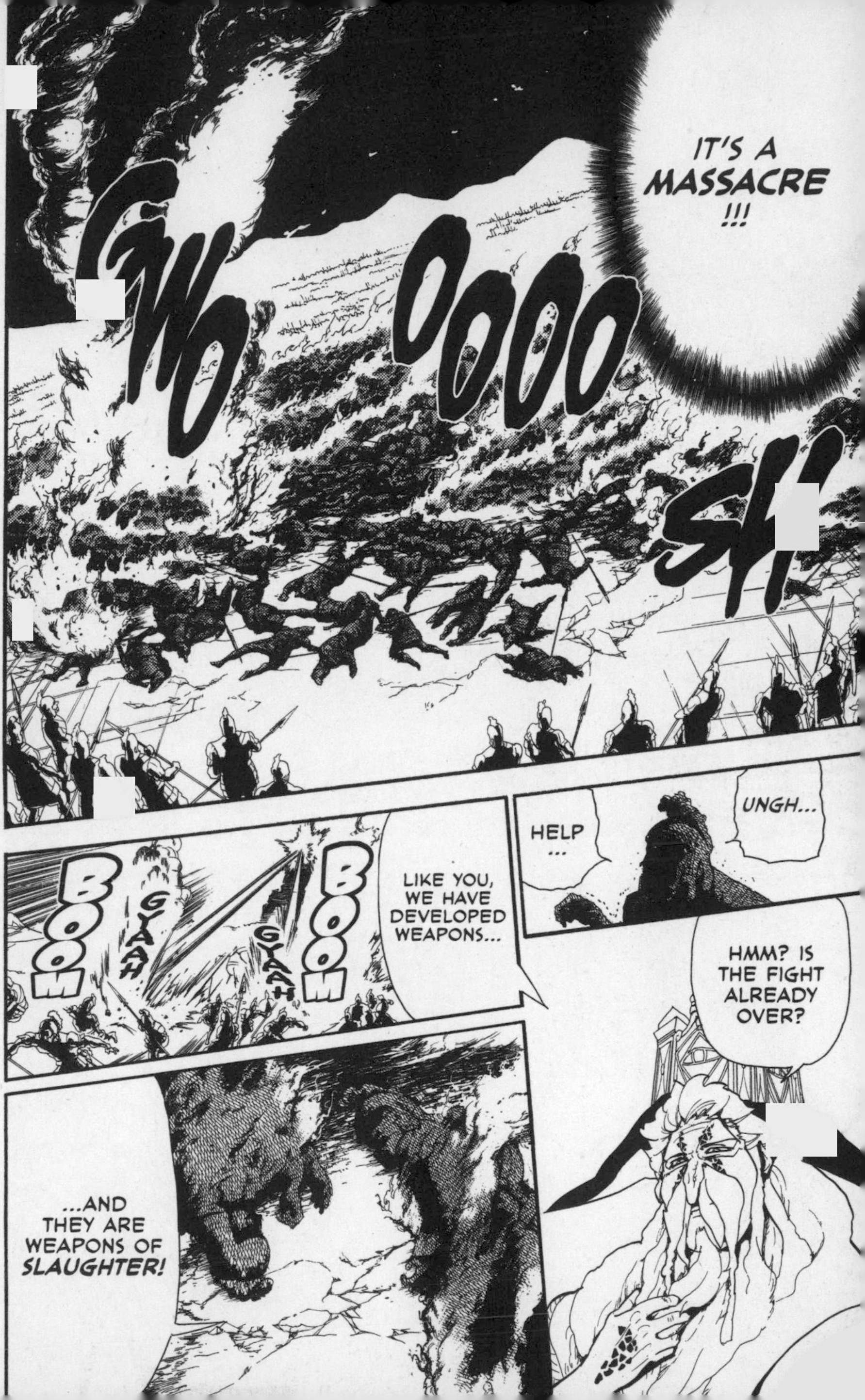
IT'S A MASSACRE !!!
GWOOOOOSH!
UNGH...
HELP...
HMM? IS THE FIGHT ALREADY OVER?
LIKE YOU, WE HAVE DEVELOPED WEAPONS...
BOOM
GYAAH
GYAAH
BOOM
...AND THEY ARE WEAPONS OF SLAUGHTER!

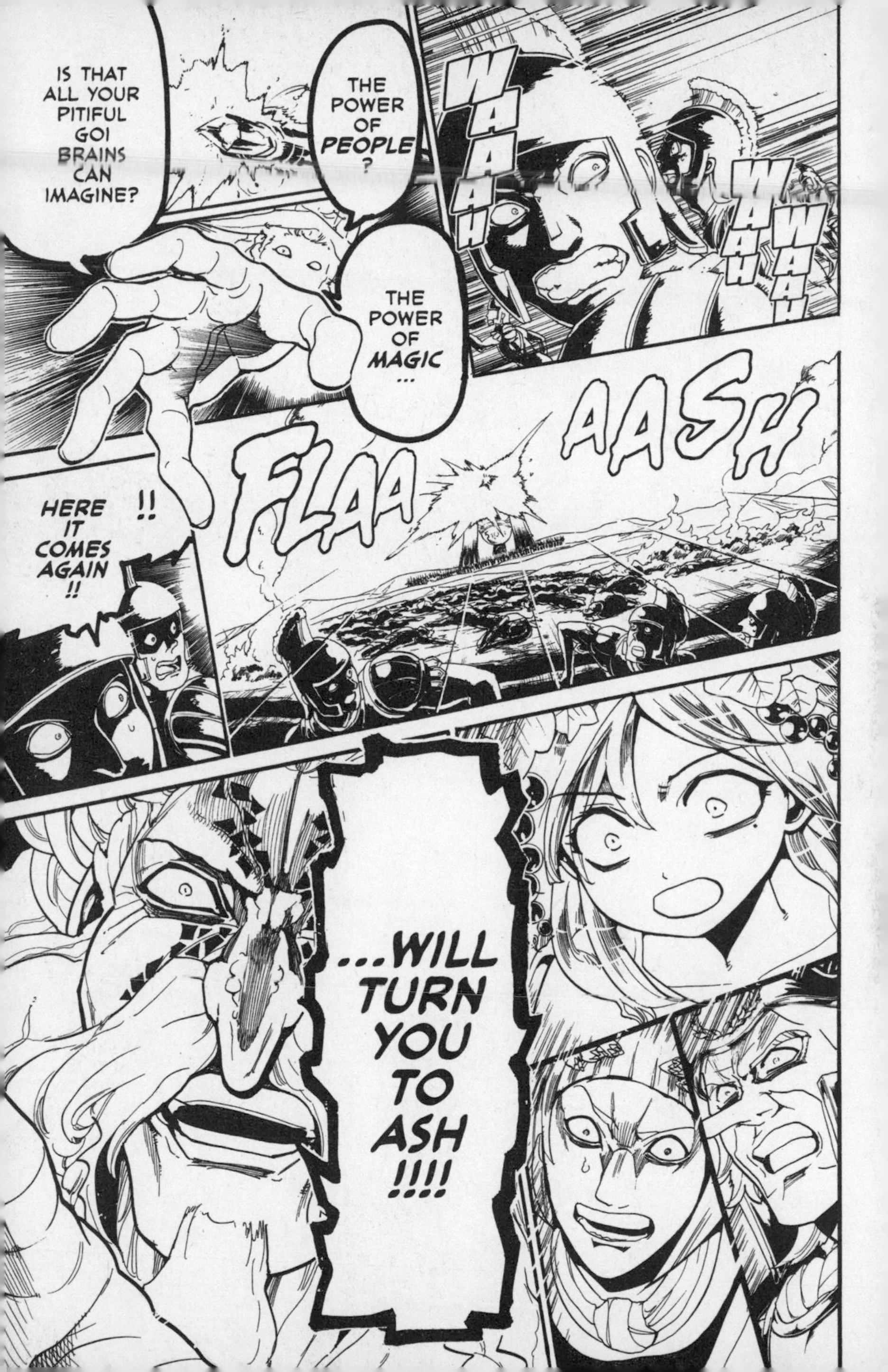
WAAAH
WAAH
WAAAH
THE POWER OF PEOPLE?
THE POWER OF MAGIC...
IS THAT ALL YOUR PITIFUL GOI BRAINS CAN IMAGINE?
FLAA AASH
HERE IT COMES AGAIN!!
!!
...WILL TURN YOU TO ASH!!!!

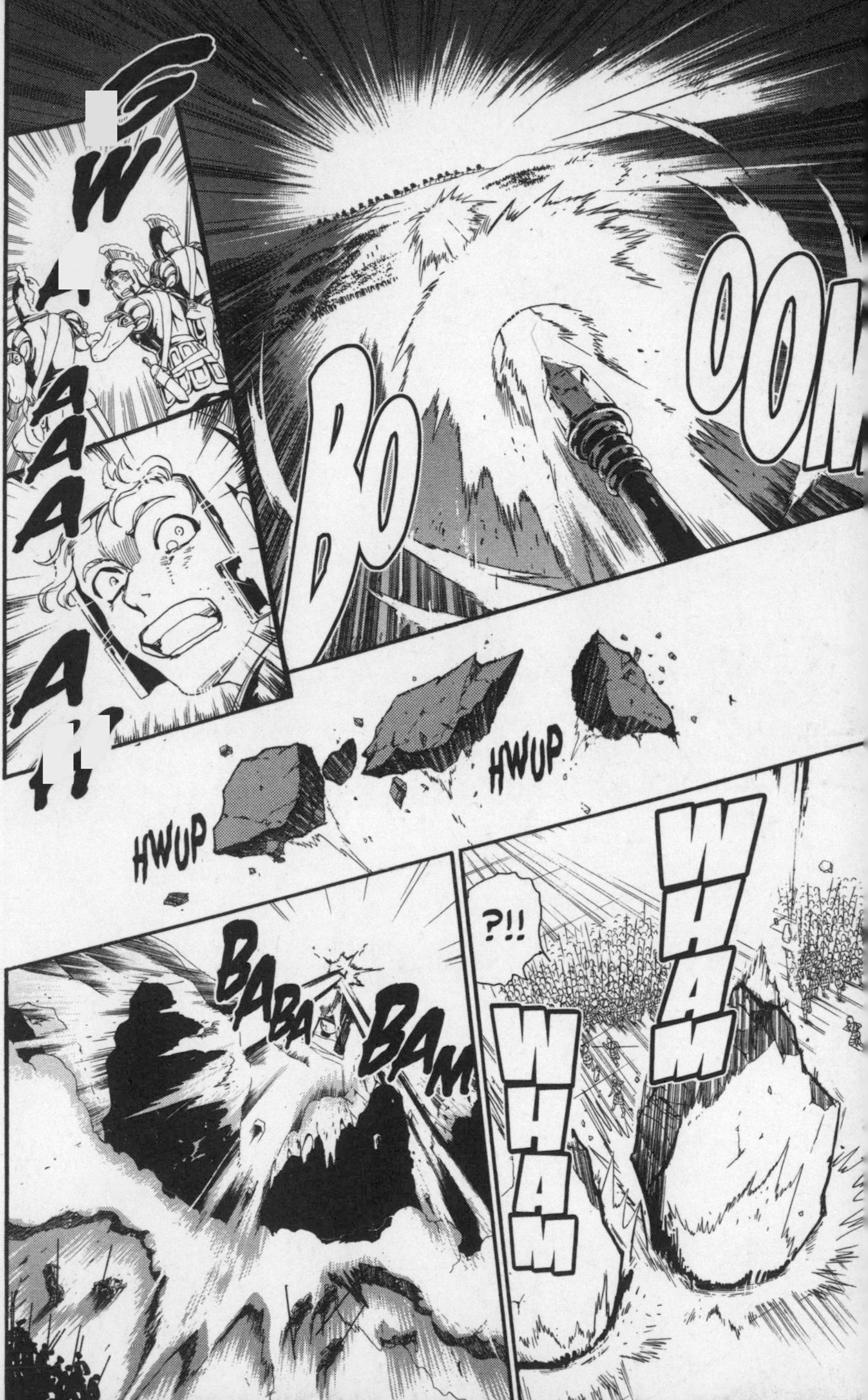
BOOOM
GWAAAAA!!
HWUP
HWUP
WHAM
?!!
WHAM
BABABAM

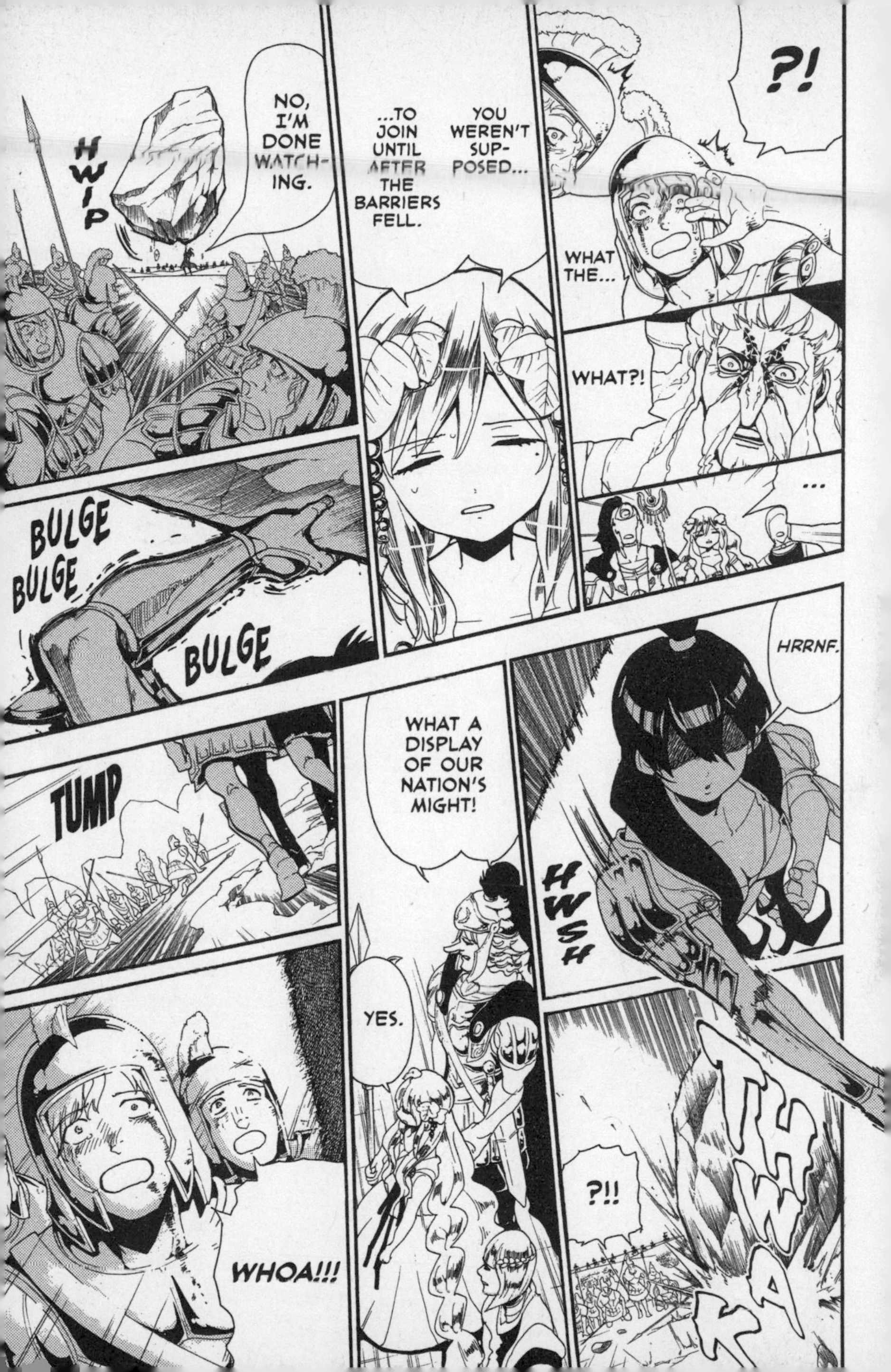
?!
WHAT THE...
WHAT?!
...
YOU WEREN'T SUPPOSED...
...TO JOIN UNTIL AFTER THE BARRIERS FELL.
NO, I'M DONE WATCHING.
HWIP
BULGE BULGE
BULGE
HRRNF.
HWSH
WHAT A DISPLAY OF OUR NATION'S MIGHT!
TUMP
?!!
THWAK
YES.
WHOA!!!

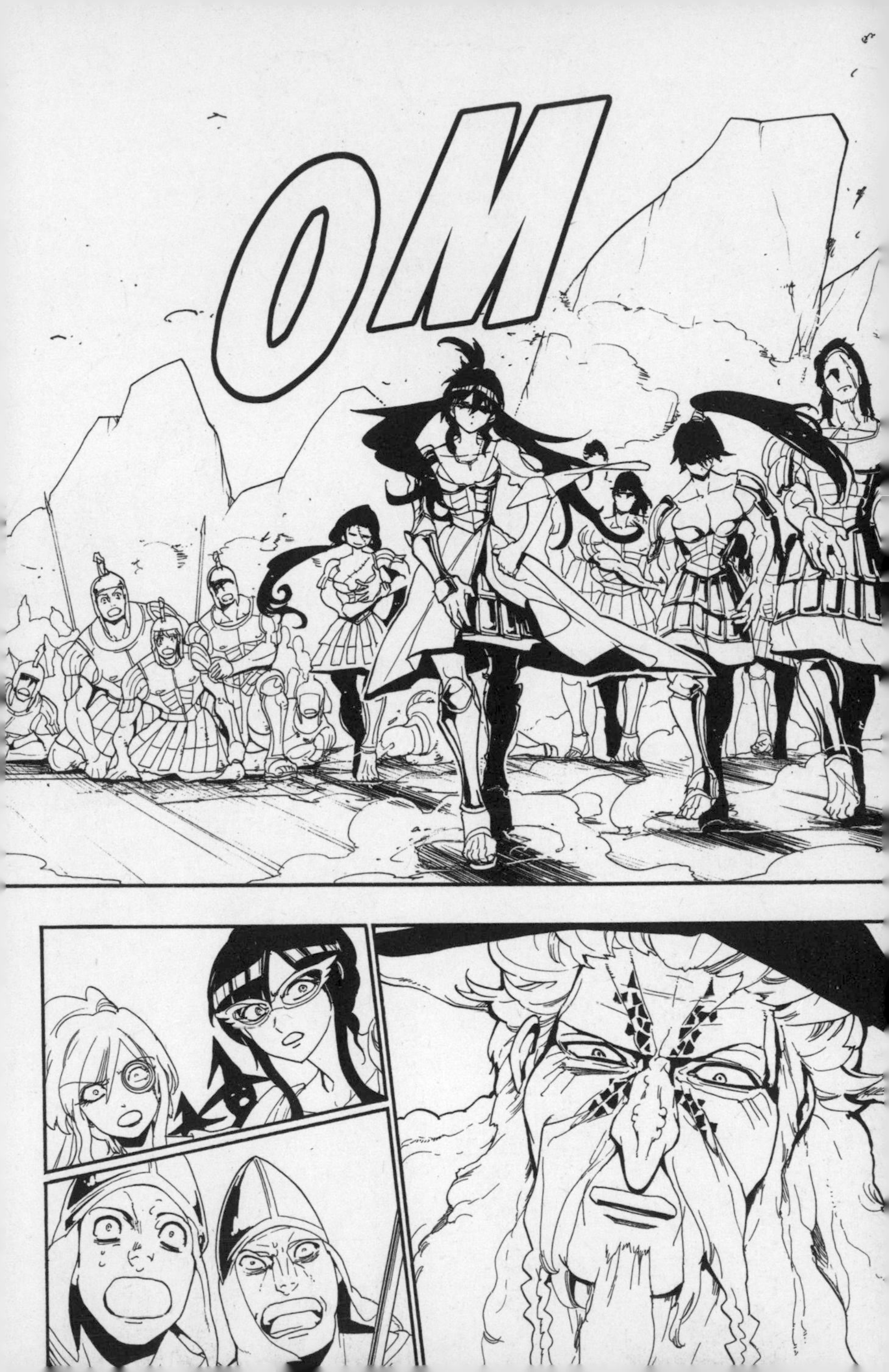
OM

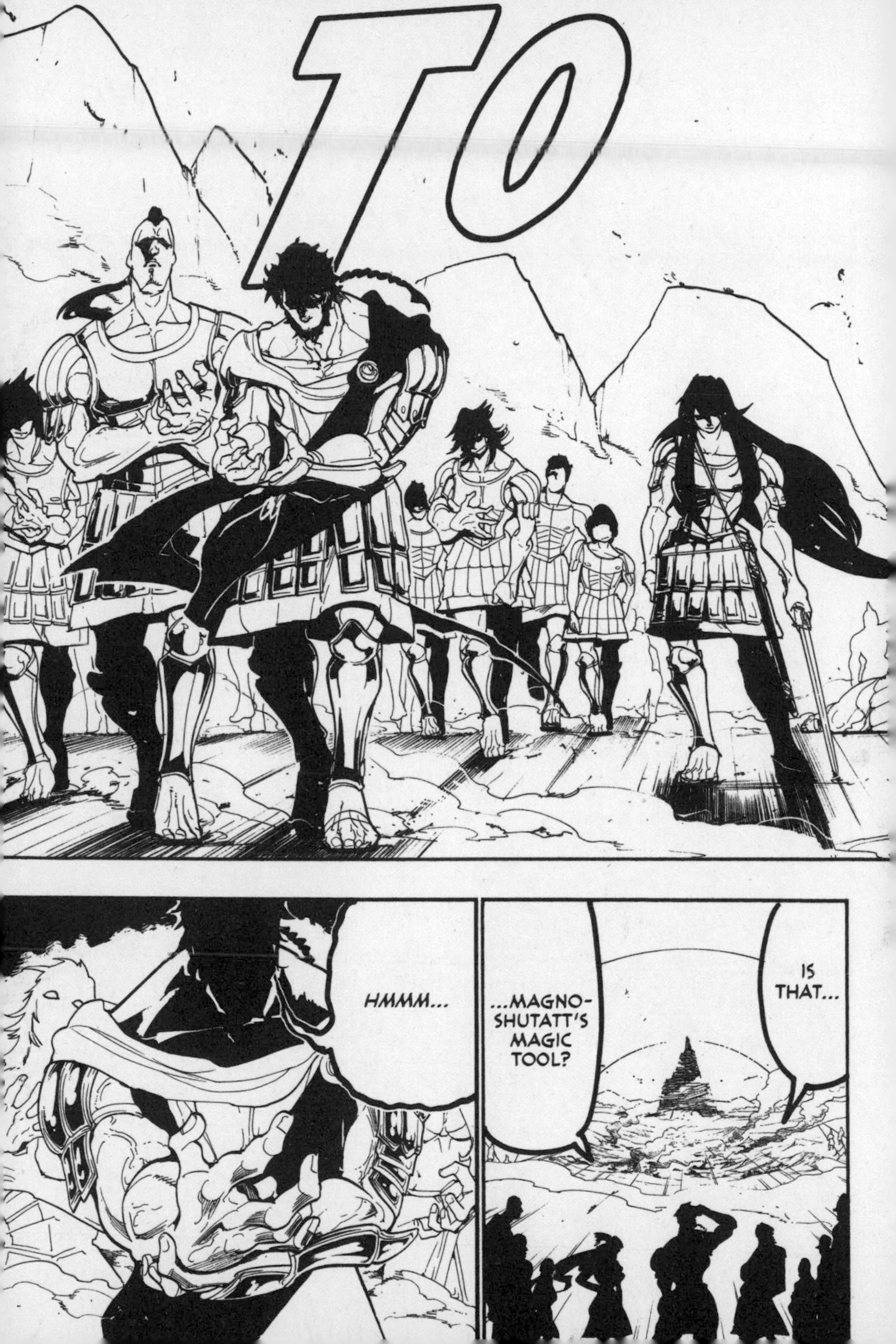
TO
IS THAT...
...MAGNO-SHUTATT'S MAGIC TOOL?
HMMM...

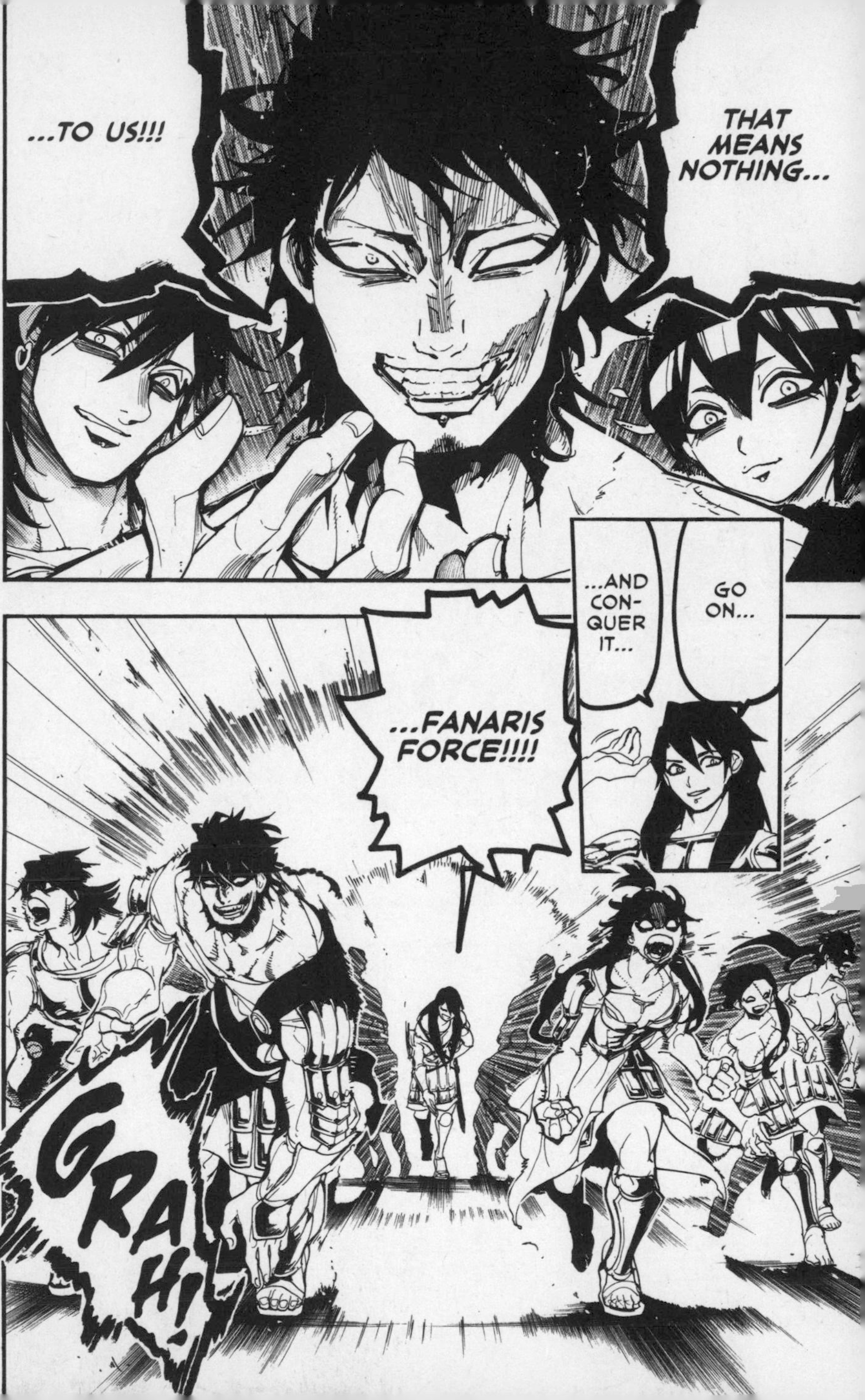
THAT MEANS NOTHING...
...TO US!!!
GO ON...
...AND CON-QUER IT...
...FANARIS FORCE!!!!
GRAH!

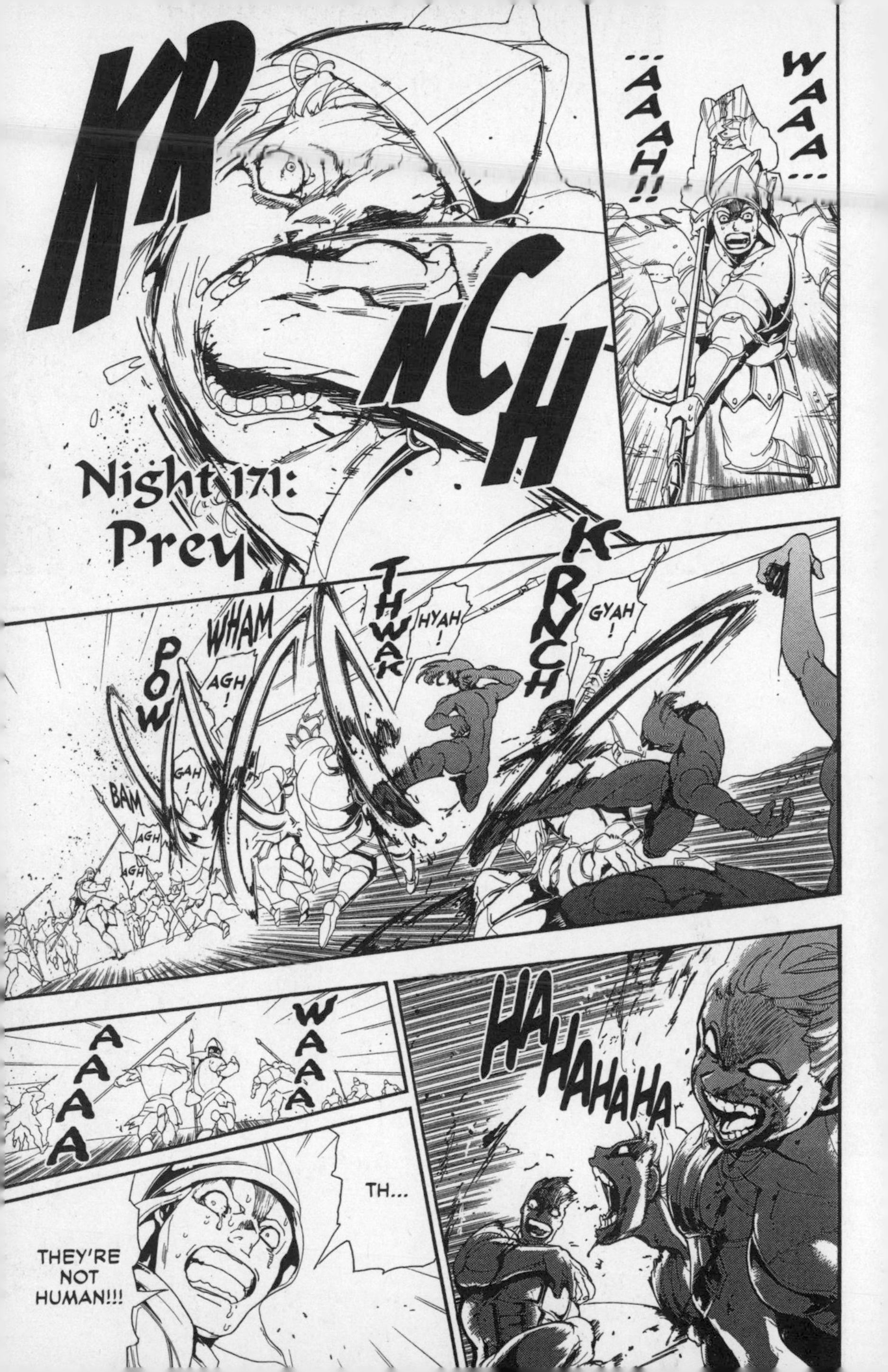
WAAA...
...AAAH!!
KR
NCH
Night 171: Prey
GYAH!
KRNCH
HYAH!
THWAK
WHAM
POW
AGH!
GAH!
BAM
AGH!
AGH!
HAHAHAHAHA
WAAA
AAAA
TH...
THEY'RE NOT HUMAN!!!

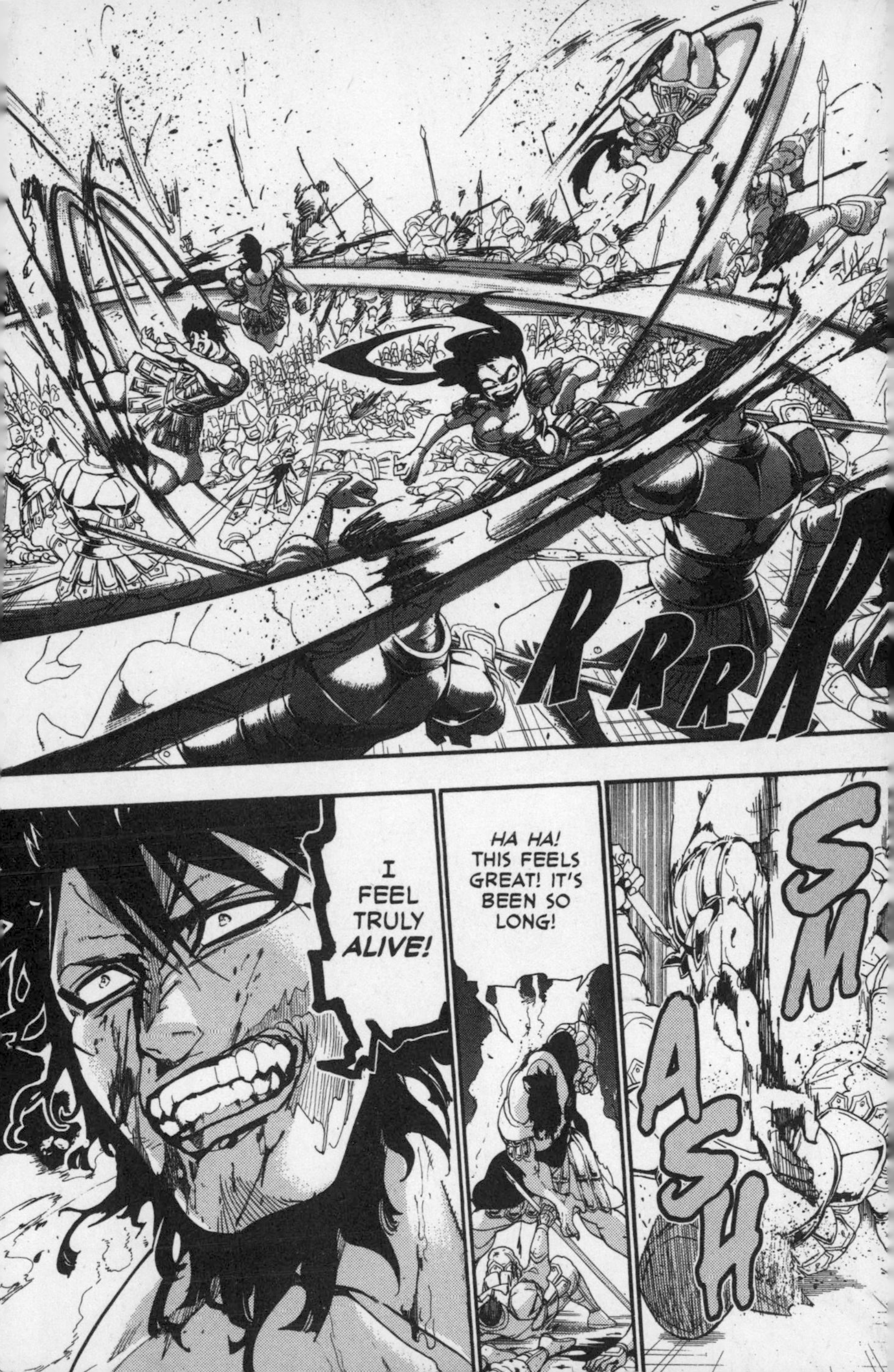
RRRK
SMASH
HA HA! THIS FEELS GREAT! IT'S BEEN SO LONG!
I FEEL TRULY ALIVE!

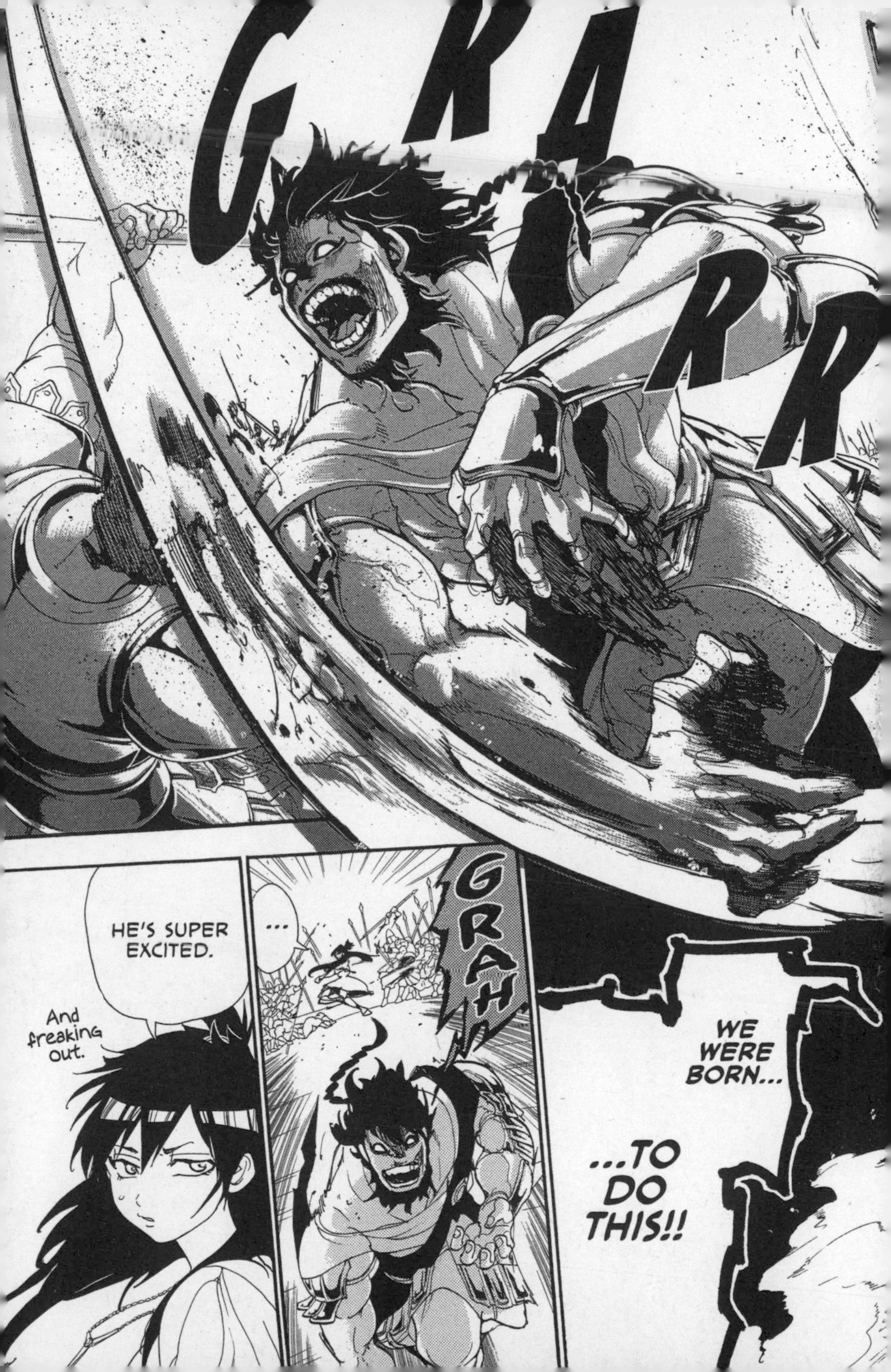
GKARR
WE WERE BORN...
...TO DO THIS!!
GRAH
...
HE'S SUPER EXCITED.
And freaking out.

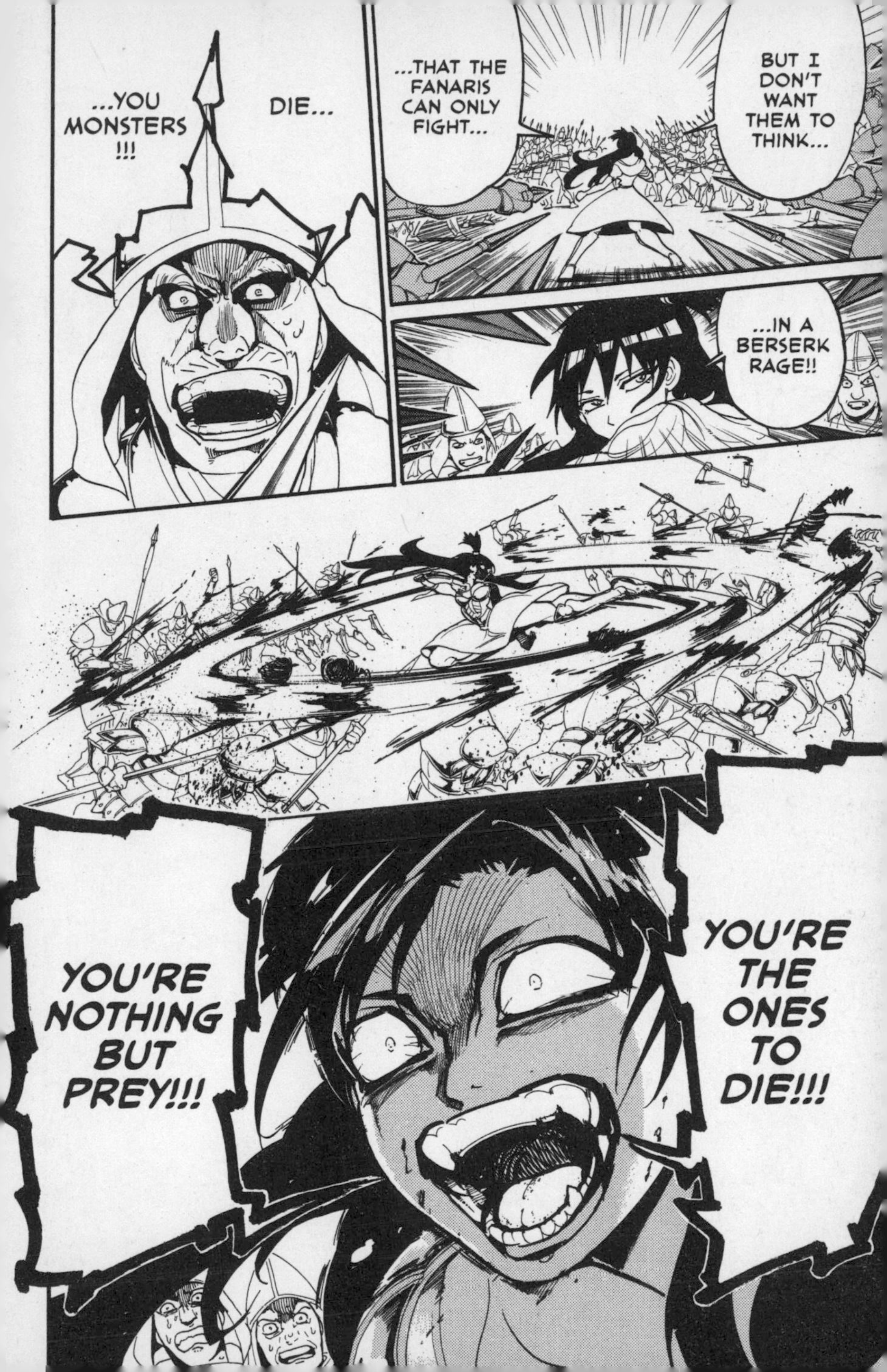

BUT I DON'T WANT THEM TO THINK...
...THAT THE FANARIS CAN ONLY FIGHT...
...IN A BERSERK RAGE!!
DIE...
...YOU MONSTERS!!!
YOU'RE THE ONES TO DIE!!!
YOU'RE NOTHING BUT PREY!!!

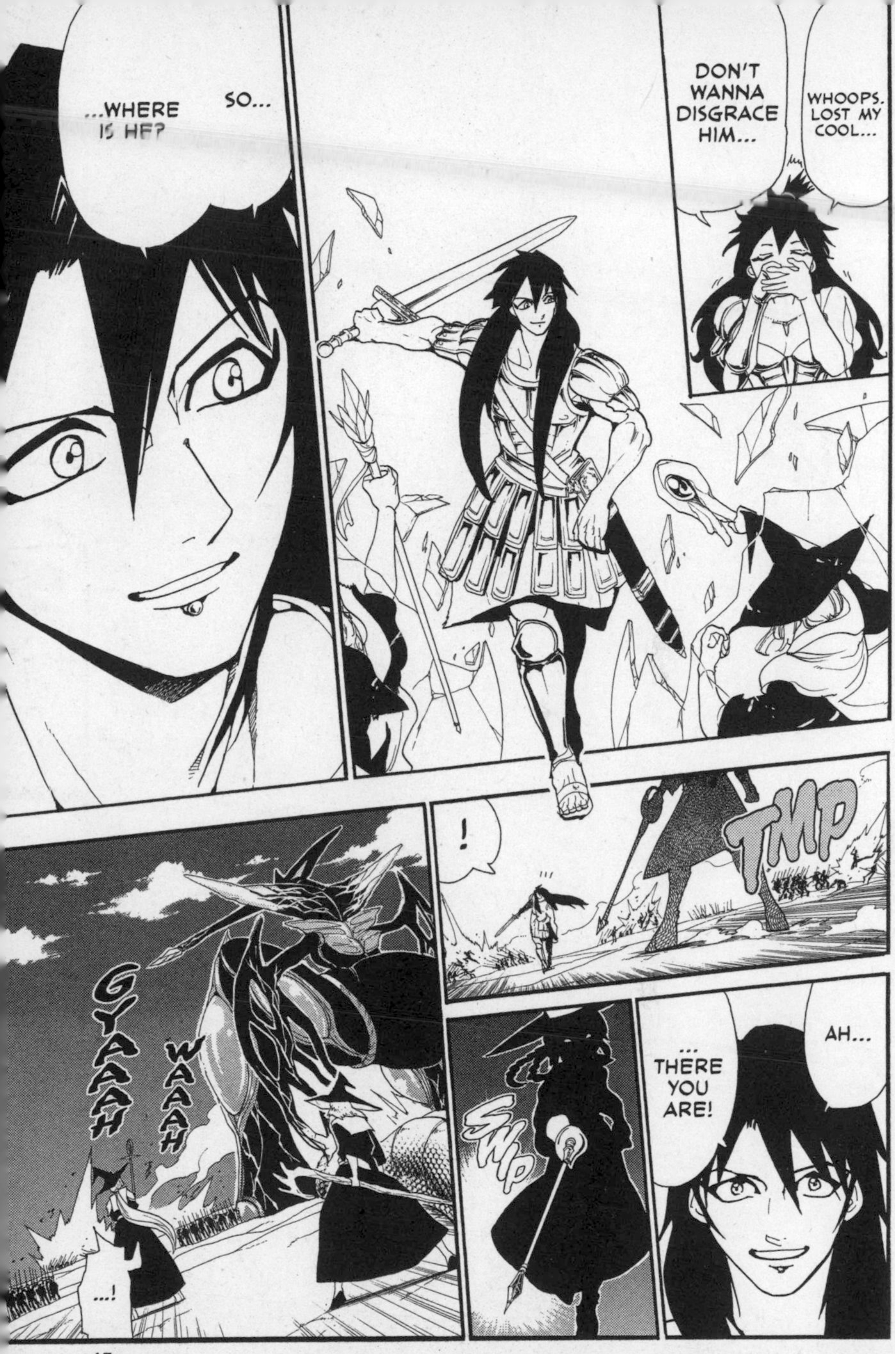
WHOOPS. LOST MY COOL...
DON'T WANNA DISGRACE HIM...
SO...
...WHERE IS HE?
TMP
!
AH...
...THERE YOU ARE!
SWP
GYAAAH
WAAAH
...!

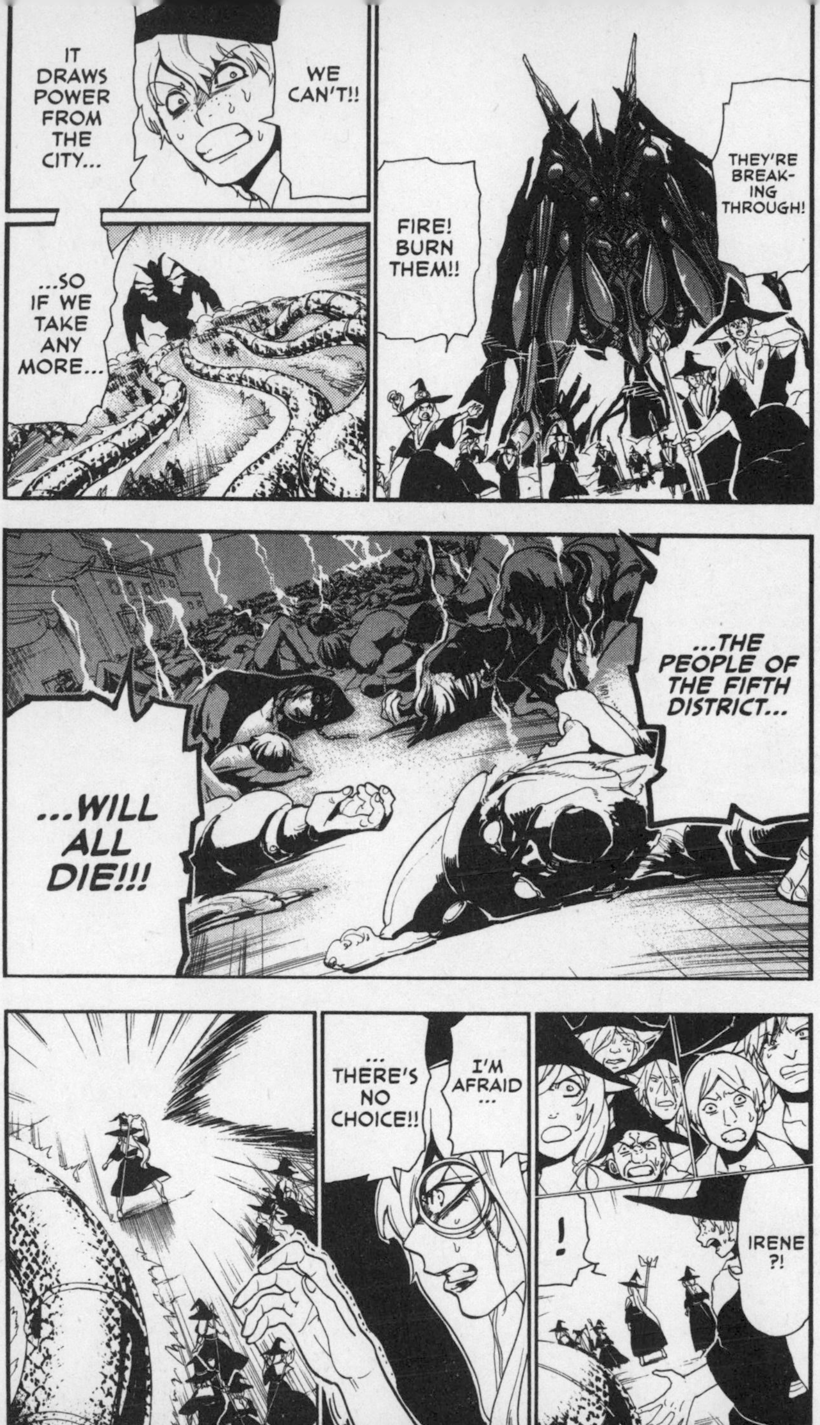
THEY'RE BREAK-ING THROUGH!
FIRE! BURN THEM!!
WE CAN'T!!
IT DRAWS POWER FROM THE CITY...
...SO IF WE TAKE ANY MORE...
...THE PEOPLE OF THE FIFTH DISTRICT...
...WILL ALL DIE!!!
!
IRENE ?!
I'M AFRAID ...
... THERE'S NO CHOICE!!

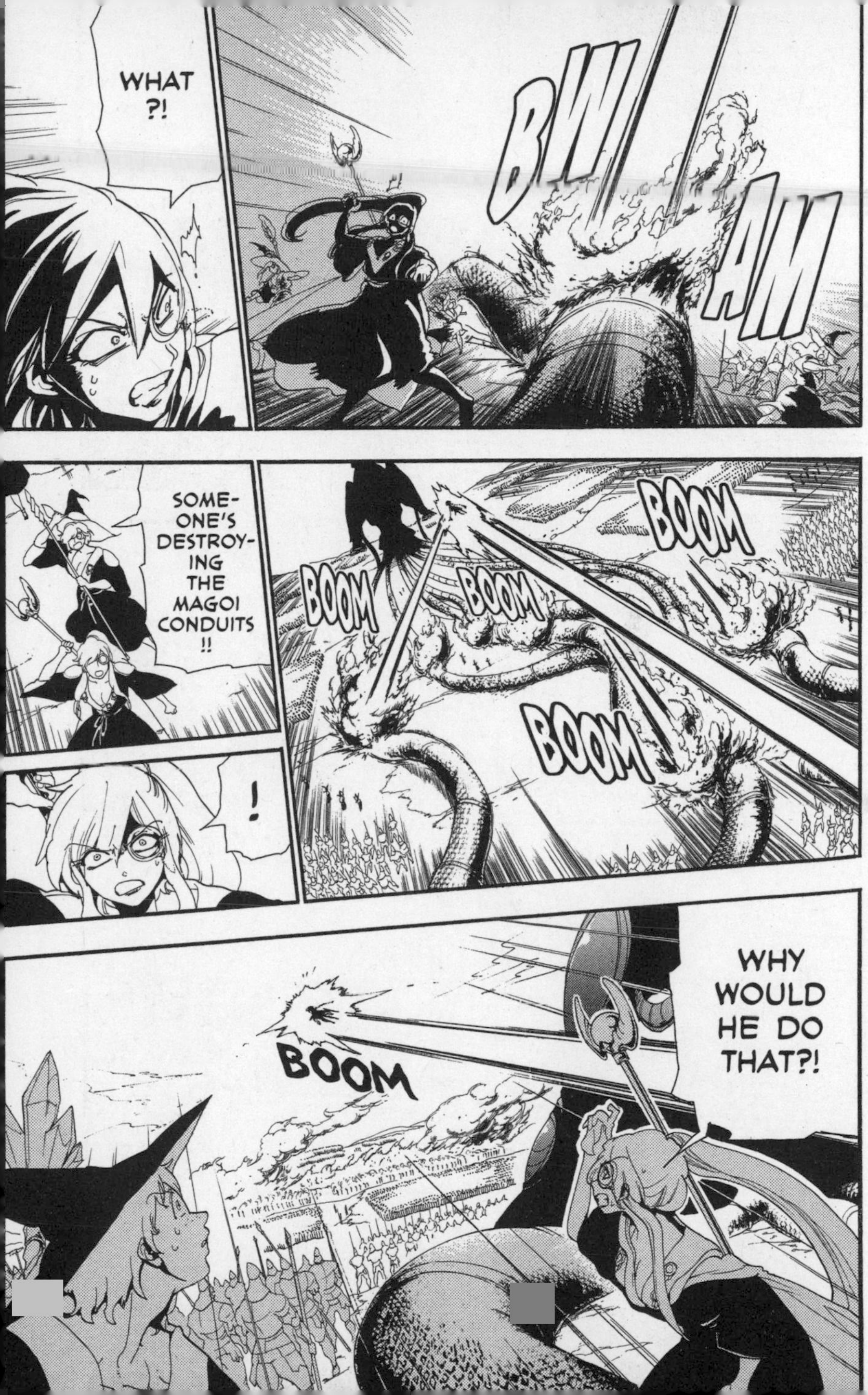
BWAM
WHAT ?!
BOOM
BOOM
BOOM
BOOM
SOME-ONE'S DESTROY-ING THE MAGOI CONDUITS !!
!
WHY WOULD HE DO THAT?!
BOOM

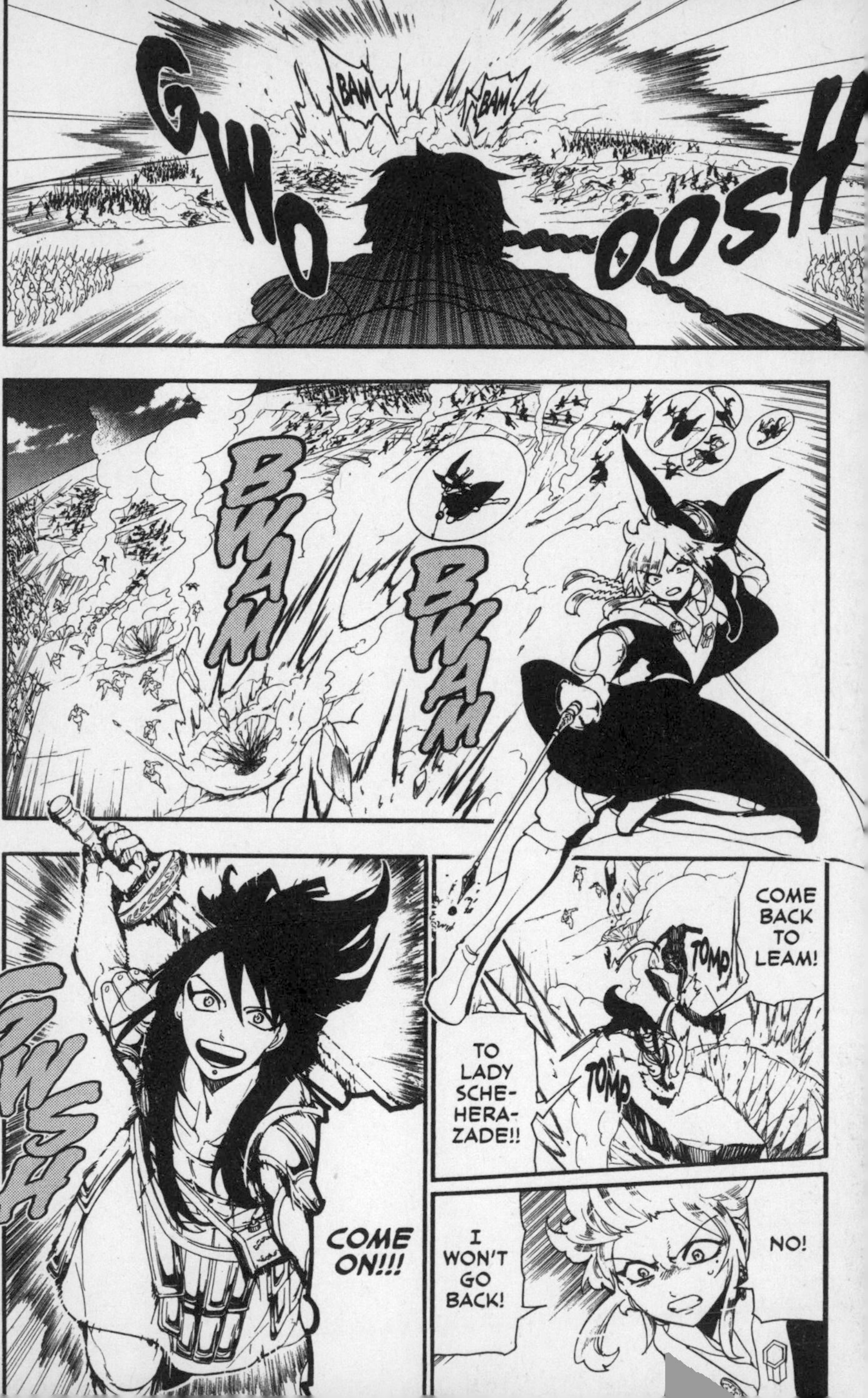
GWOOOSH
BAM
BAM
BWAM
BWAM
COME BACK TO LEAM!
TOMP
TO LADY SCHEHERAZADE!!
TOMP
NO!
I WON'T GO BACK!
GWSH
COME ON!!!

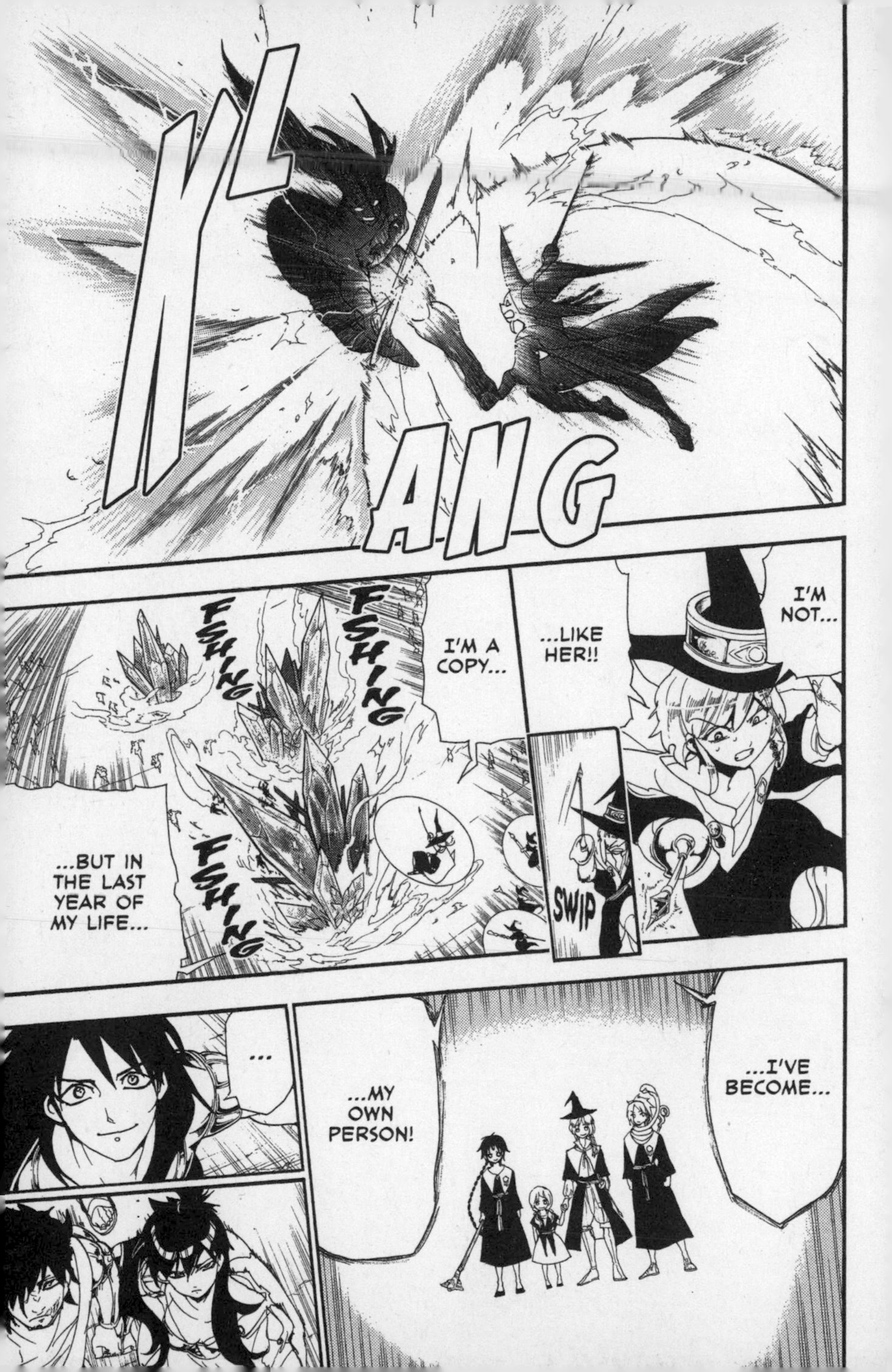
KLANG
I'M NOT...
...LIKE HER!!
SWIP
I'M A COPY...
FSHING
FSHING
FSHING
...BUT IN THE LAST YEAR OF MY LIFE...
...I'VE BECOME...
...MY OWN PERSON!
...

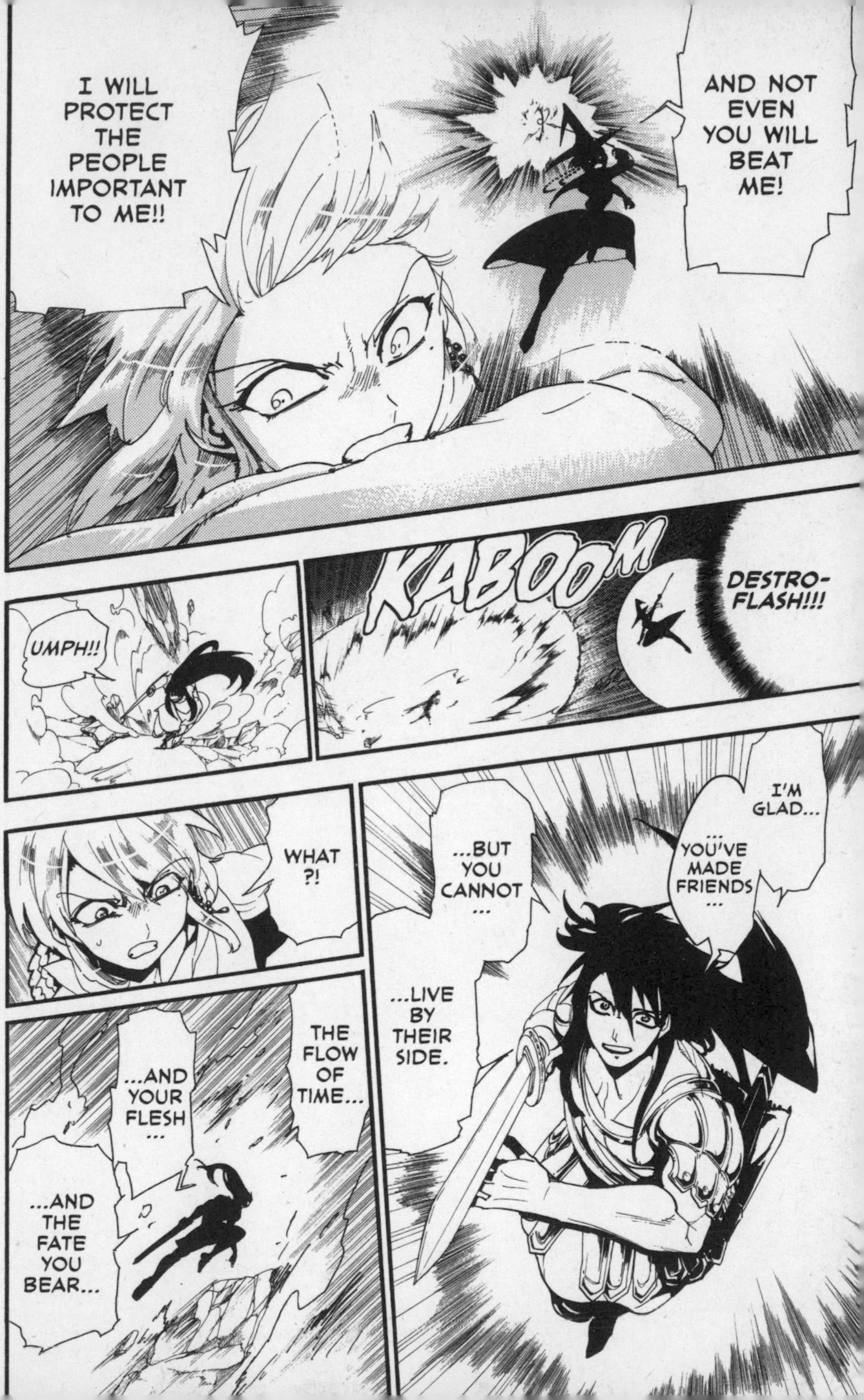
AND NOT EVEN YOU WILL BEAT ME!
I WILL PROTECT THE PEOPLE IMPORTANT TO ME!!
DESTRO-FLASH!!!
KABOOM
UMPH!!
I'M GLAD...
...YOU'VE MADE FRIENDS...
...BUT YOU CANNOT...
...LIVE BY THEIR SIDE.
WHAT?!
THE FLOW OF TIME...
...AND YOUR FLESH...
...AND THE FATE YOU BEAR...

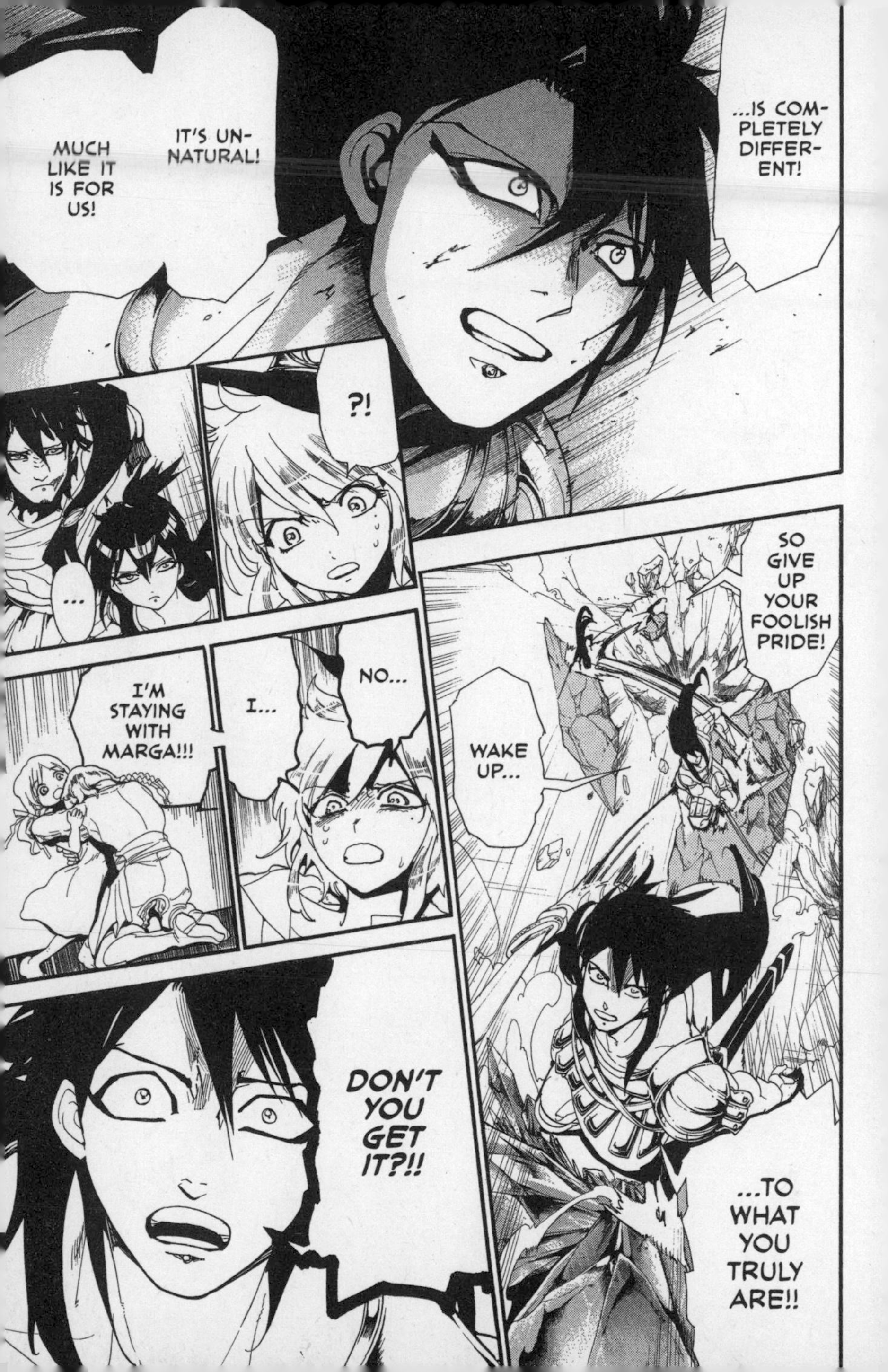
...IS COMPLETELY DIFFERENT!
IT'S UNNATURAL!
MUCH LIKE IT IS FOR US!
?!
...
SO GIVE UP YOUR FOOLISH PRIDE!
WAKE UP...
NO...
I...
I'M STAYING WITH MARGA!!!
DON'T YOU GET IT?!!
...TO WHAT YOU TRULY ARE!!

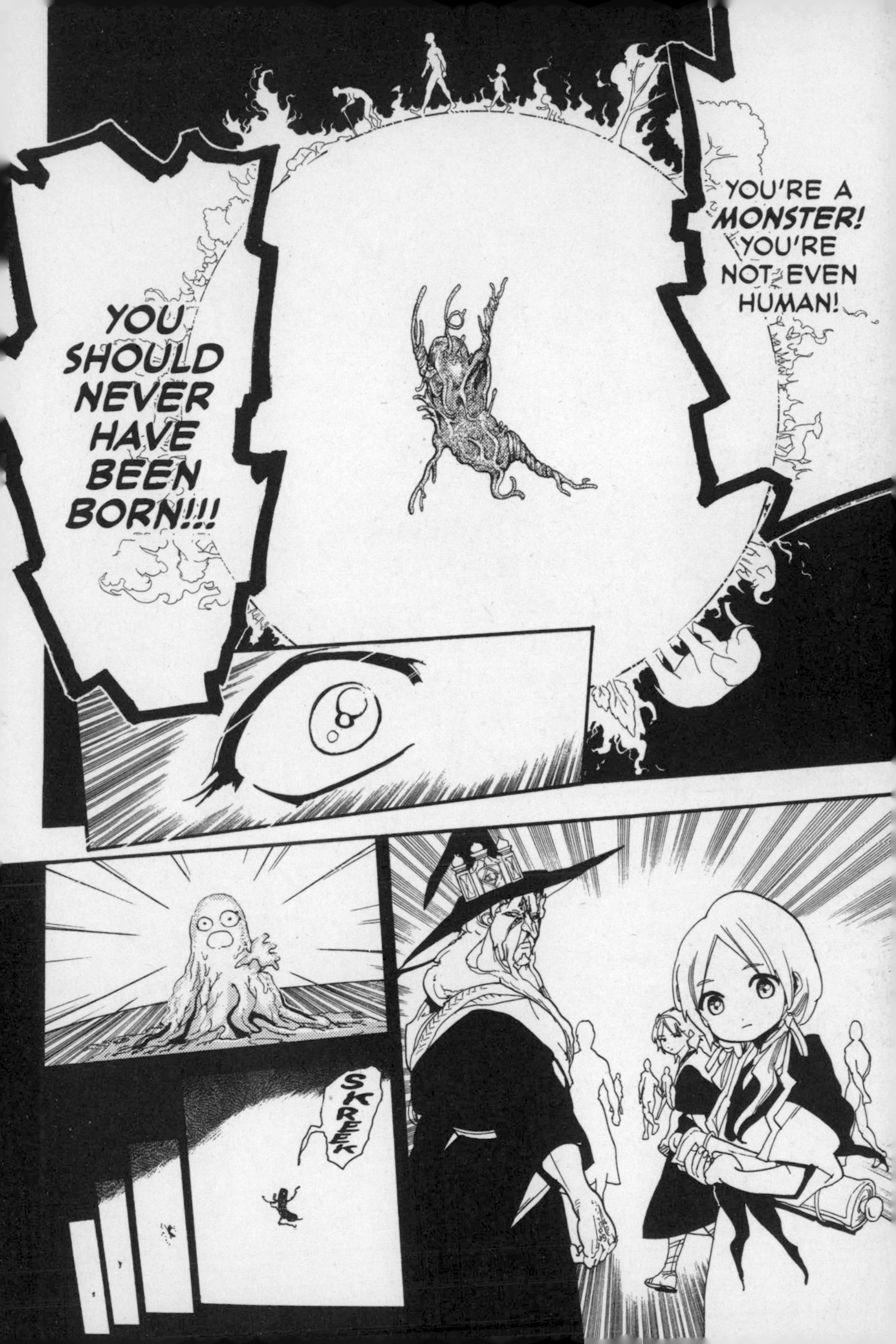

YOU'RE A MONSTER! YOU'RE NOT EVEN HUMAN!
YOU SHOULD NEVER HAVE BEEN BORN!!!
SKREEK

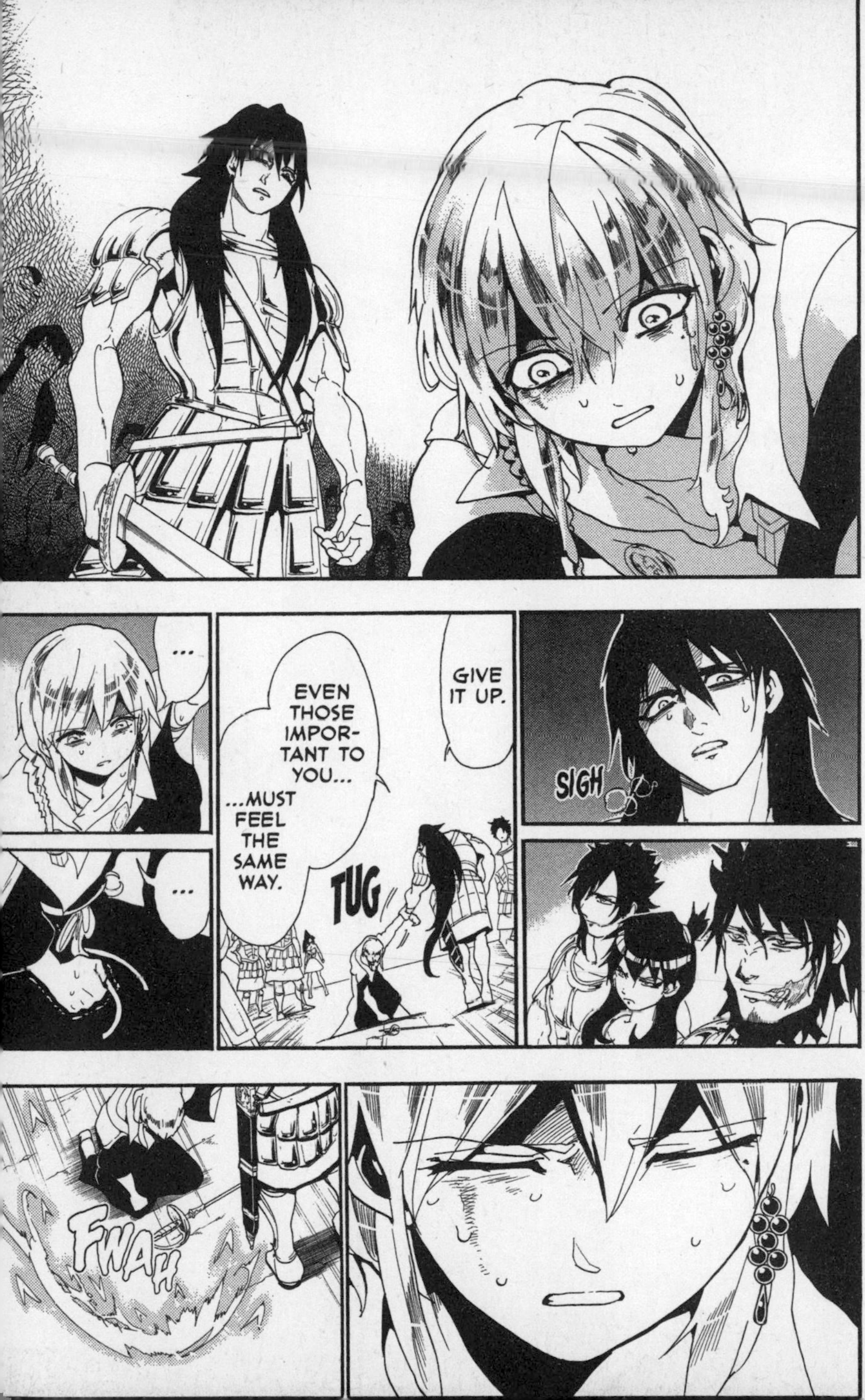
SIGH
GIVE IT UP.
EVEN THOSE IMPORTANT TO YOU...
...MUST FEEL THE SAME WAY.
TUG
...
...
FWAH

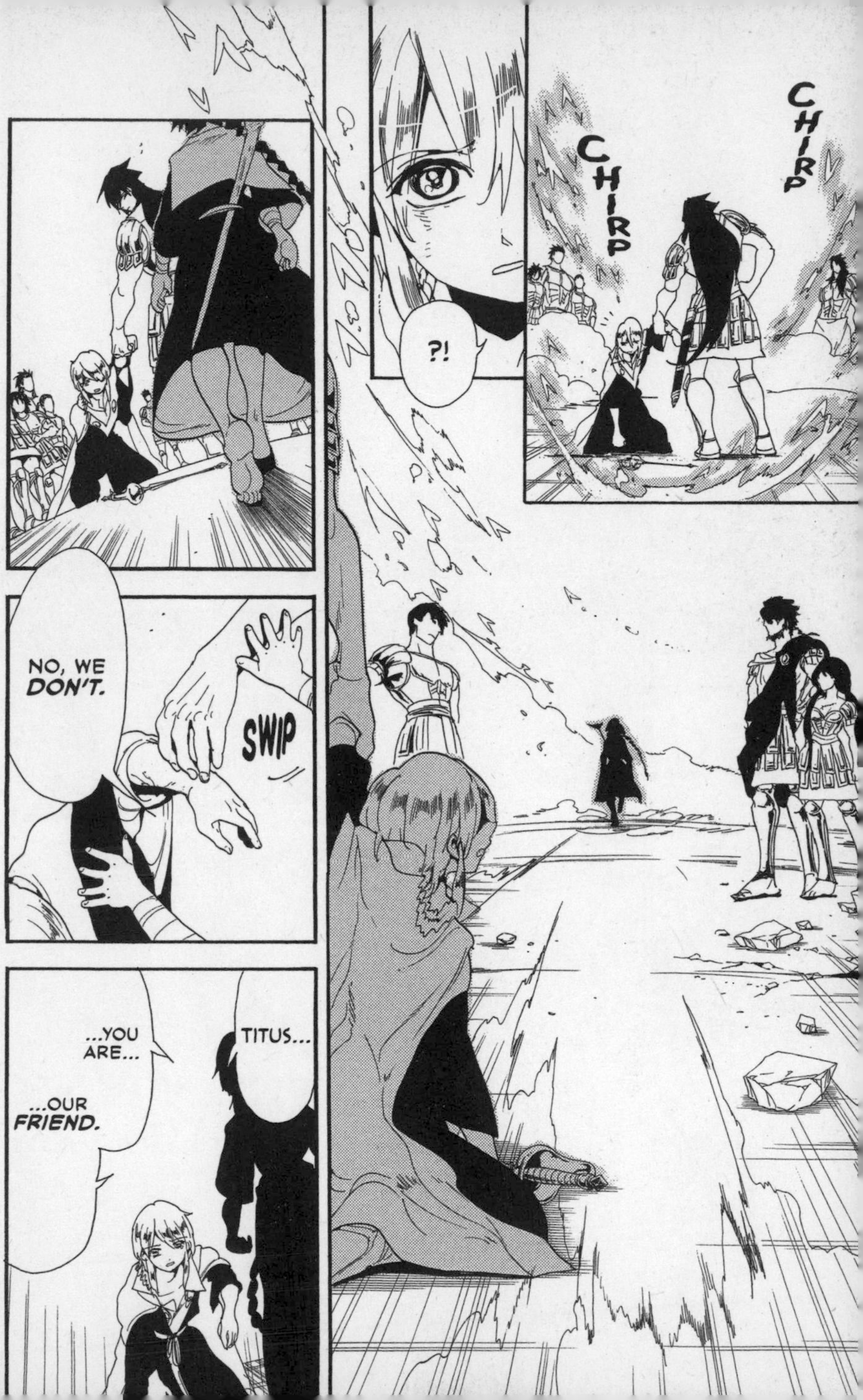
CHIRP
CHIRP
?!
NO, WE DON'T.
SWIP
TITUS...
...YOU ARE...
...OUR FRIEND.

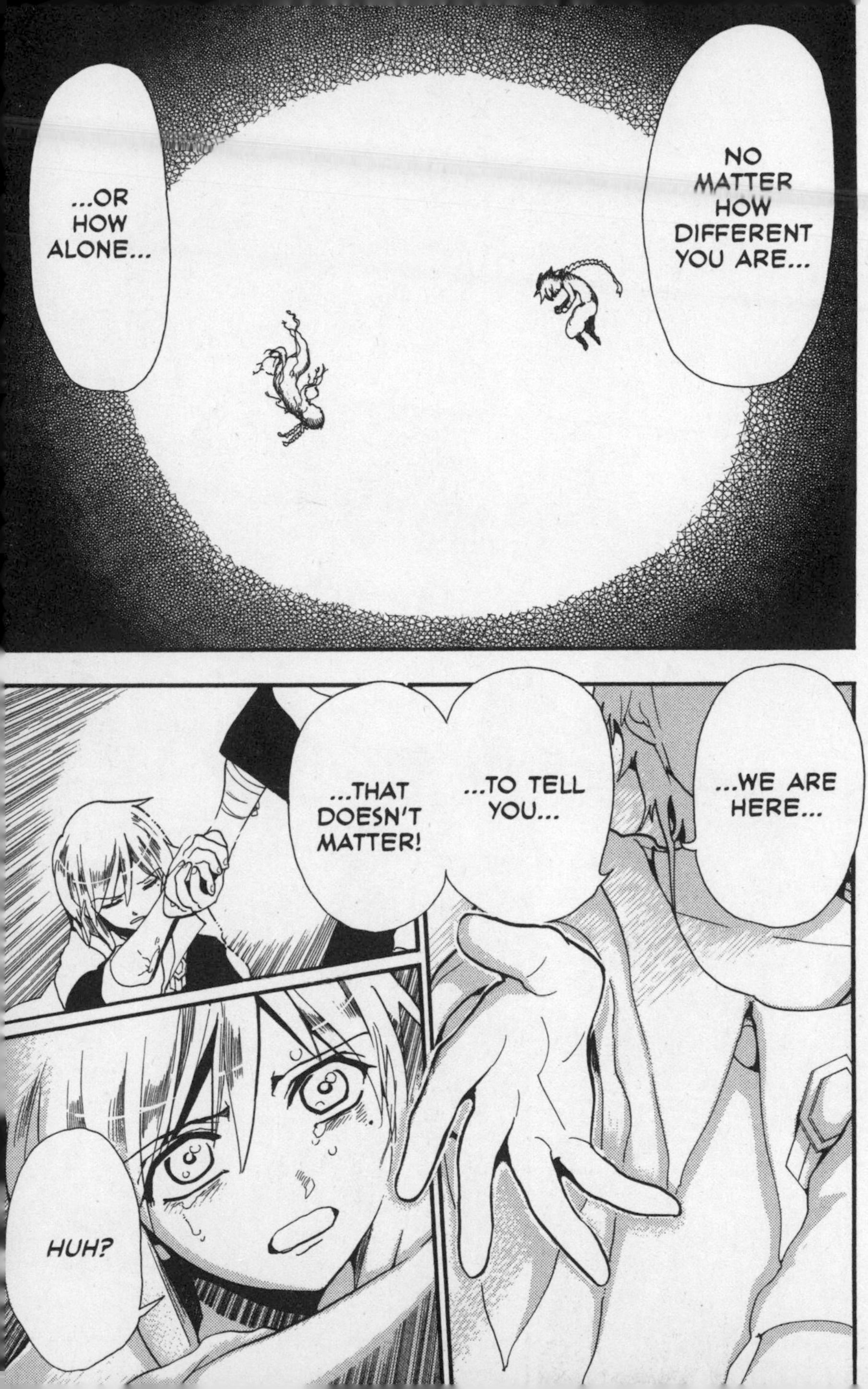
NO MATTER HOW DIFFERENT YOU ARE...
...OR HOW ALONE...
...WE ARE HERE...
...TO TELL YOU...
...THAT DOESN'T MATTER!
HUH?

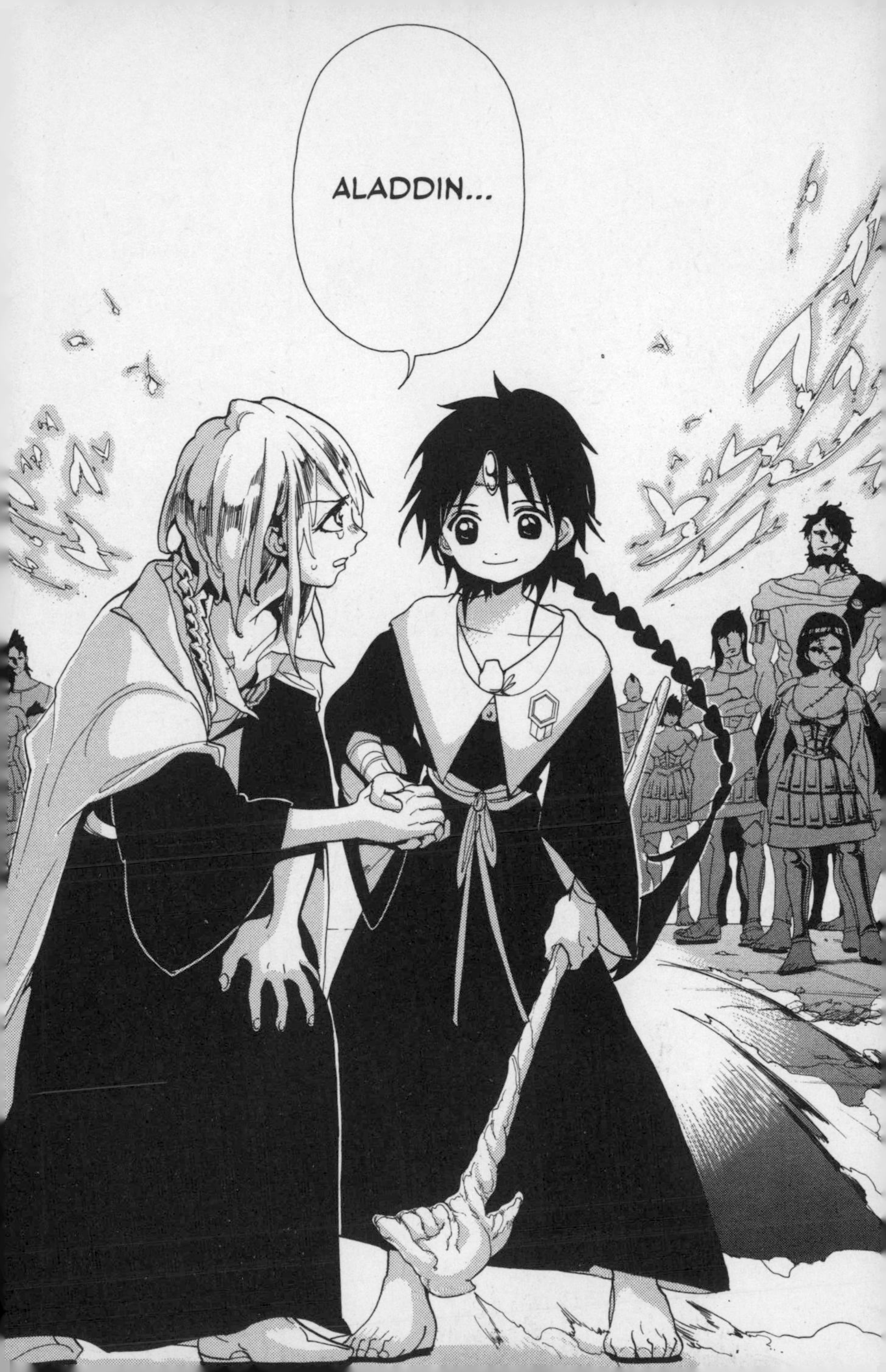
ALADDIN...

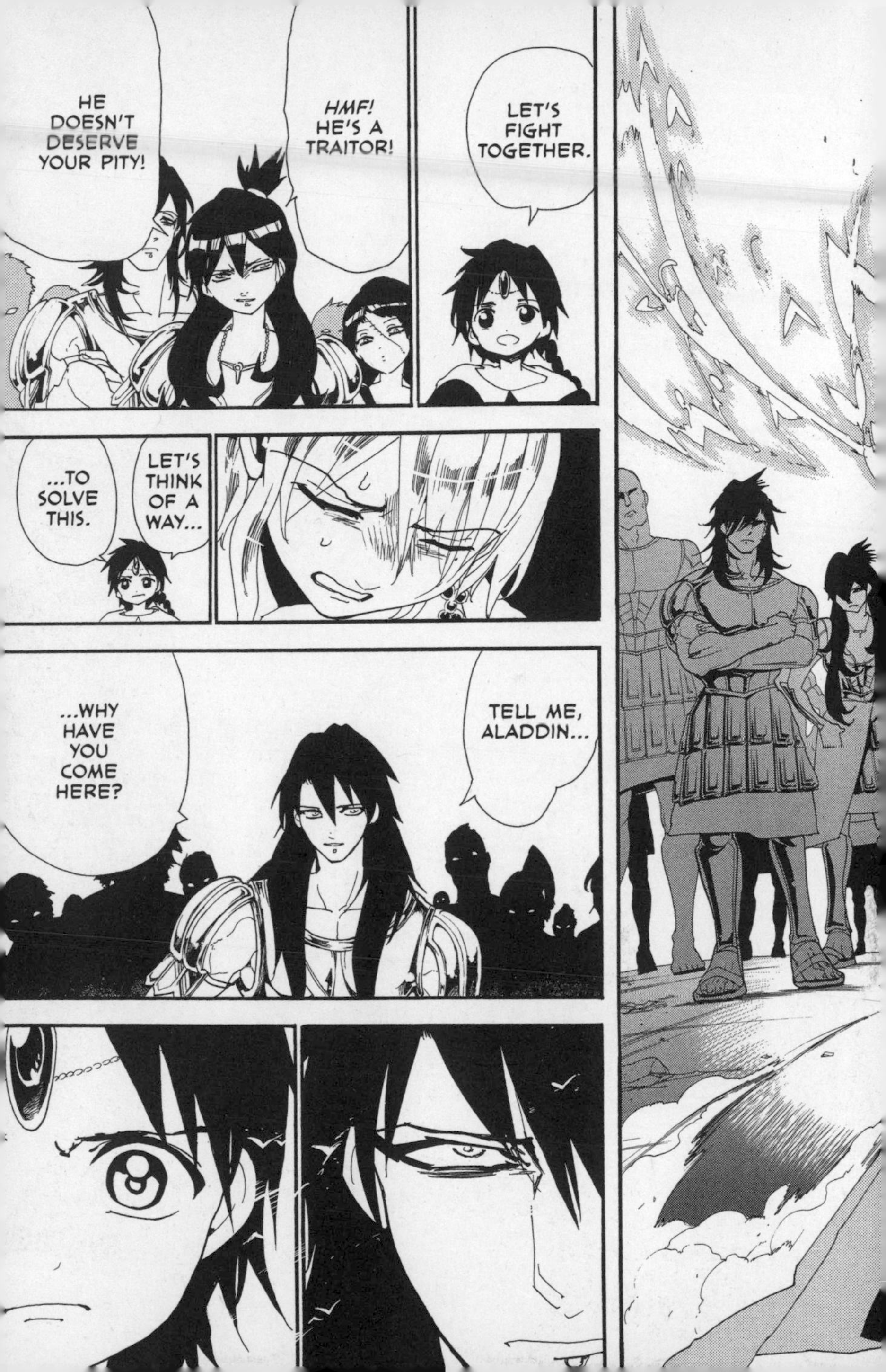
LET'S FIGHT TOGETHER.
HMF! HE'S A TRAITOR!
HE DOESN'T DESERVE YOUR PITY!
LET'S THINK OF A WAY...
...TO SOLVE THIS.
TELL ME, ALADDIN...
...WHY HAVE YOU COME HERE?

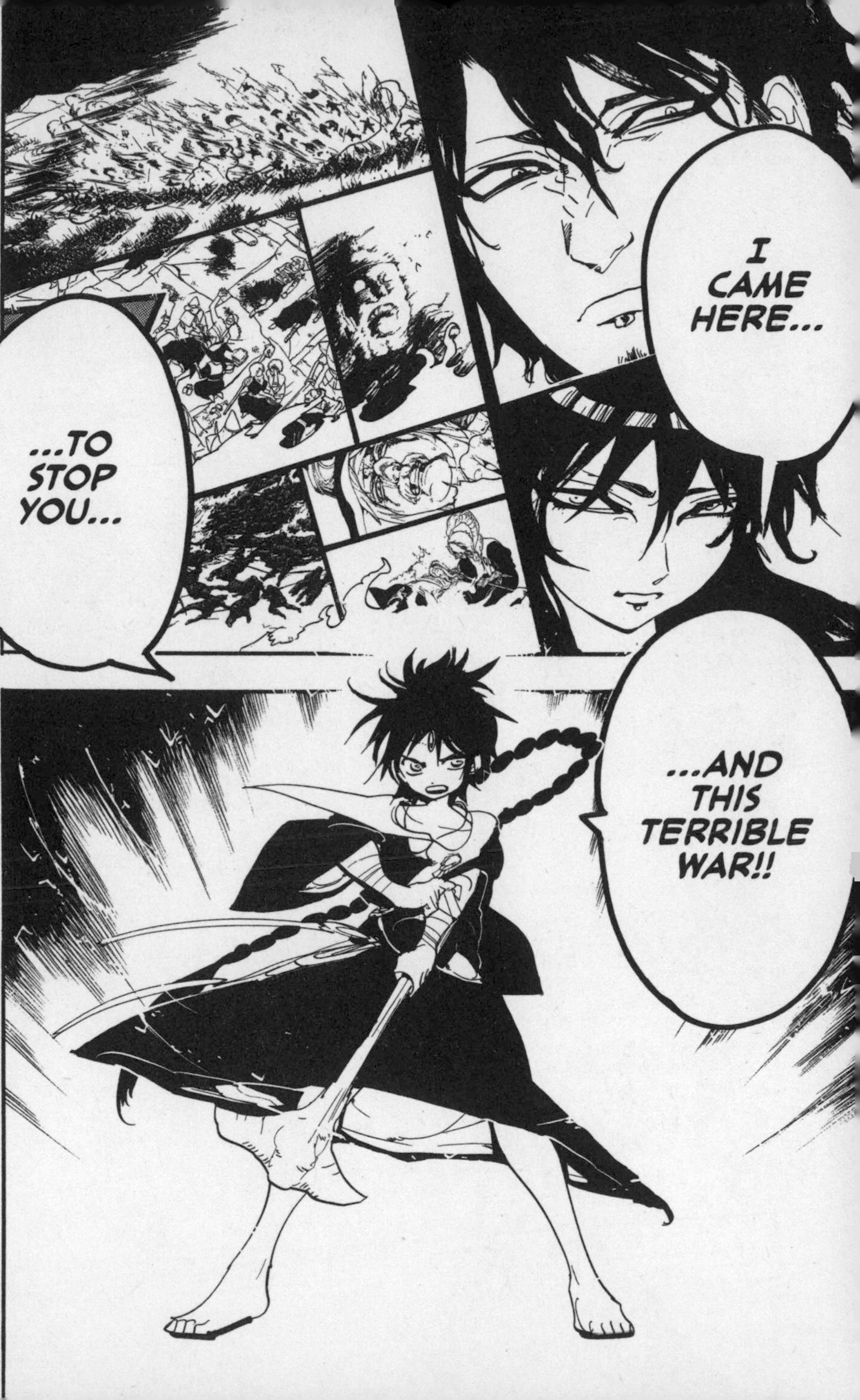
I CAME HERE...
...TO STOP YOU...
...AND THIS TERRIBLE WAR!!

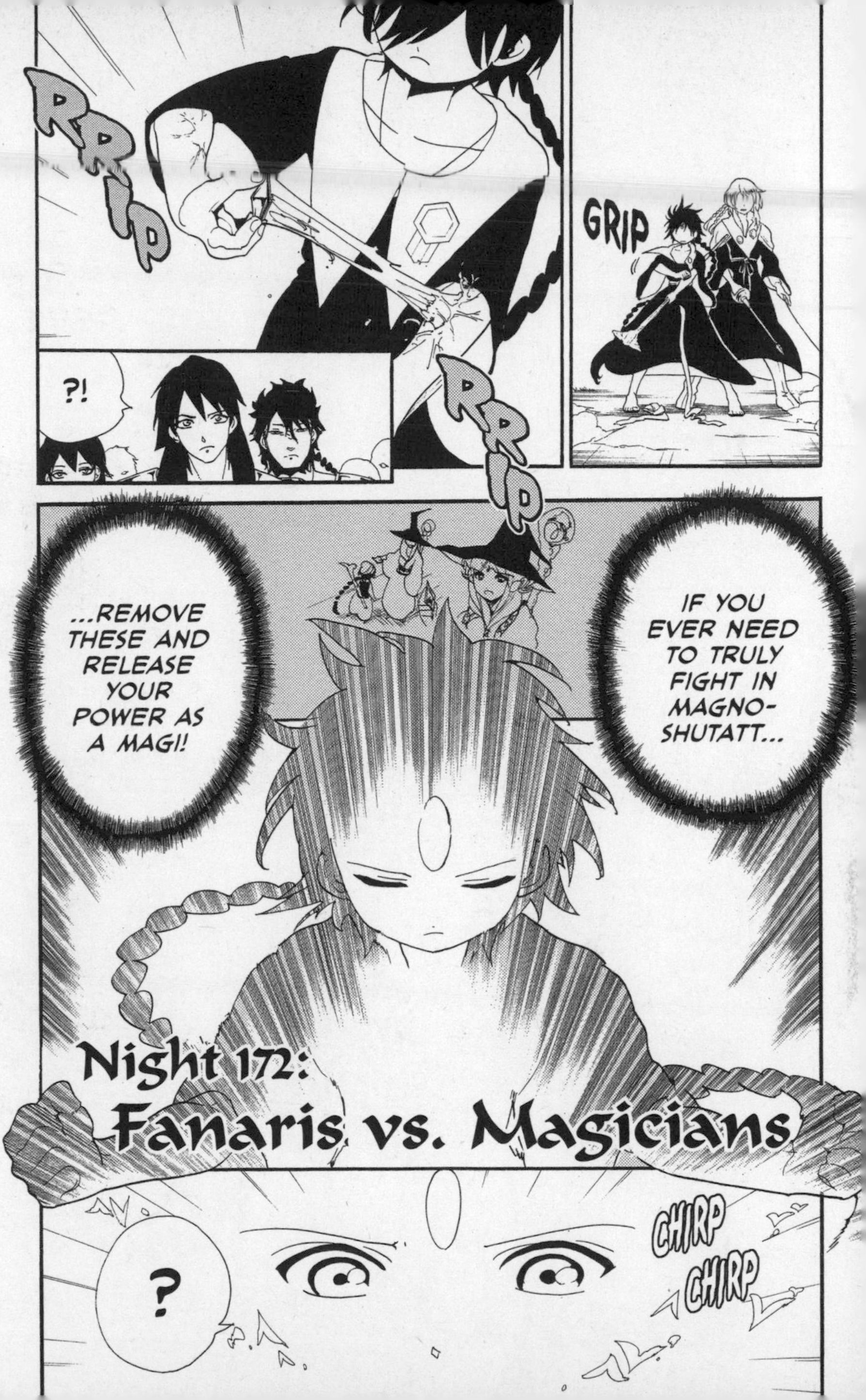
GRIP
RRIP
RRIP
?!
IF YOU EVER NEED TO TRULY FIGHT IN MAGNOSHUTATT...
...REMOVE THESE AND RELEASE YOUR POWER AS A MAGI!
Night 172:
Fanaris vs. Magicians
CHIRP
CHIRP
?

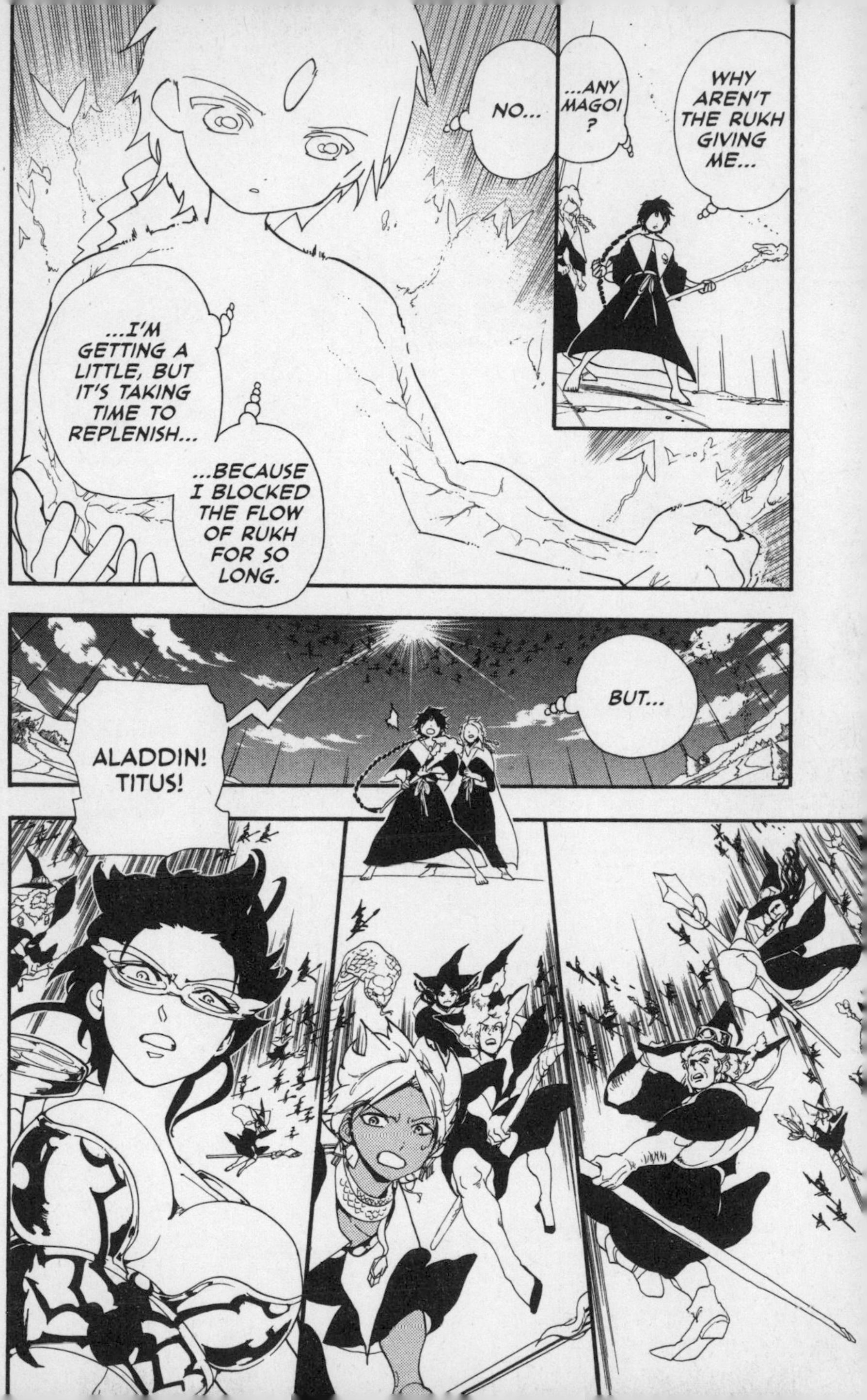
WHY AREN'T THE RUKH GIVING ME...
...ANY MAGOI?
NO...
...I'M GETTING A LITTLE, BUT IT'S TAKING TIME TO REPLENISH...
...BECAUSE I BLOCKED THE FLOW OF RUKH FOR SO LONG.
BUT...
ALADDIN! TITUS!

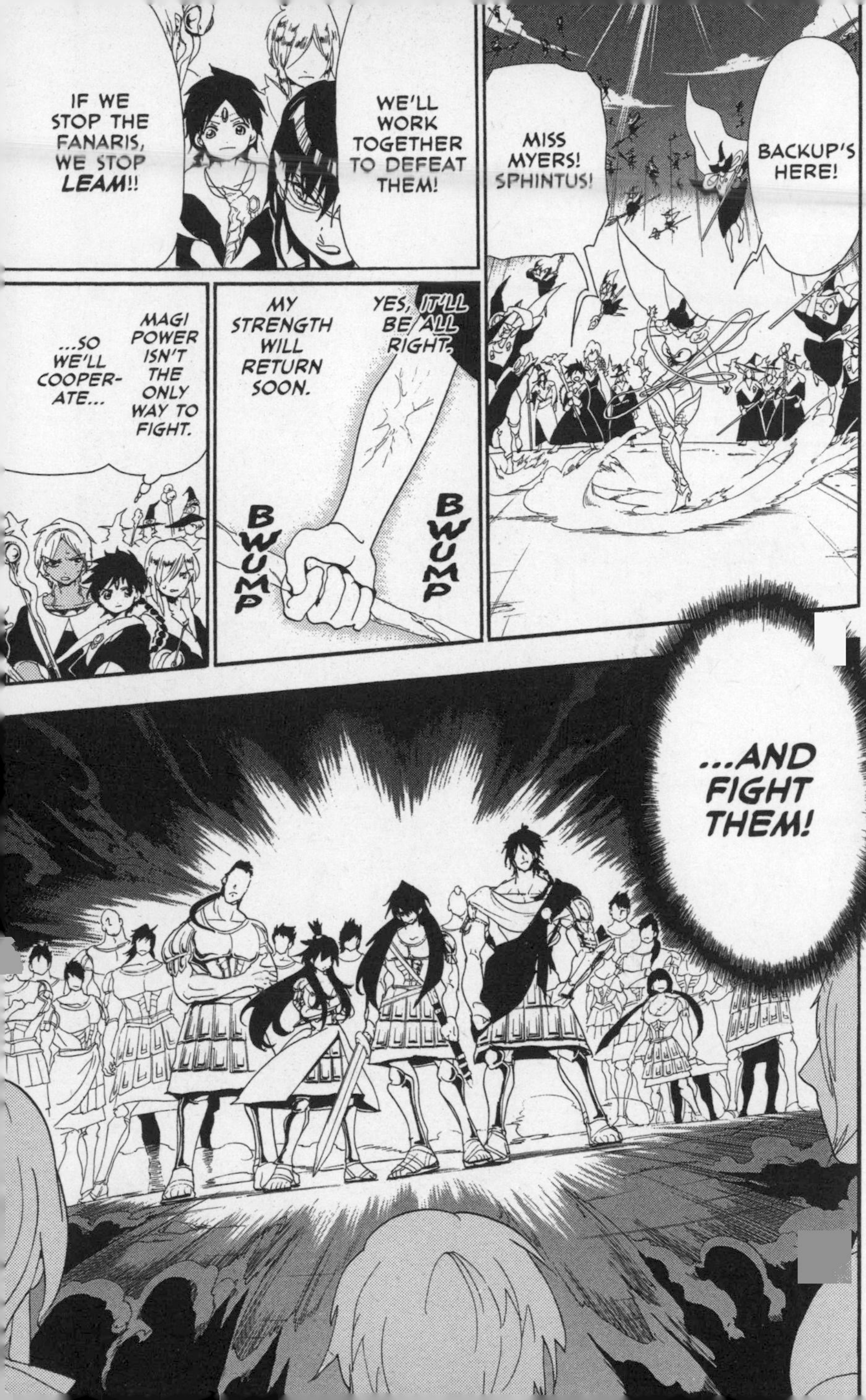
BACKUP'S HERE!
MISS MYERS! SPHINTUS!
WE'LL WORK TOGETHER TO DEFEAT THEM!
IF WE STOP THE FANARIS, WE STOP LEAM!!
YES, IT'LL BE ALL RIGHT.
BWUMP
MY STRENGTH WILL RETURN SOON.
BWUMP
MAGI POWER ISN'T THE ONLY WAY TO FIGHT.
...SO WE'LL COOPER-ATE...
...AND FIGHT THEM!

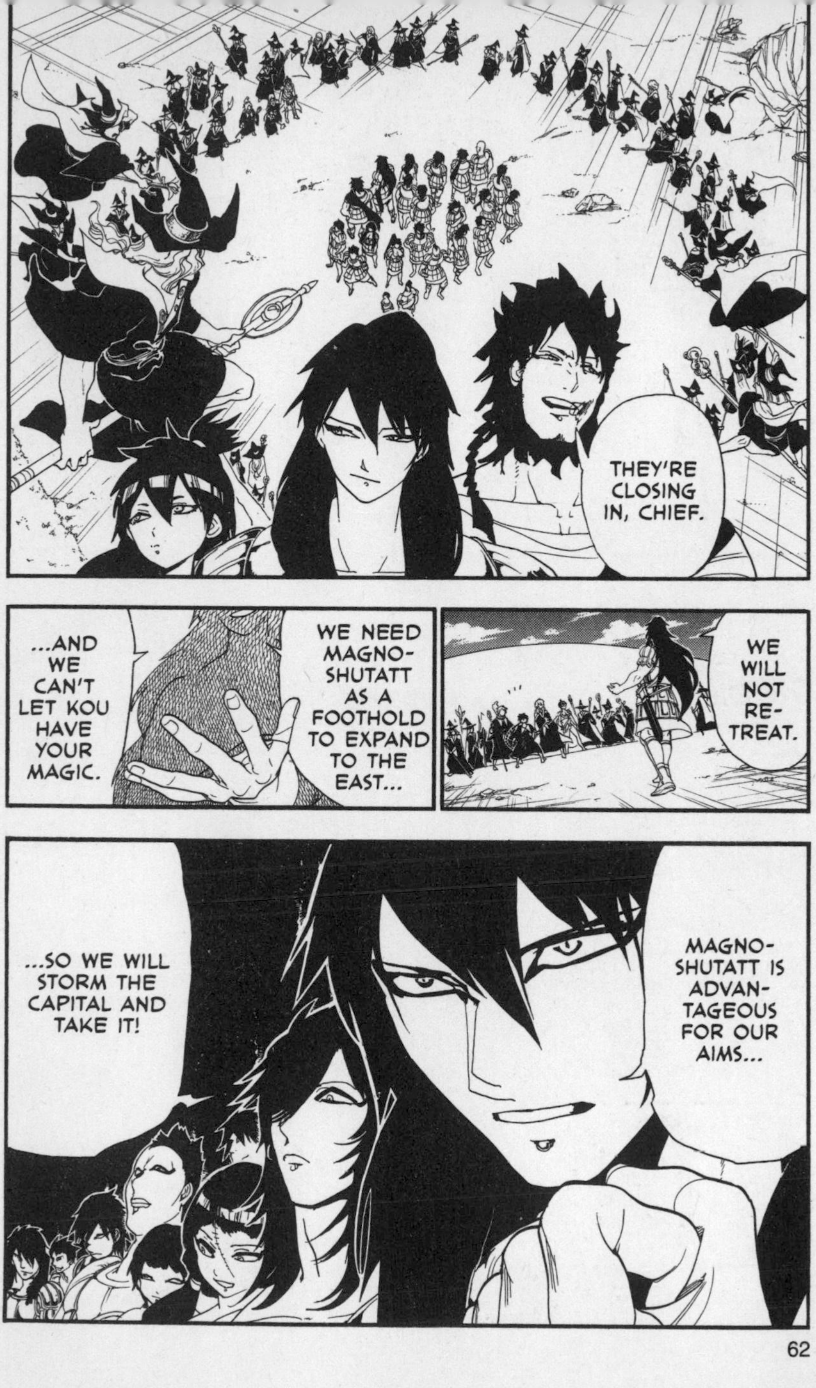
THEY'RE CLOSING IN, CHIEF.
WE WILL NOT RE-TREAT.
WE NEED MAGNO-SHUTATT AS A FOOTHOLD TO EXPAND TO THE EAST...
...AND WE CAN'T LET KOU HAVE YOUR MAGIC.
MAGNO-SHUTATT IS ADVAN-TAGEOUS FOR OUR AIMS...
...SO WE WILL STORM THE CAPITAL AND TAKE IT!

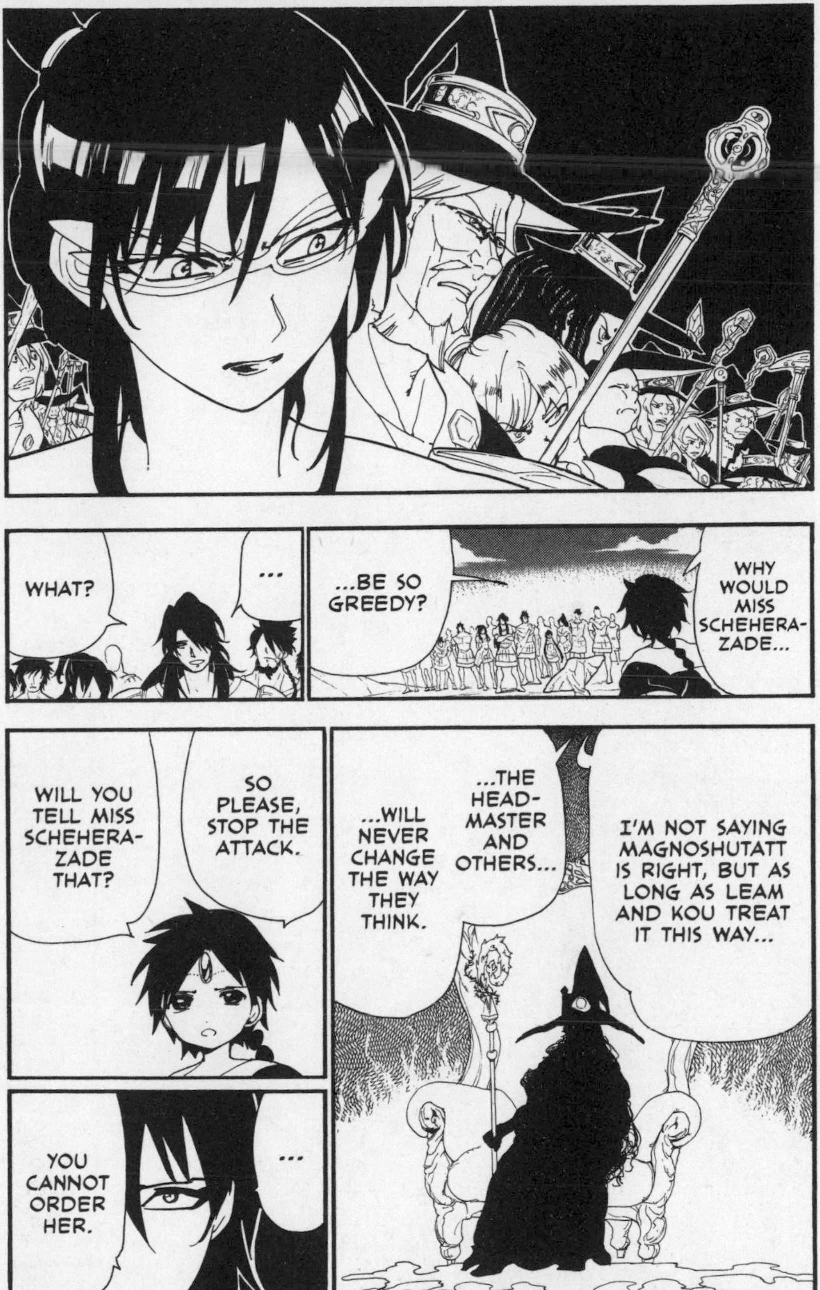
WHY WOULD MISS SCHEHERAZADE...
...BE SO GREEDY?
...
WHAT?
I'M NOT SAYING MAGNOSHUTATT IS RIGHT, BUT AS LONG AS LEAM AND KOU TREAT IT THIS WAY...
...THE HEADMASTER AND OTHERS...
...WILL NEVER CHANGE THE WAY THEY THINK.
SO PLEASE, STOP THE ATTACK.
WILL YOU TELL MISS SCHEHERAZADE THAT?
...
YOU CANNOT ORDER HER.

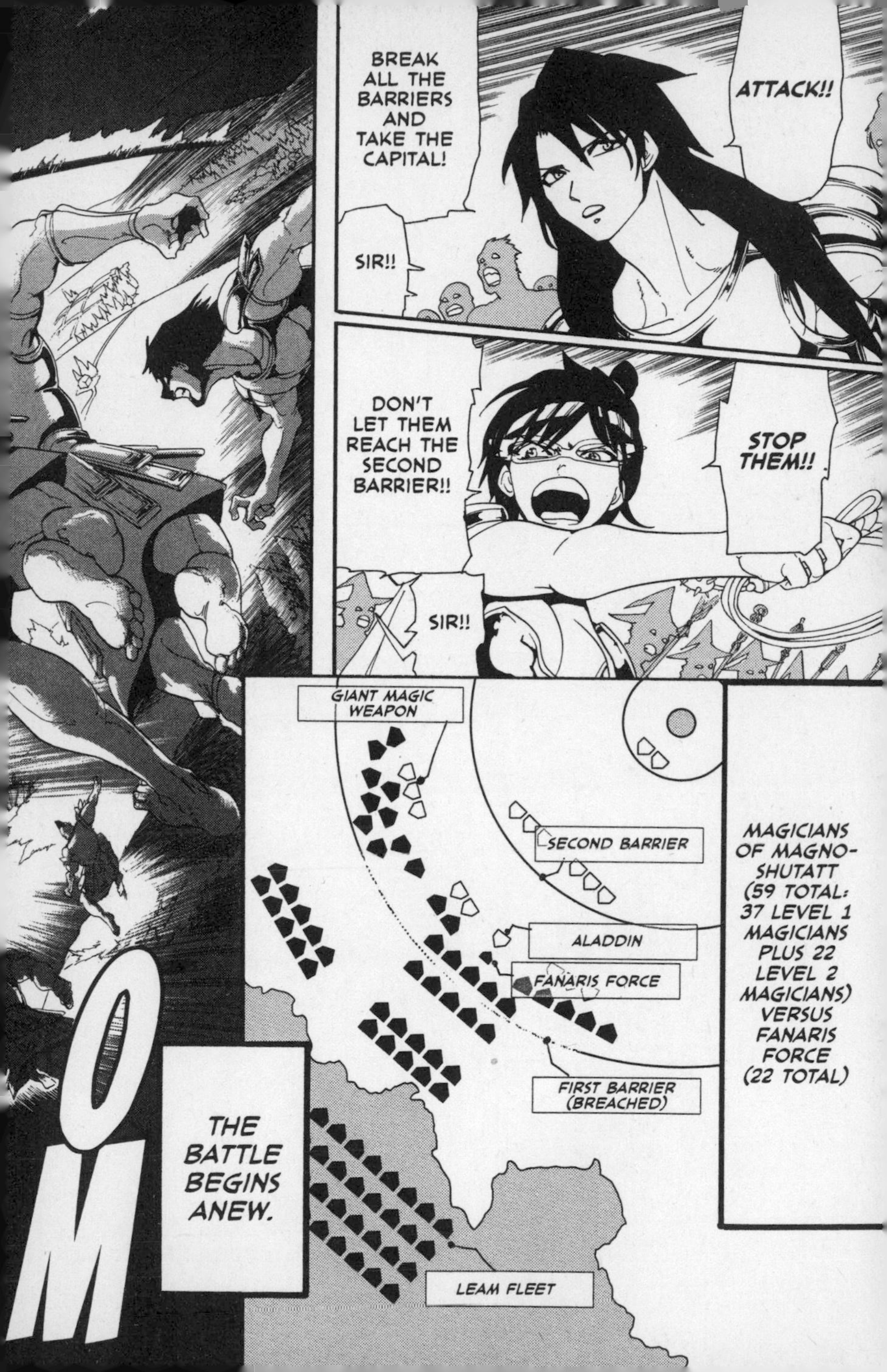
ATTACK!!
BREAK ALL THE BARRIERS AND TAKE THE CAPITAL!
SIR!!
STOP THEM!!
DON'T LET THEM REACH THE SECOND BARRIER!!
SIR!!
MAGICIANS OF MAGNO-SHUTATT (59 TOTAL: 37 LEVEL 1 MAGICIANS PLUS 22 LEVEL 2 MAGICIANS) VERSUS FANARIS FORCE (22 TOTAL)
GIANT MAGIC WEAPON
SECOND BARRIER
ALADDIN
FANARIS FORCE
FIRST BARRIER (BREACHED)
LEAM FLEET
OM
THE BATTLE BEGINS ANEW.

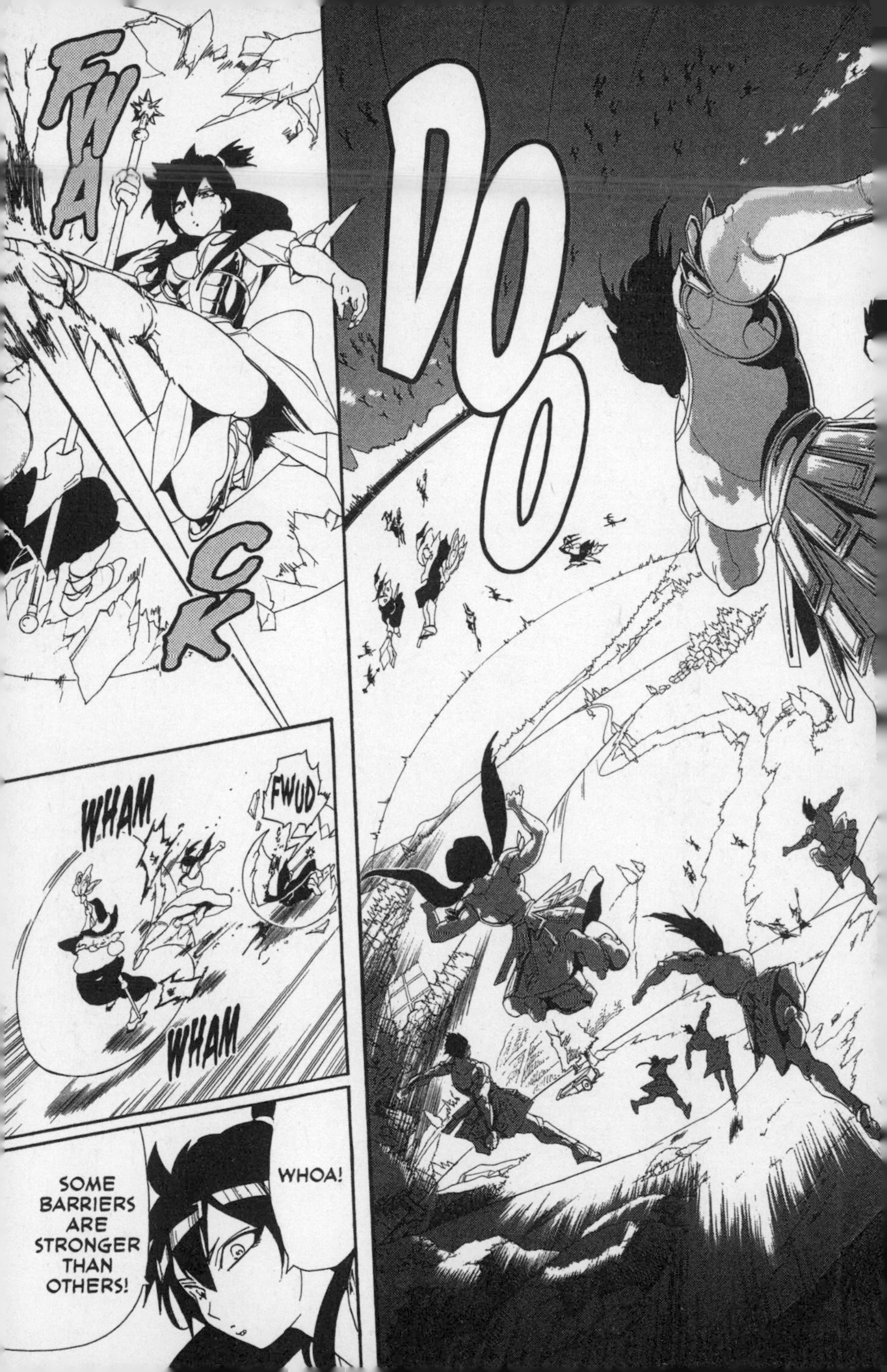
DOOO
FWA
CK
FWUD
WHAM
WHAM
WHOA!
SOME BARRIERS ARE STRONGER THAN OTHERS!

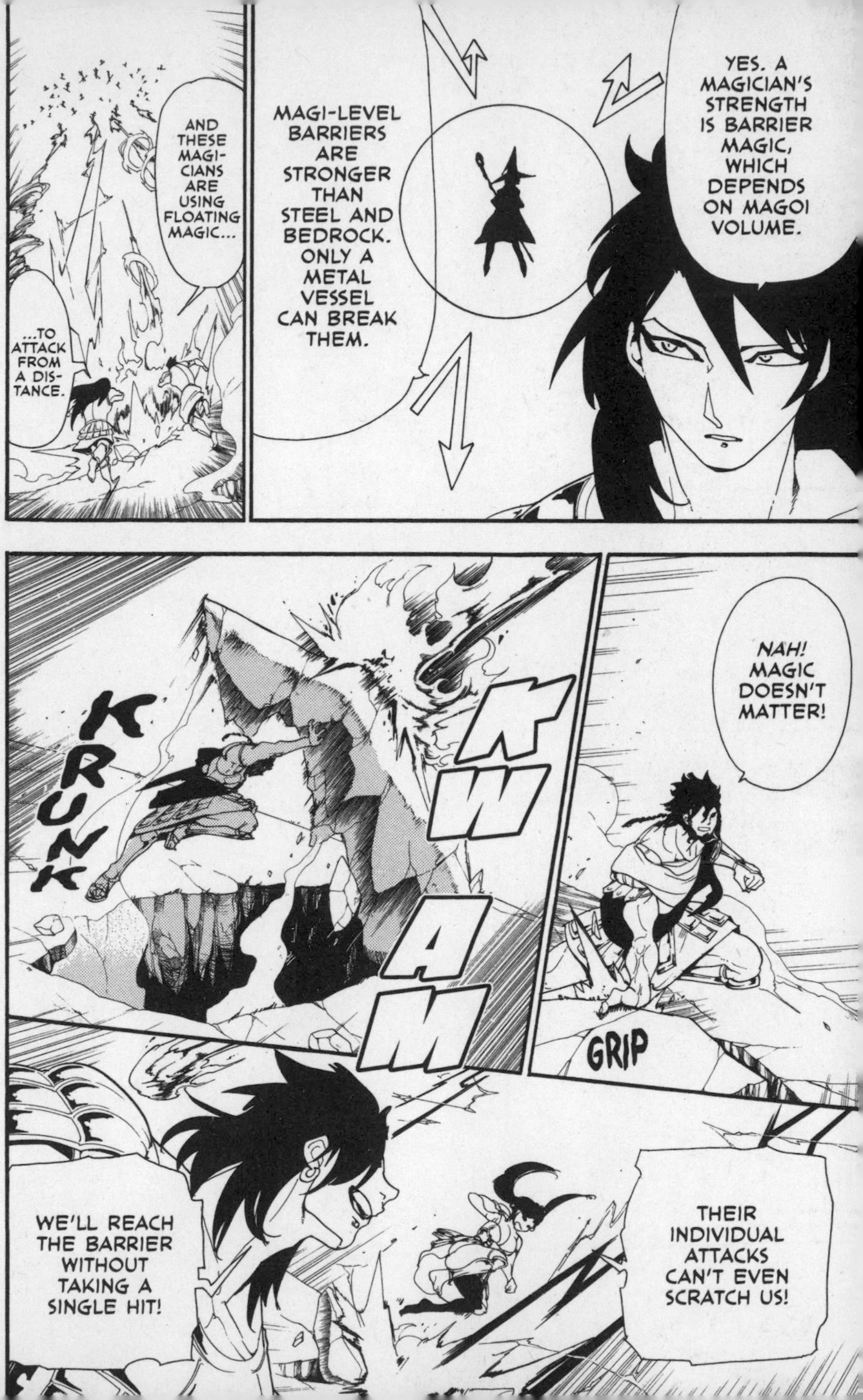
YES. A MAGICIAN'S STRENGTH IS BARRIER MAGIC, WHICH DEPENDS ON MAGOI VOLUME.
MAGI-LEVEL BARRIERS ARE STRONGER THAN STEEL AND BEDROCK. ONLY A METAL VESSEL CAN BREAK THEM.
AND THESE MAGI-CIANS ARE USING FLOATING MAGIC...
...TO ATTACK FROM A DIS-TANCE.
NAH! MAGIC DOESN'T MATTER!
GRIP
KWAM
KRUNK
THEIR INDIVIDUAL ATTACKS CAN'T EVEN SCRATCH US!
WE'LL REACH THE BARRIER WITHOUT TAKING A SINGLE HIT!

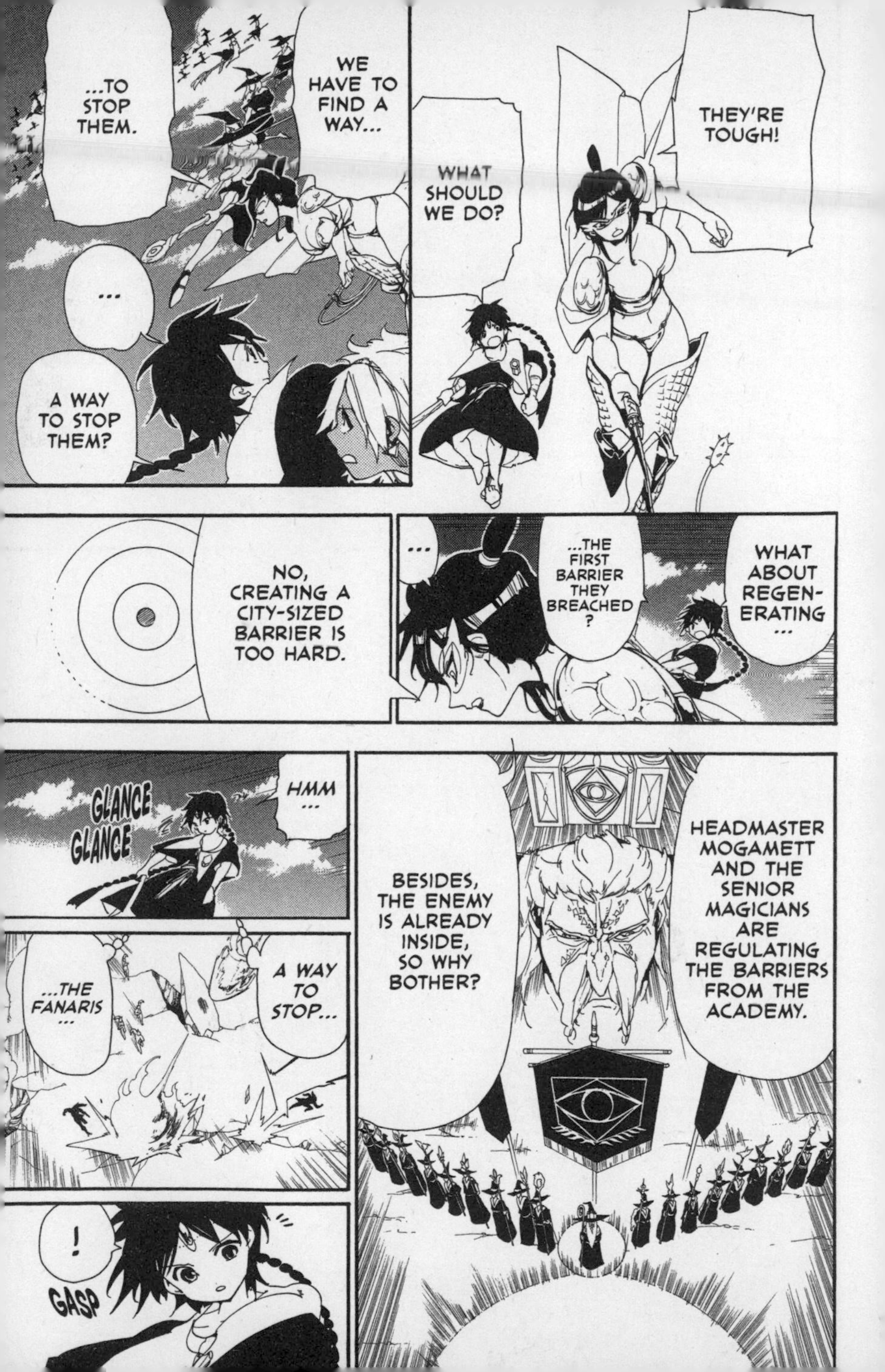
THEY'RE TOUGH!
WHAT SHOULD WE DO?
WE HAVE TO FIND A WAY...
...TO STOP THEM.
...
A WAY TO STOP THEM?
WHAT ABOUT REGEN-ERATING...
...THE FIRST BARRIER THEY BREACHED?
...
NO, CREATING A CITY-SIZED BARRIER IS TOO HARD.
HEADMASTER MOGAMETT AND THE SENIOR MAGICIANS ARE REGULATING THE BARRIERS FROM THE ACADEMY.
BESIDES, THE ENEMY IS ALREADY INSIDE, SO WHY BOTHER?
HMM...
GLANCE GLANCE
A WAY TO STOP...
...THE FANARIS...
!
GASP

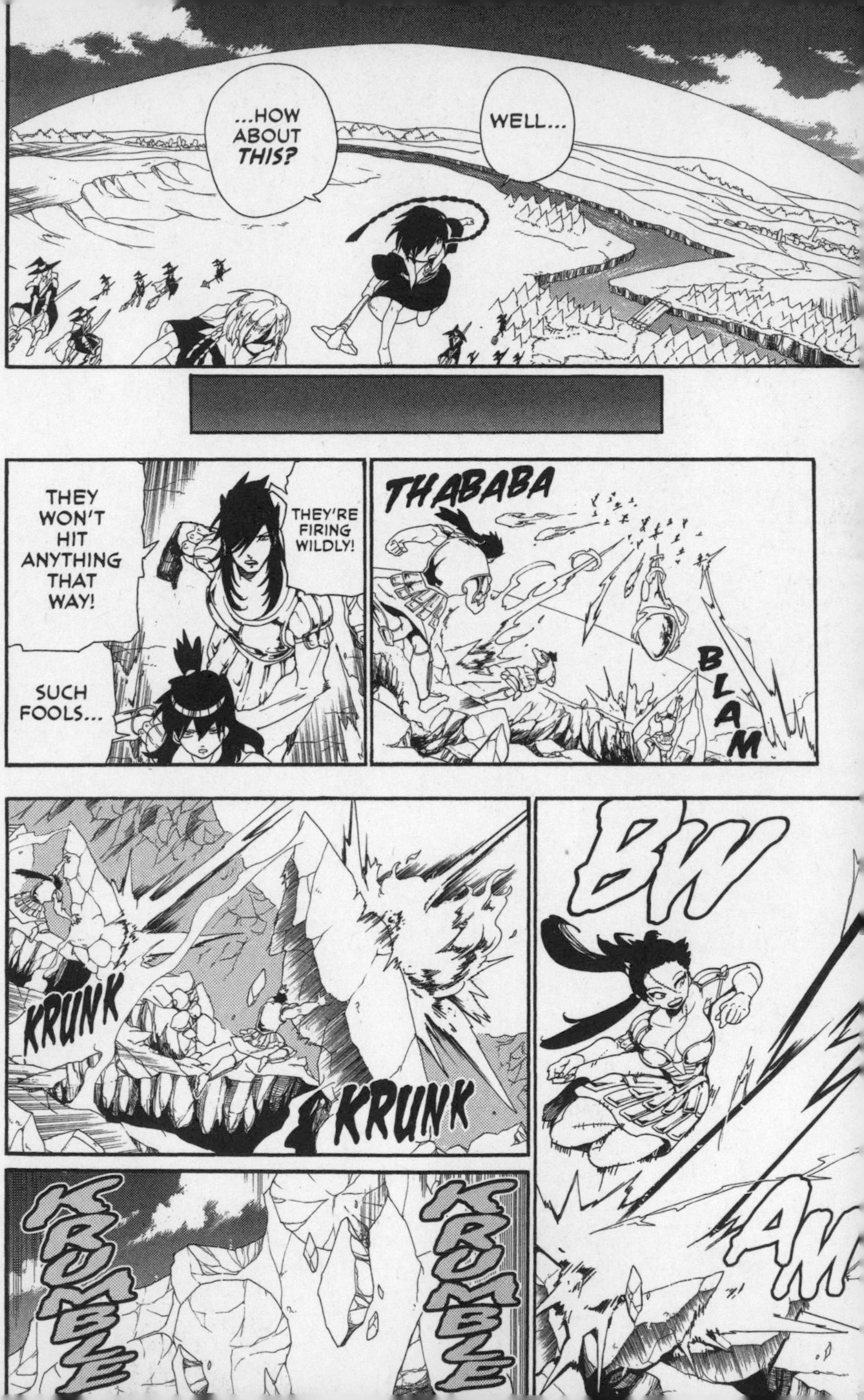
WELL...
...HOW ABOUT THIS?
THABABA
BLAM
THEY'RE FIRING WILDLY!
THEY WON'T HIT ANYTHING THAT WAY!
SUCH FOOLS...
BW
AM
KRUNK
KRUNK
KRUMBLE
KRUMBLE

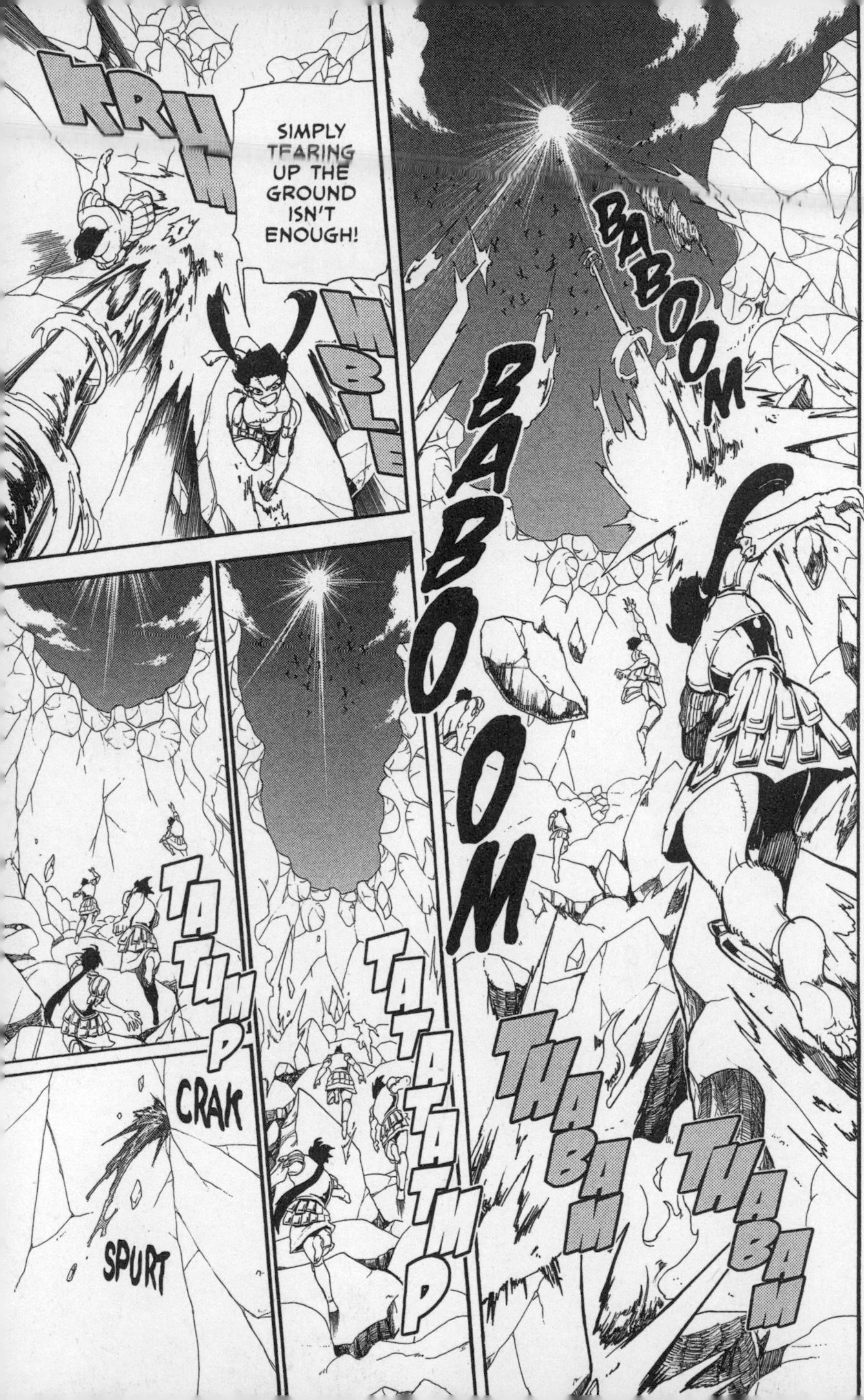
BABOOM
BABOOM
THABAM
THABAM
SIMPLY TEARING UP THE GROUND ISN'T ENOUGH!
KRUMMBLE
TATATATMP
TATUMP
CRAK
SPURT

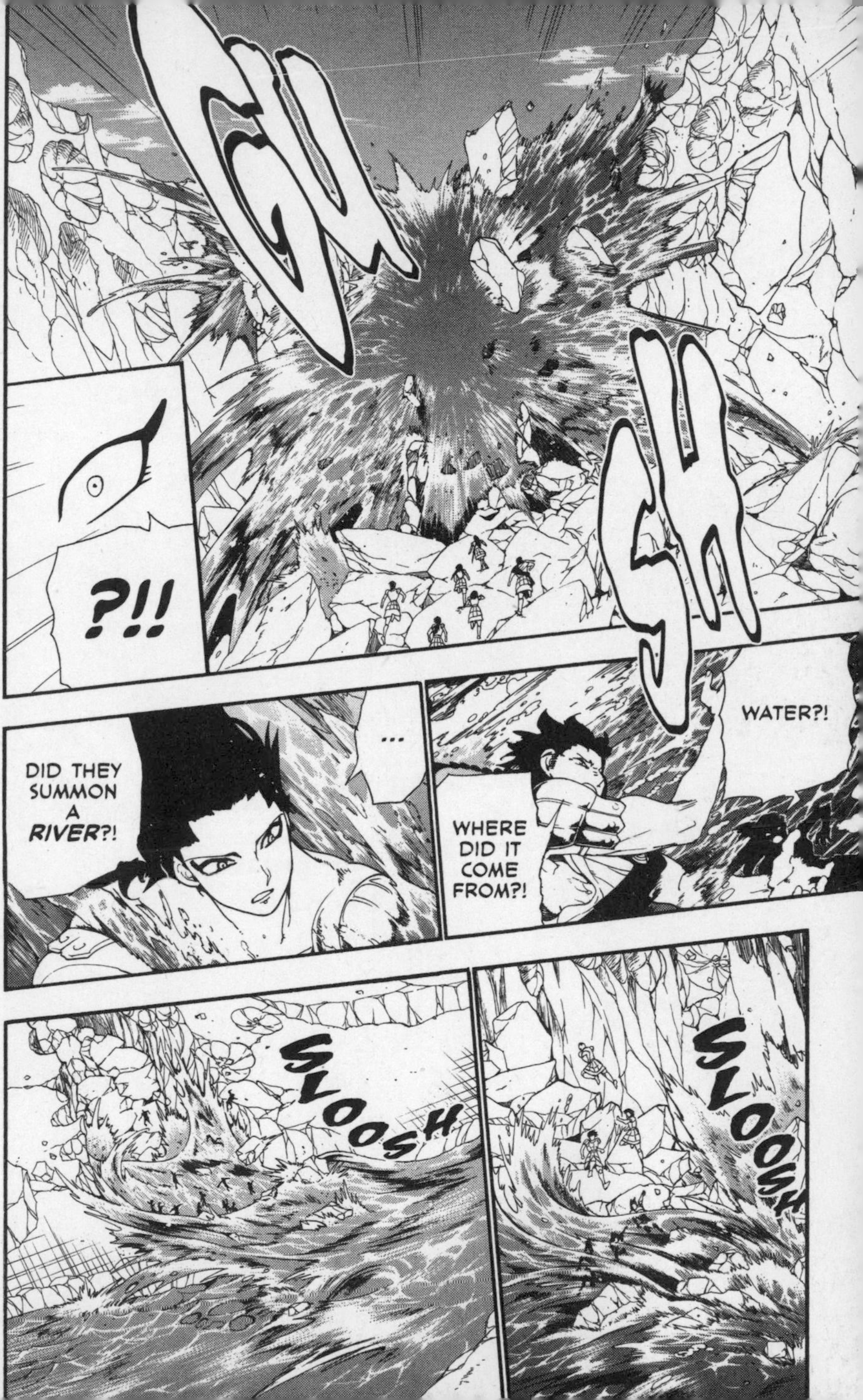
GU
SH
?!!
WATER?!
WHERE DID IT COME FROM?!
...
DID THEY SUMMON A *RIVER*?!
SLOOSH
SLOOSH

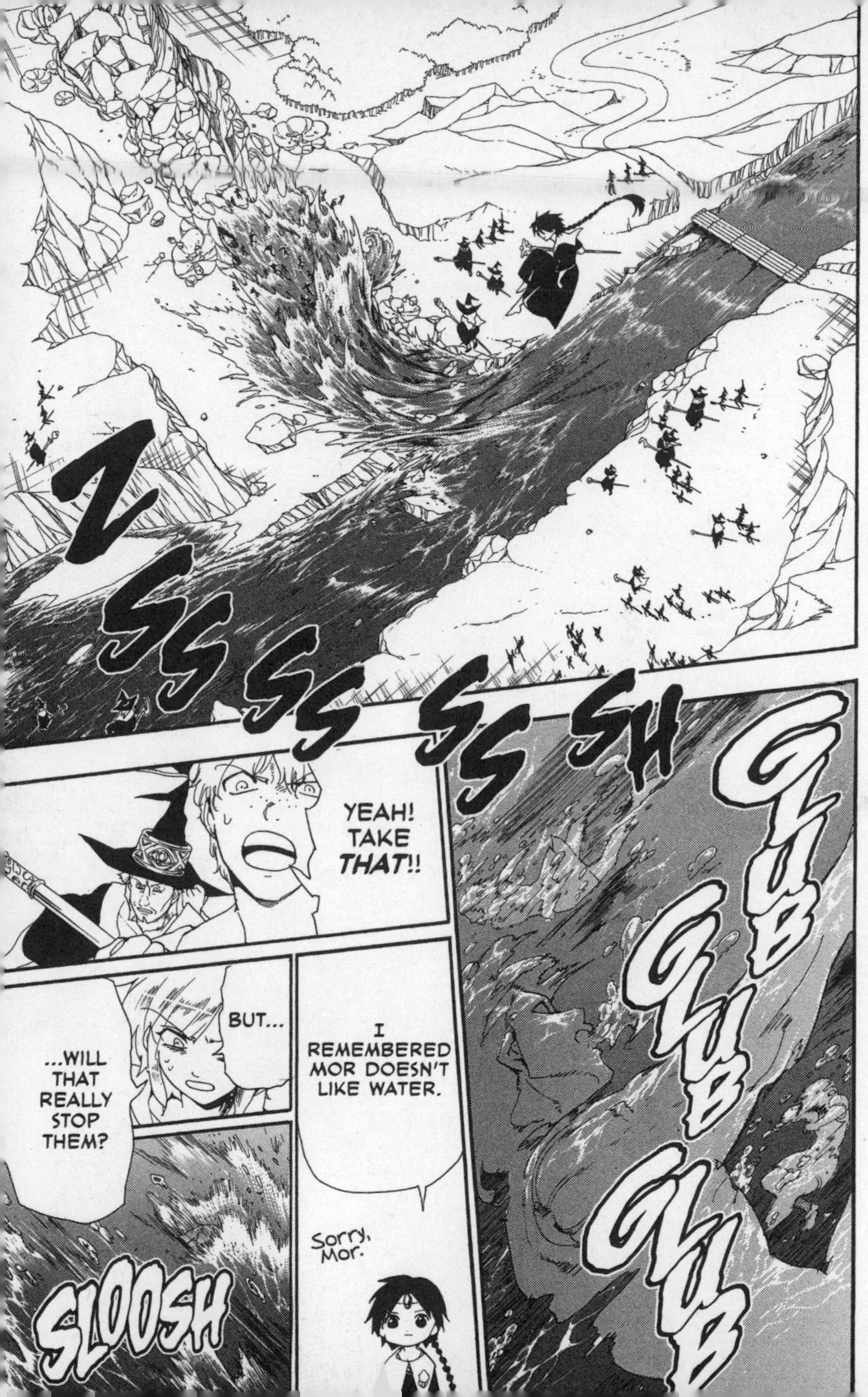
ZSSSSSSSSH
GLUB GLUB GLUB
YEAH! TAKE *THAT*!!
I REMEMBERED MOR DOESN'T LIKE WATER.
Sorry, Mor.
BUT...
...WILL THAT REALLY STOP THEM?
SLOOSH

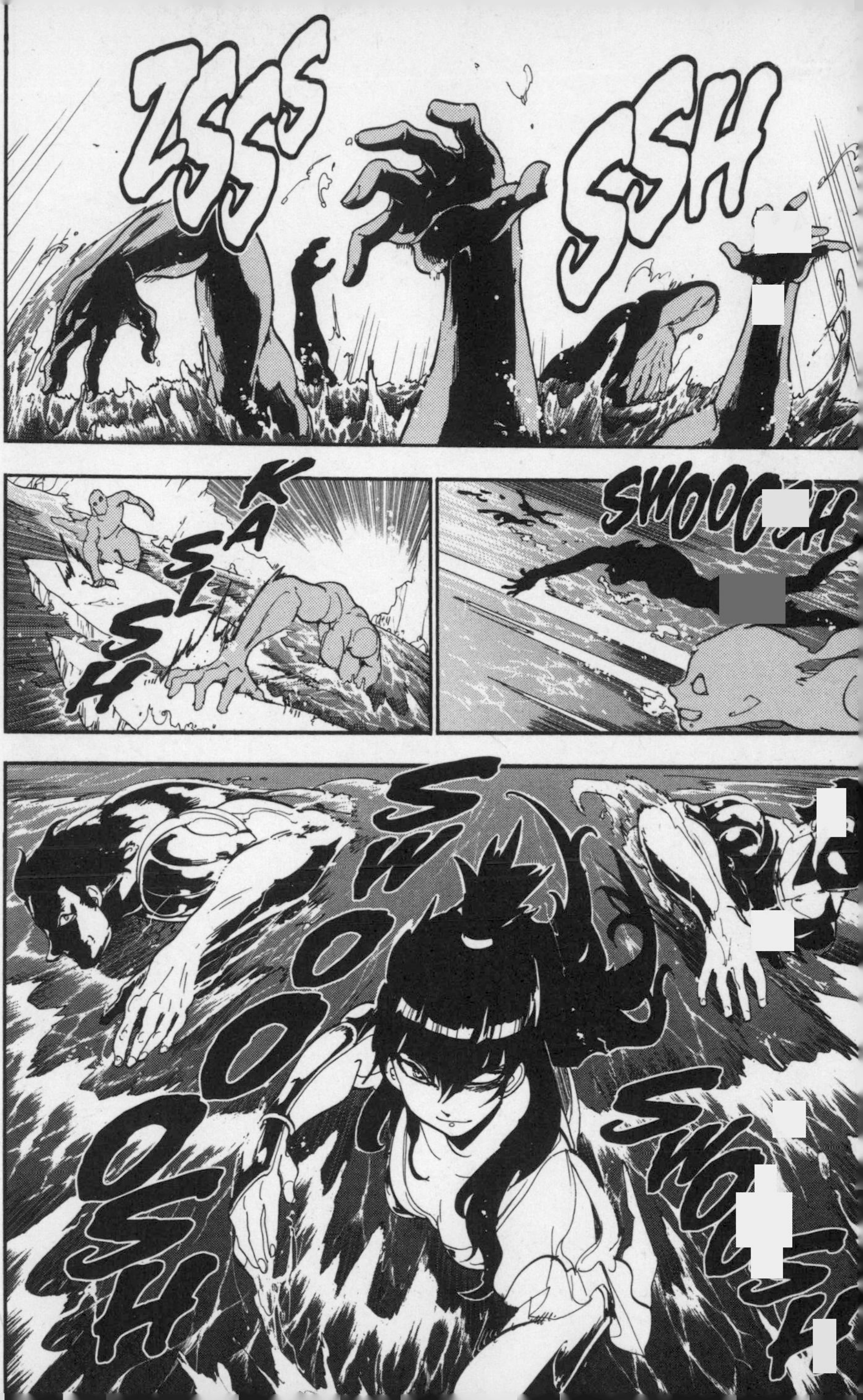
ZSSS
SSH
SWOOO
KASLSH
SWOOSH
SWOOOOOSH

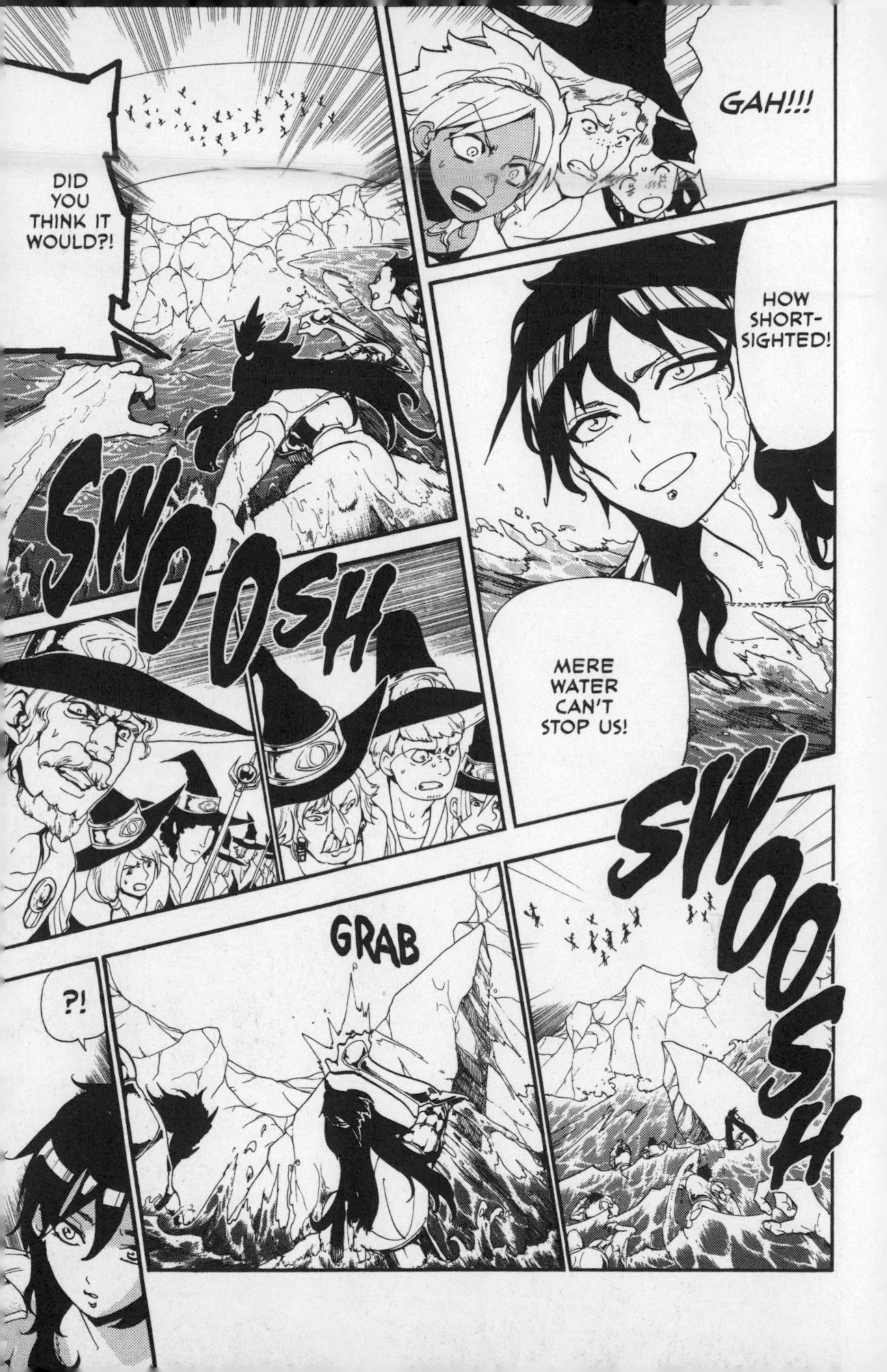
GAH!!!
HOW SHORT-SIGHTED!
MERE WATER CAN'T STOP US!
DID YOU THINK IT WOULD?!
SWOOSH
SWOOSH
GRAB
?!

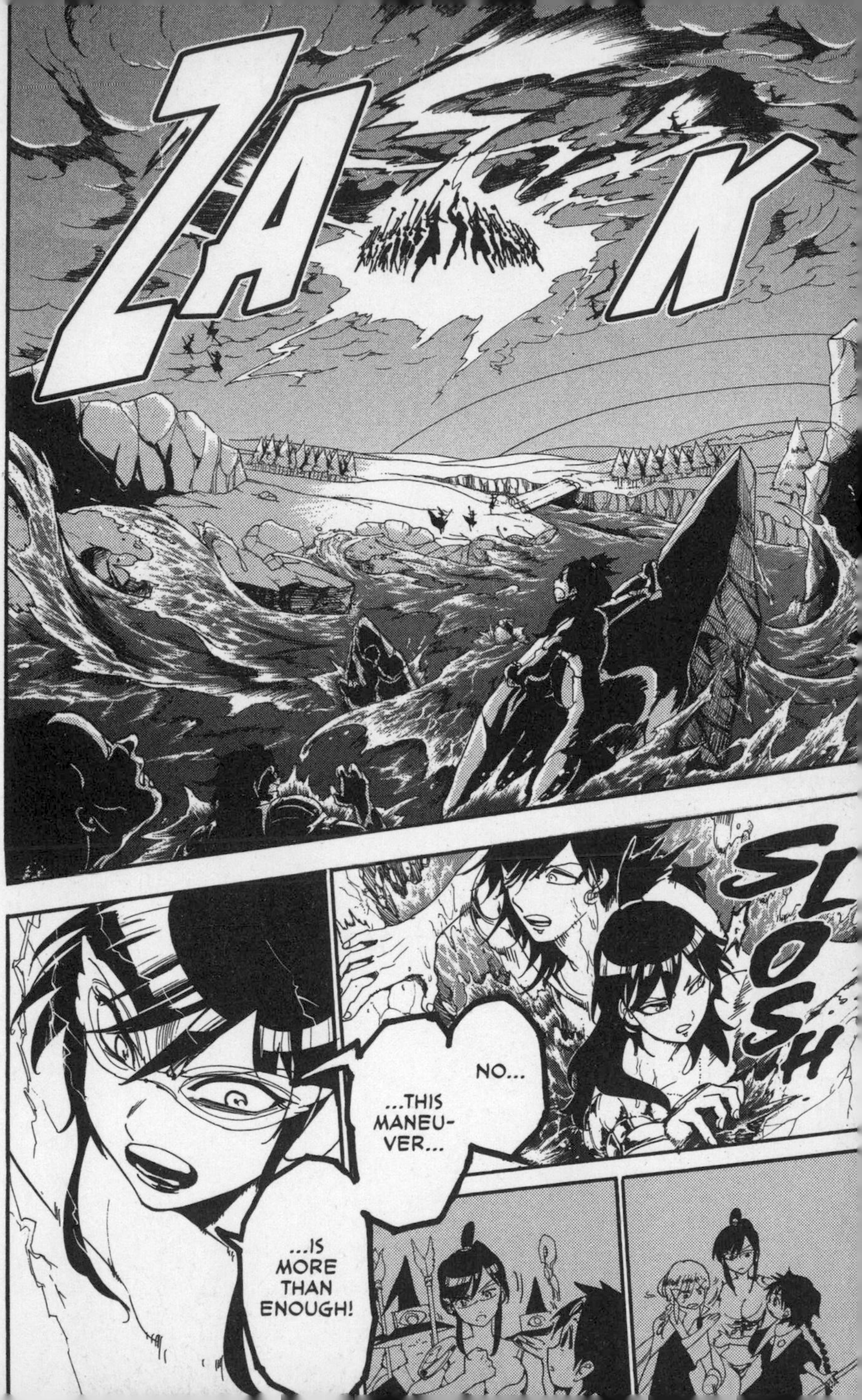
ZA-K
SLOSH
NO...
...THIS MANEUVER...
...IS MORE THAN ENOUGH!

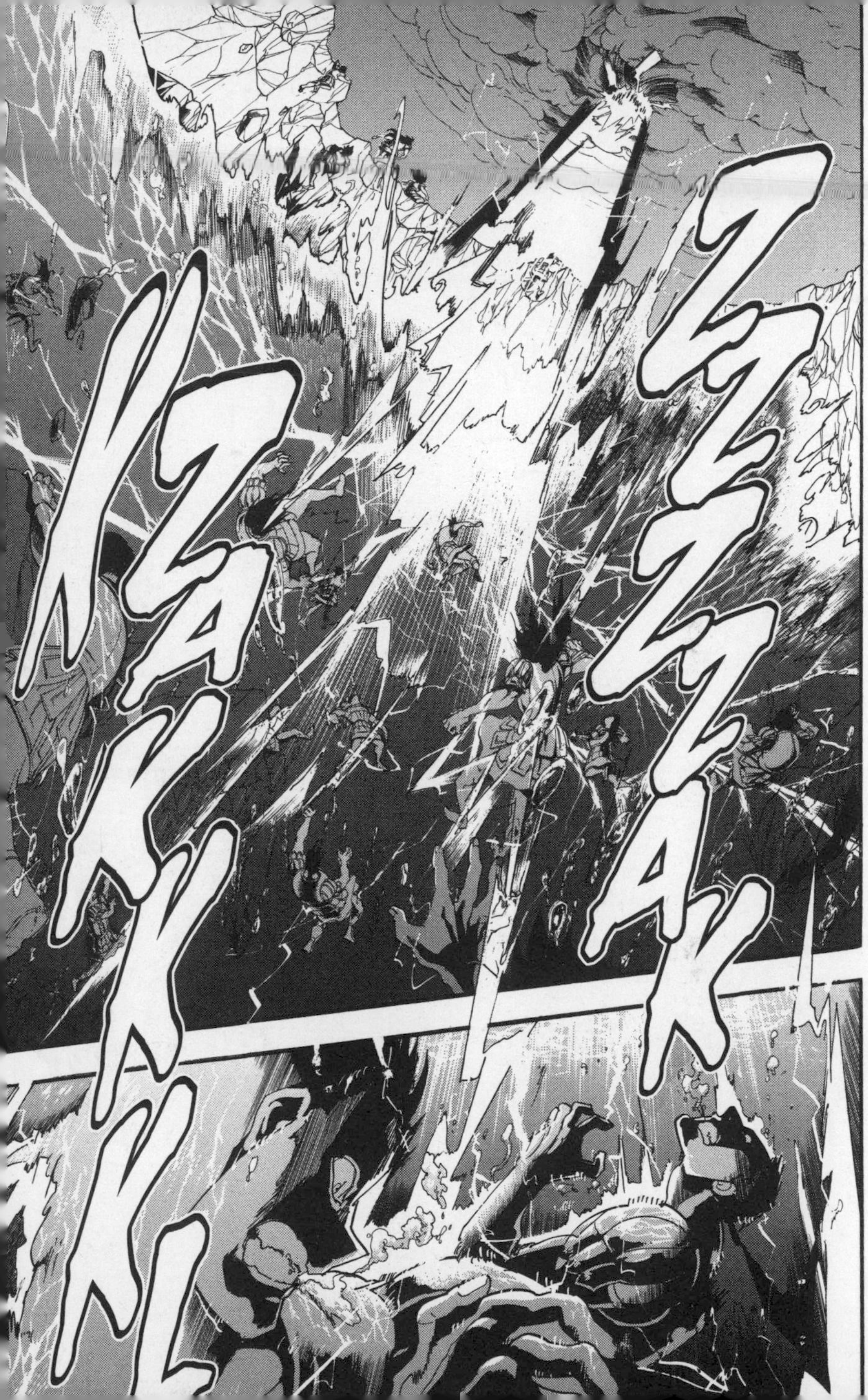

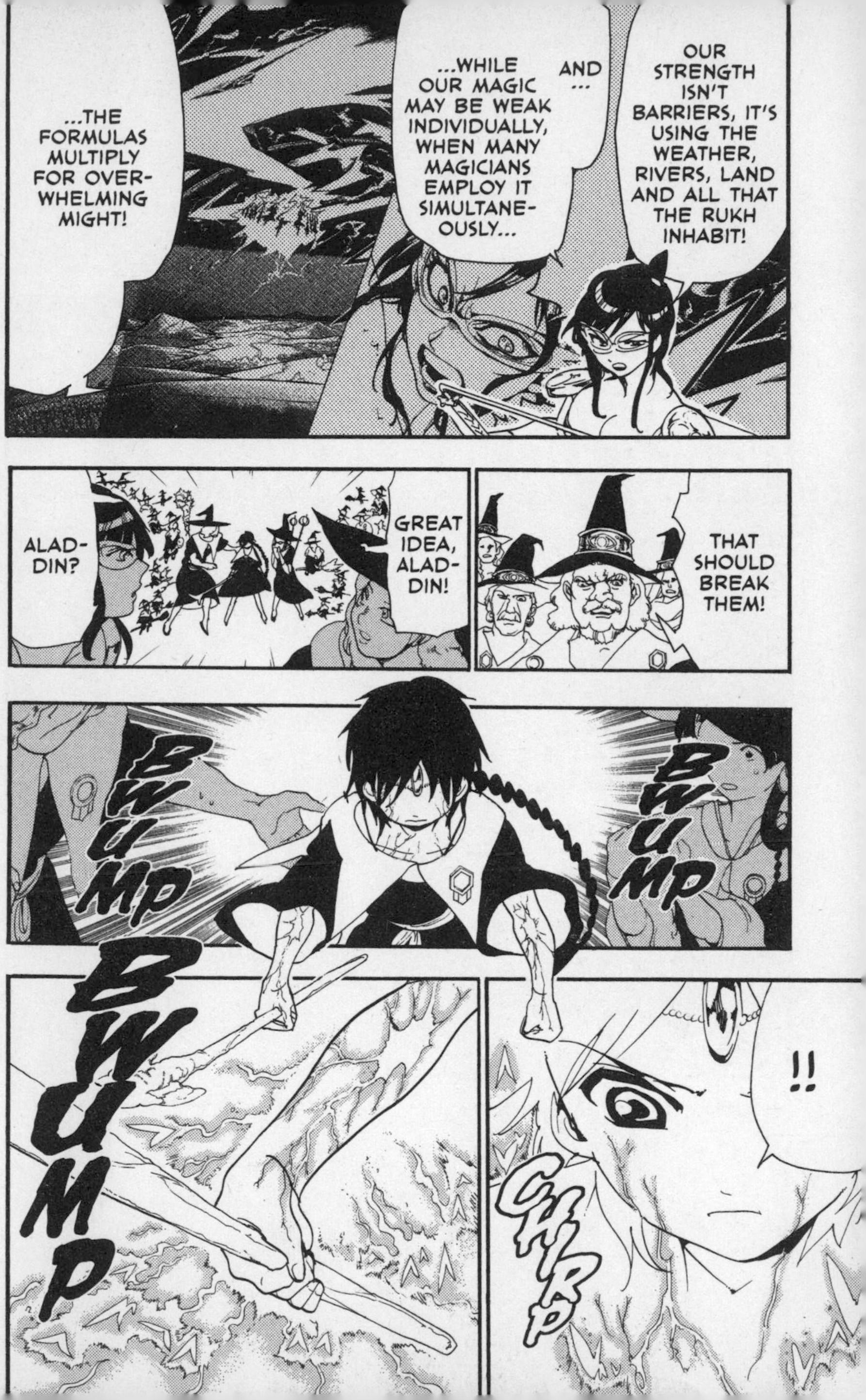
OUR STRENGTH ISN'T BARRIERS, IT'S USING THE WEATHER, RIVERS, LAND AND ALL THAT THE RUKH INHABIT!
AND ...
...WHILE OUR MAGIC MAY BE WEAK INDIVIDUALLY, WHEN MANY MAGICIANS EMPLOY IT SIMULTANE-OUSLY...
...THE FORMULAS MULTIPLY FOR OVER-WHELMING MIGHT!
THAT SHOULD BREAK THEM!
GREAT IDEA, ALAD-DIN!
ALAD-DIN?
BWUMP
BWUMP
!!
CHIRP
BWUMP

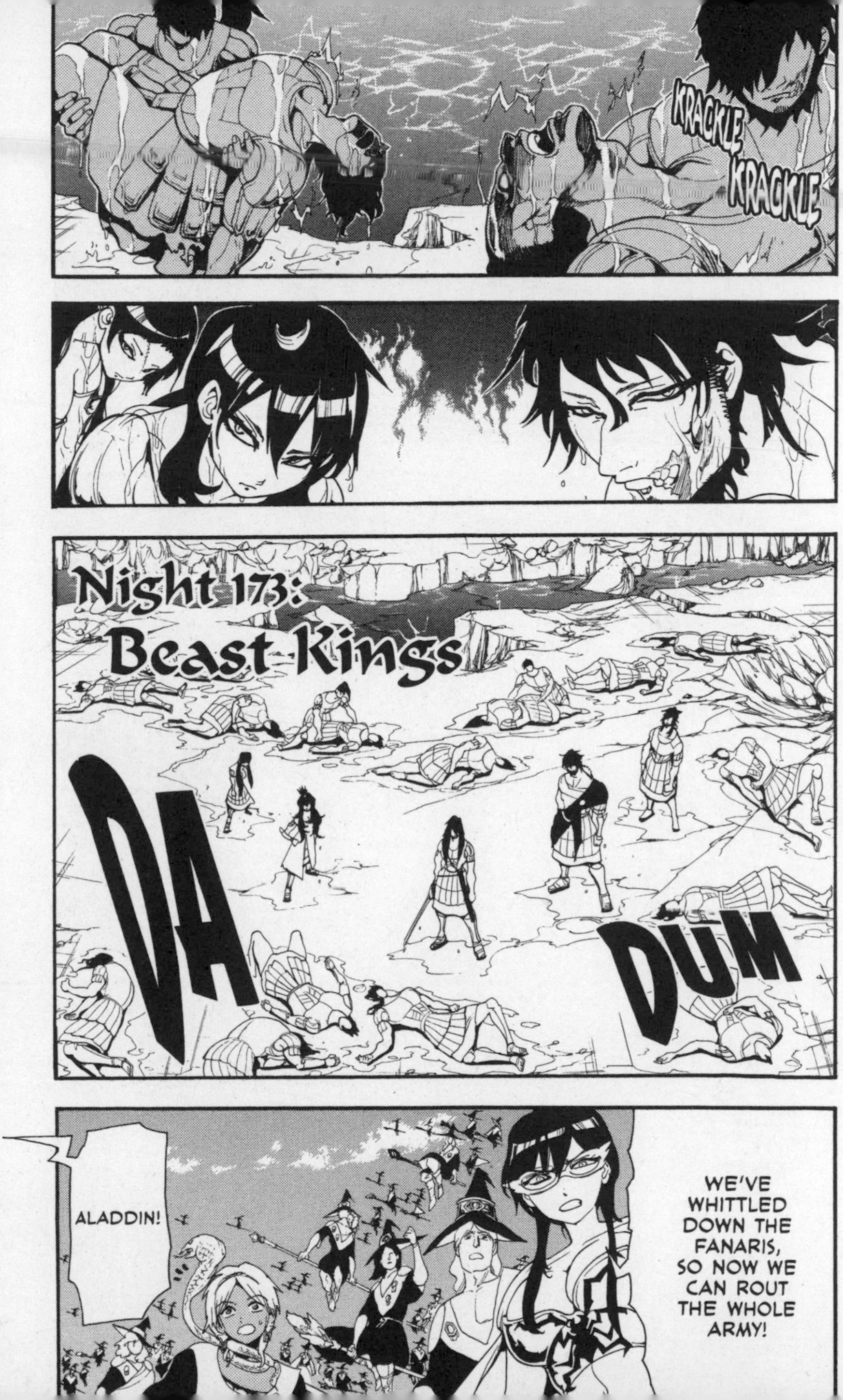
KRACKLE
KRACKLE
Night 173: Beast Kings
DA
DUM
WE'VE WHITTLED DOWN THE FANARIS, SO NOW WE CAN ROUT THE WHOLE ARMY!
ALADDIN!

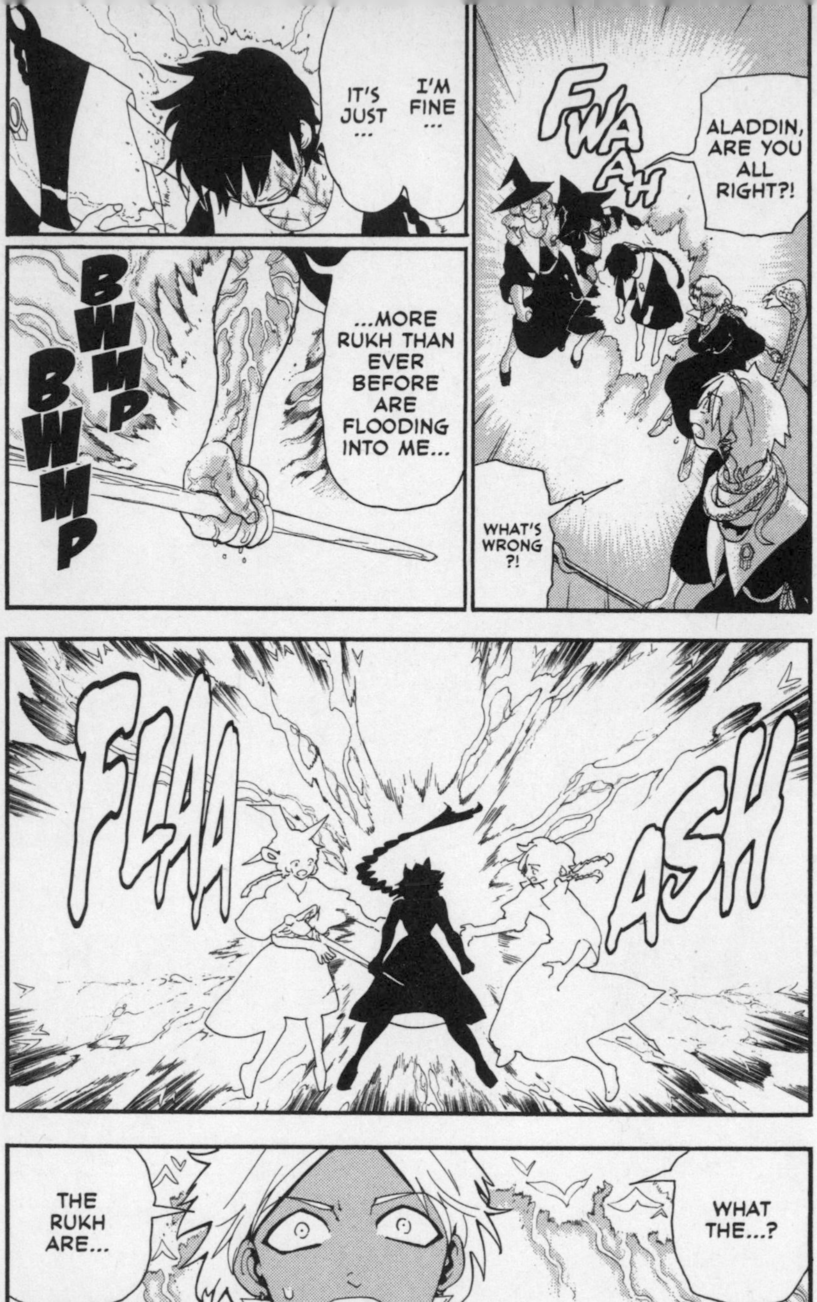
FWAAH
ALADDIN, ARE YOU ALL RIGHT?!
WHAT'S WRONG ?!
I'M FINE ...
IT'S JUST ...
BWWMP
BWWMP
...MORE RUKH THAN EVER BEFORE ARE FLOODING INTO ME...
FLAASH
WHAT THE...?
THE RUKH ARE...

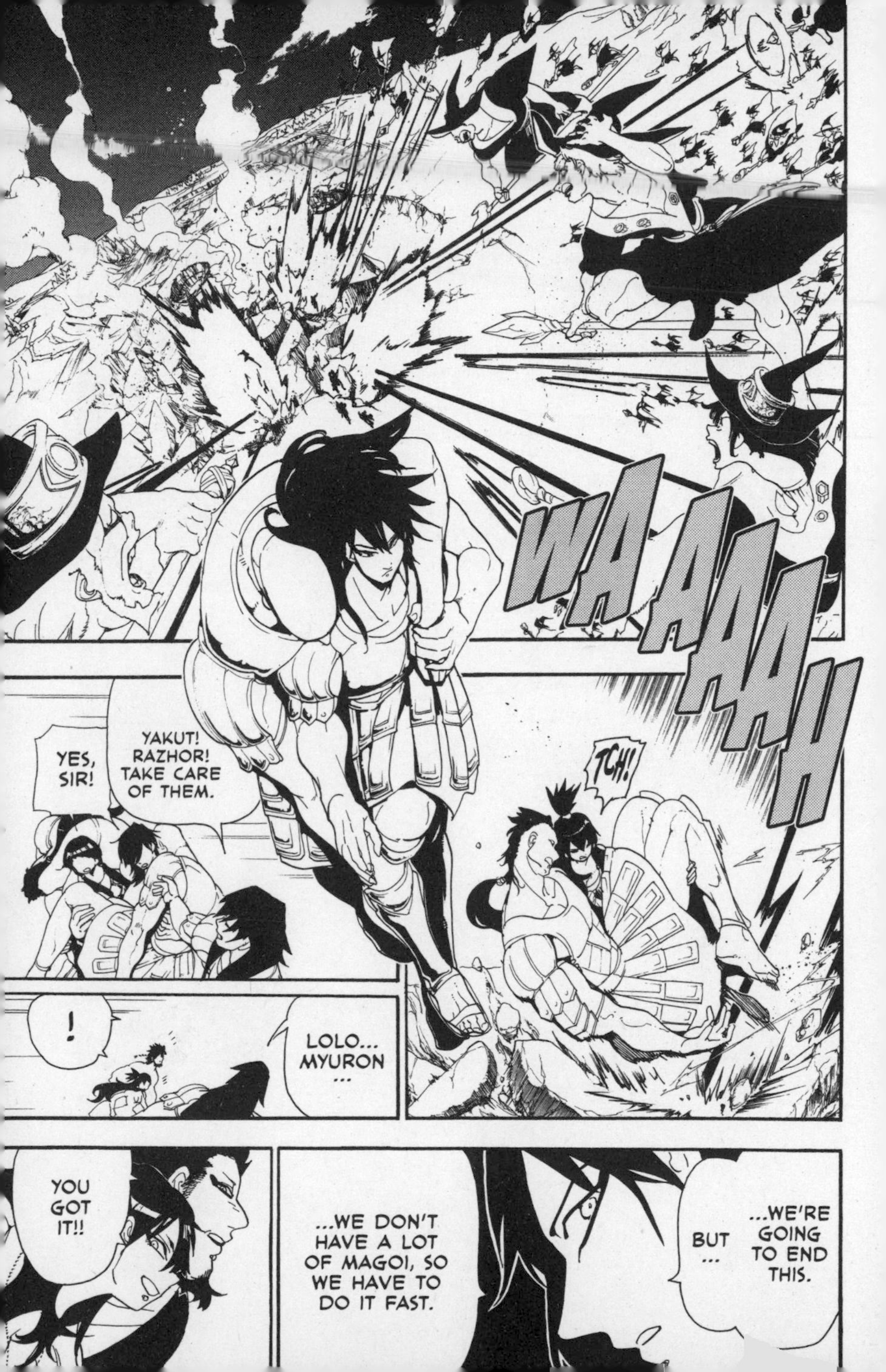
WAAAAAH
TCH!
YAKUT! RAZHOR! TAKE CARE OF THEM.
YES, SIR!
LOLO... MYURON...
!
...WE'RE GOING TO END THIS.
BUT...
...WE DON'T HAVE A LOT OF MAGOI, SO WE HAVE TO DO IT FAST.
YOU GOT IT!!

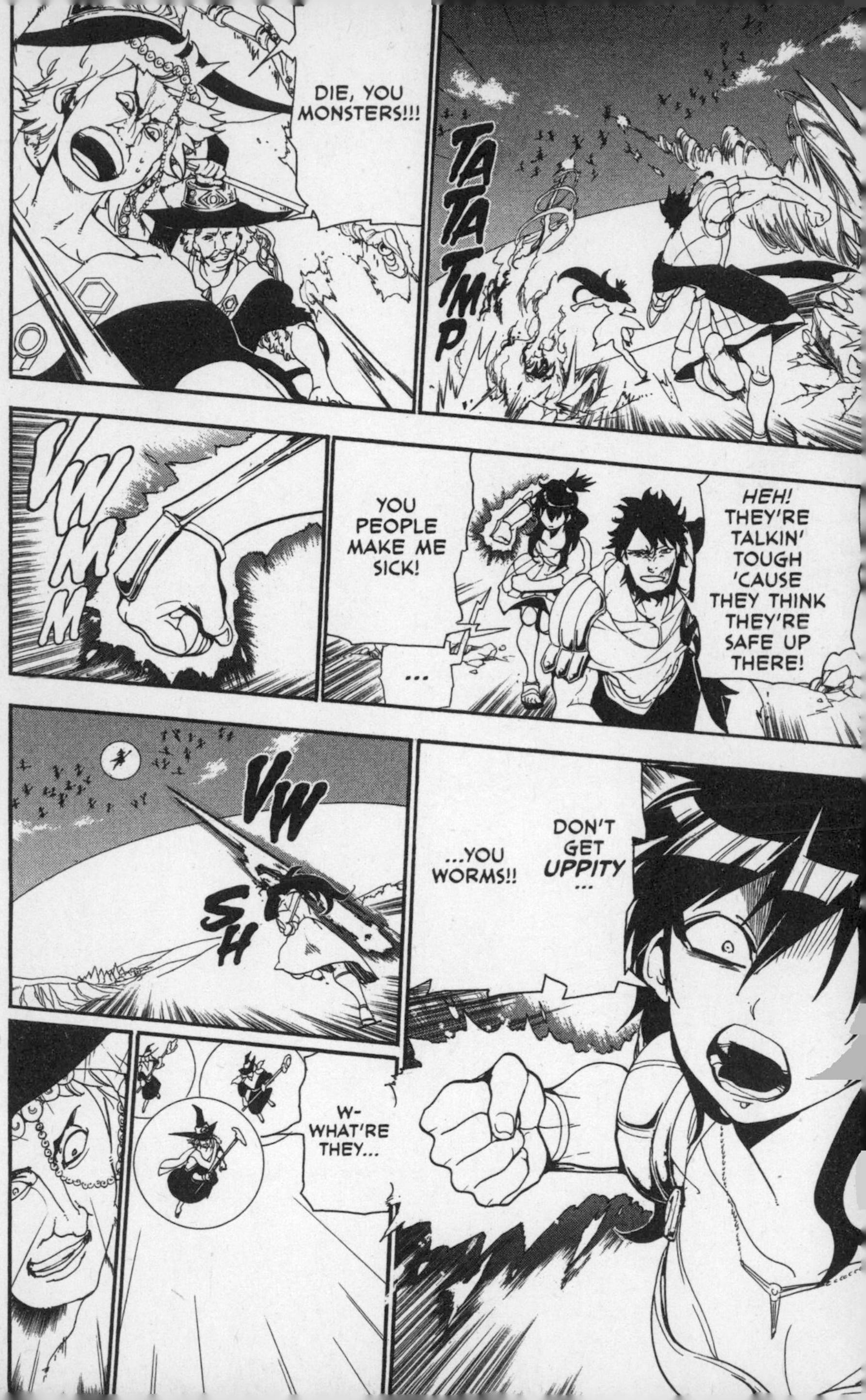
TATATMP
DIE, YOU MONSTERS!!!
HEH! THEY'RE TALKIN' TOUGH 'CAUSE THEY THINK THEY'RE SAFE UP THERE!
YOU PEOPLE MAKE ME SICK!
...
VWMMM
DON'T GET UPPITY ...
...YOU WORMS!!
VW
SH
W- WHAT'RE THEY...

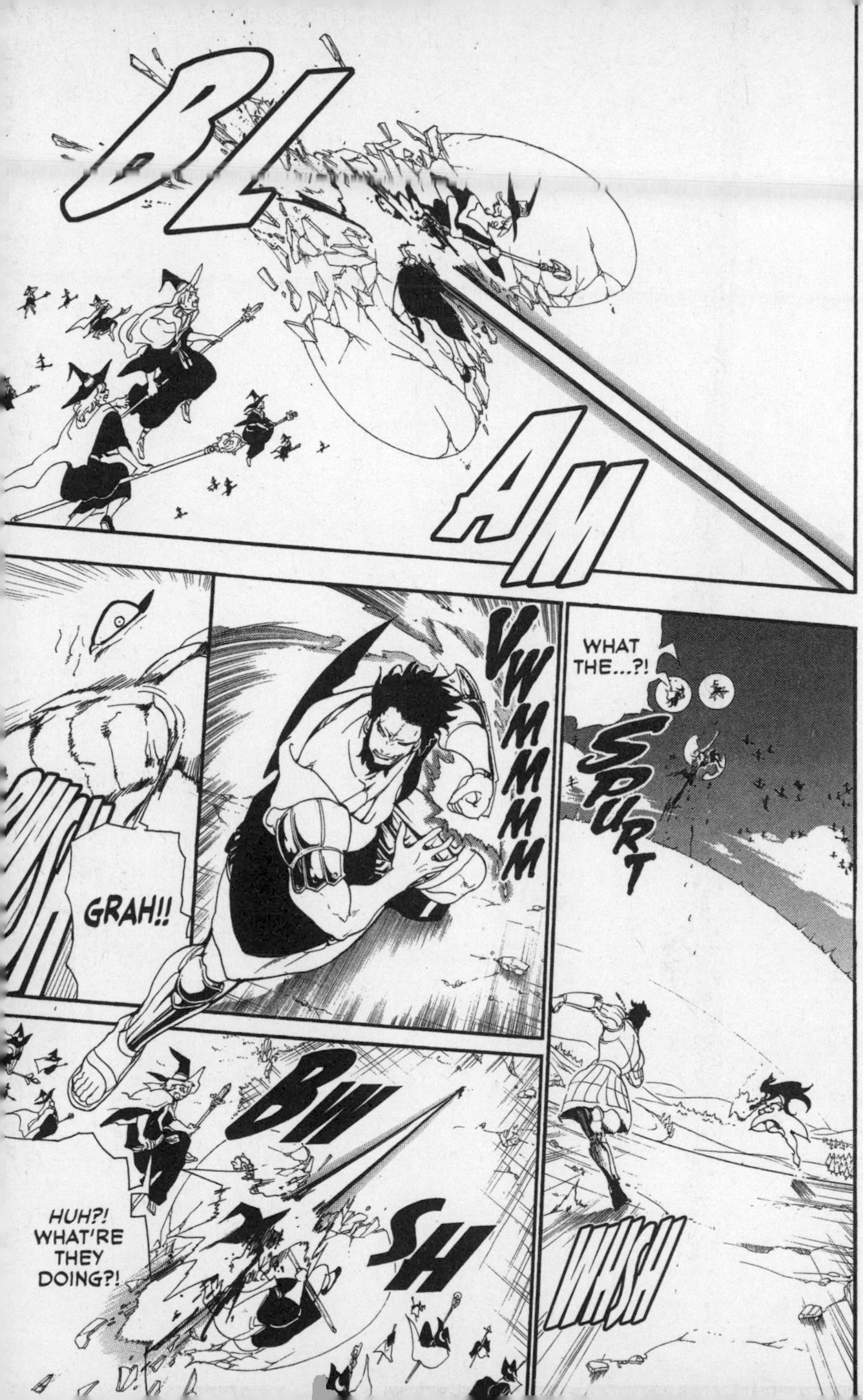
BLAM
WHAT THE...?!
SPURT
WHSH
VWMMMMM
GRAH!!
BWSH
HUH?! WHAT'RE THEY DOING?!

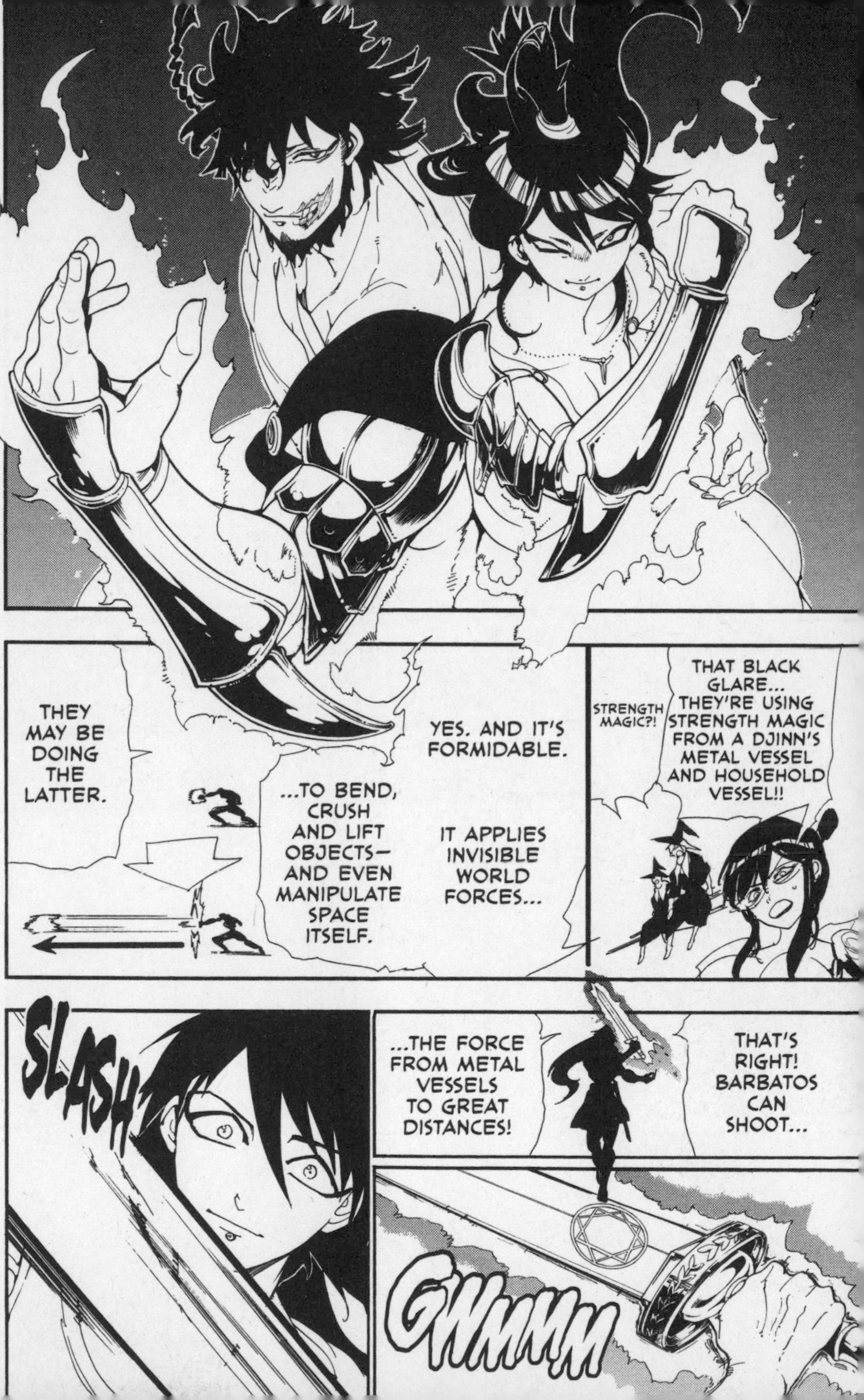
THAT BLACK GLARE... THEY'RE USING STRENGTH MAGIC FROM A DJINN'S METAL VESSEL AND HOUSEHOLD VESSEL!!
STRENGTH MAGIC?!
YES. AND IT'S FORMIDABLE.
IT APPLIES INVISIBLE WORLD FORCES...
...TO BEND, CRUSH AND LIFT OBJECTS—AND EVEN MANIPULATE SPACE ITSELF.
THEY MAY BE DOING THE LATTER.
THAT'S RIGHT! BARBATOS CAN SHOOT...
...THE FORCE FROM METAL VESSELS TO GREAT DISTANCES!
GWMMM
SLASH

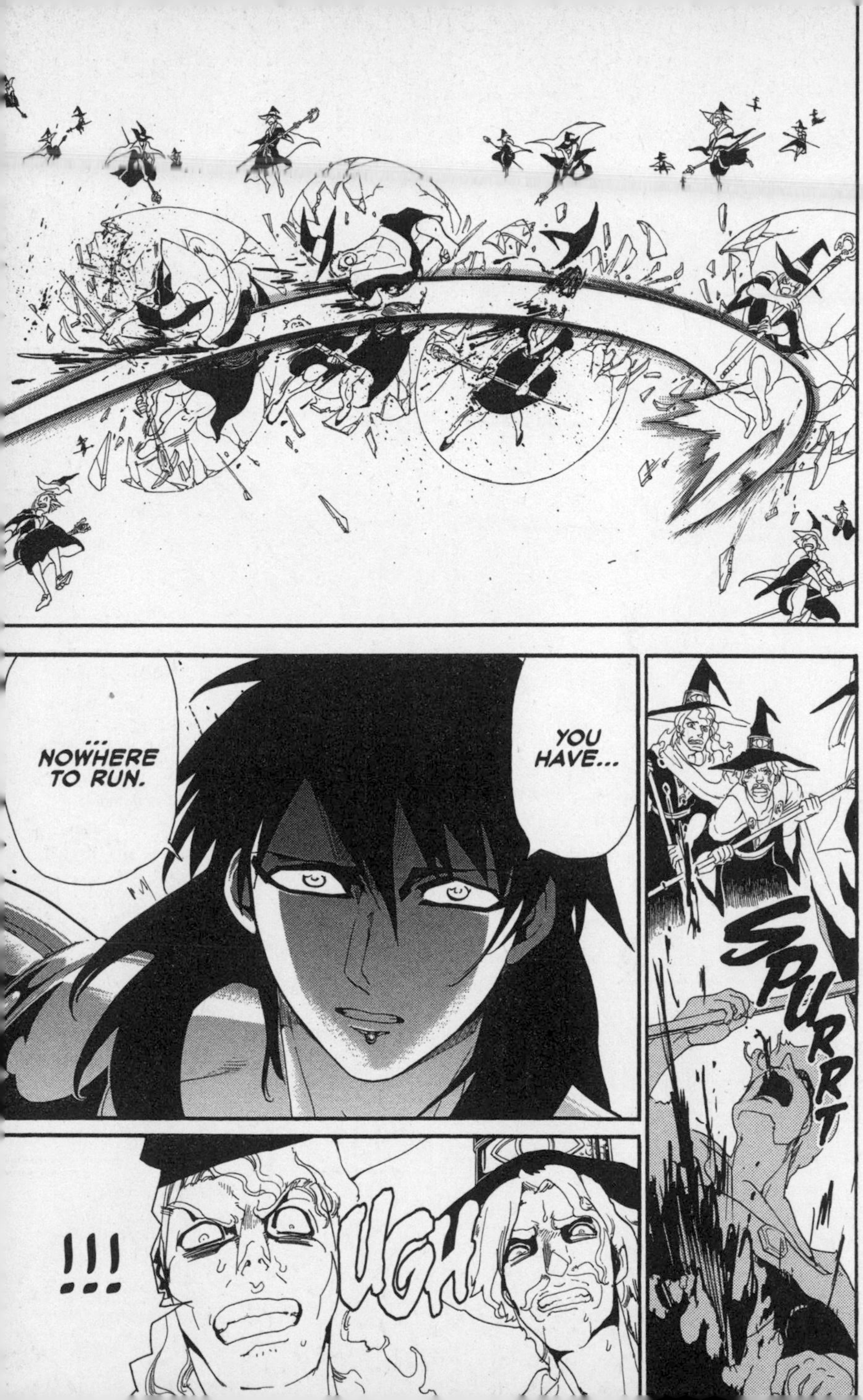
SPURRT
YOU HAVE...
...NOWHERE TO RUN.
UGH
!!!

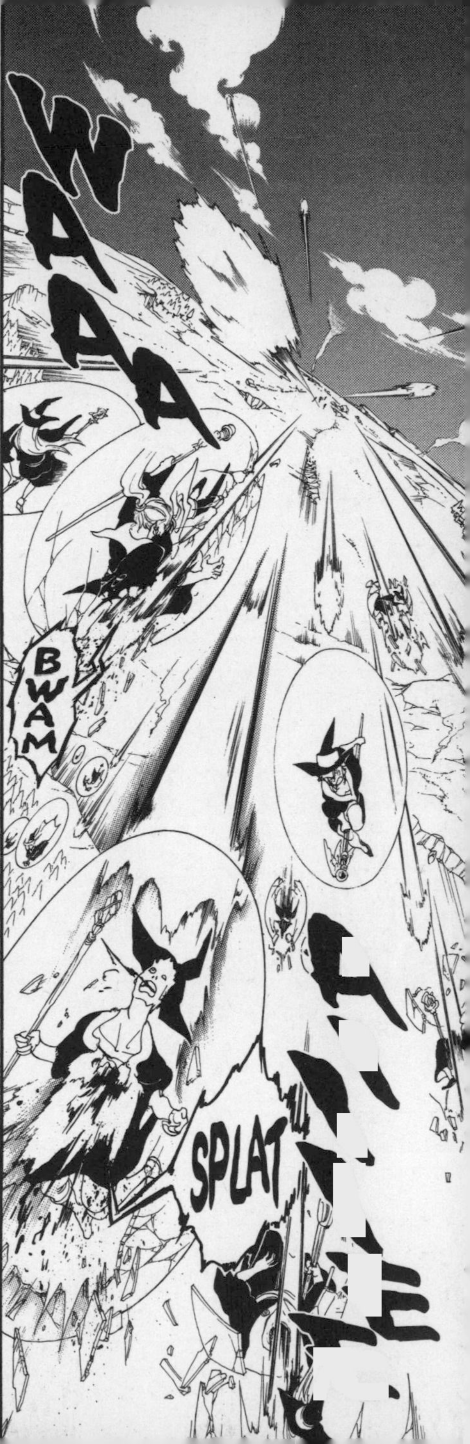
WAAA
BWAM
SPLAT

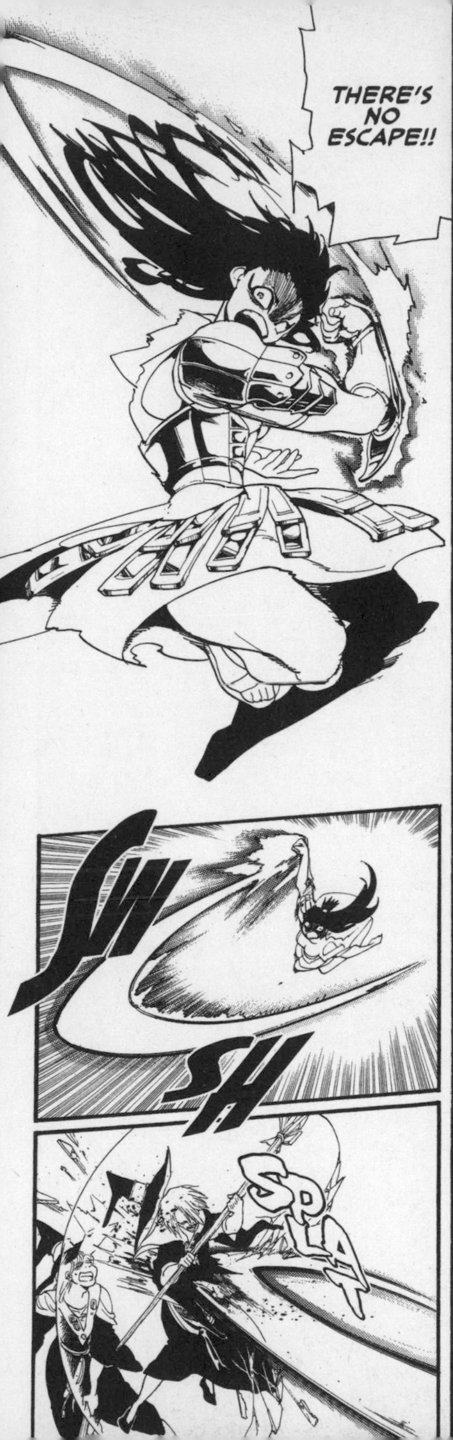
THERE'S NO ESCAPE!!
SWISH
SPLAT

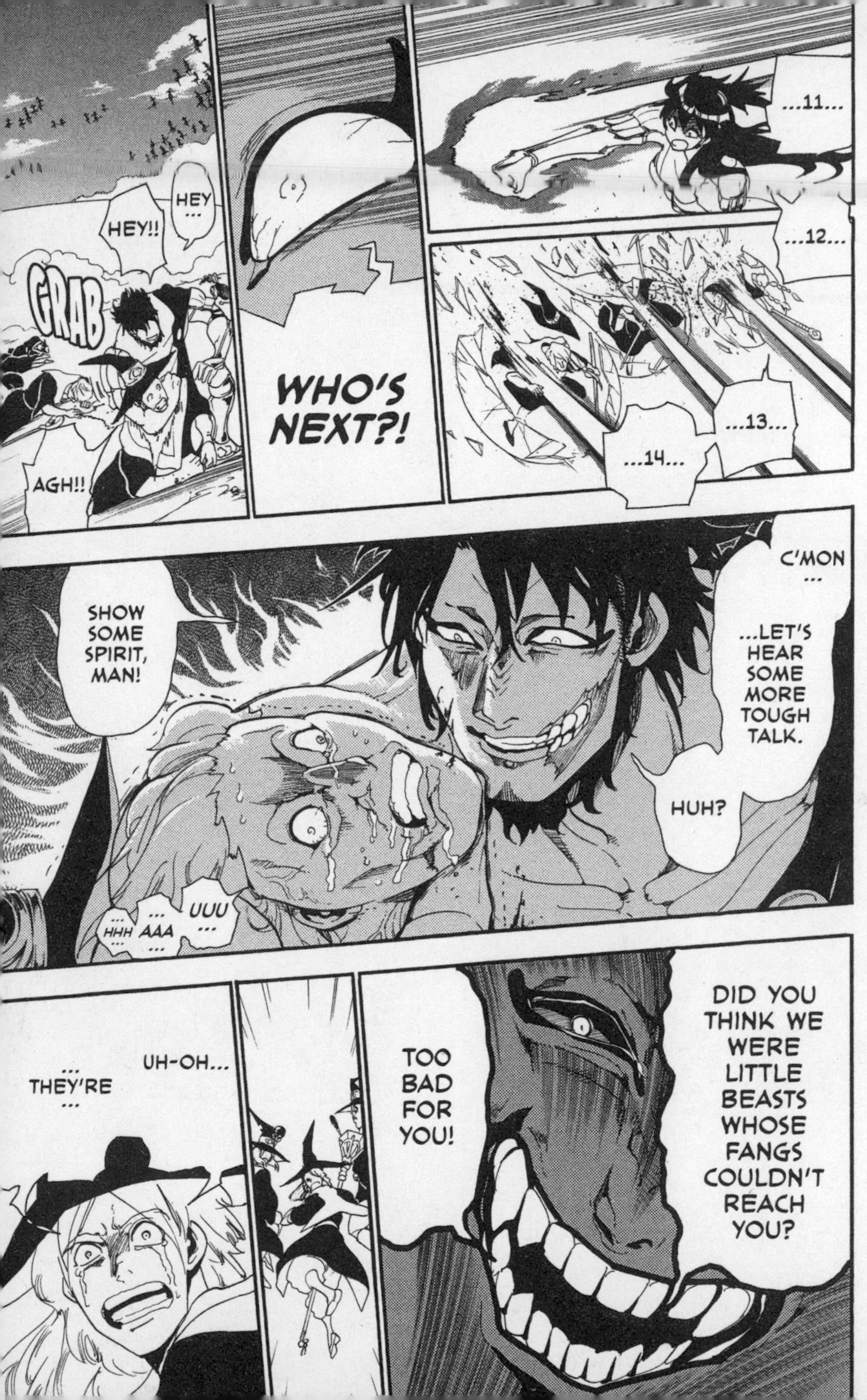
...11...
...12...
...13...
...14...
WHO'S NEXT?!
HEY ...
HEY!!
GRAB
AGH!!
C'MON ...
...LET'S HEAR SOME MORE TOUGH TALK.
SHOW SOME SPIRIT, MAN!
HUH?
UUU ...
... AAA ...
... HHH ...
DID YOU THINK WE WERE LITTLE BEASTS WHOSE FANGS COULDN'T REACH YOU?
TOO BAD FOR YOU!
UH-OH...
... THEY'RE ...

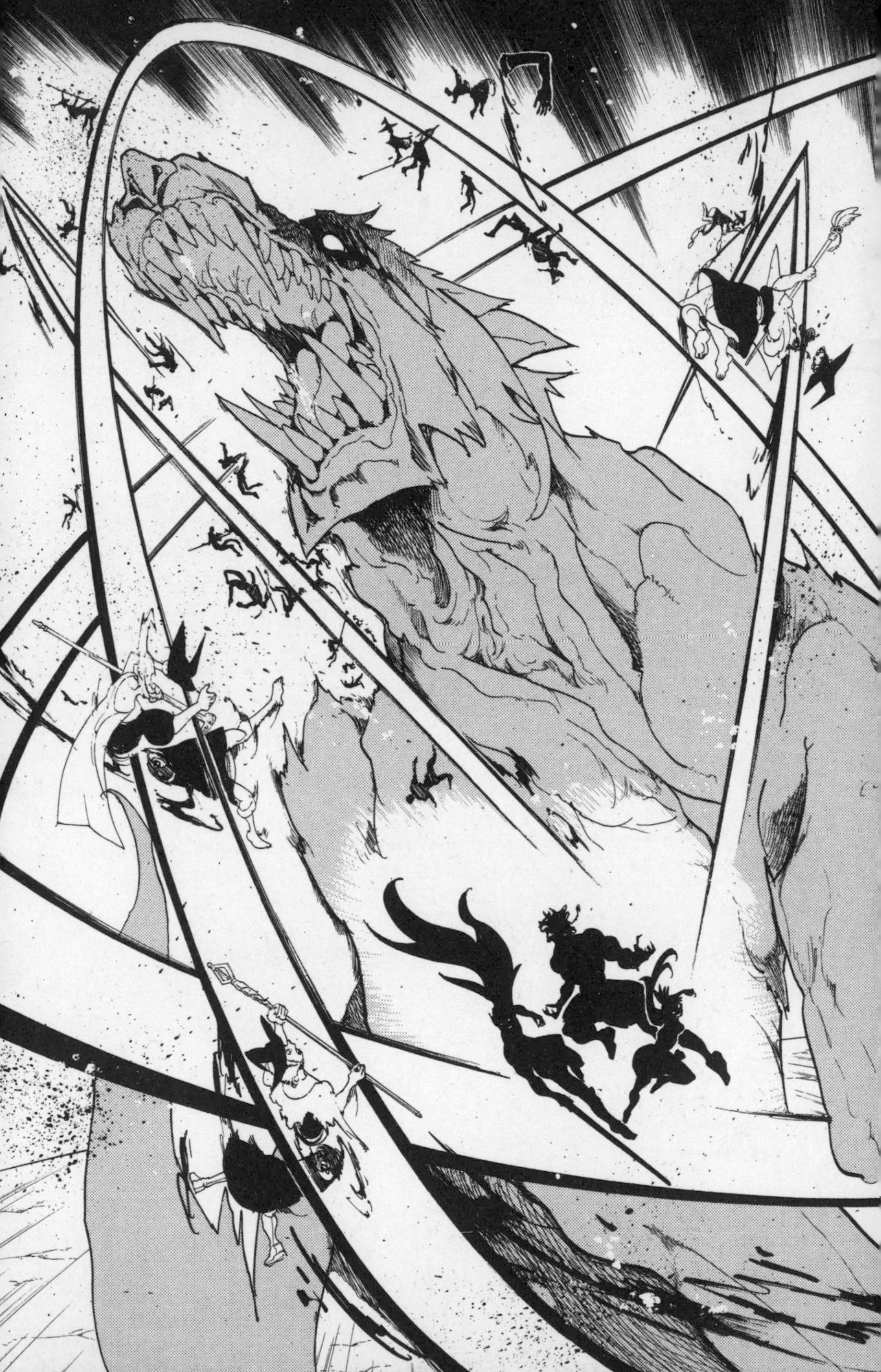

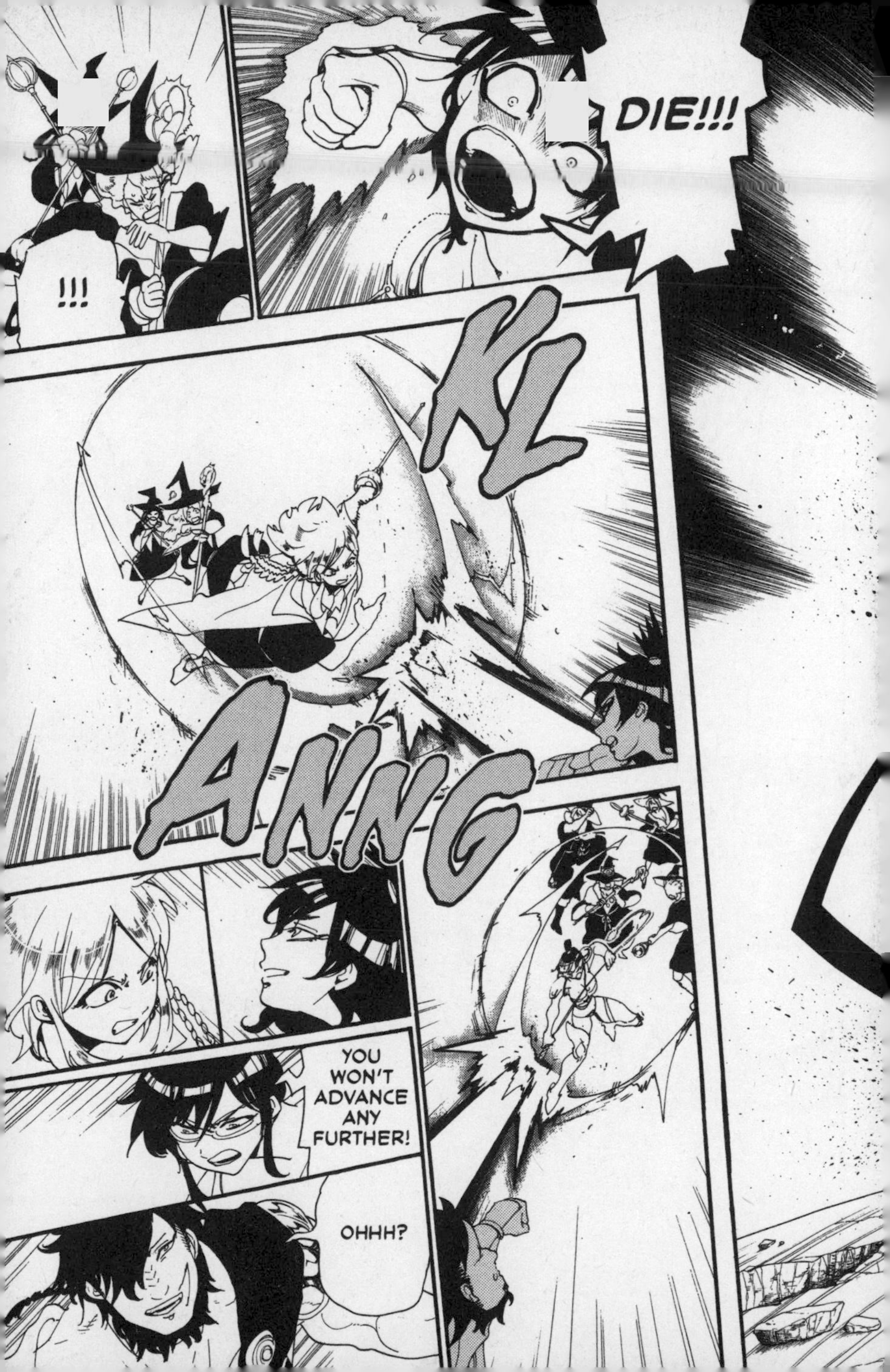
DIE!!!
!!!
KL ANNG
YOU WON'T ADVANCE ANY FURTHER!
OHHH?

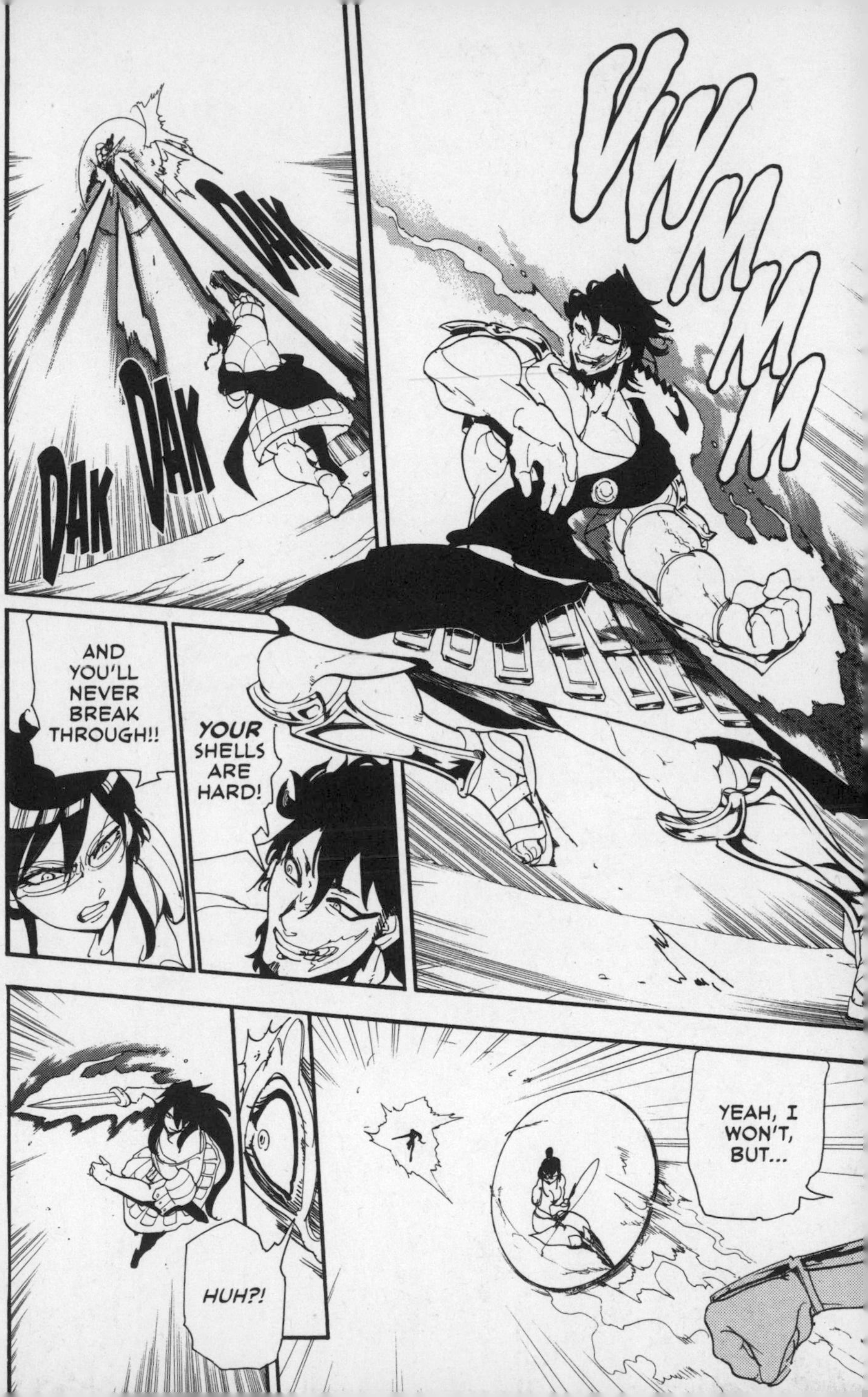
DAK
DAK
DAK
YOUR SHELLS ARE HARD!
AND YOU'LL NEVER BREAK THROUGH!!
YEAH, I WON'T, BUT...
HUH?!

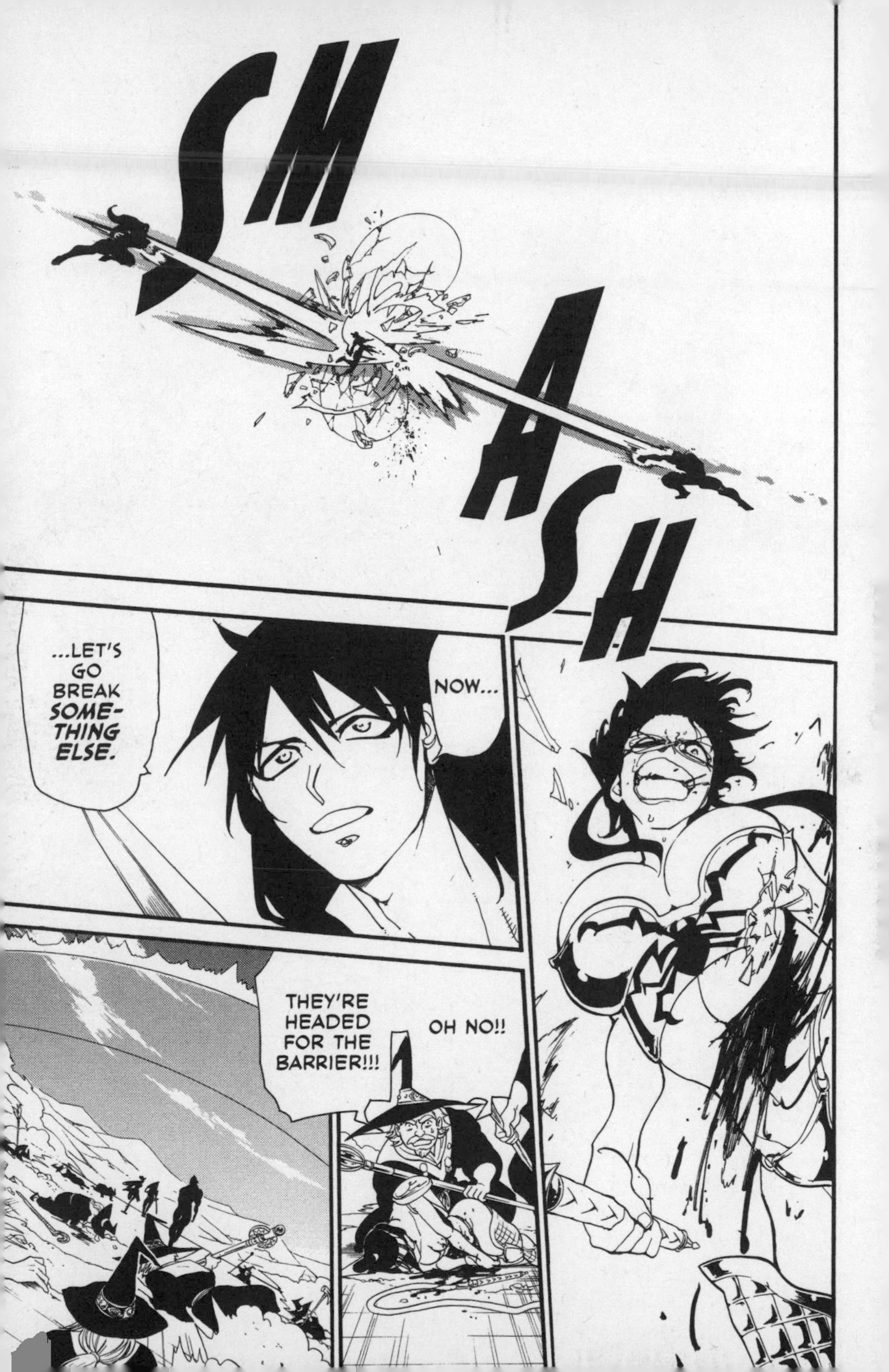
SMASH
NOW...
...LET'S GO BREAK SOMETHING ELSE.
OH NO!!
THEY'RE HEADED FOR THE BARRIER!!!

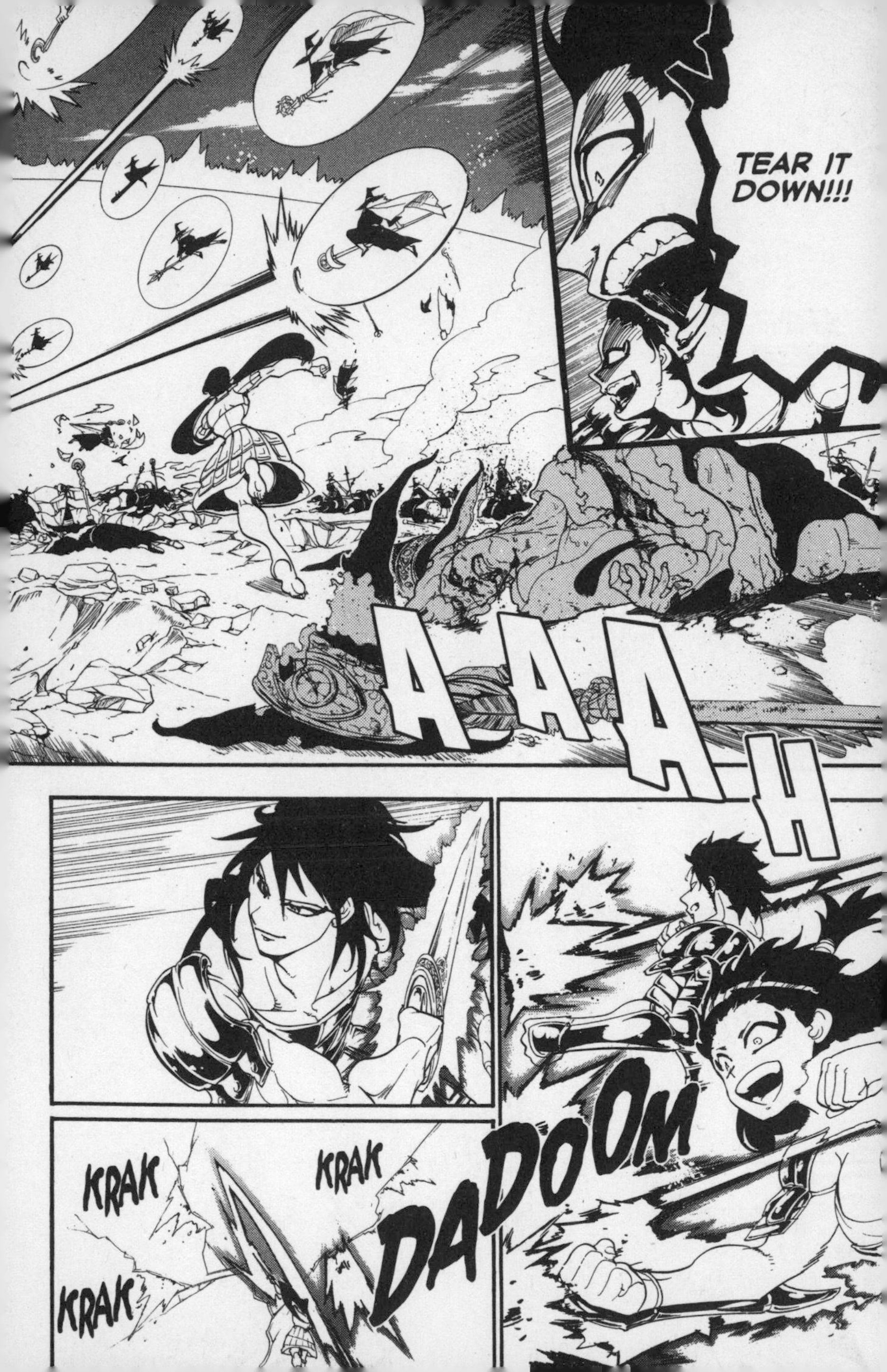
TEAR IT DOWN!!!
AAAAH
DADOOM
KRAK
KRAK
KRAK

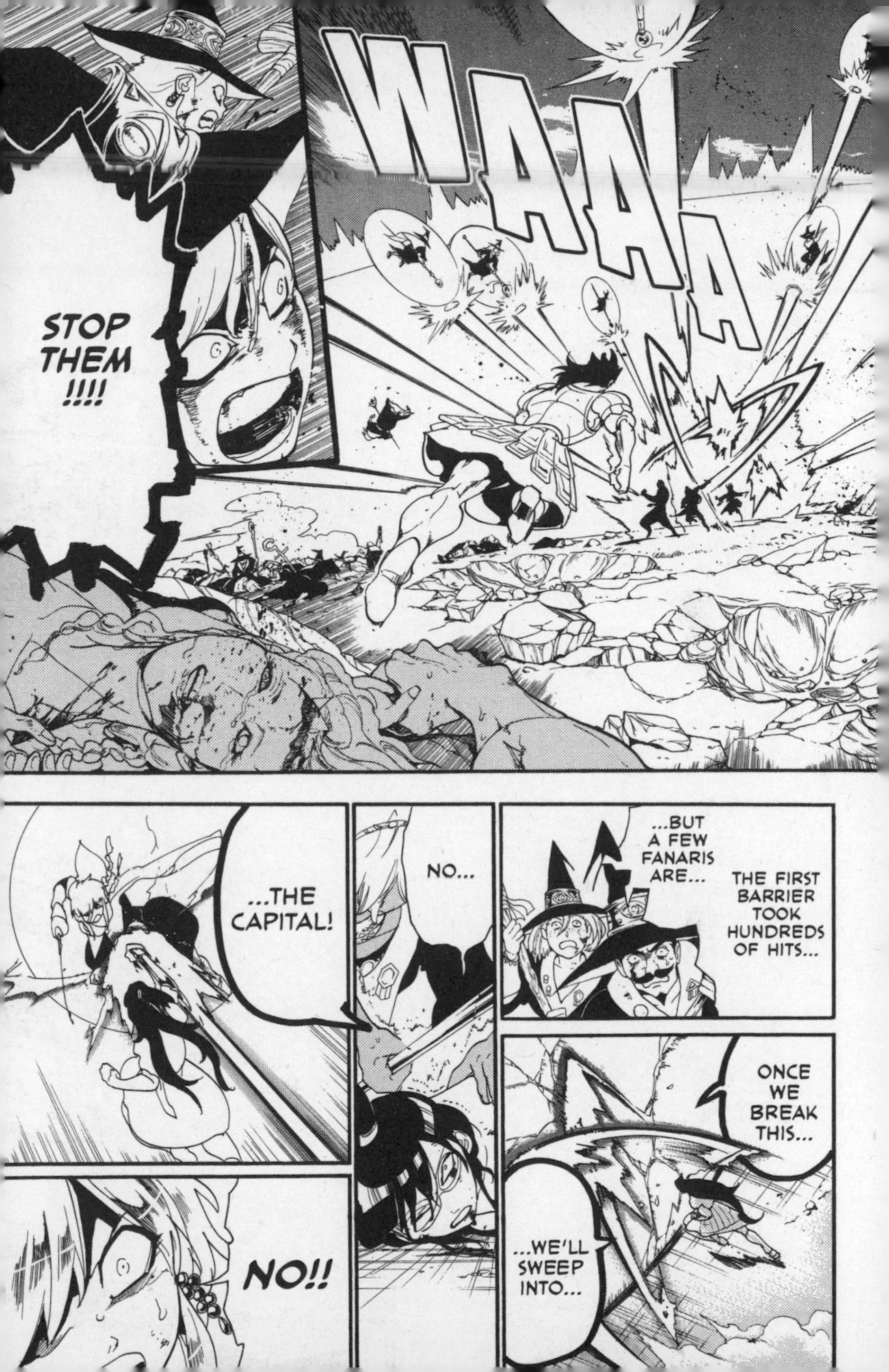
WAAA
STOP THEM !!!!
THE FIRST BARRIER TOOK HUNDREDS OF HITS...
...BUT A FEW FANARIS ARE...
ONCE WE BREAK THIS...
...WE'LL SWEEP INTO...
NO...
...THE CAPITAL!
NO!!

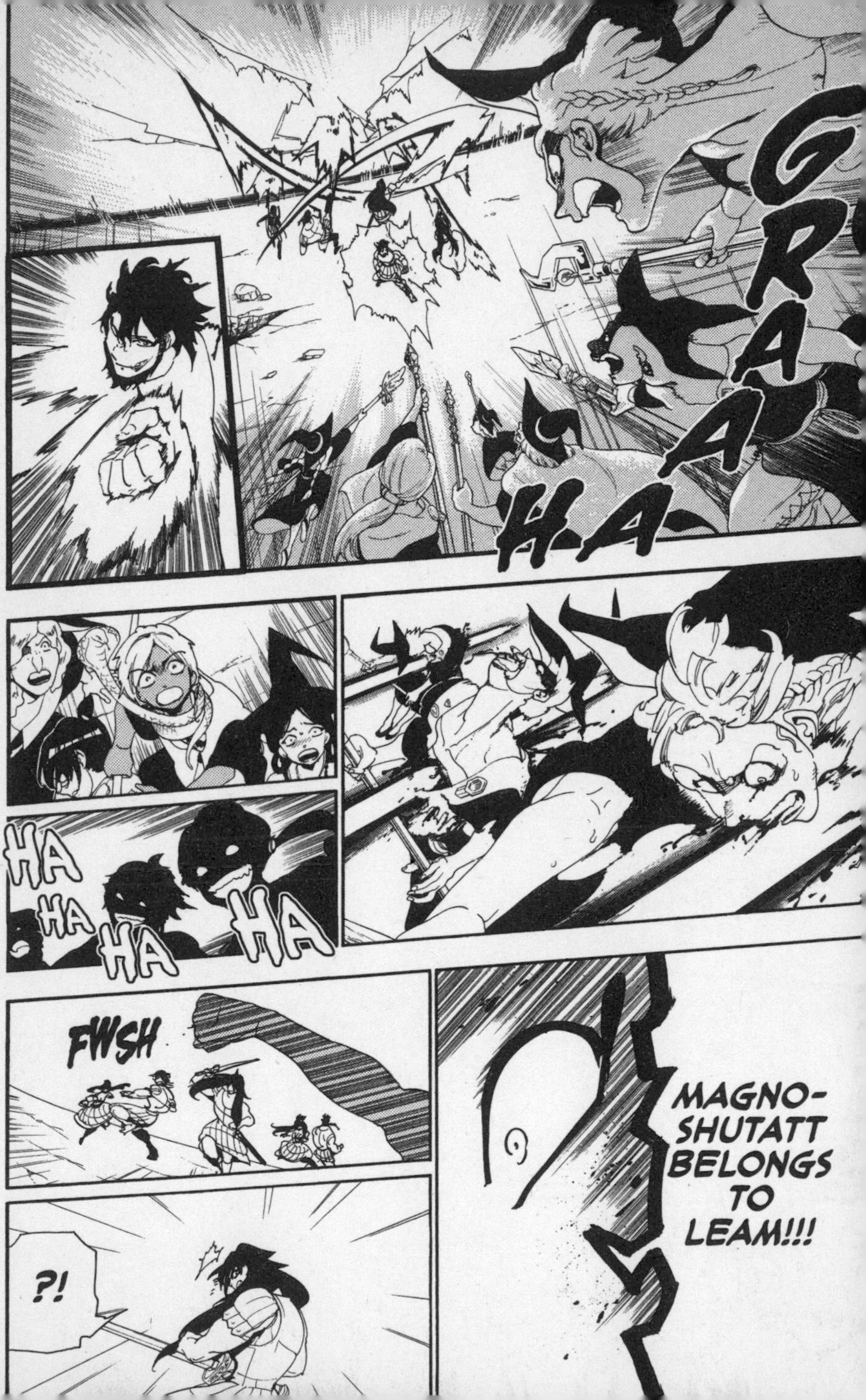

GRAAAHA
HA HA HA HA
FWSH
MAGNO-SHUTATT BELONGS TO LEAM!!!
?!

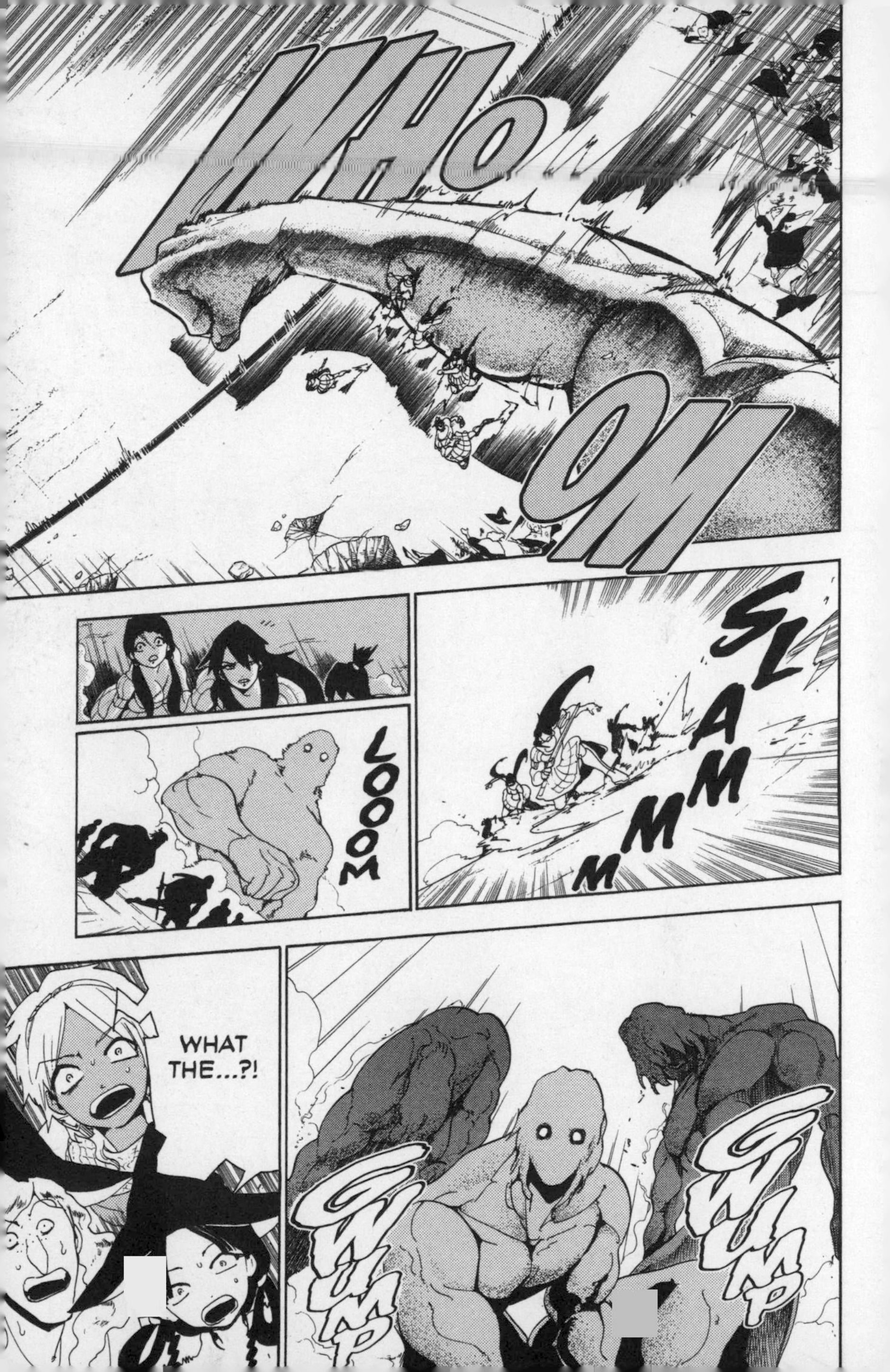
WHO
OM
SLAMMMM
LOOOM
GWUMP
GWUMP
WHAT THE...?!

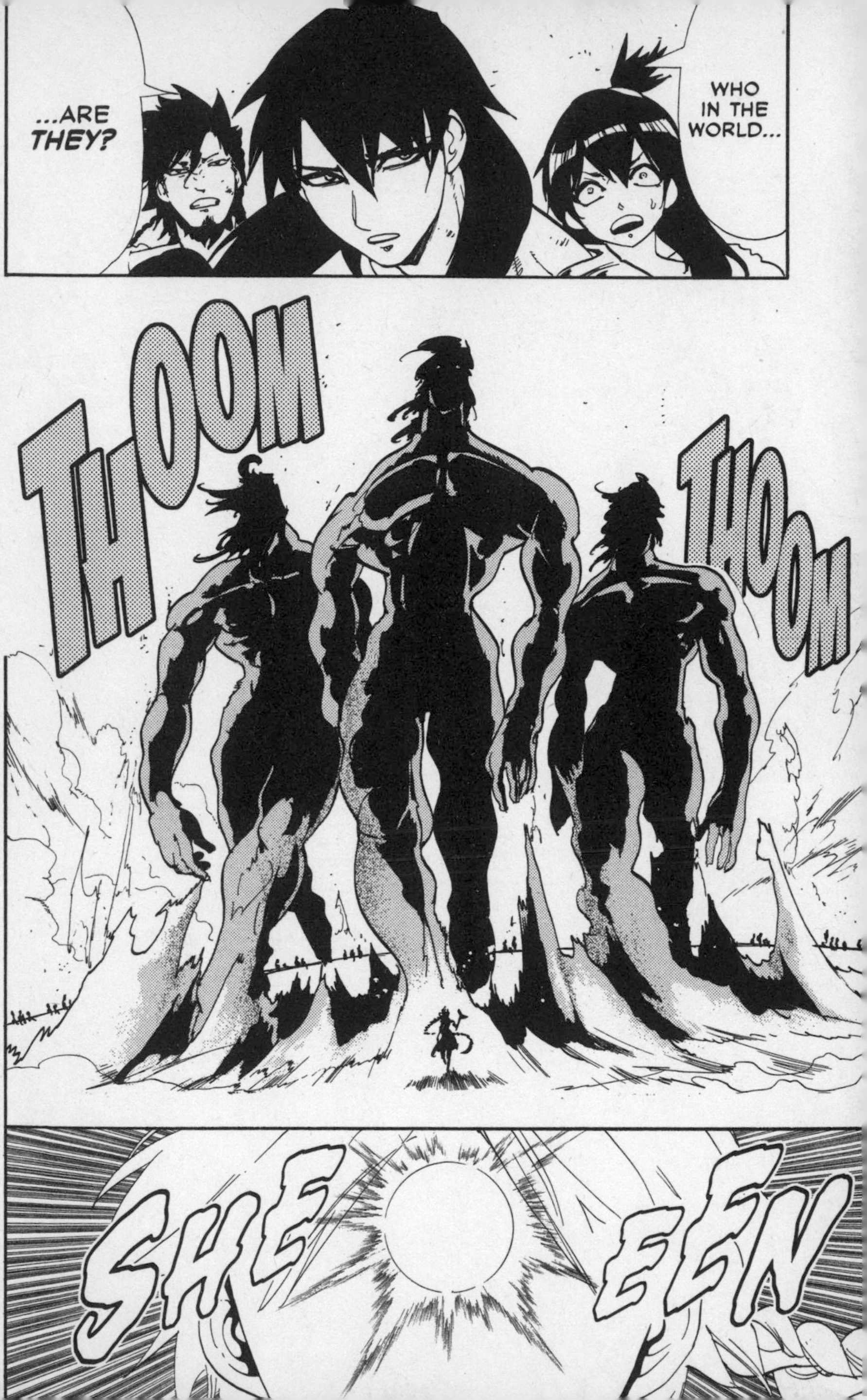
WHO IN THE WORLD...
...ARE THEY?
THOOM
THOOM
SHE EEN

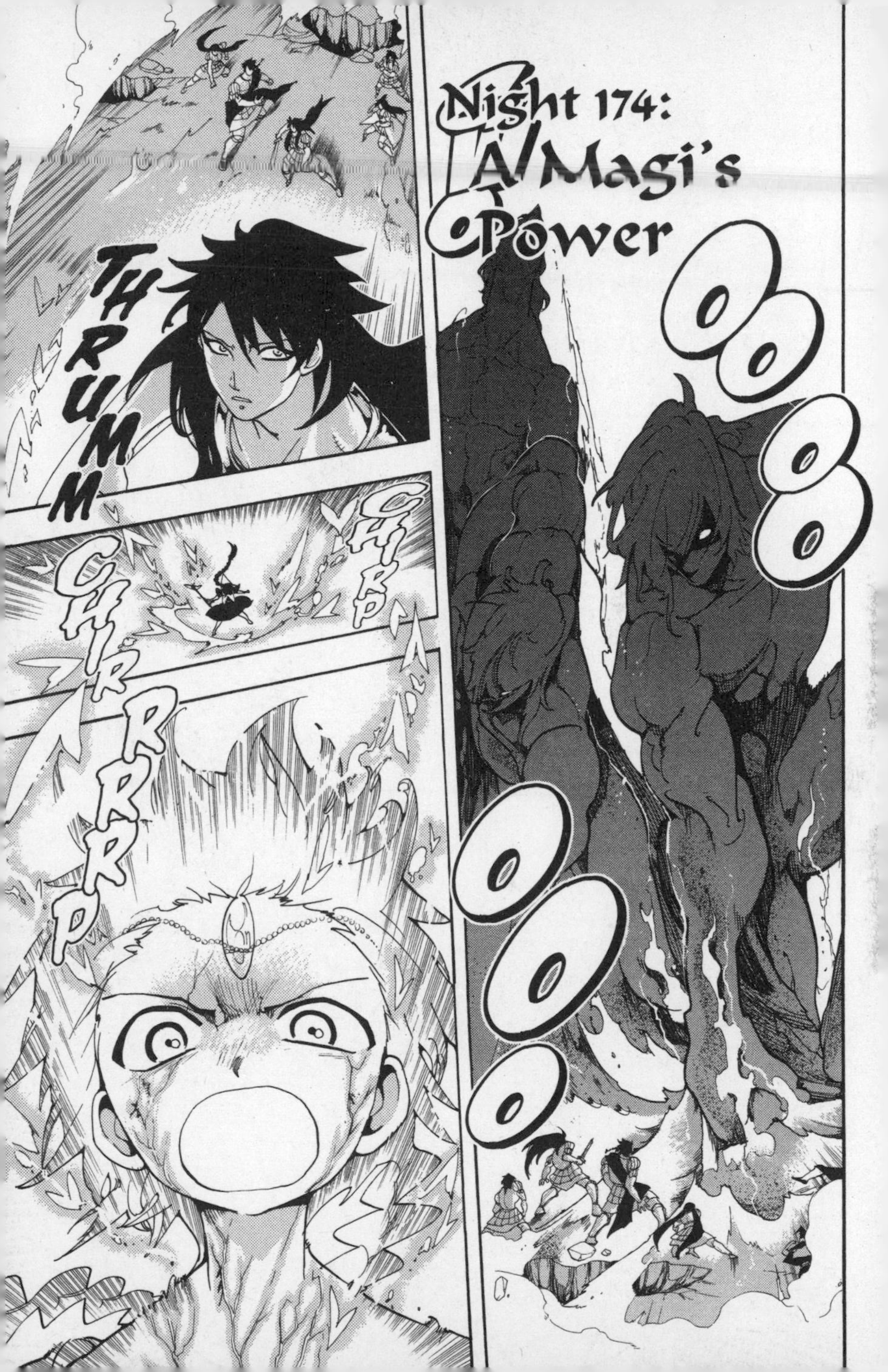

Night 174: A Magi's Power
OOOOO
OOOOO
THRUMM
CHIRP
CHIRRRRP

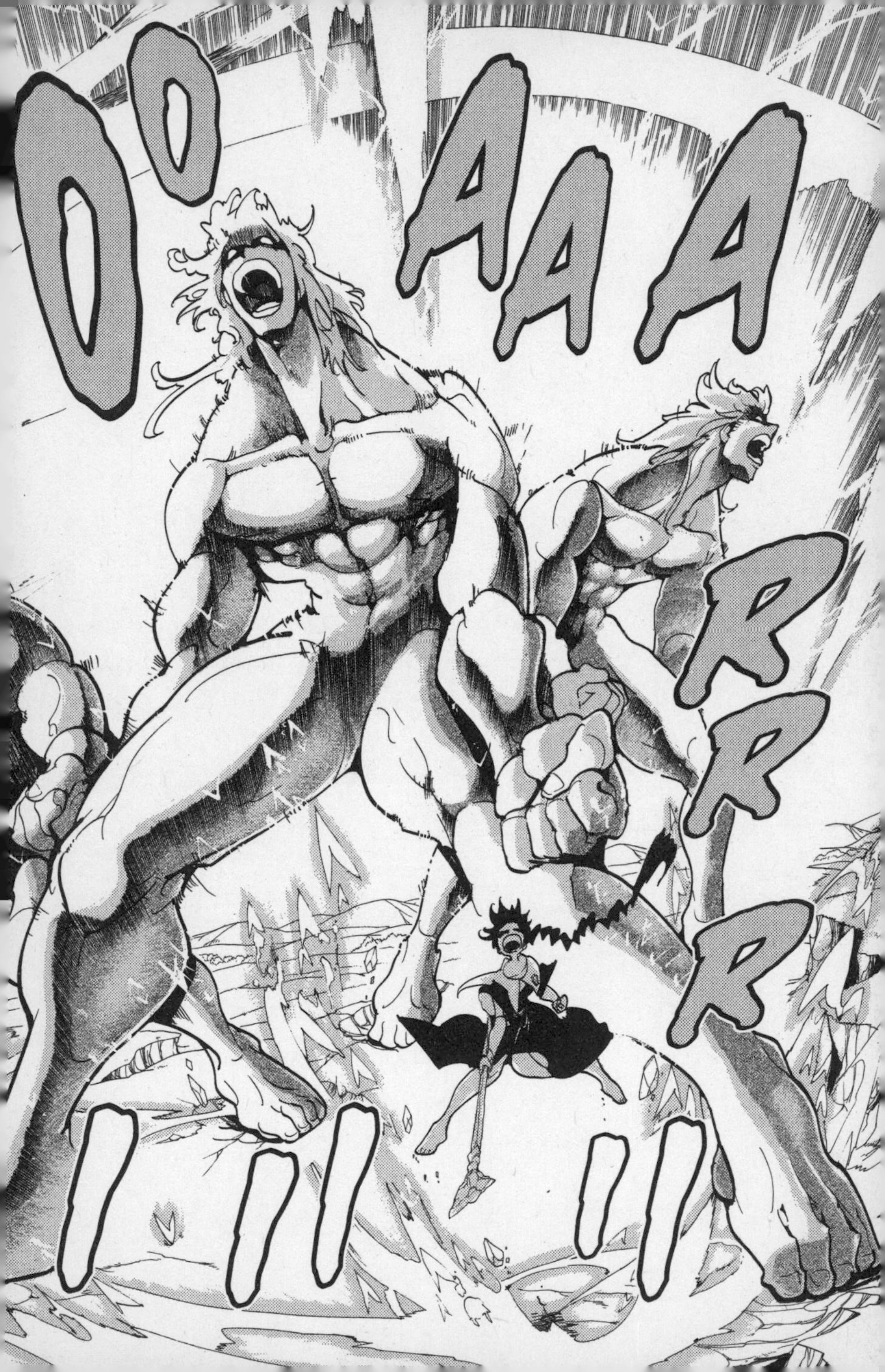
OOAAARRR

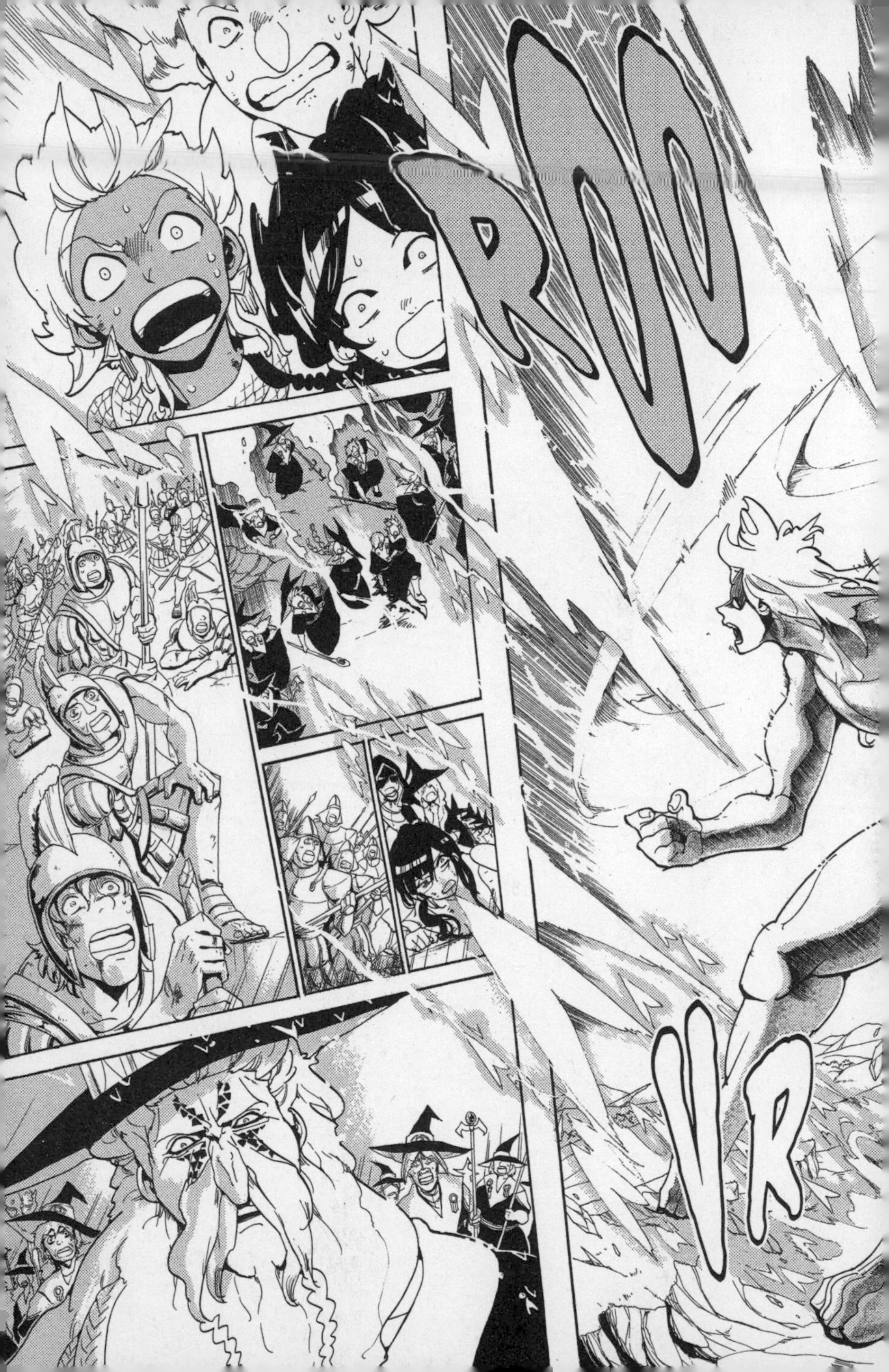

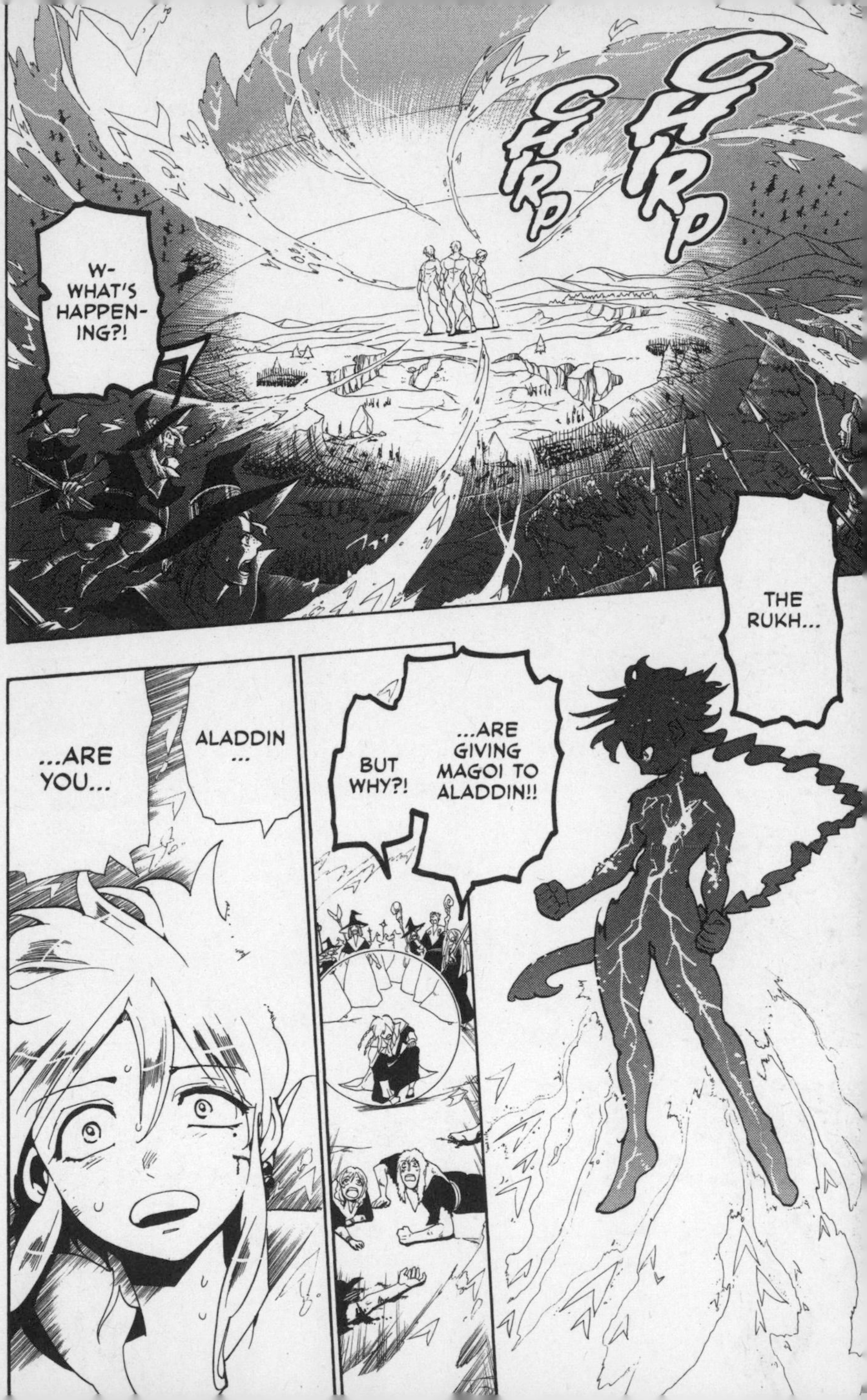

CHIRP
CHIRP
W-WHAT'S HAPPENING?!
THE RUKH...
...ARE GIVING MAGOI TO ALADDIN!!
BUT WHY?!
ALADDIN...
...ARE YOU...

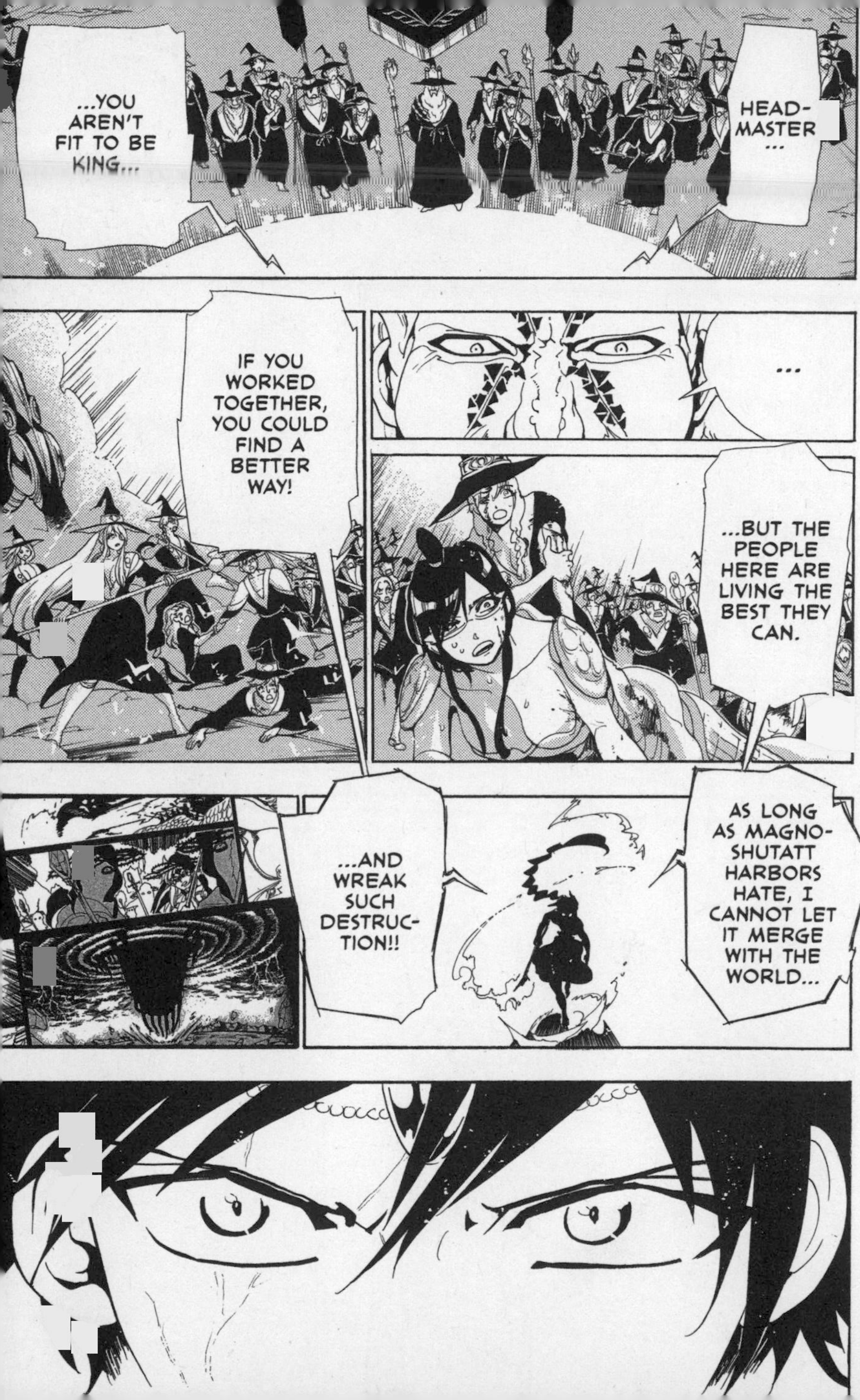
HEAD-MASTER...
...YOU AREN'T FIT TO BE KING...
...
...BUT THE PEOPLE HERE ARE LIVING THE BEST THEY CAN.
IF YOU WORKED TOGETHER, YOU COULD FIND A BETTER WAY!
AS LONG AS MAGNO-SHUTATT HARBORS HATE, I CANNOT LET IT MERGE WITH THE WORLD...
...AND WREAK SUCH DESTRUCTION!!

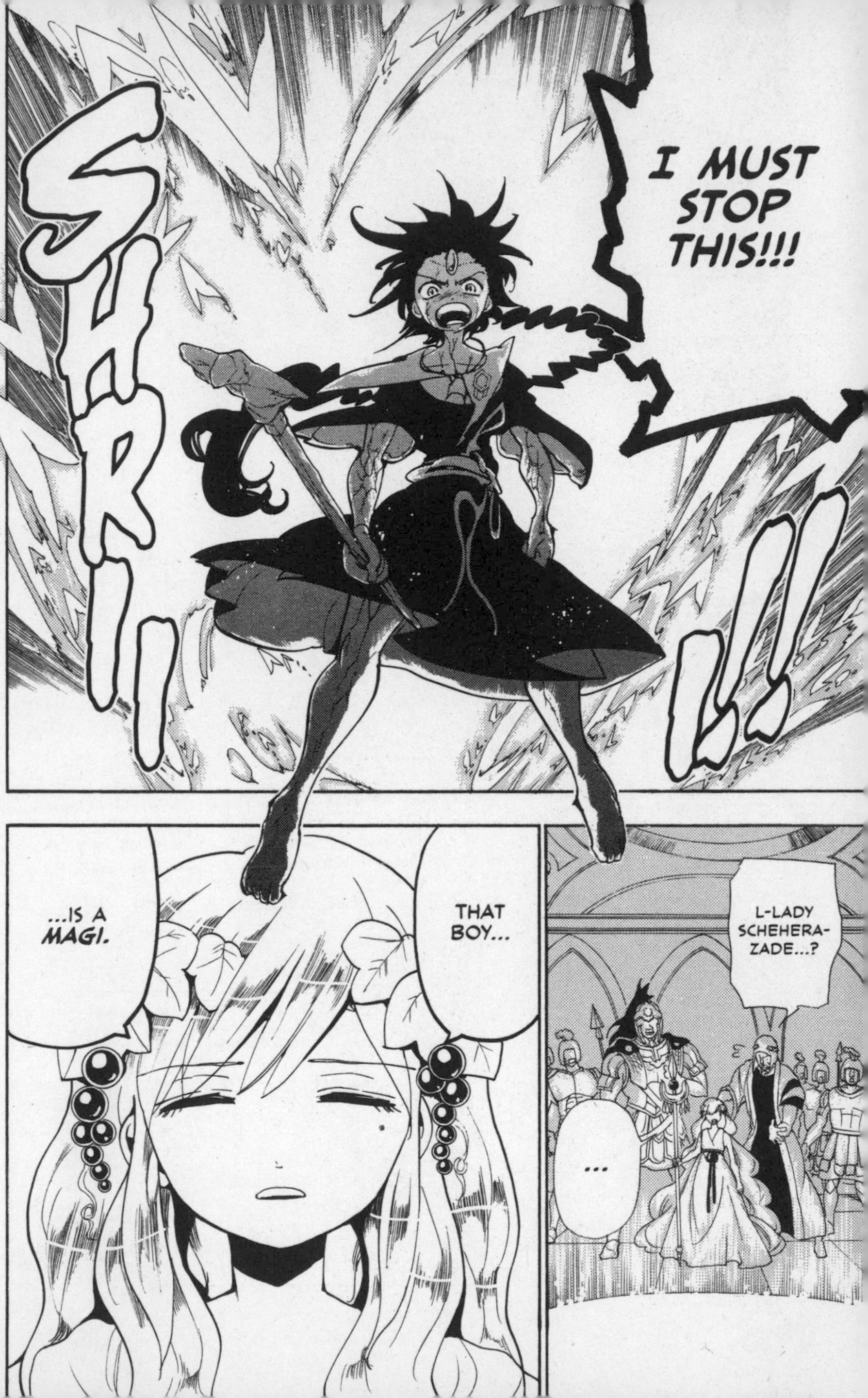
I MUST STOP THIS!!!
SHRI!!
L-LADY SCHEHERA-ZADE...?
...
THAT BOY...
...IS A MAGI.

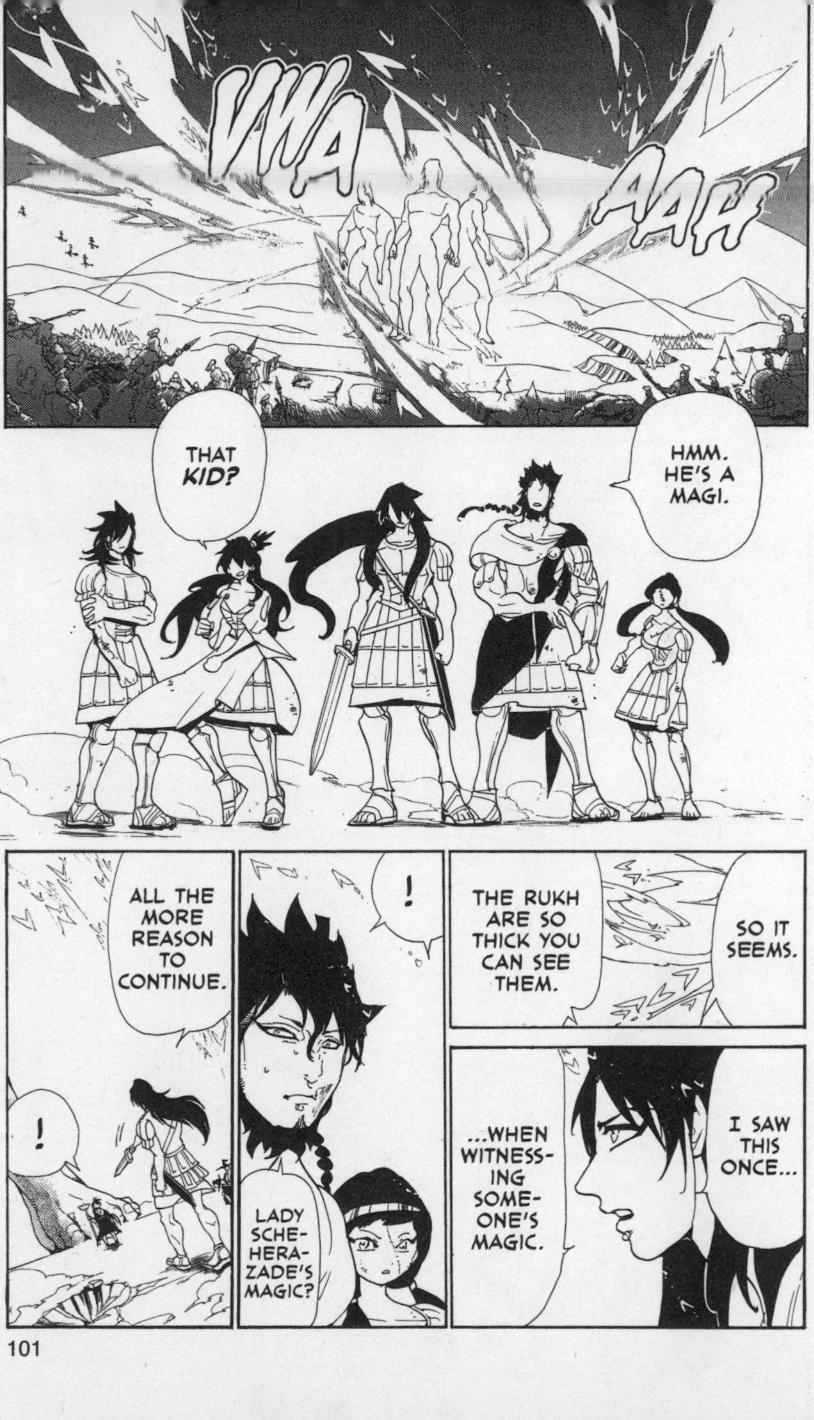
VWA
AAH
HMM. HE'S A MAGI.
THAT KID?
SO IT SEEMS.
THE RUKH ARE SO THICK YOU CAN SEE THEM.
I SAW THIS ONCE...
...WHEN WITNESSING SOMEONE'S MAGIC.
!
LADY SCHEHERAZADE'S MAGIC?
ALL THE MORE REASON TO CONTINUE.
!

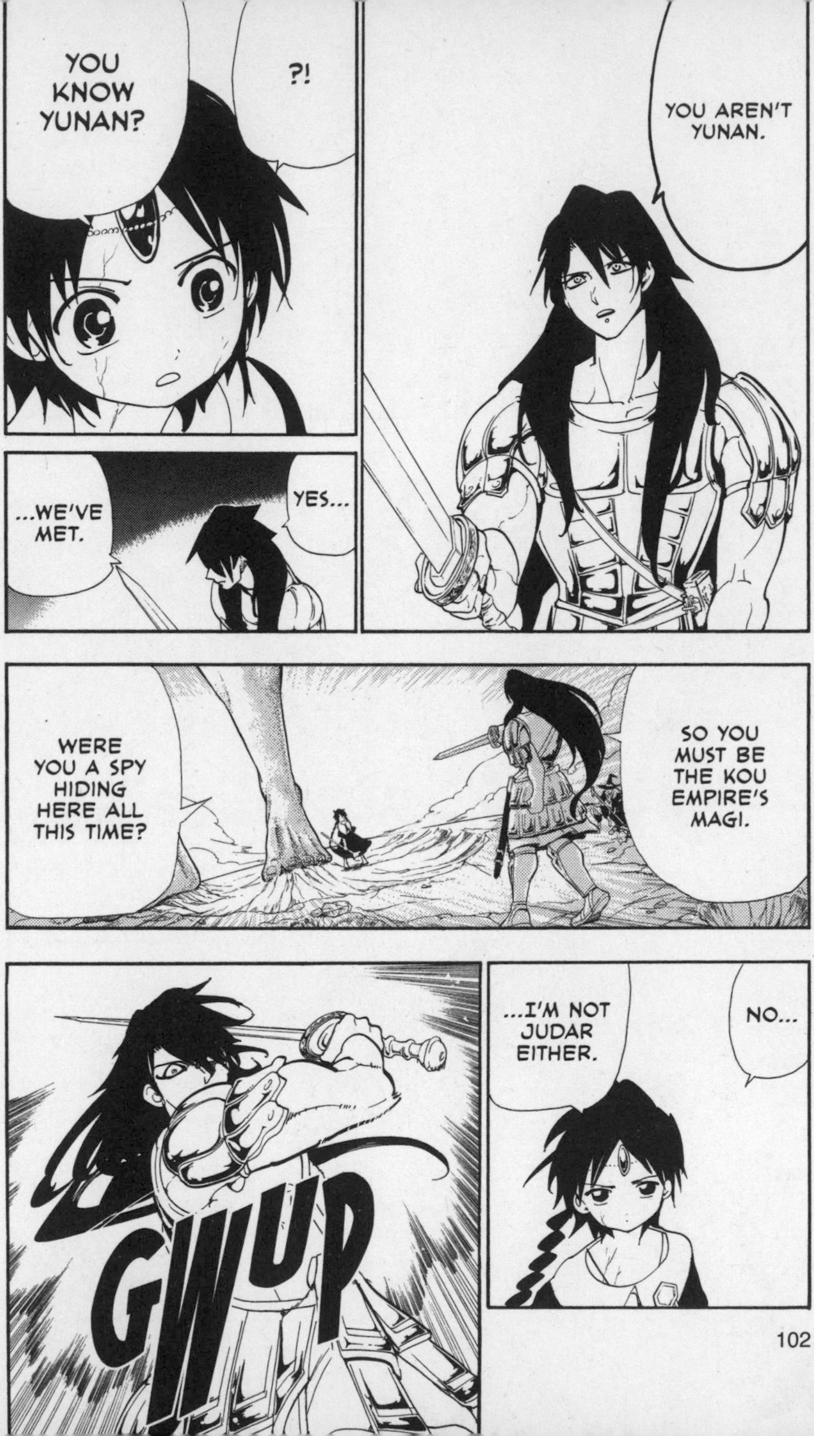
YOU AREN'T YUNAN.
?!
YOU KNOW YUNAN?
YES...
...WE'VE MET.
SO YOU MUST BE THE KOU EMPIRE'S MAGI.
WERE YOU A SPY HIDING HERE ALL THIS TIME?
NO...
...I'M NOT JUDAR EITHER.
GWUP

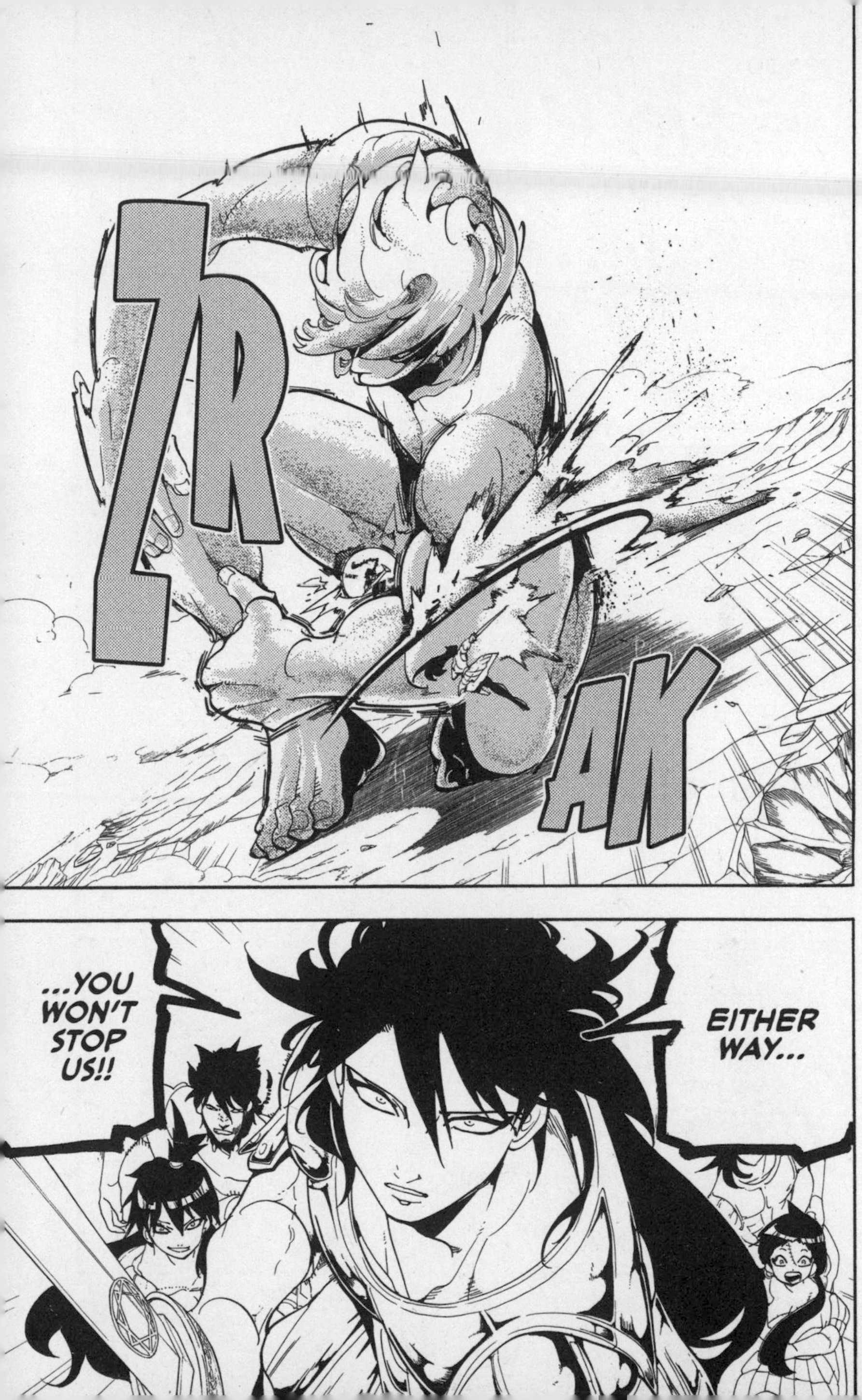
ZRAK
EITHER WAY...
...YOU WON'T STOP US!!

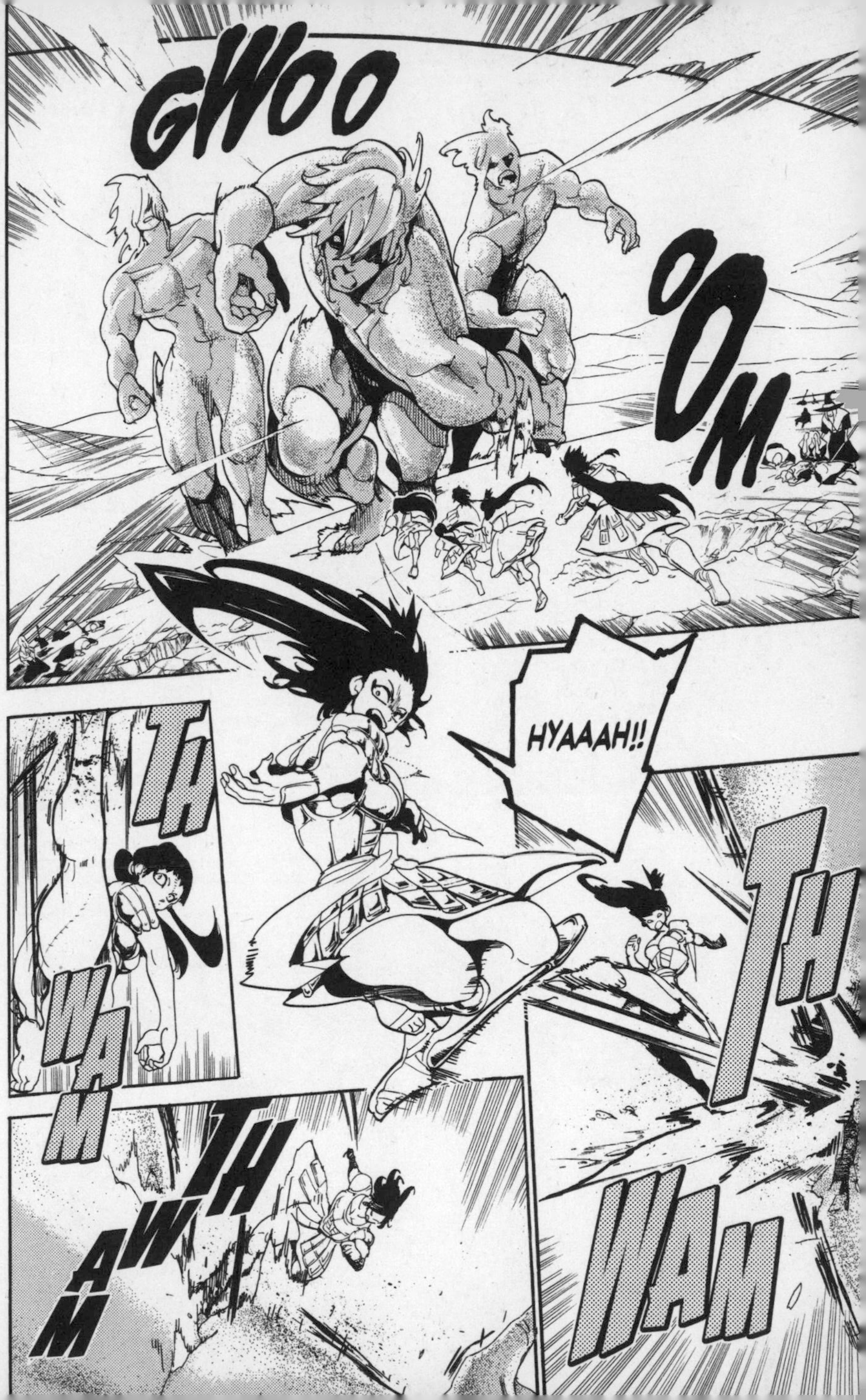
GWOO
OOM
HYAAAH!!
THWAM
THWAM
THWAM

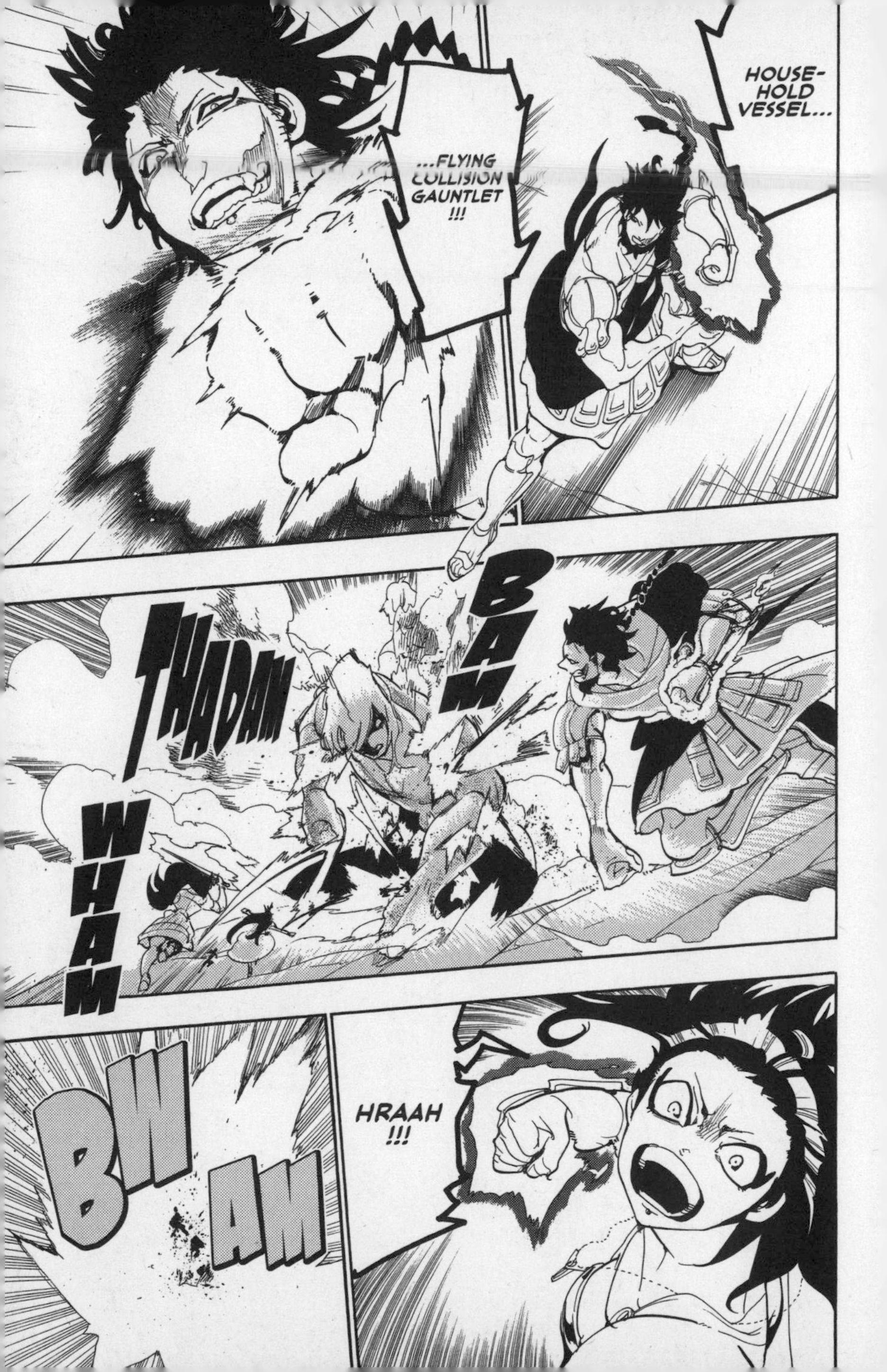
HOUSE-HOLD VESSEL...
...FLYING COLLISION GAUNTLET!!!
BAM
THADAM
WHAM
HRAAH!!!
BWAM

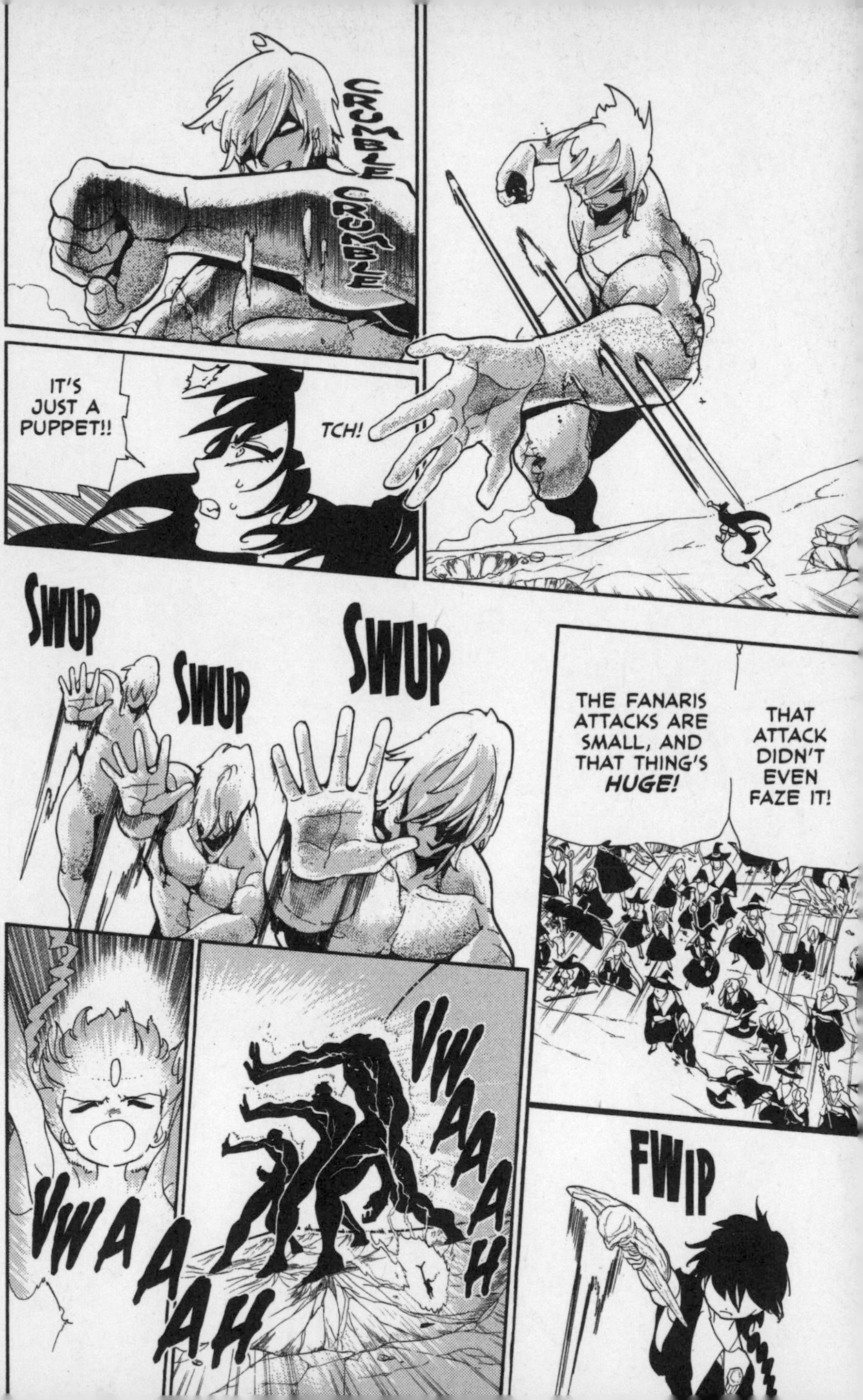
CRUMBLE CRUMBLE
TCH!
IT'S JUST A PUPPET!!
THAT ATTACK DIDN'T EVEN FAZE IT!
THE FANARIS ATTACKS ARE SMALL, AND THAT THING'S *HUGE!*
SWUP
SWUP
SWUP
FWIP
VWAAAAH
VWAAAH

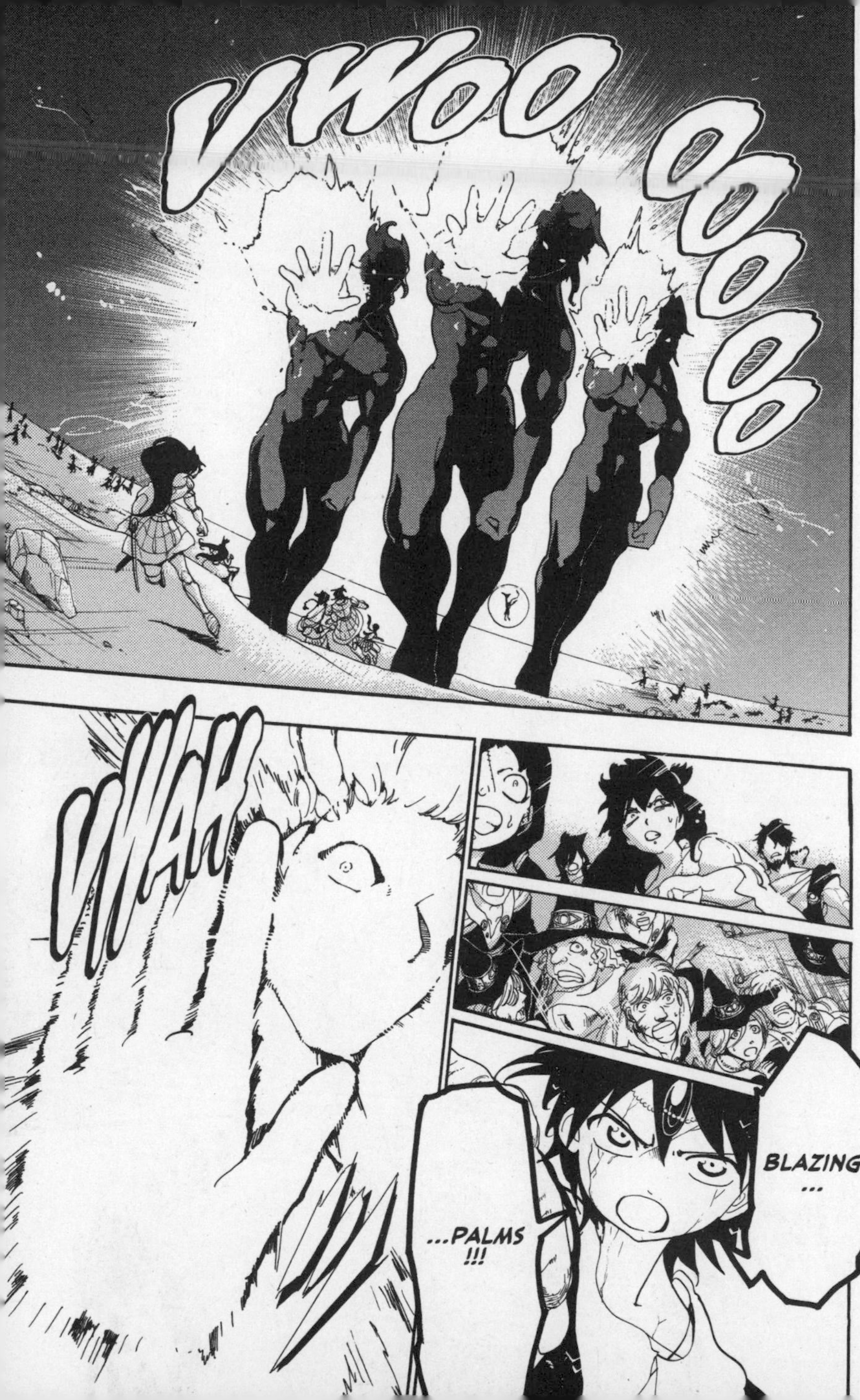
VWOOOOOOOO
BLAZING...
...PALMS!!!
WAH

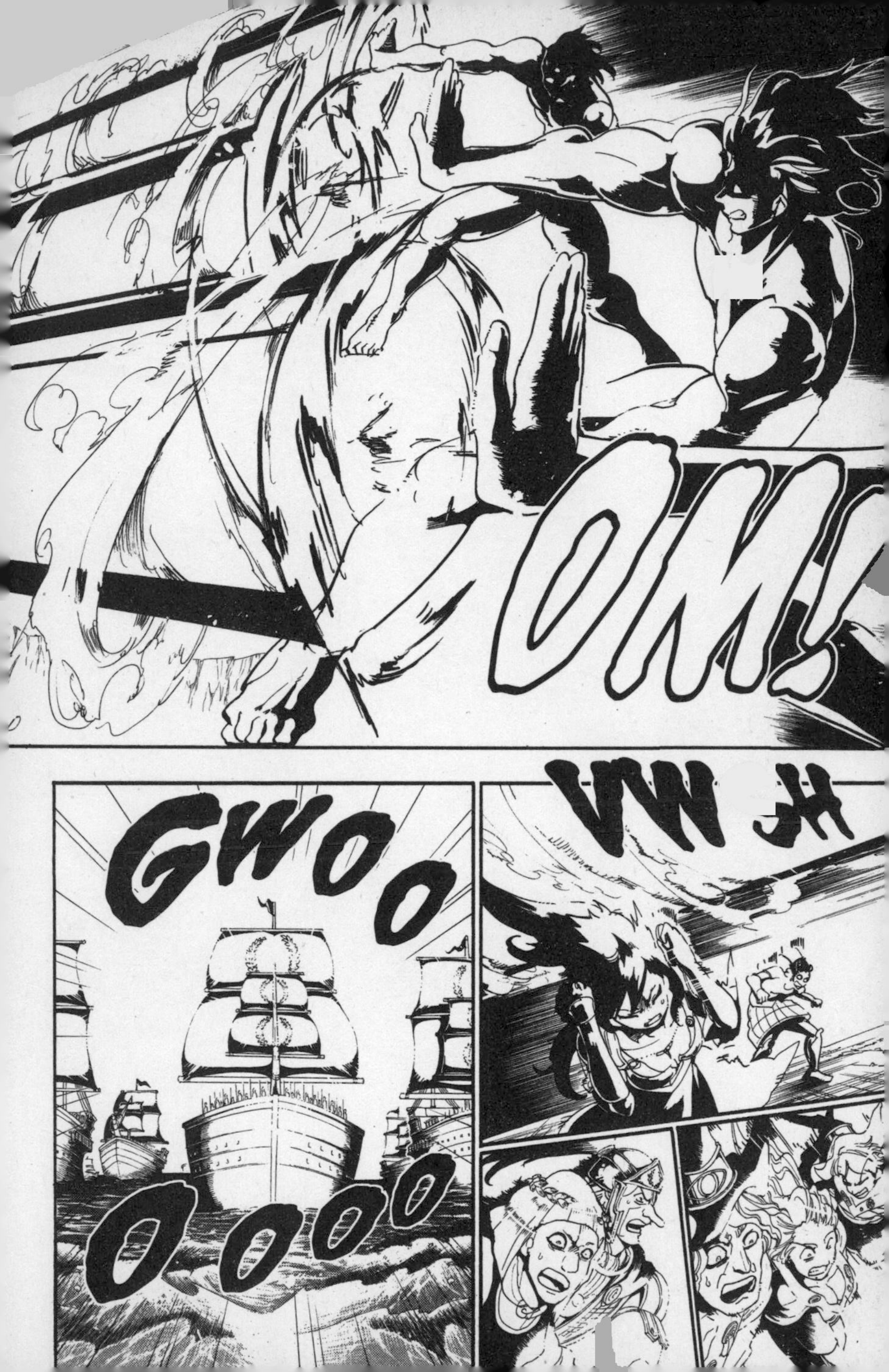
OM!
VW
GWOOOOOOO

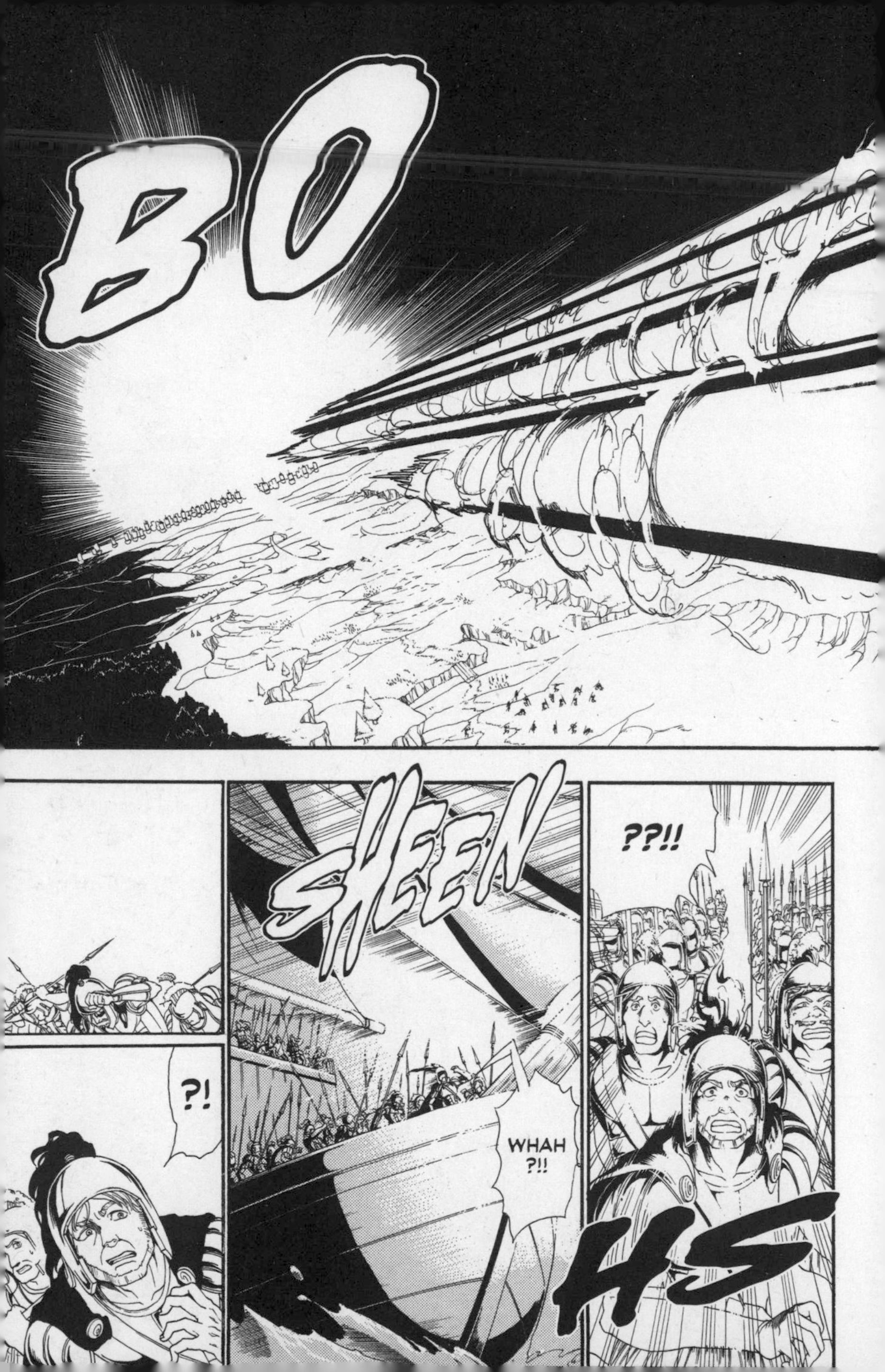
BO
??!!
HS
SHEEN
WHAH ?!!
?!

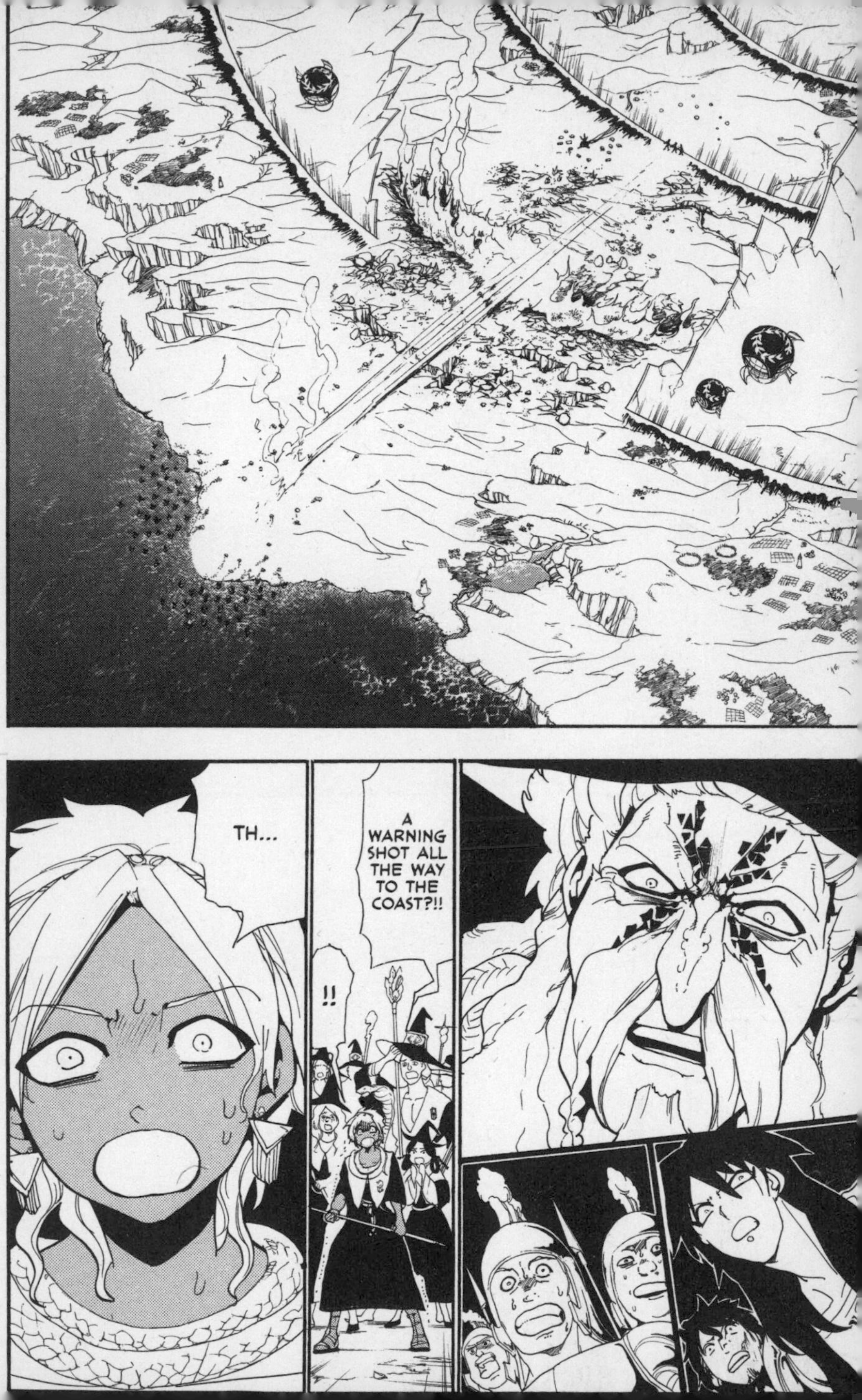
A WARNING SHOT ALL THE WAY TO THE COAST?!!
!!
TH...

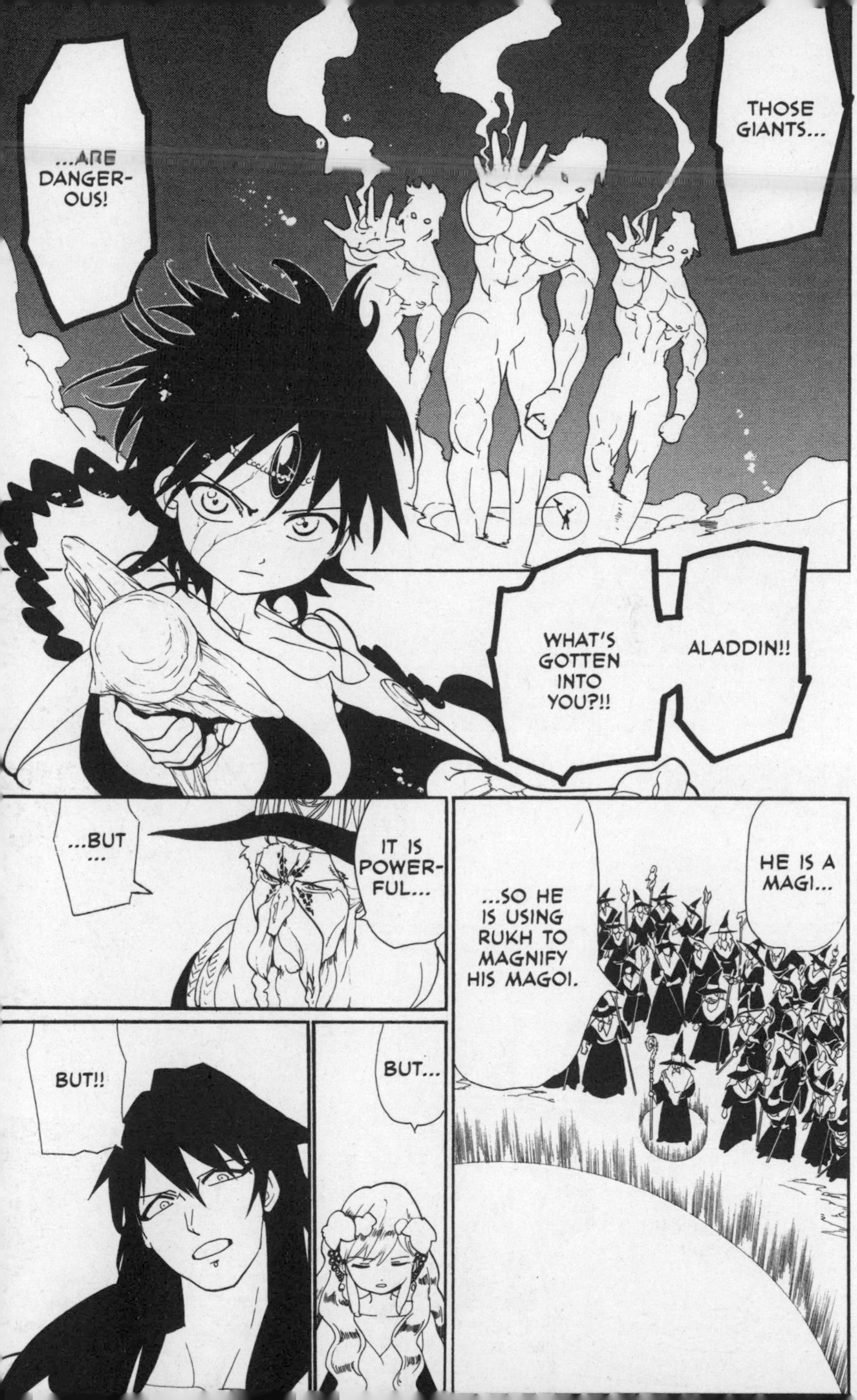
THOSE GIANTS...
...ARE DANGER-OUS!
ALADDIN!!
WHAT'S GOTTEN INTO YOU?!!
HE IS A MAGI...
...SO HE IS USING RUKH TO MAGNIFY HIS MAGOI.
IT IS POWER-FUL...
...BUT ...
BUT...
BUT!!

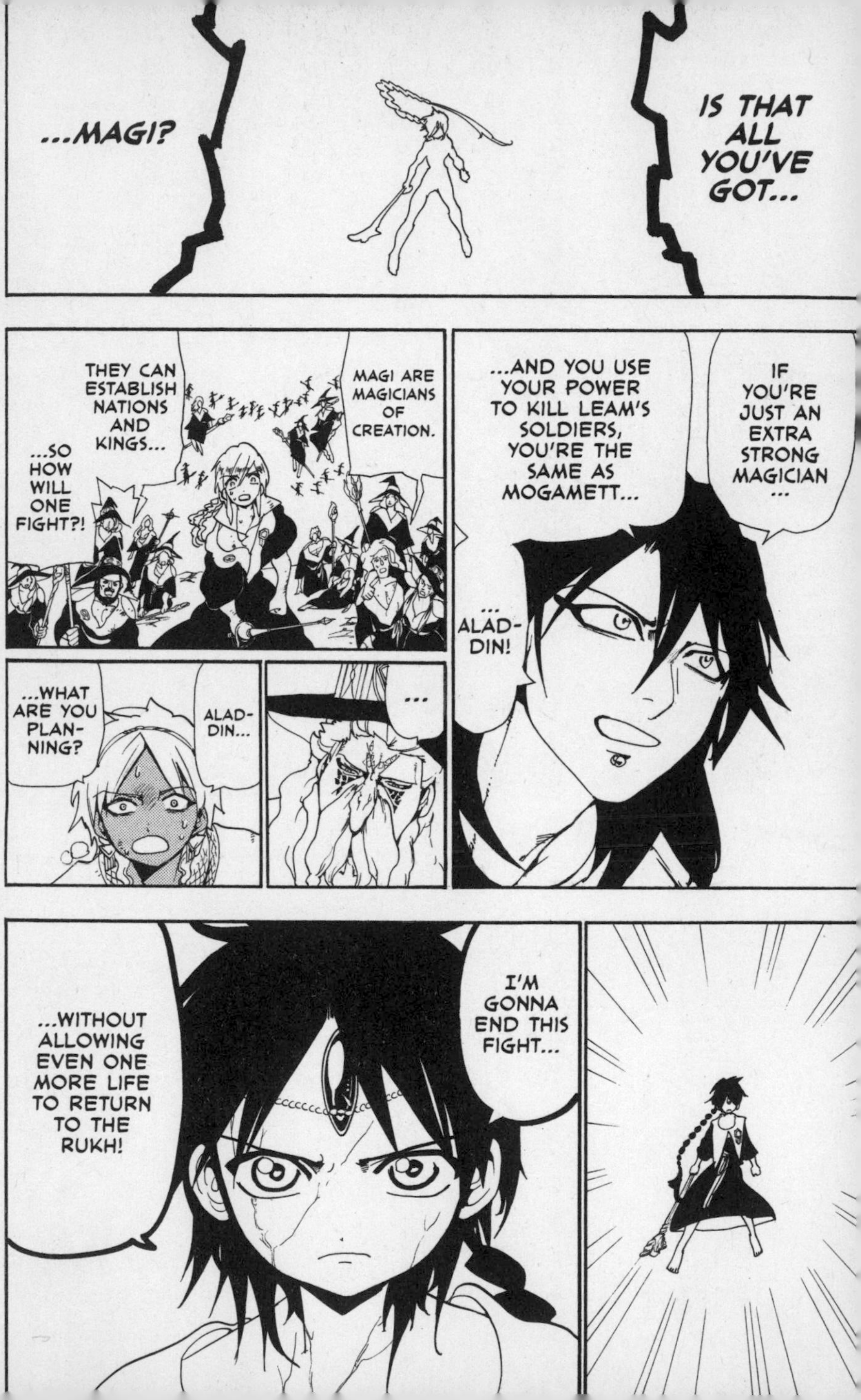
IS THAT ALL YOU'VE GOT...
...MAGI?
IF YOU'RE JUST AN EXTRA STRONG MAGICIAN ...
...AND YOU USE YOUR POWER TO KILL LEAM'S SOLDIERS, YOU'RE THE SAME AS MOGAMETT...
... ALAD-DIN!
MAGI ARE MAGICIANS OF CREATION.
THEY CAN ESTABLISH NATIONS AND KINGS...
...SO HOW WILL ONE FIGHT?!
...
ALAD-DIN...
...WHAT ARE YOU PLAN-NING?
I'M GONNA END THIS FIGHT...
...WITHOUT ALLOWING EVEN ONE MORE LIFE TO RETURN TO THE RUKH!

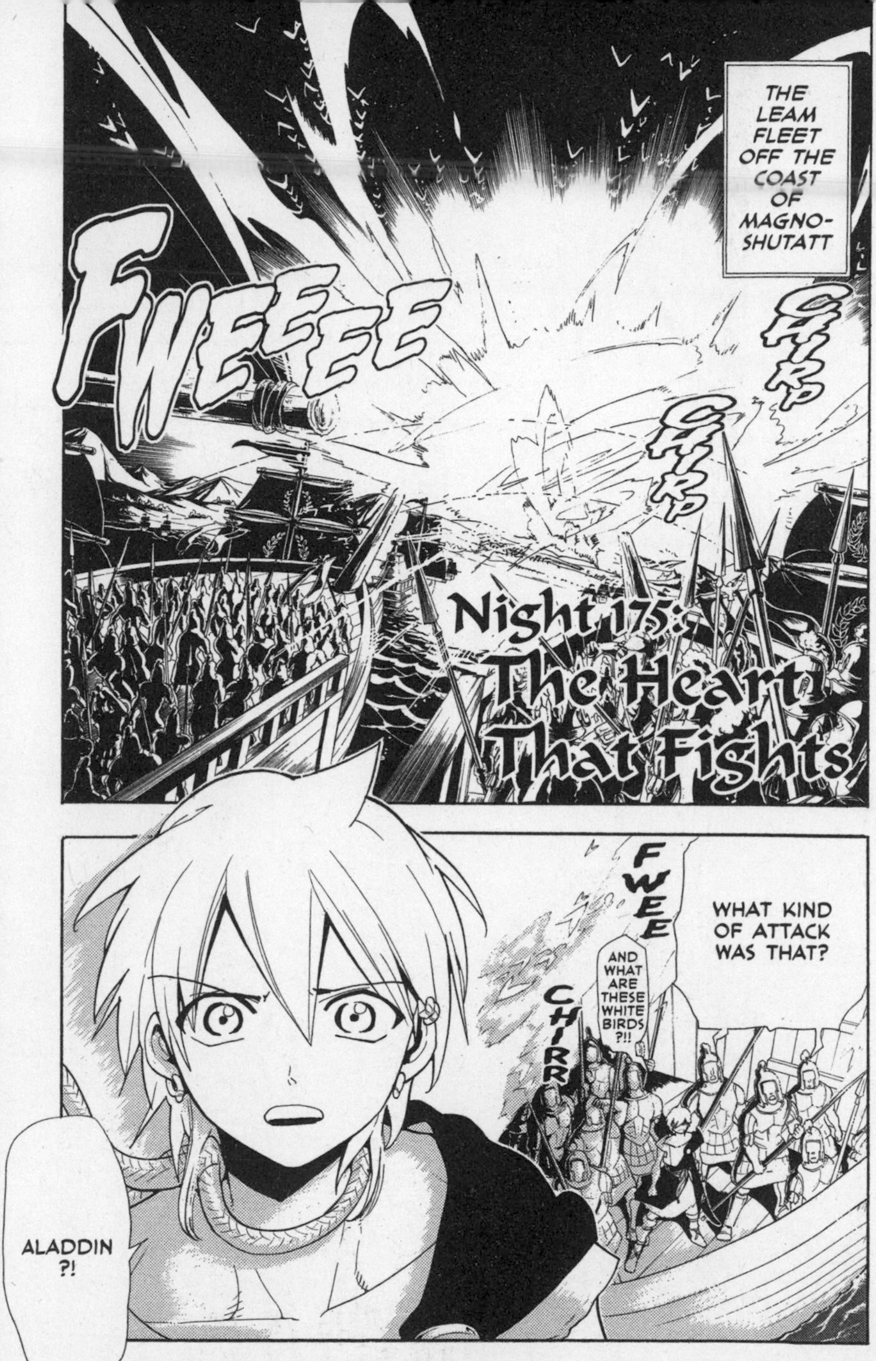
THE LEAM FLEET OFF THE COAST OF MAGNO-SHUTATT
CHIRP
CHIRP
FWEEEE
Night 175: The Heart That Fights
WHAT KIND OF ATTACK WAS THAT?
FWEE
AND WHAT ARE THESE WHITE BIRDS ?!!
CHIRR
ALADDIN ?!

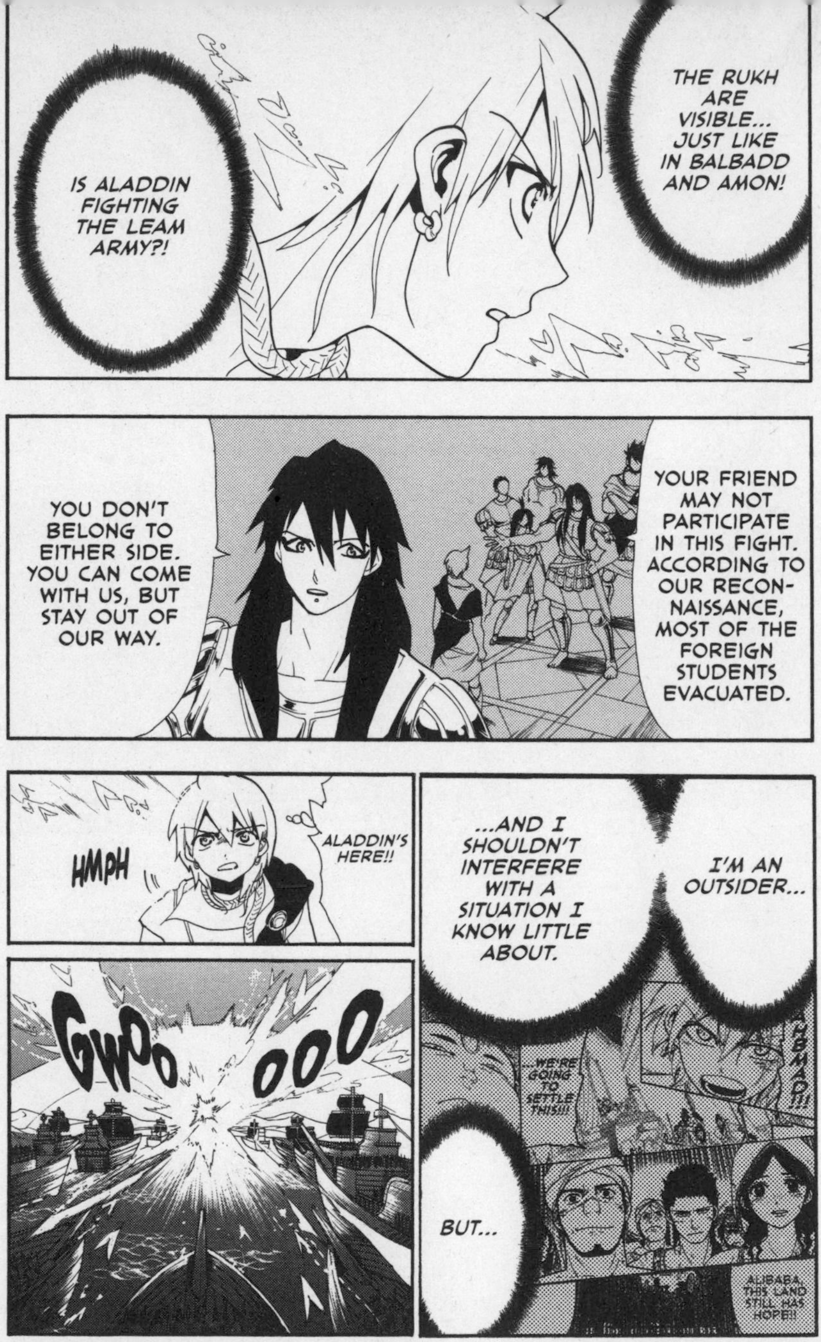
THE RUKH ARE VISIBLE... JUST LIKE IN BALBADD AND AMON!
IS ALADDIN FIGHTING THE LEAM ARMY?!
YOUR FRIEND MAY NOT PARTICIPATE IN THIS FIGHT. ACCORDING TO OUR RECON-NAISSANCE, MOST OF THE FOREIGN STUDENTS EVACUATED.
YOU DON'T BELONG TO EITHER SIDE. YOU CAN COME WITH US, BUT STAY OUT OF OUR WAY.
I'M AN OUTSIDER...
...AND I SHOULDN'T INTERFERE WITH A SITUATION I KNOW LITTLE ABOUT.
AHBMAD!!!
...WE'RE GOING TO SETTLE THIS!!!
BUT...
ALIBABA, THIS LAND STILL HAS HOPE!!
ALADDIN'S HERE!!
HMPH
GWOOOOO

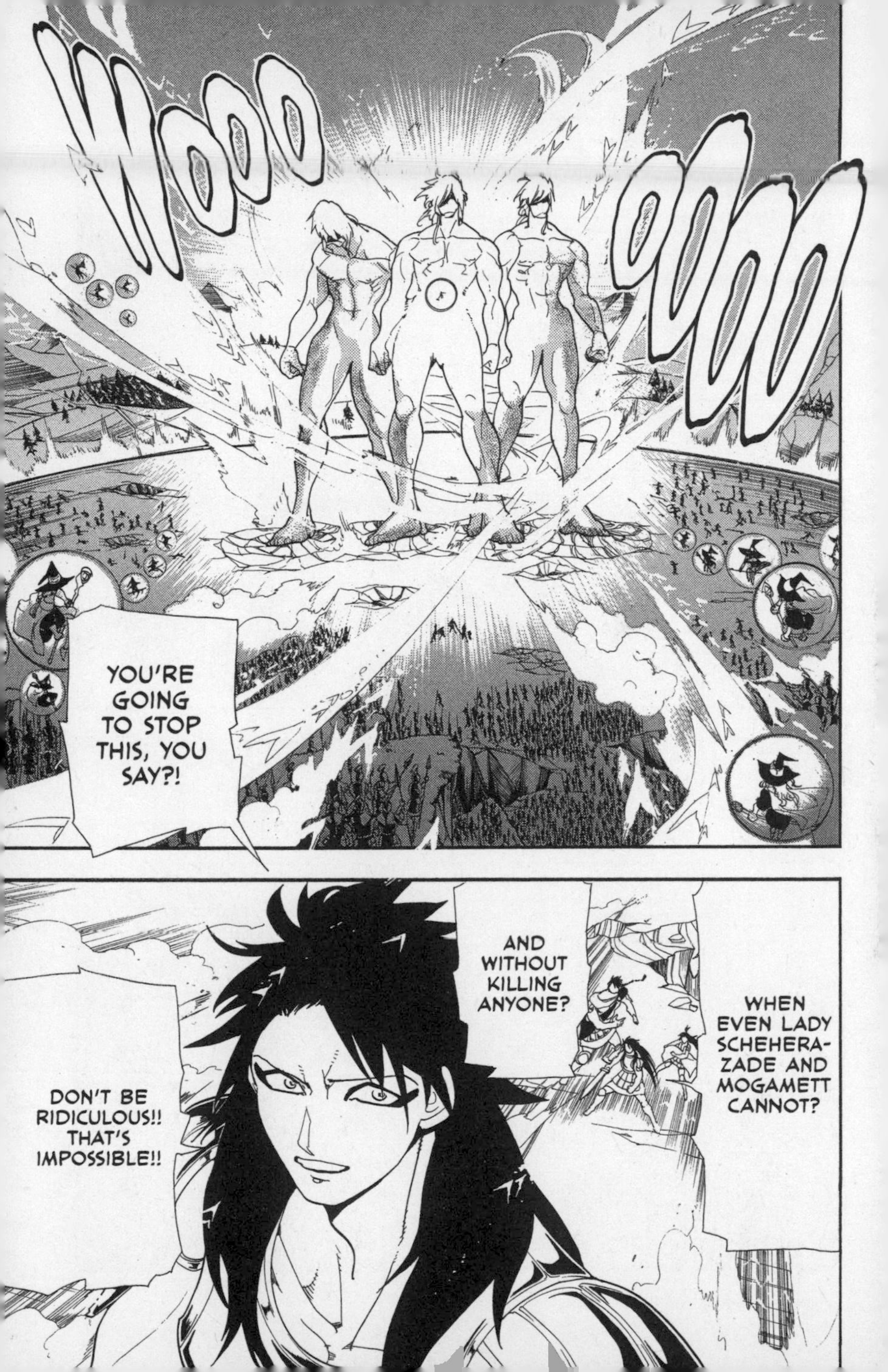
WOOOOOOOOO
YOU'RE GOING TO STOP THIS, YOU SAY?!
AND WITHOUT KILLING ANYONE?
WHEN EVEN LADY SCHEHERAZADE AND MOGAMETT CANNOT?
DON'T BE RIDICULOUS!! THAT'S IMPOSSIBLE!!

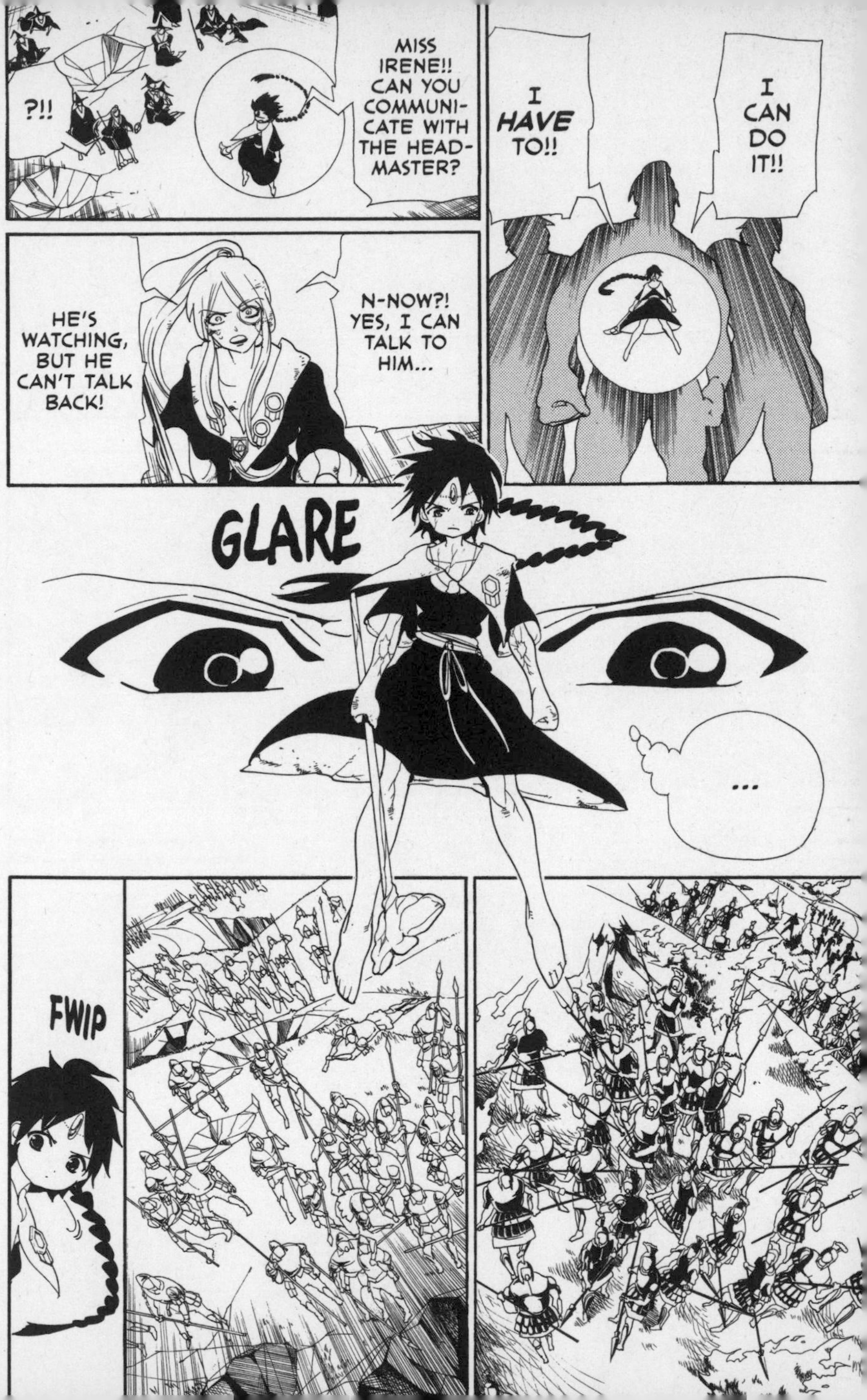

I CAN DO IT!!
I *HAVE* TO!!
MISS IRENE!! CAN YOU COMMUNICATE WITH THE HEADMASTER?
?!!
N-NOW?! YES, I CAN TALK TO HIM...
HE'S WATCHING, BUT HE CAN'T TALK BACK!
...
GLARE
FWIP

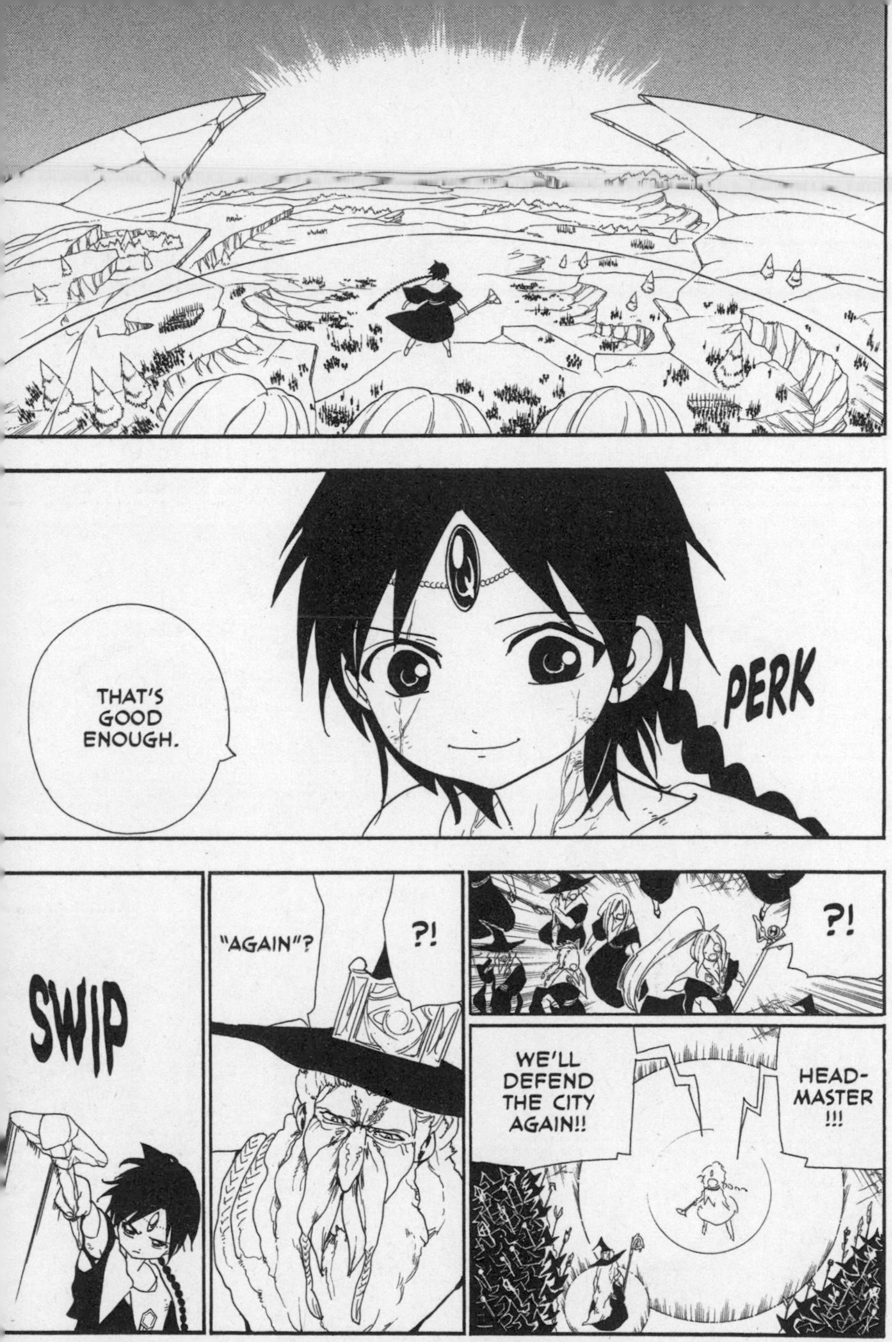
PERK
THAT'S GOOD ENOUGH.
?!
HEAD-MASTER!!!
WE'LL DEFEND THE CITY AGAIN!!
?!
"AGAIN"?
SWIP

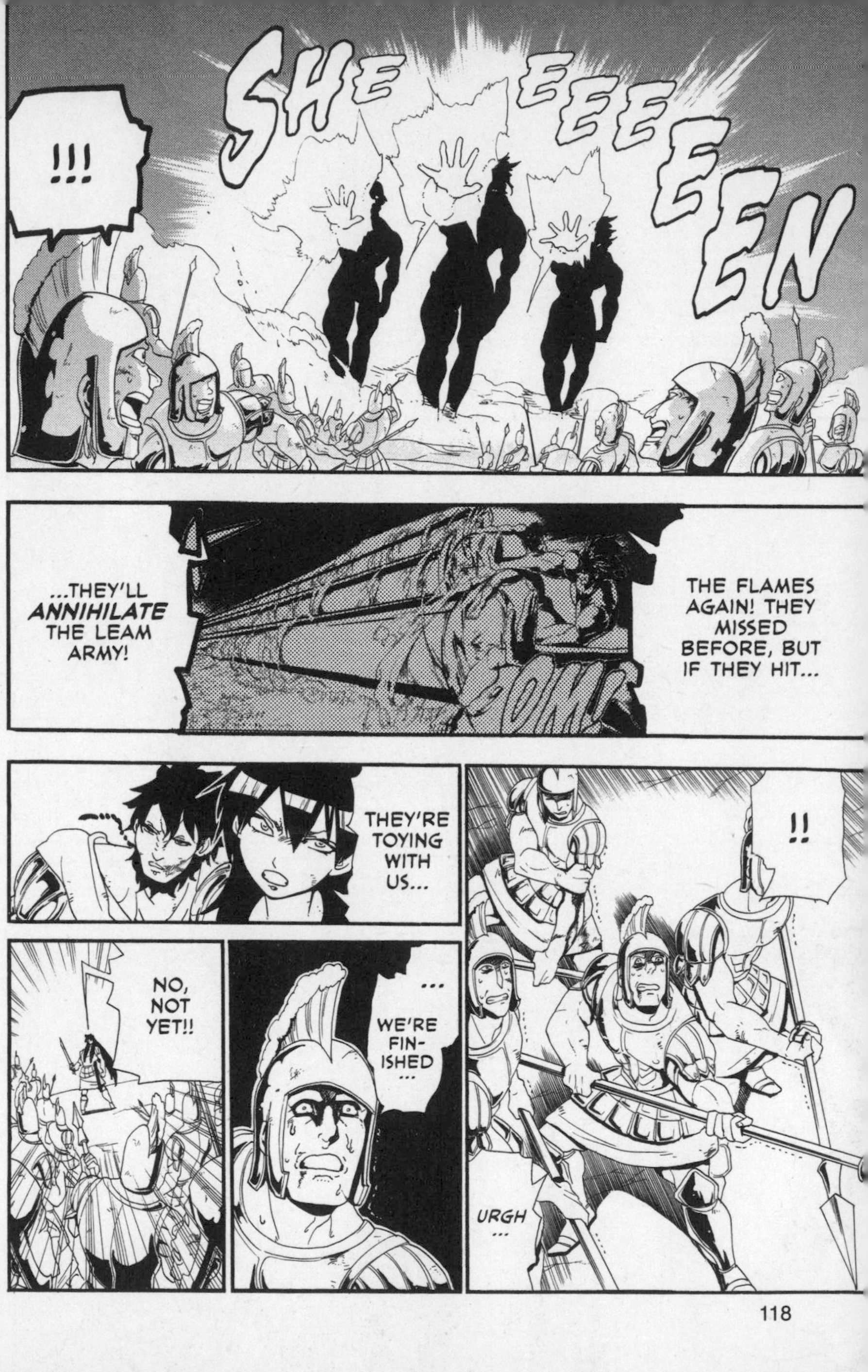
SHEEEEEEEN
!!!
THE FLAMES AGAIN! THEY MISSED BEFORE, BUT IF THEY HIT...
...THEY'LL ANNIHILATE THE LEAM ARMY!
!!
URGH ...
THEY'RE TOYING WITH US...
... WE'RE FIN-ISHED ...
NO, NOT YET!!

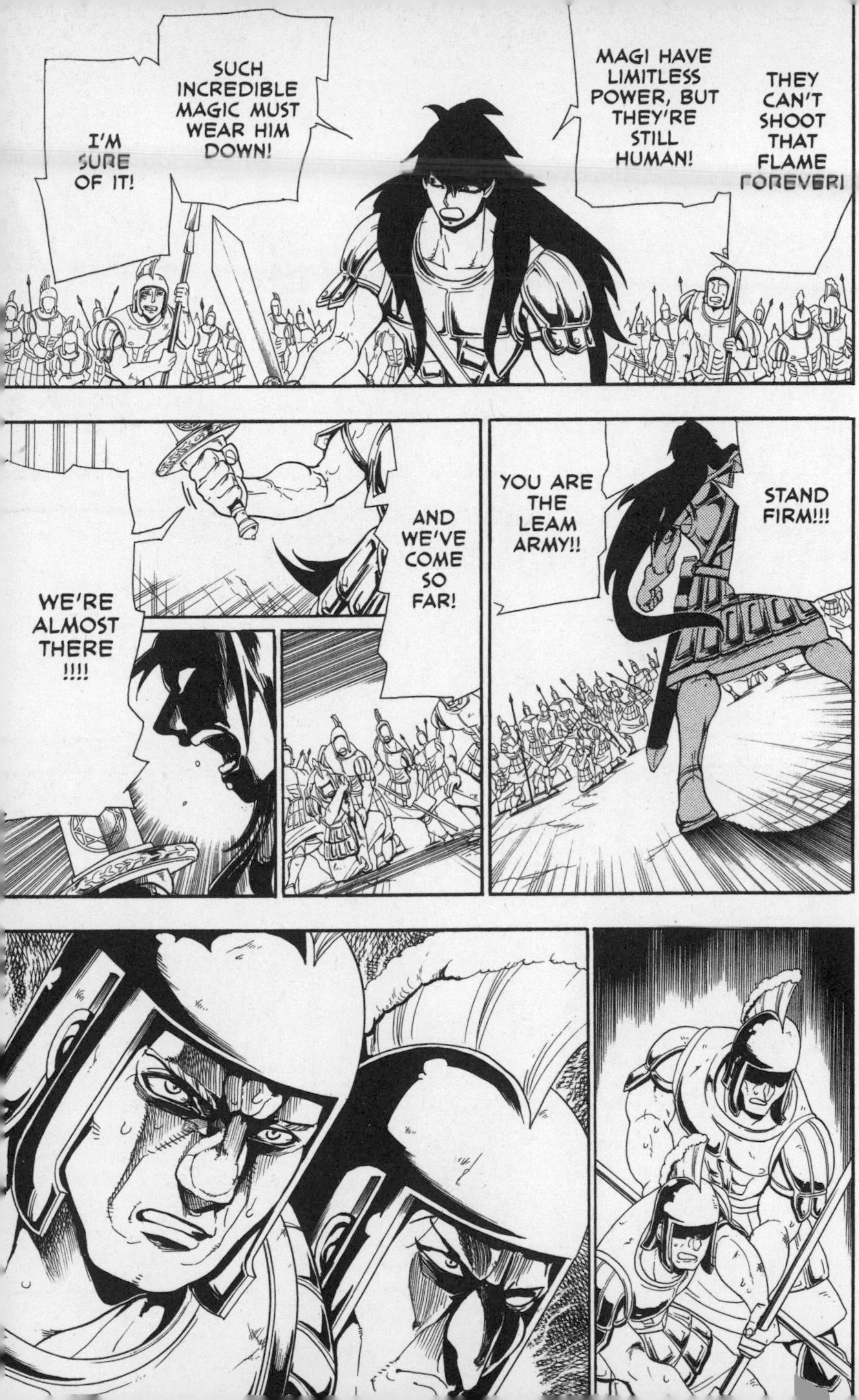
THEY CAN'T SHOOT THAT FLAME FOREVER!
MAGI HAVE LIMITLESS POWER, BUT THEY'RE STILL HUMAN!
SUCH INCREDIBLE MAGIC MUST WEAR HIM DOWN!
I'M SURE OF IT!
STAND FIRM!!!
YOU ARE THE LEAM ARMY!!
AND WE'VE COME SO FAR!
WE'RE ALMOST THERE !!!!

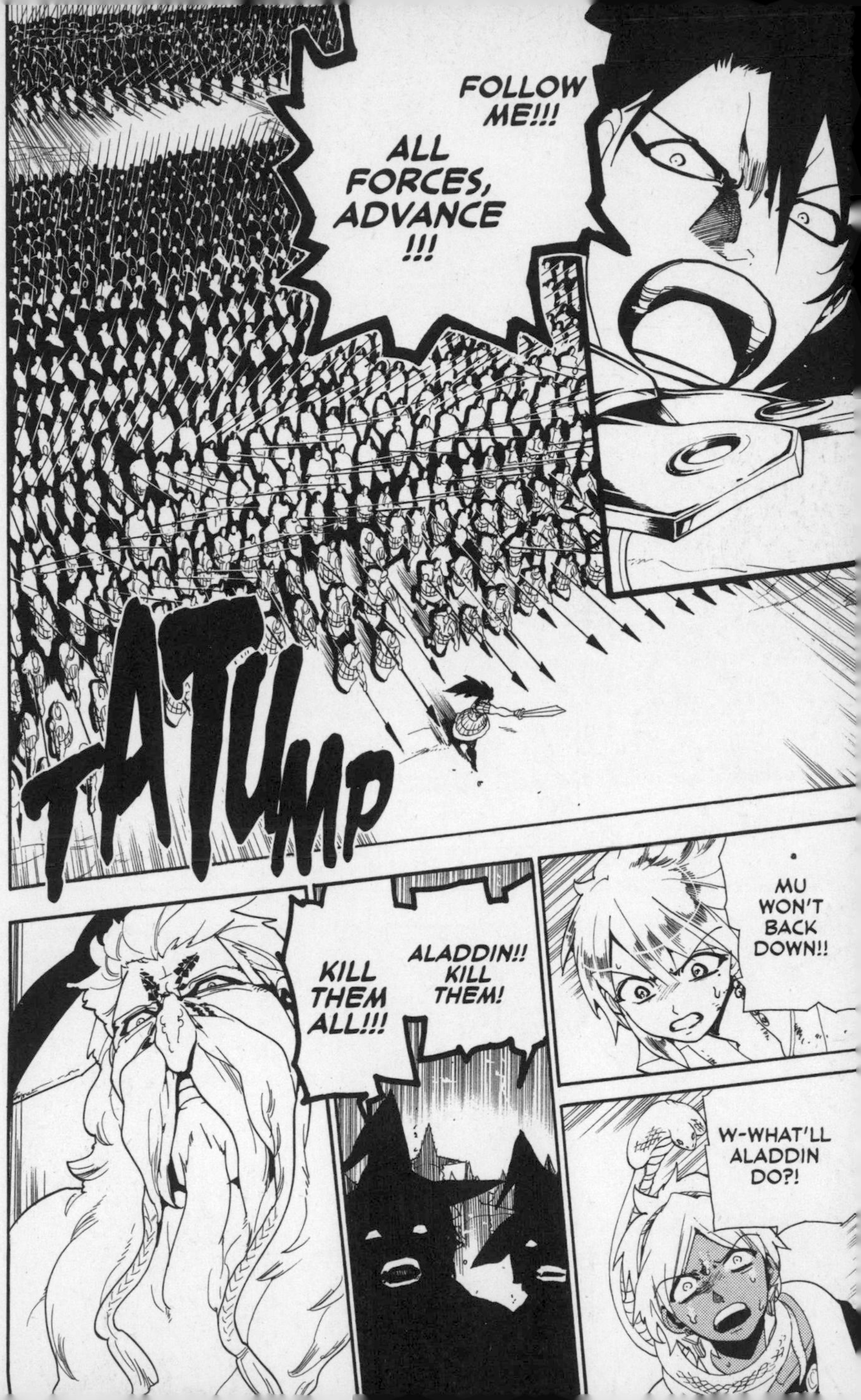
FOLLOW ME!!!
ALL FORCES, ADVANCE!!!
TATUMP
MU WON'T BACK DOWN!!
W-WHAT'LL ALADDIN DO?!
ALADDIN!! KILL THEM!
KILL THEM ALL!!!

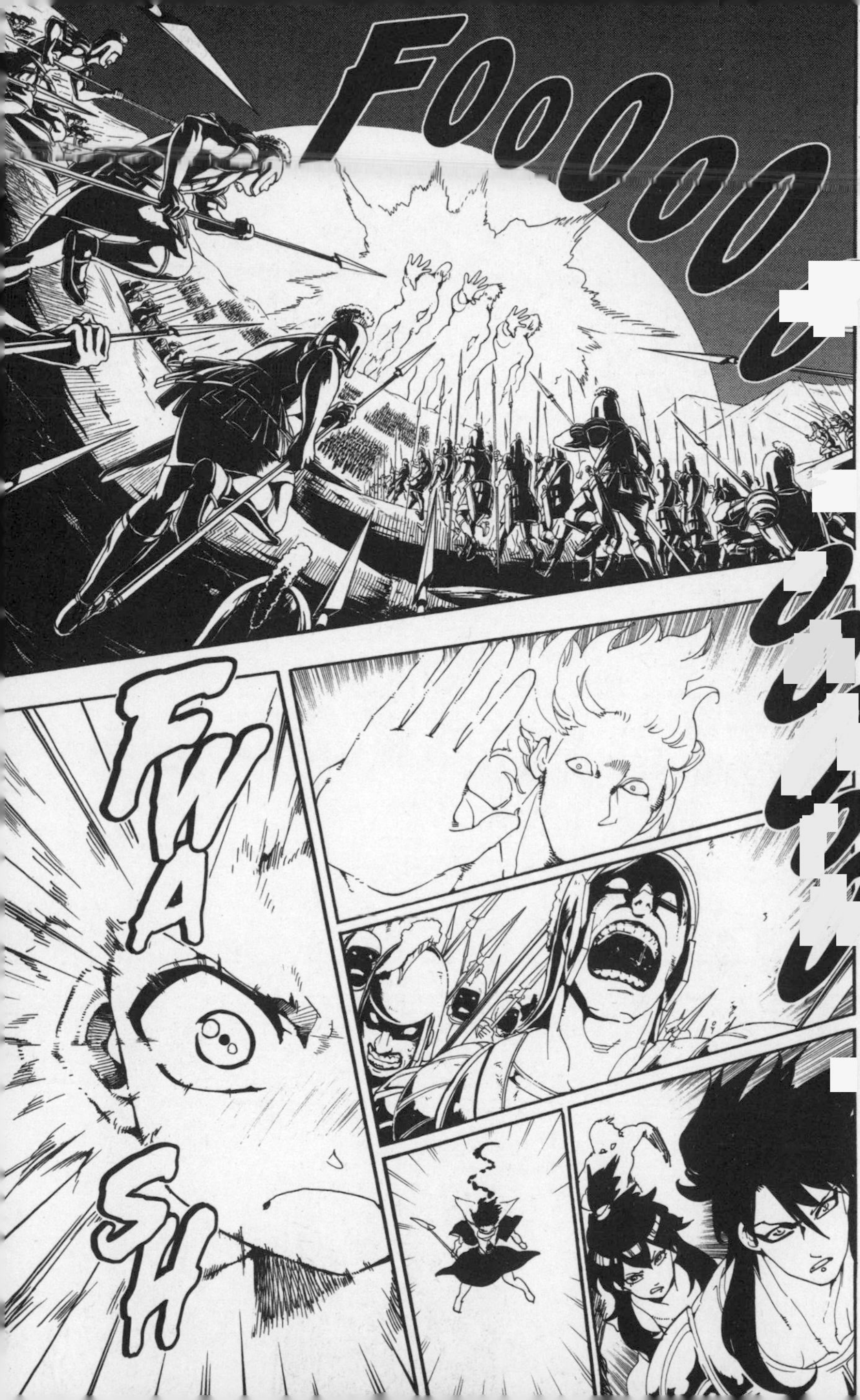
FOOOOO
FWASH

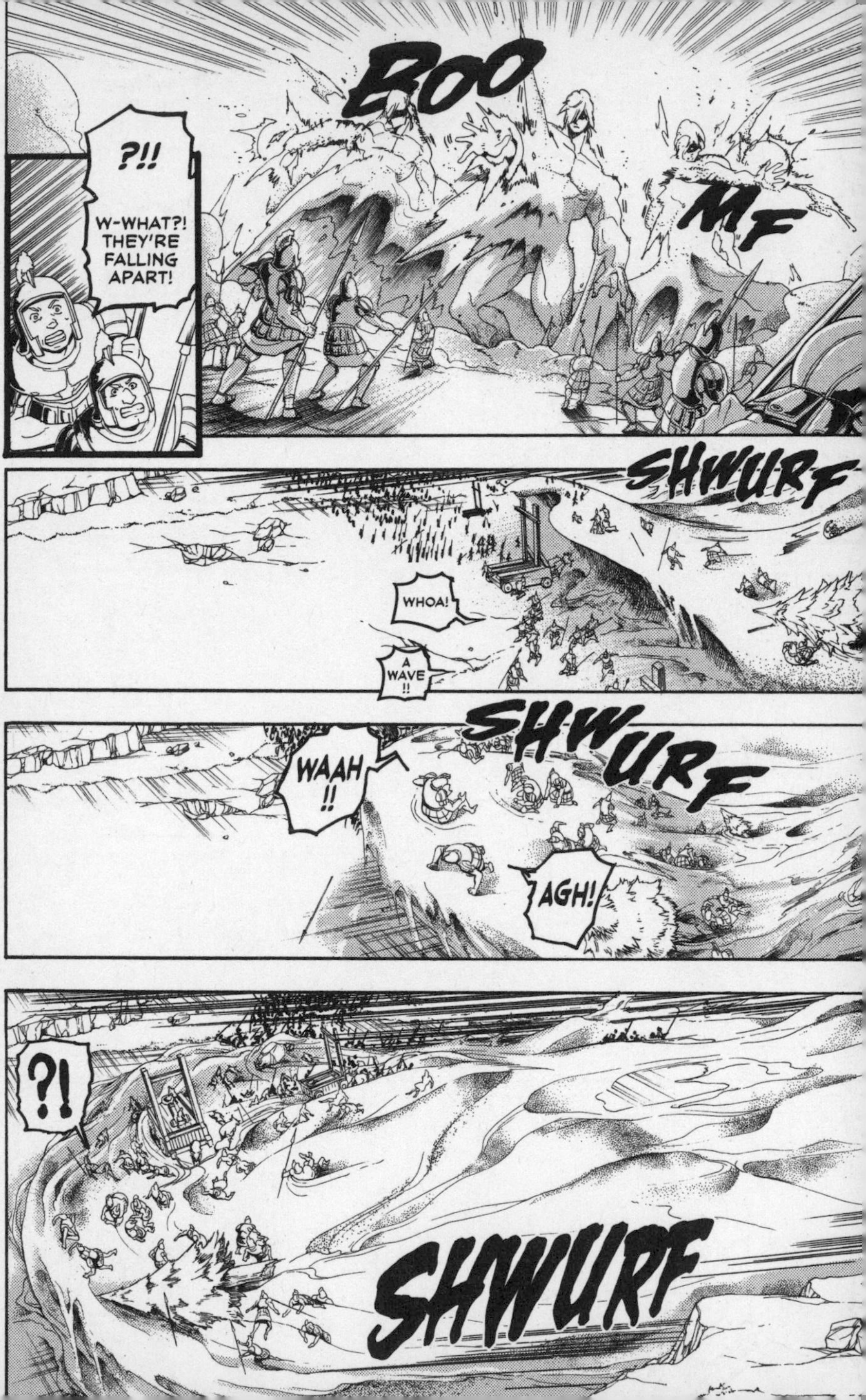
BOOMF
?!!
W-WHAT?! THEY'RE FALLING APART!
SHWURF
WHOA!
A WAVE!!
SHWURF
WAAH!!
AGH!
?!
SHWURF

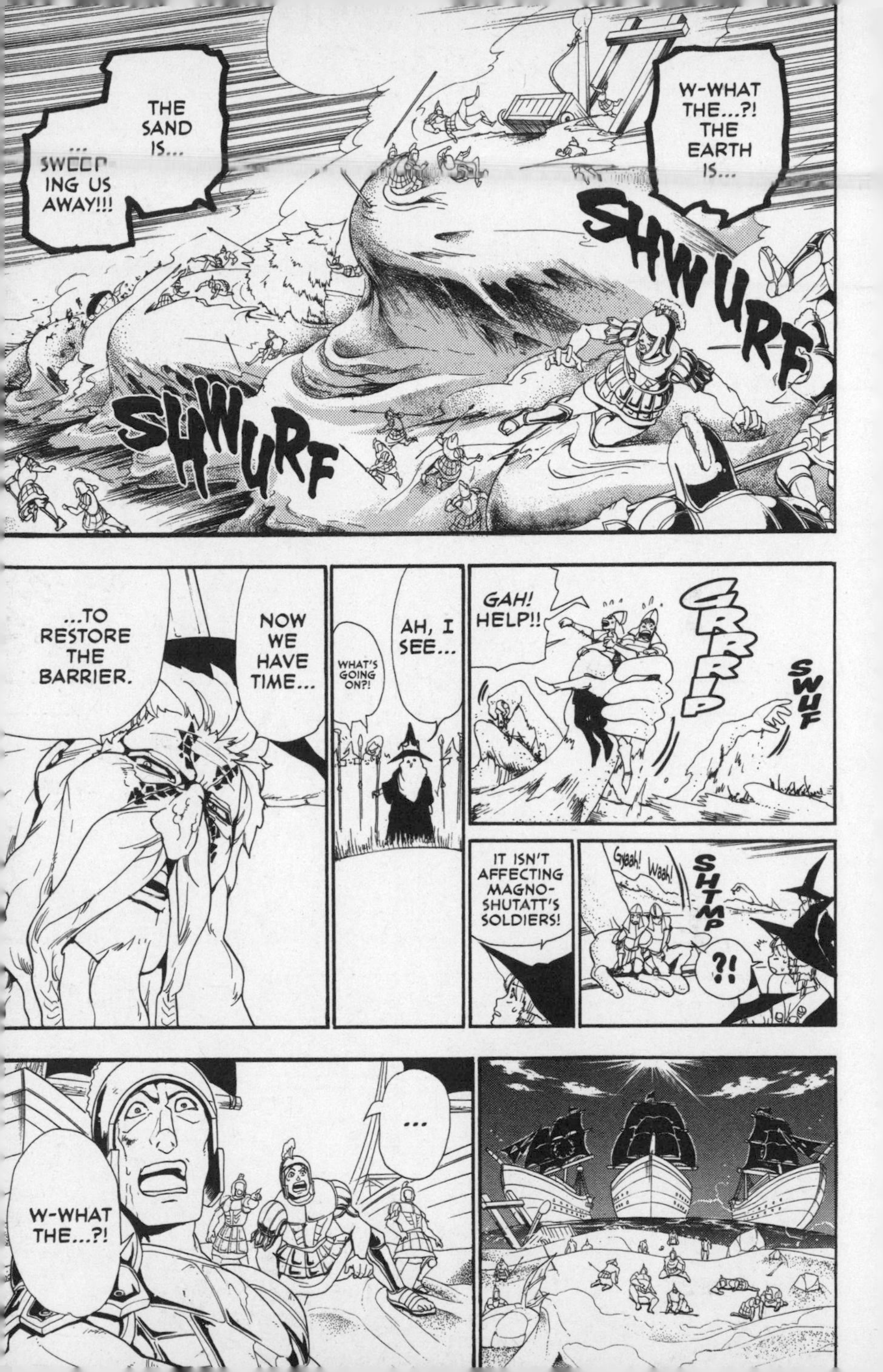

W-WHAT THE...?! THE EARTH IS...
THE SAND IS... ...SWEEPING US AWAY!!!
SHWURF
SHWURF
GRRRIP
SWUF
GAH! HELP!!
Gyaah! Waah!
SHTMP
?!
IT ISN'T AFFECTING MAGNO-SHUTATT'S SOLDIERS!
AH, I SEE...
WHAT'S GOING ON?!
NOW WE HAVE TIME...
...TO RESTORE THE BARRIER.
...
W-WHAT THE...?!

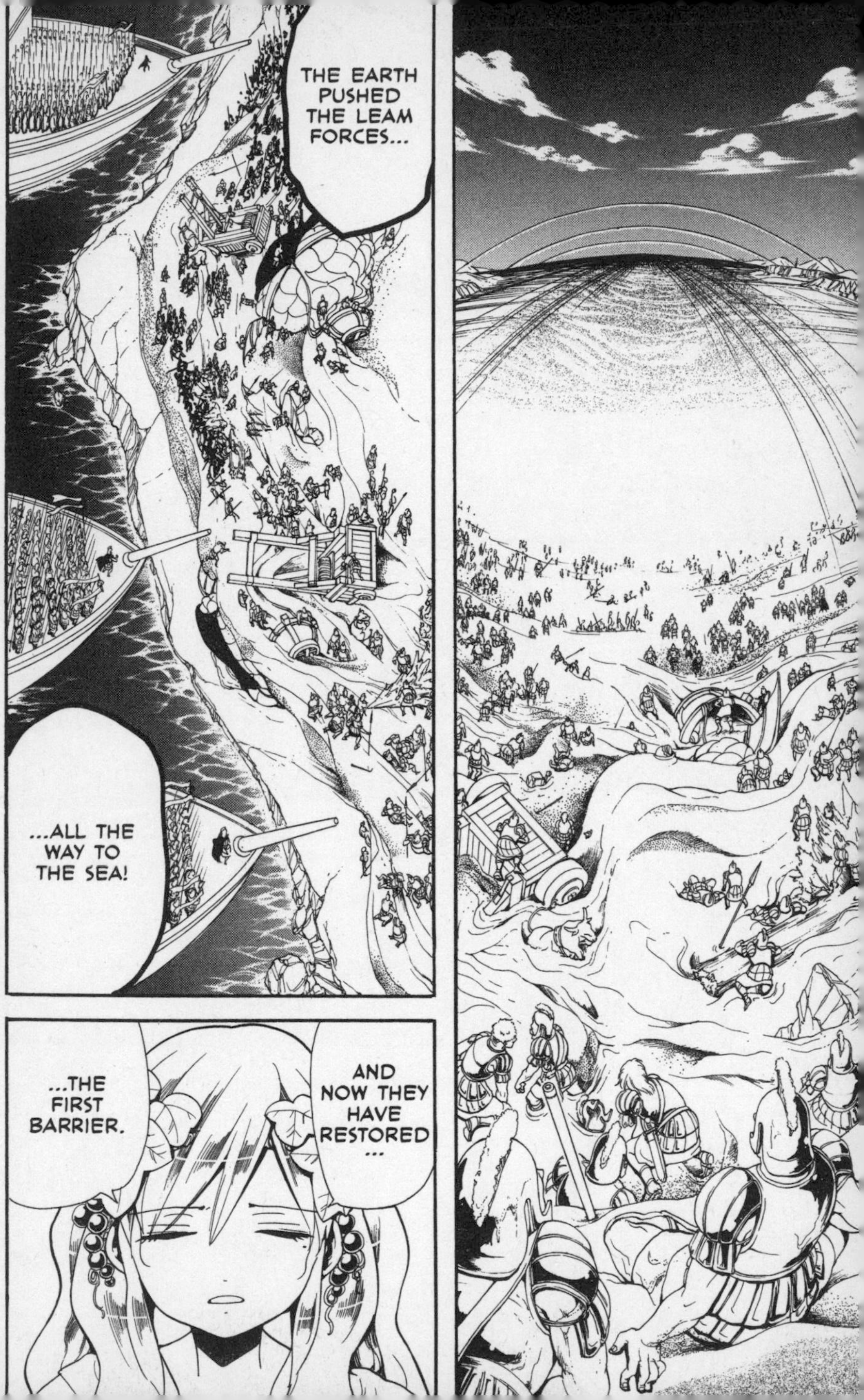
THE EARTH PUSHED THE LEAM FORCES...
...ALL THE WAY TO THE SEA!
AND NOW THEY HAVE RESTORED...
...THE FIRST BARRIER.

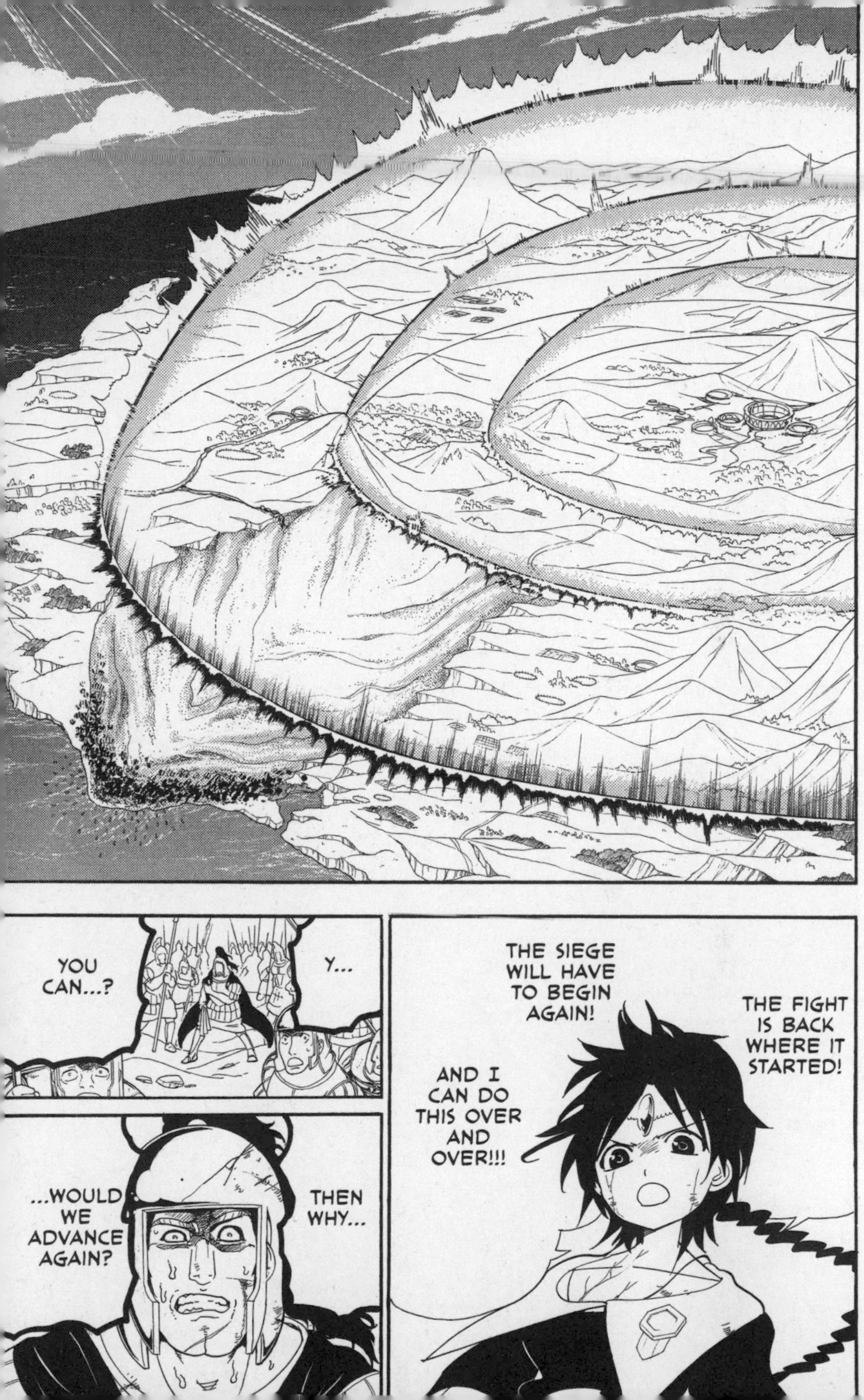
THE SIEGE WILL HAVE TO BEGIN AGAIN!
THE FIGHT IS BACK WHERE IT STARTED!
AND I CAN DO THIS OVER AND OVER!!!
Y...
YOU CAN...?
THEN WHY...
...WOULD WE ADVANCE AGAIN?

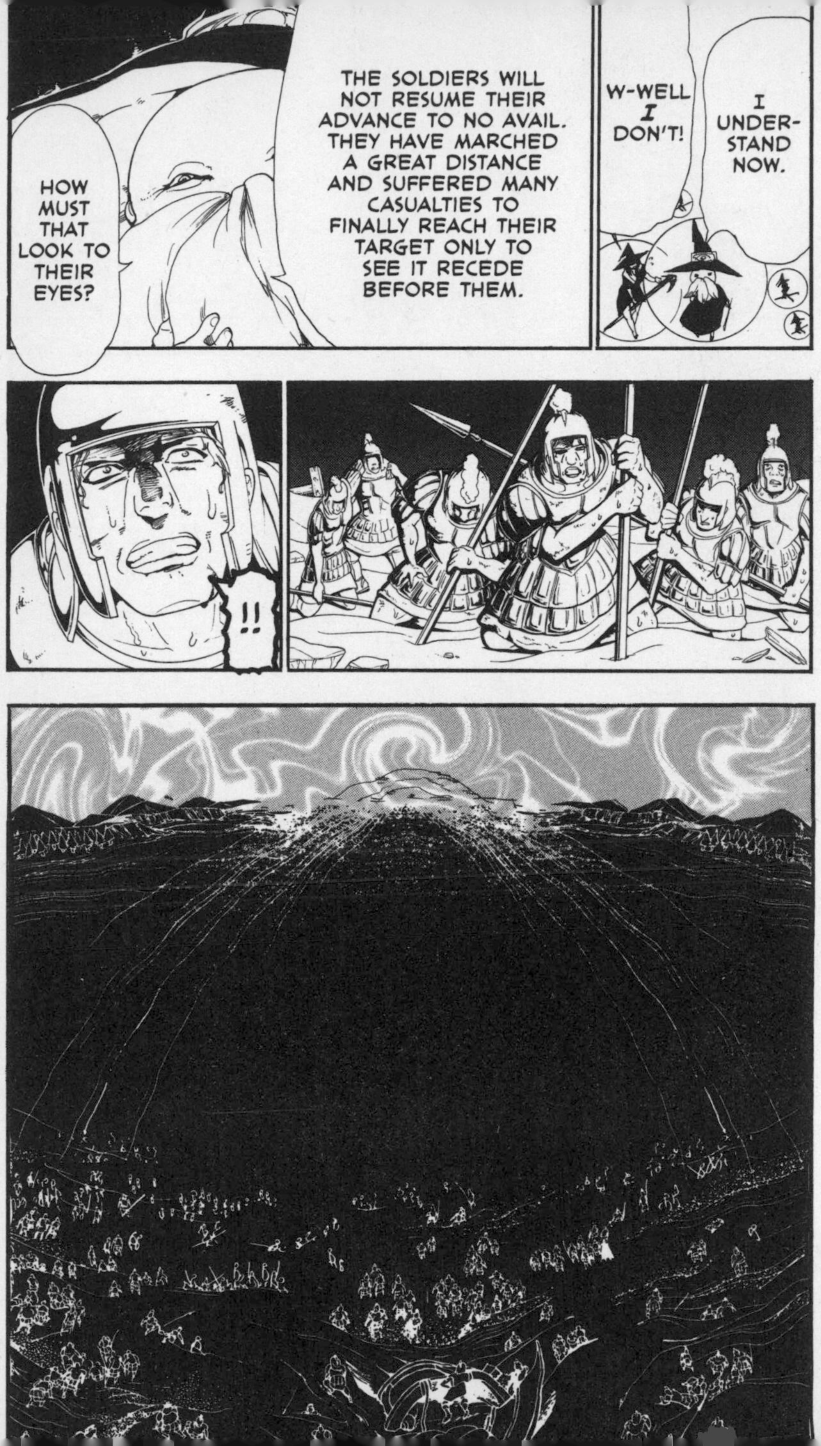
I UNDERSTAND NOW.
W-WELL I DON'T!
THE SOLDIERS WILL NOT RESUME THEIR ADVANCE TO NO AVAIL. THEY HAVE MARCHED A GREAT DISTANCE AND SUFFERED MANY CASUALTIES TO FINALLY REACH THEIR TARGET ONLY TO SEE IT RECEDE BEFORE THEM.
HOW MUST THAT LOOK TO THEIR EYES?
!!

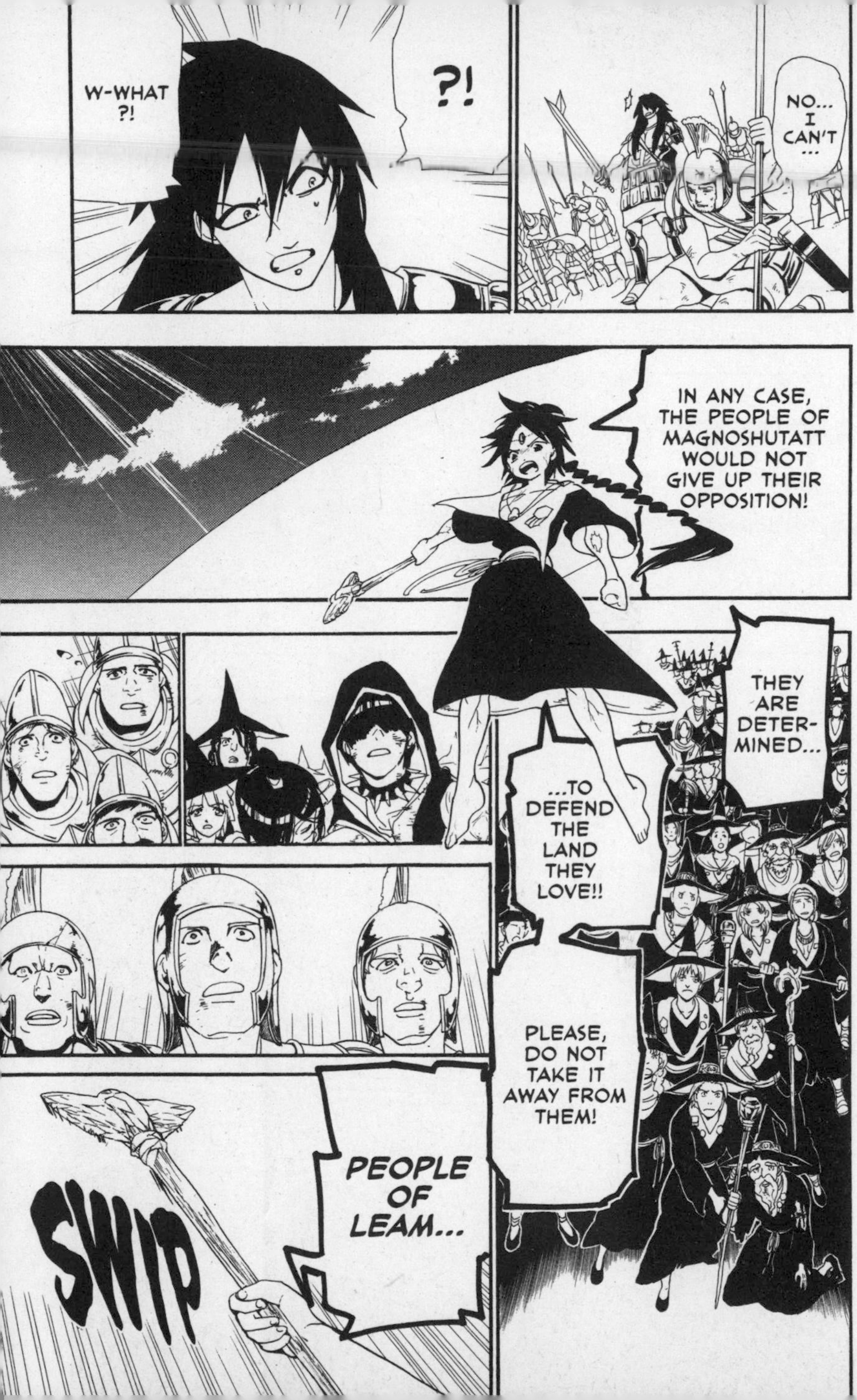
NO... I CAN'T ...
?!
W-WHAT ?!
IN ANY CASE, THE PEOPLE OF MAGNOSHUTATT WOULD NOT GIVE UP THEIR OPPOSITION!
THEY ARE DETERMINED...
...TO DEFEND THE LAND THEY LOVE!!
PLEASE, DO NOT TAKE IT AWAY FROM THEM!
PEOPLE OF LEAM...
SWIP

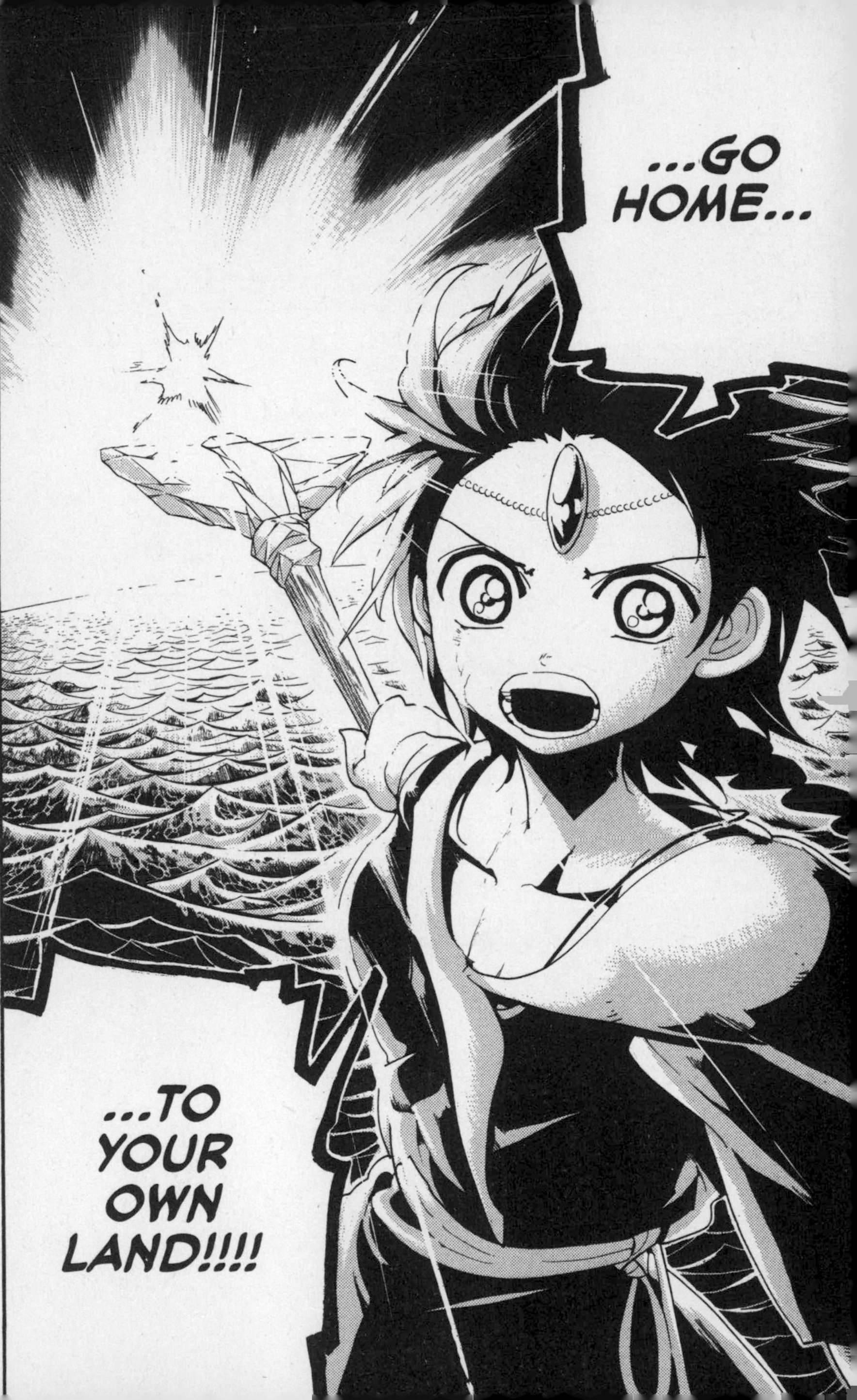
...GO HOME...
...TO YOUR OWN LAND!!!!

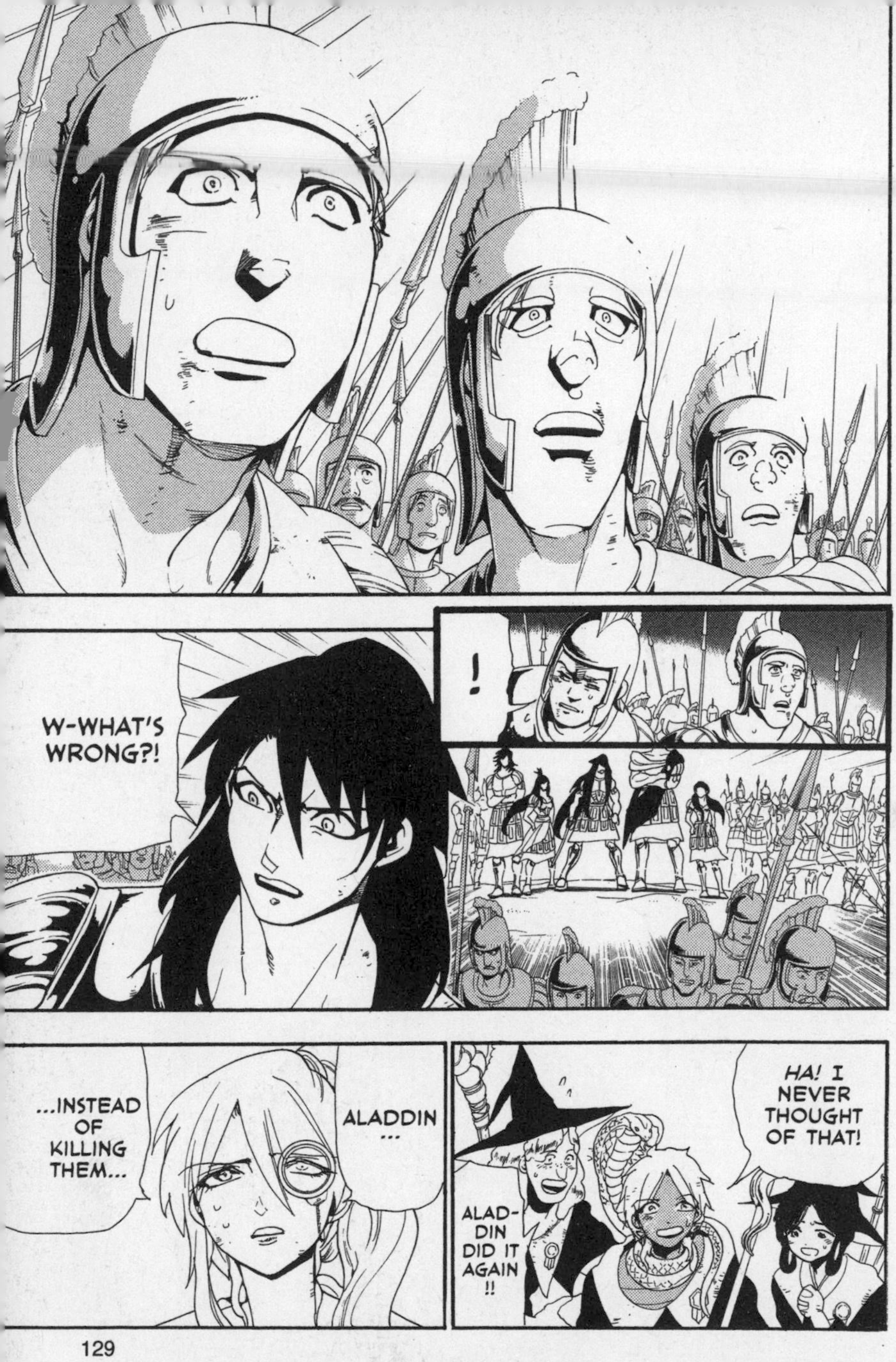
!
W-WHAT'S WRONG?!
HA! I NEVER THOUGHT OF THAT!
ALADDIN DID IT AGAIN!!
ALADDIN...
...INSTEAD OF KILLING THEM...

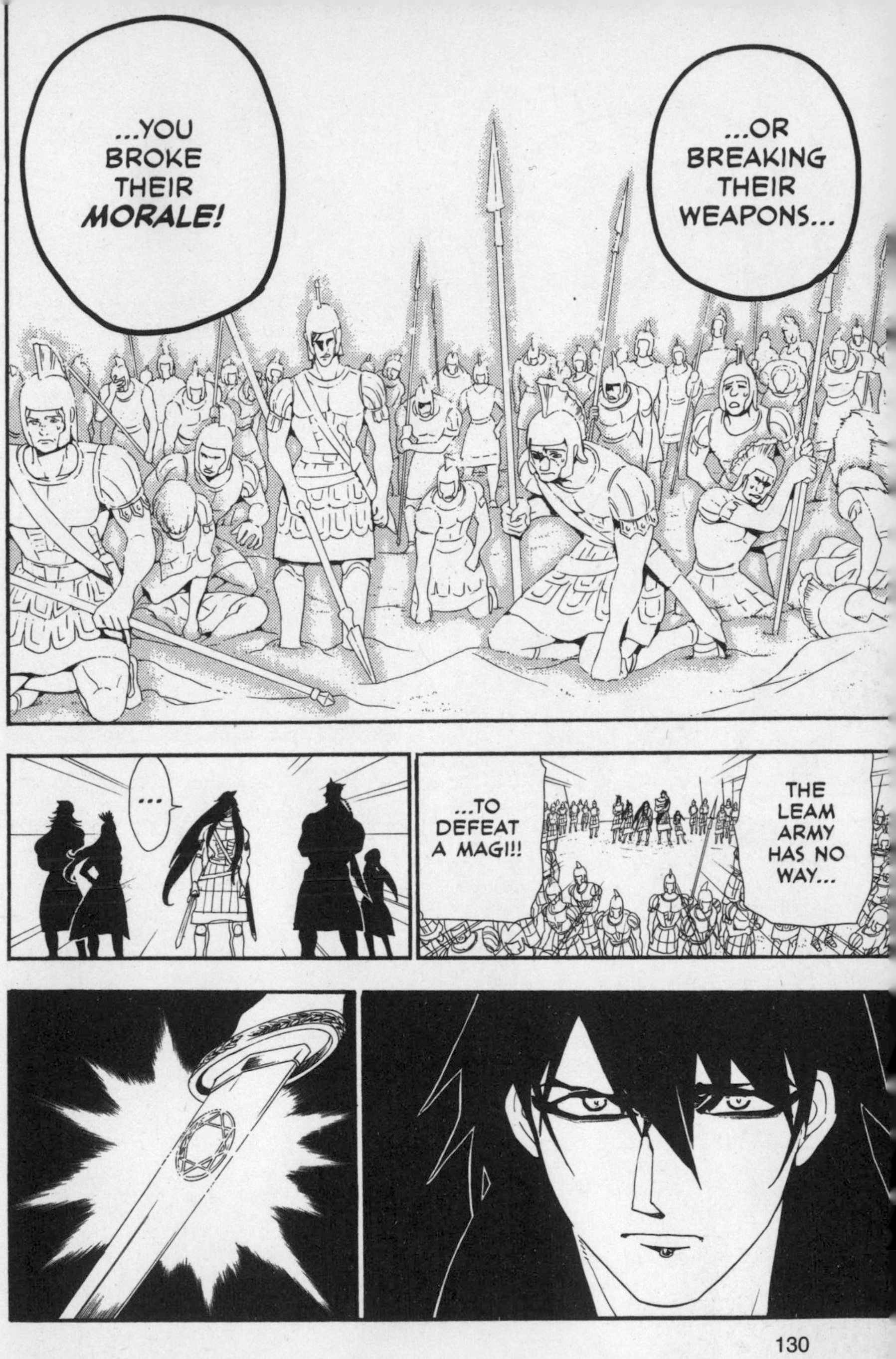
...OR BREAKING THEIR WEAPONS...
...YOU BROKE THEIR *MORALE!*
THE LEAM ARMY HAS NO WAY...
...TO DEFEAT A MAGI!!
...

Night 176: Barbatos

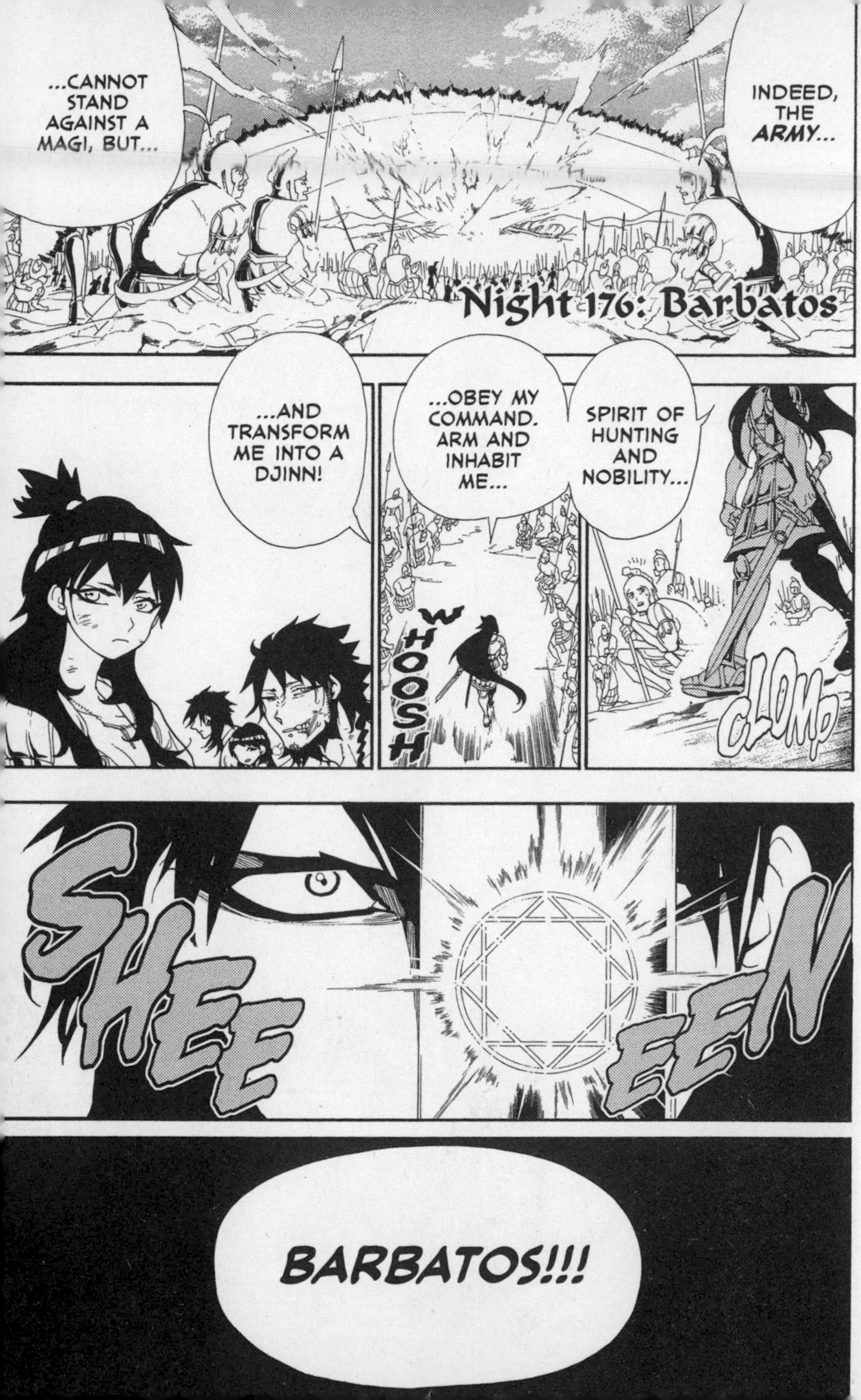
INDEED, THE ARMY...
...CANNOT STAND AGAINST A MAGI, BUT...
SPIRIT OF HUNTING AND NOBILITY...
CLOMP
...OBEY MY COMMAND. ARM AND INHABIT ME...
WHOOSH
...AND TRANSFORM ME INTO A DJINN!
SHEEEEN
BARBATOS!!!

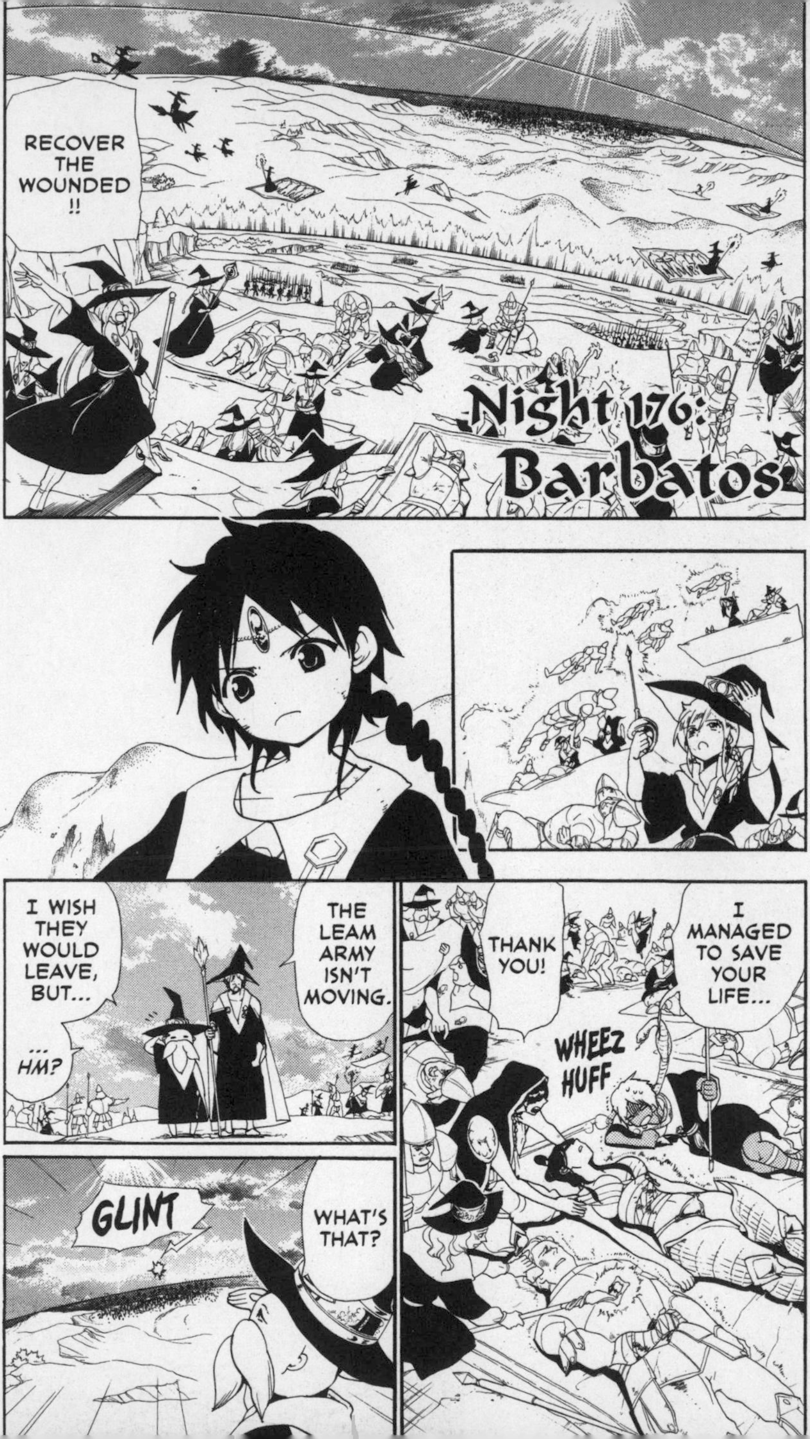
RECOVER THE WOUNDED!!
Night 176: Barbatos
I MANAGED TO SAVE YOUR LIFE...
THANK YOU!
WHEEZ HUFF
THE LEAM ARMY ISN'T MOVING.
I WISH THEY WOULD LEAVE, BUT...
...HM?
WHAT'S THAT?
GLINT

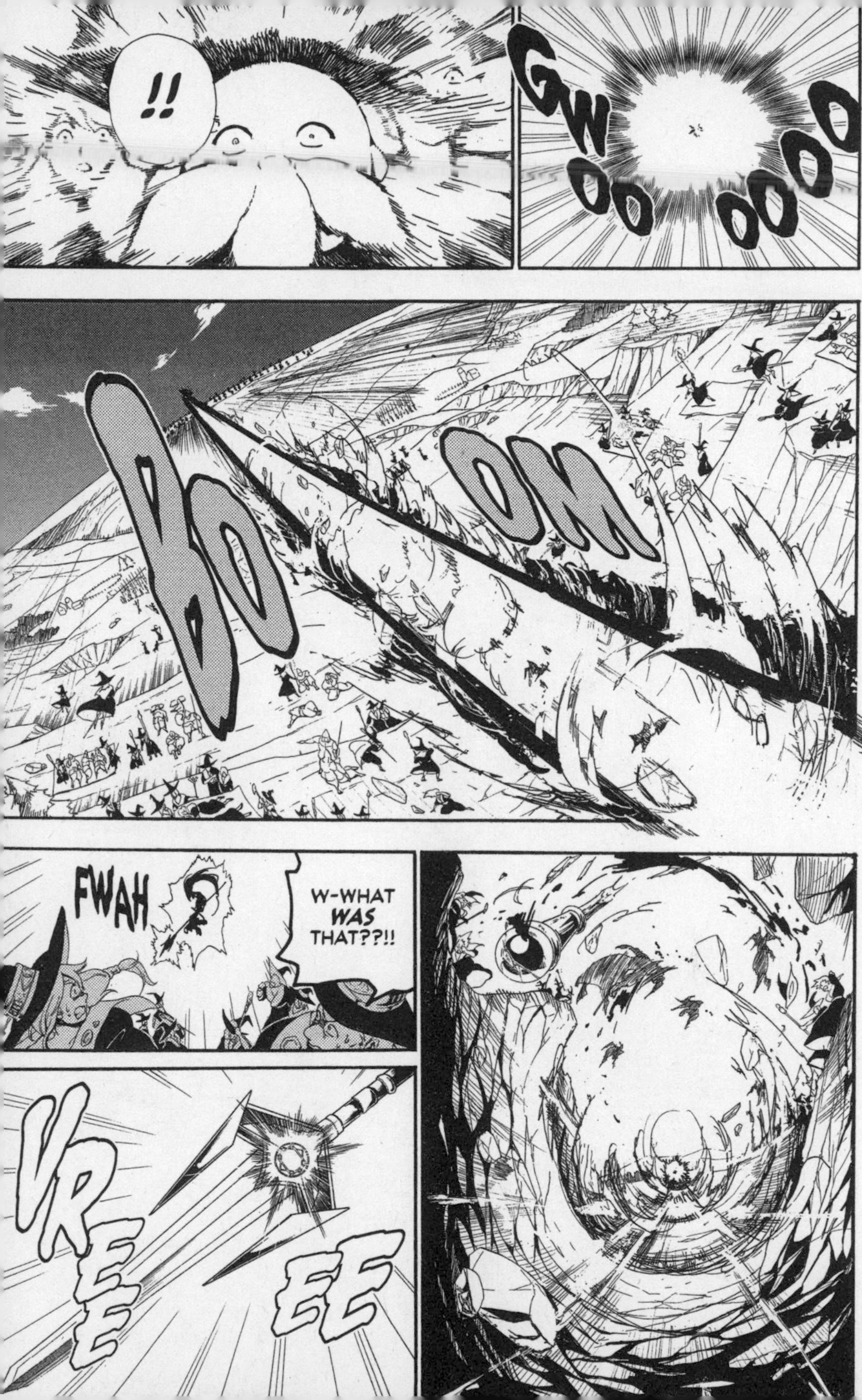
GWOOOOOO
!!
BOOM
FWAH
W-WHAT WAS THAT??!!
VREEEEE

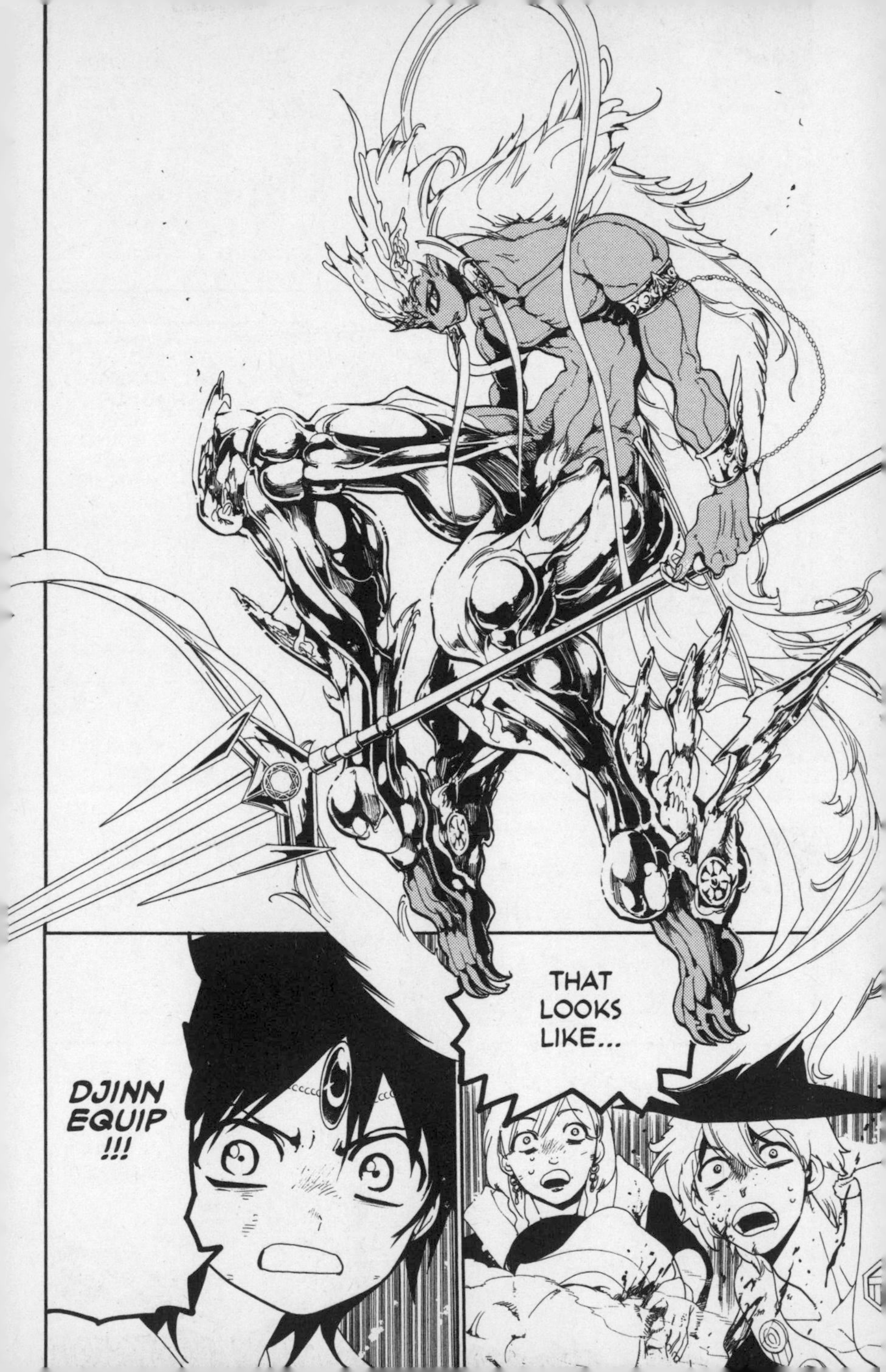
THAT LOOKS LIKE...
DJINN EQUIP !!!

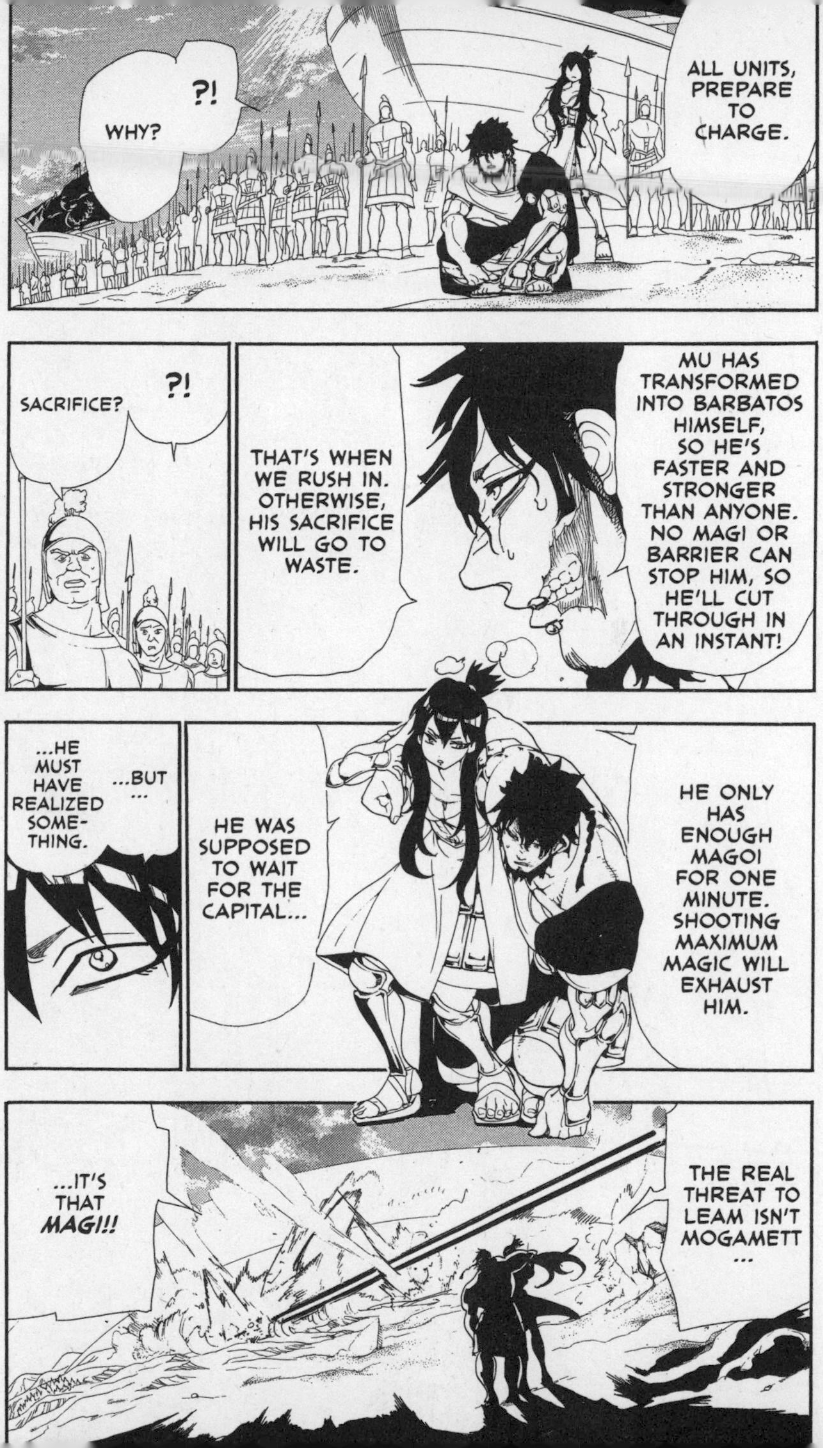
ALL UNITS, PREPARE TO CHARGE.
?!
WHY?
MU HAS TRANSFORMED INTO BARBATOS HIMSELF, SO HE'S FASTER AND STRONGER THAN ANYONE. NO MAGI OR BARRIER CAN STOP HIM, SO HE'LL CUT THROUGH IN AN INSTANT!
THAT'S WHEN WE RUSH IN. OTHERWISE, HIS SACRIFICE WILL GO TO WASTE.
?!
SACRIFICE?
HE ONLY HAS ENOUGH MAGOI FOR ONE MINUTE. SHOOTING MAXIMUM MAGIC WILL EXHAUST HIM.
HE WAS SUPPOSED TO WAIT FOR THE CAPITAL...
...BUT...
...HE MUST HAVE REALIZED SOMETHING.
THE REAL THREAT TO LEAM ISN'T MOGAMETT...
...IT'S THAT *MAGI!!*

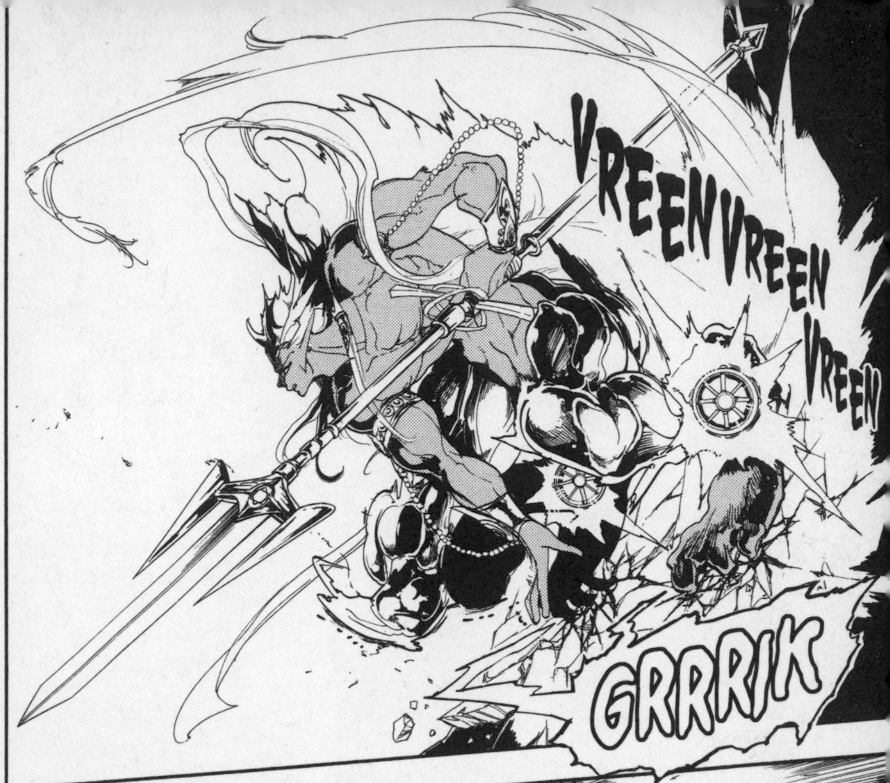
VREENVREEN
VREEN
GRRRIK
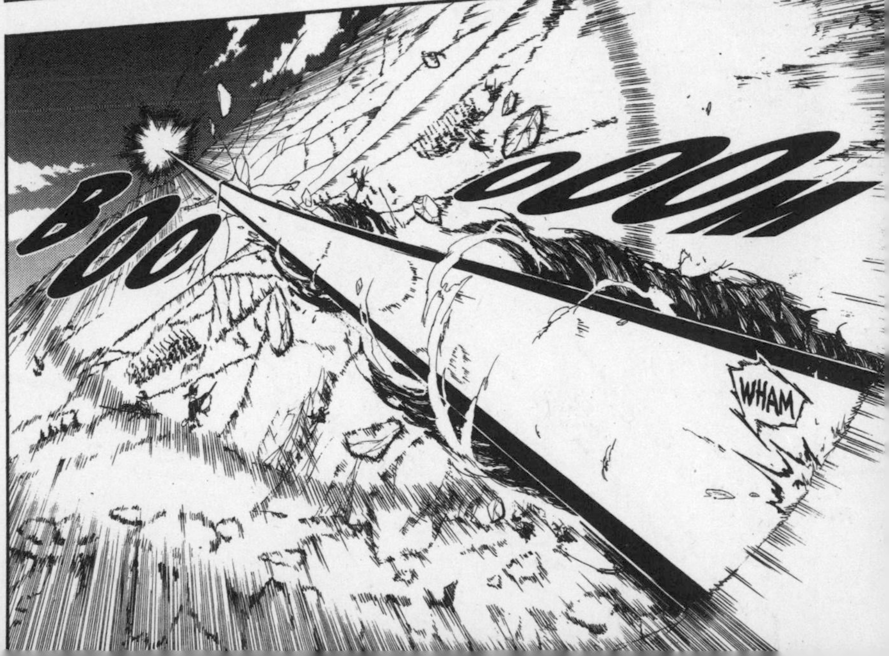
BOO
OOM
WHAM

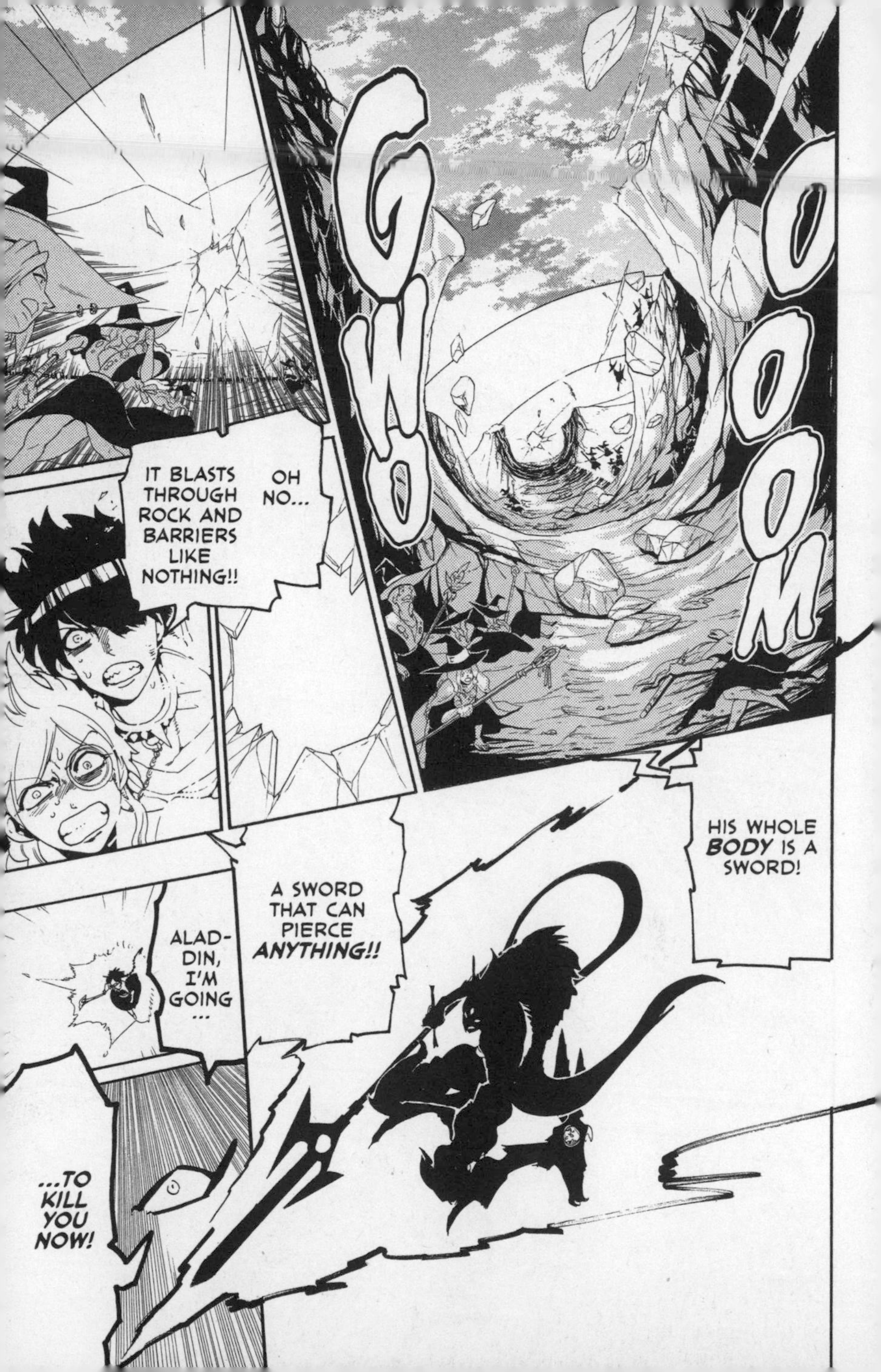
GWOOOOOOM
OH NO...
IT BLASTS THROUGH ROCK AND BARRIERS LIKE NOTHING!!
HIS WHOLE *BODY* IS A SWORD!
A SWORD THAT CAN PIERCE ***ANYTHING!!***
ALAD-DIN, I'M GOING ...
...TO KILL YOU NOW!

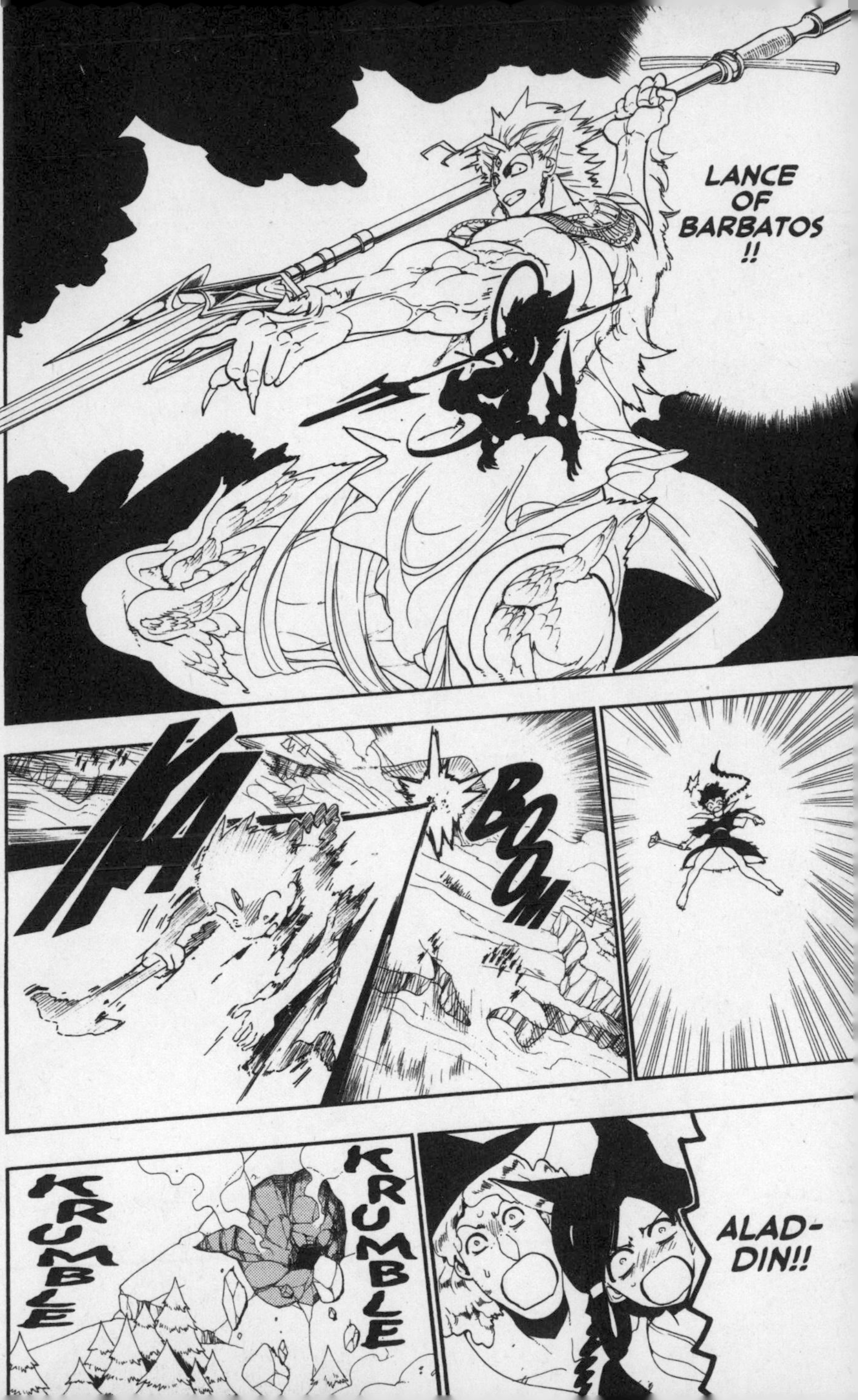
LANCE OF BARBATOS !!
BOOM
ALAD-DIN!!
KRUMBLE
KRUMBLE

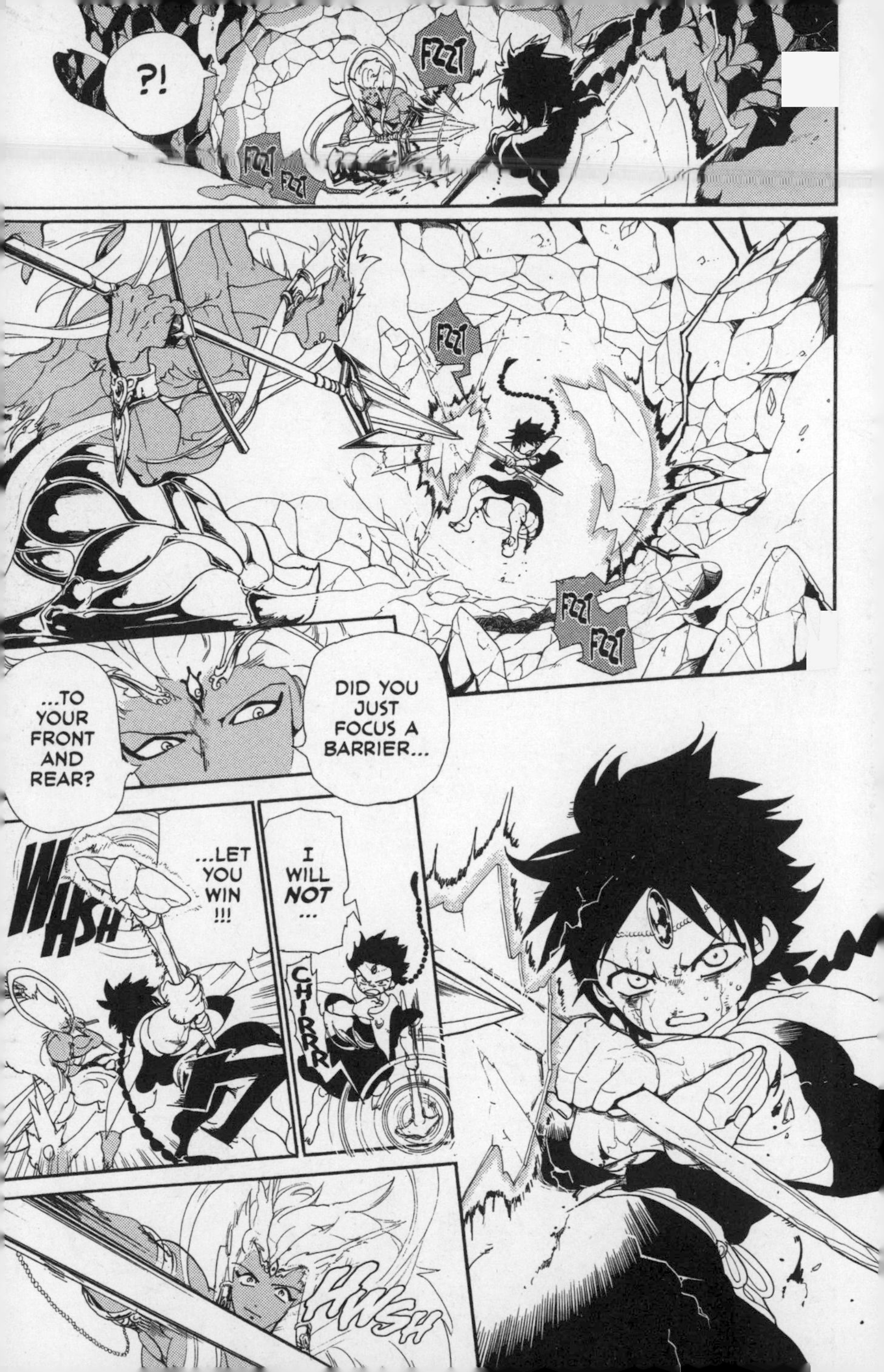
FZZT
?!
FZZT
FZZT
FZZT
FZZT
FZZT
DID YOU JUST FOCUS A BARRIER...
...TO YOUR FRONT AND REAR?
I WILL NOT ...
CHIRRR
...LET YOU WIN !!!
WHSH
WHSH

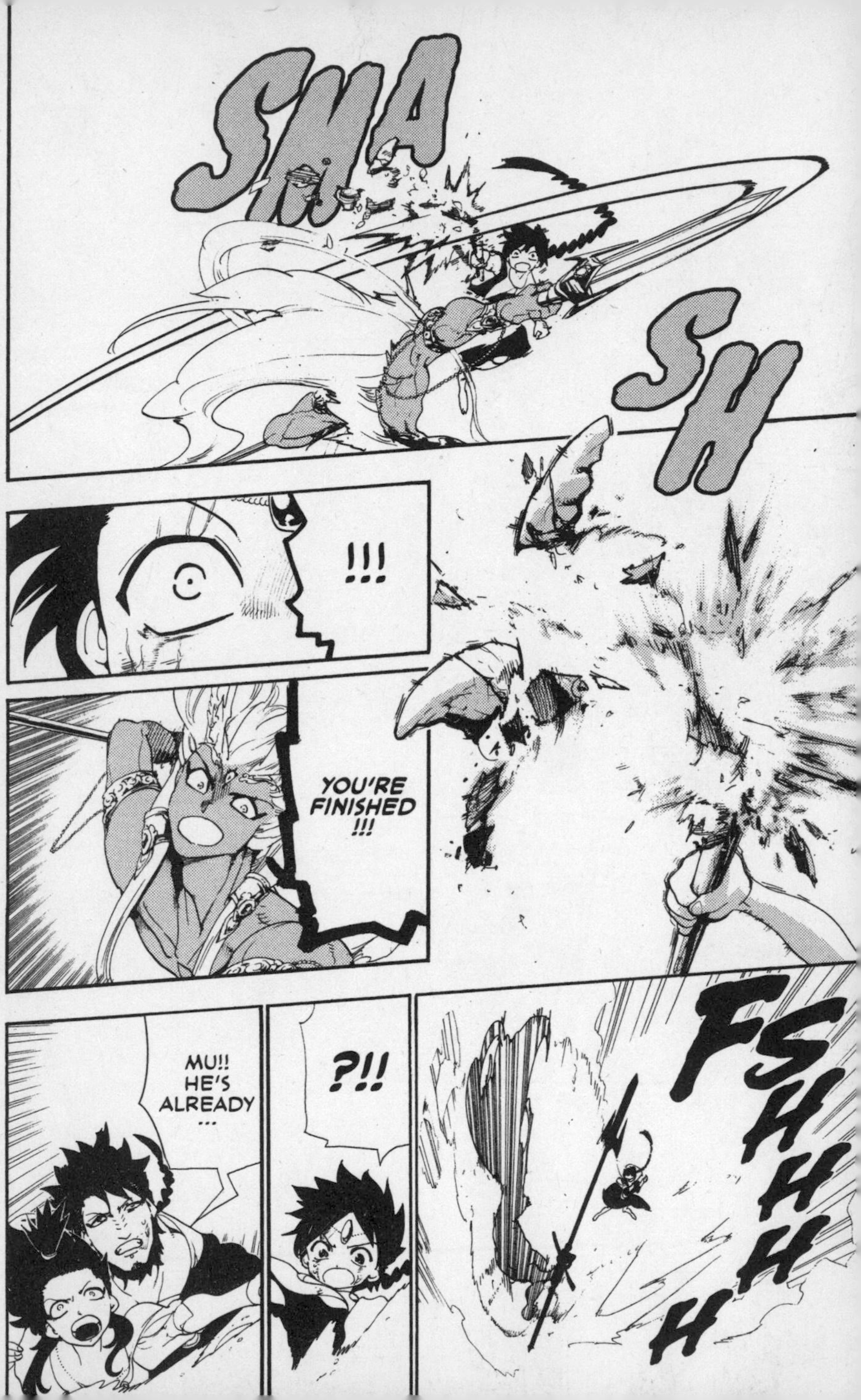
SHA
SH
!!!
YOU'RE FINISHED !!!
FSHHHHH
?!!
MU!! HE'S ALREADY ...

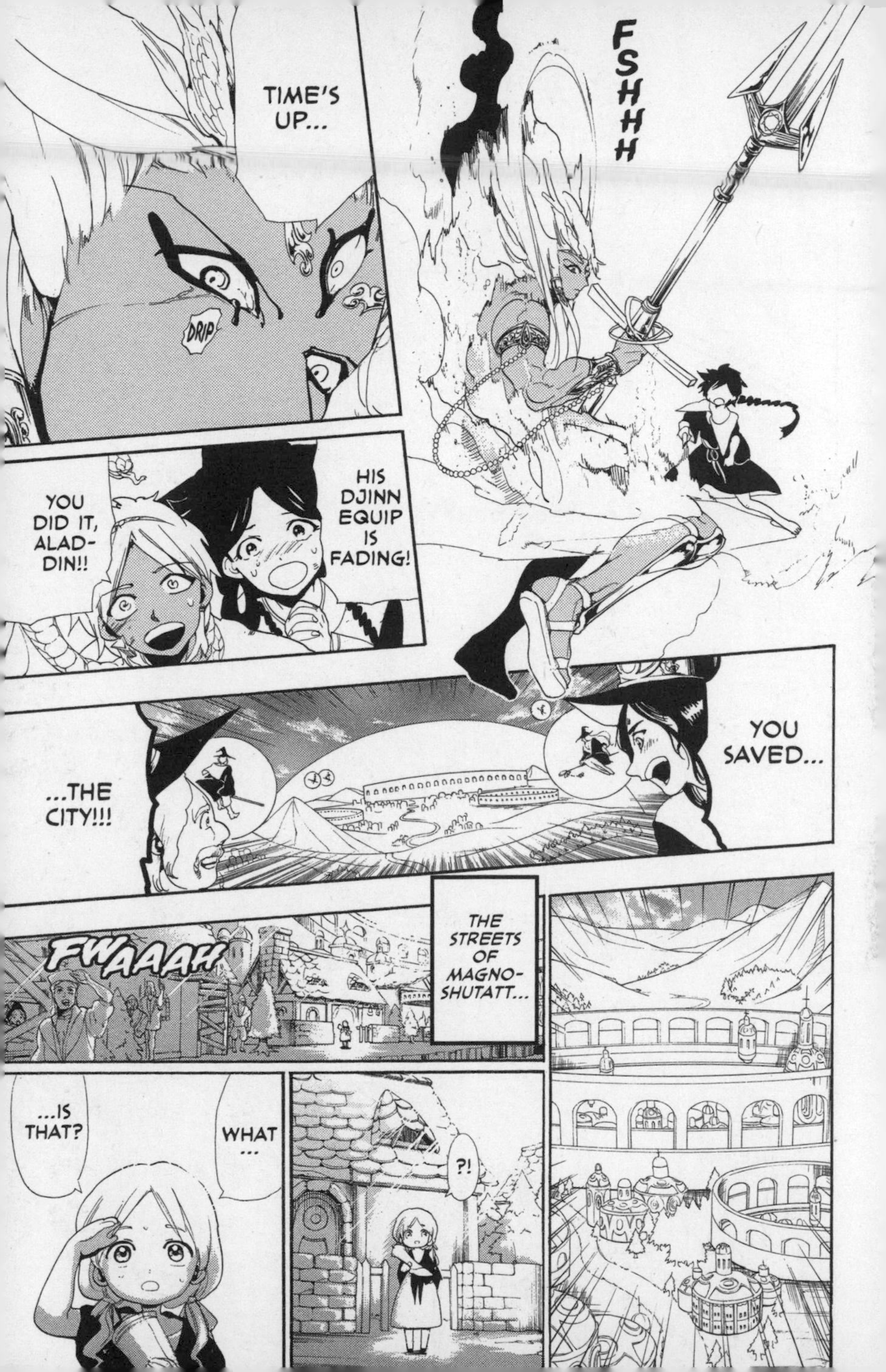
FSHHH
TIME'S UP...
DRIP
HIS DJINN EQUIP IS FADING!
YOU DID IT, ALAD-DIN!!
YOU SAVED...
...THE CITY!!!
THE STREETS OF MAGNO-SHUTATT...
FWAAAH
?!
WHAT...
...IS THAT?

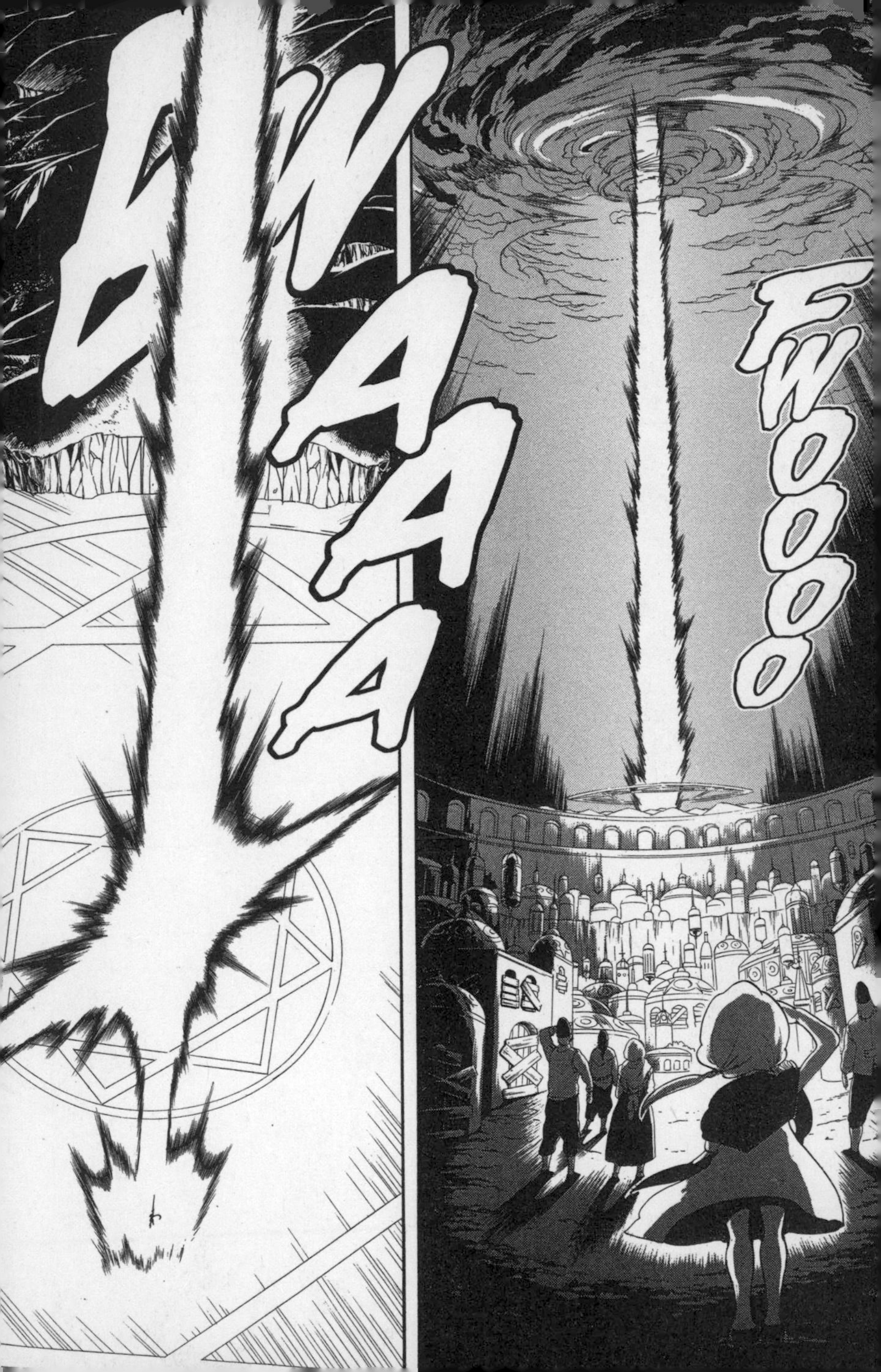
FWOOOO
GWAAA

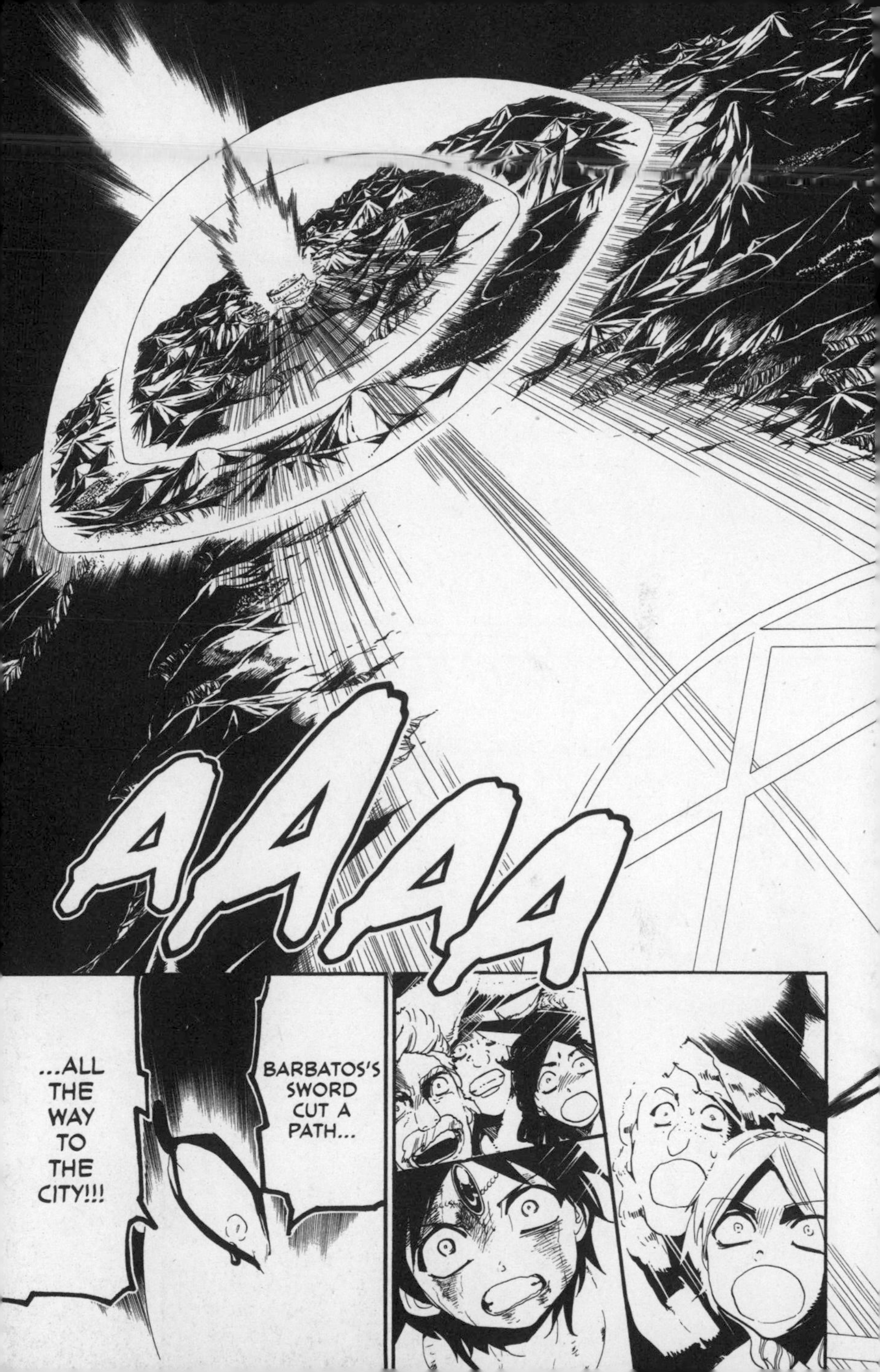
AAAA
BARBATOS'S SWORD CUT A PATH...
...ALL THE WAY TO THE CITY!!!

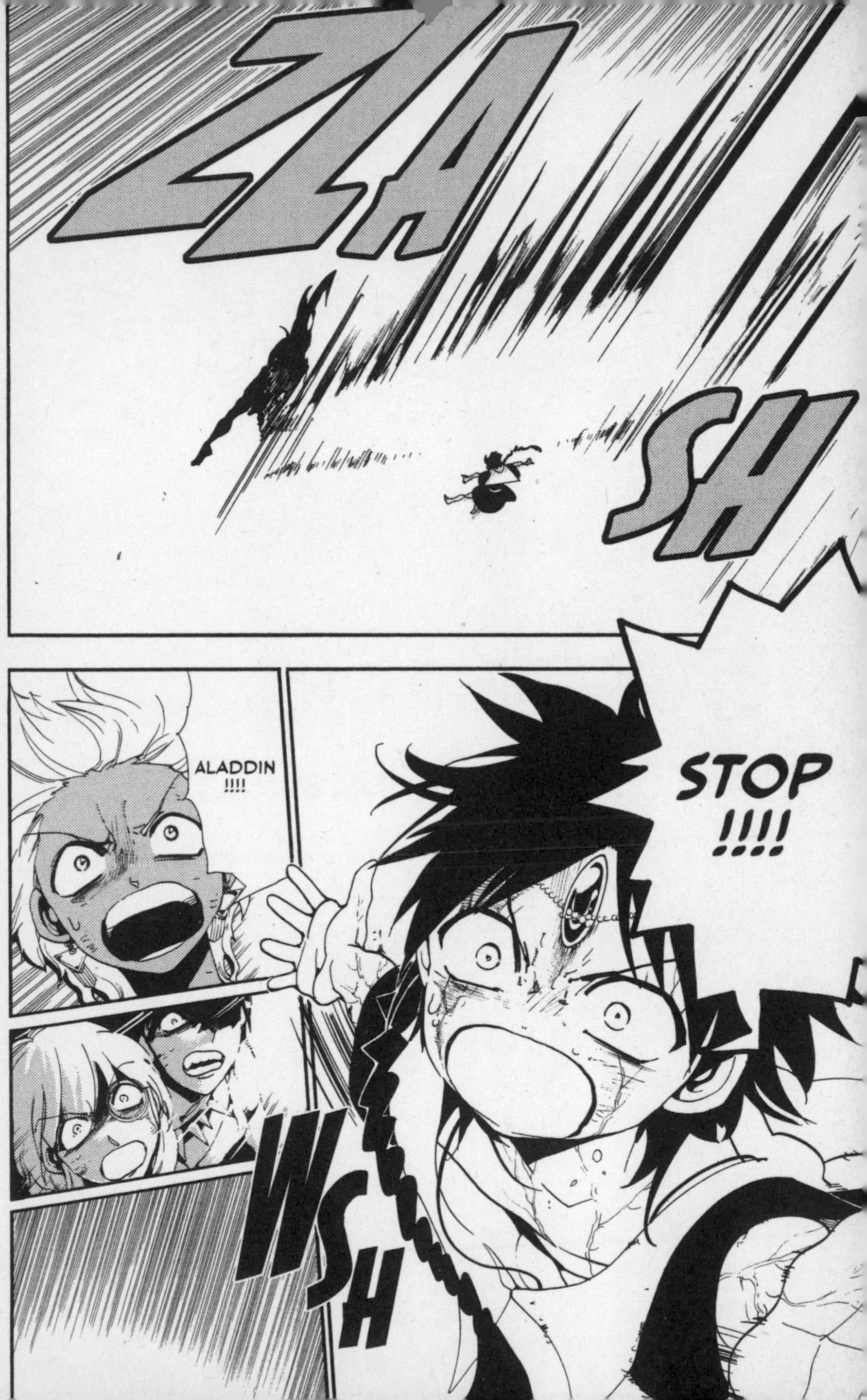
ZA
SH
STOP !!!!
WSH
ALADDIN !!!!

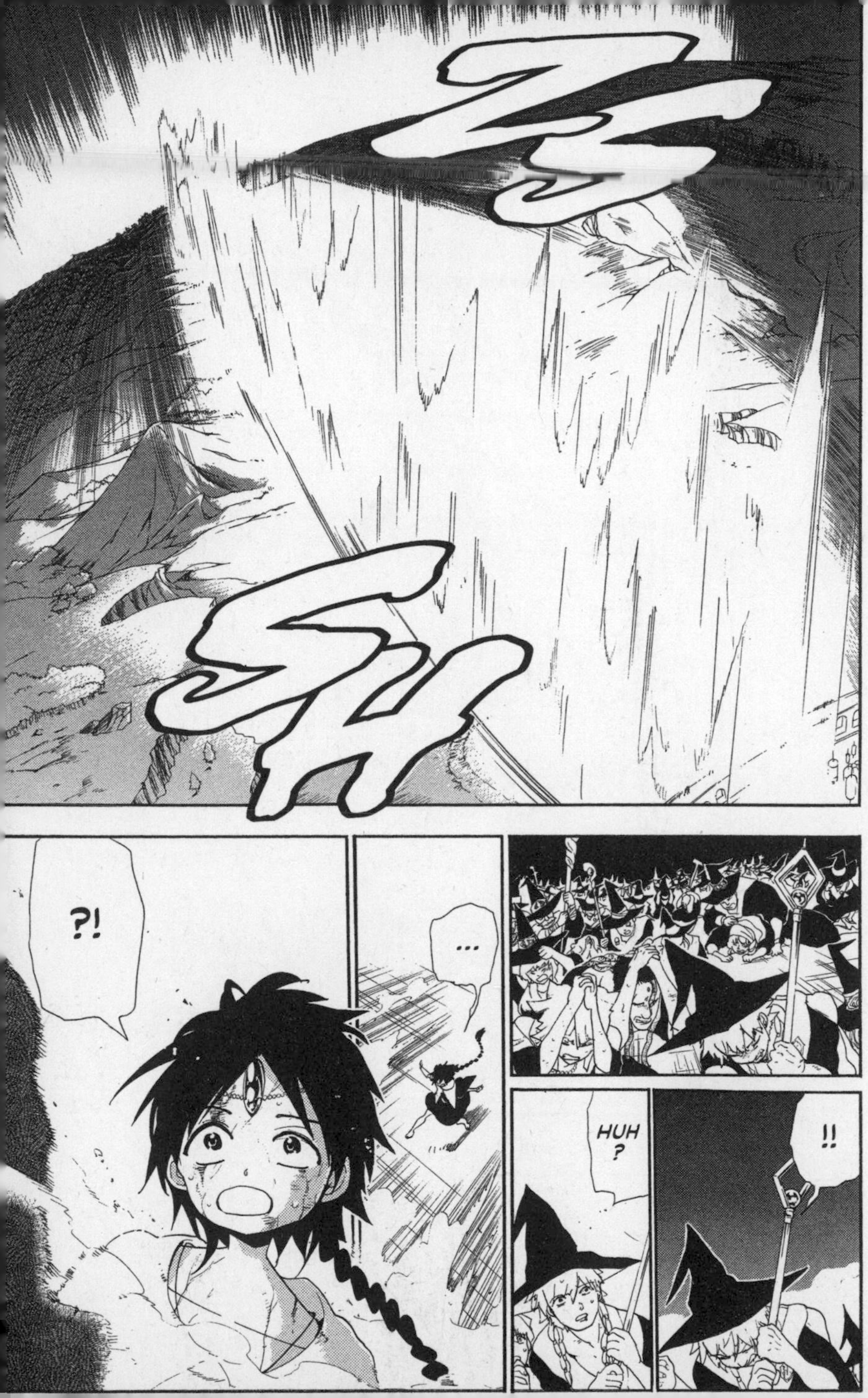
!!
HUH?
...
?!

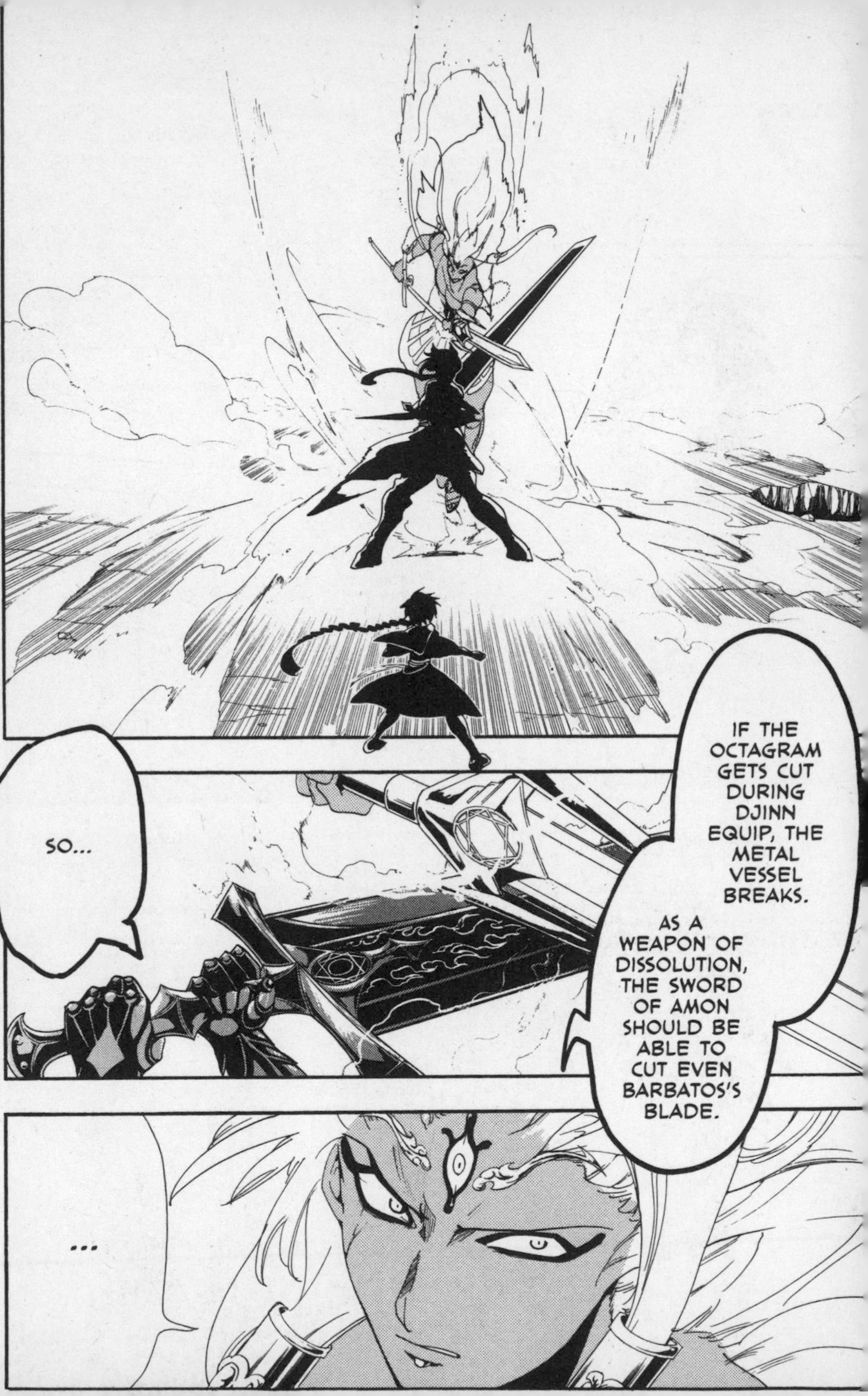
IF THE OCTAGRAM GETS CUT DURING DJINN EQUIP, THE METAL VESSEL BREAKS.
AS A WEAPON OF DISSOLUTION, THE SWORD OF AMON SHOULD BE ABLE TO CUT EVEN BARBATOS'S BLADE.
SO...
...

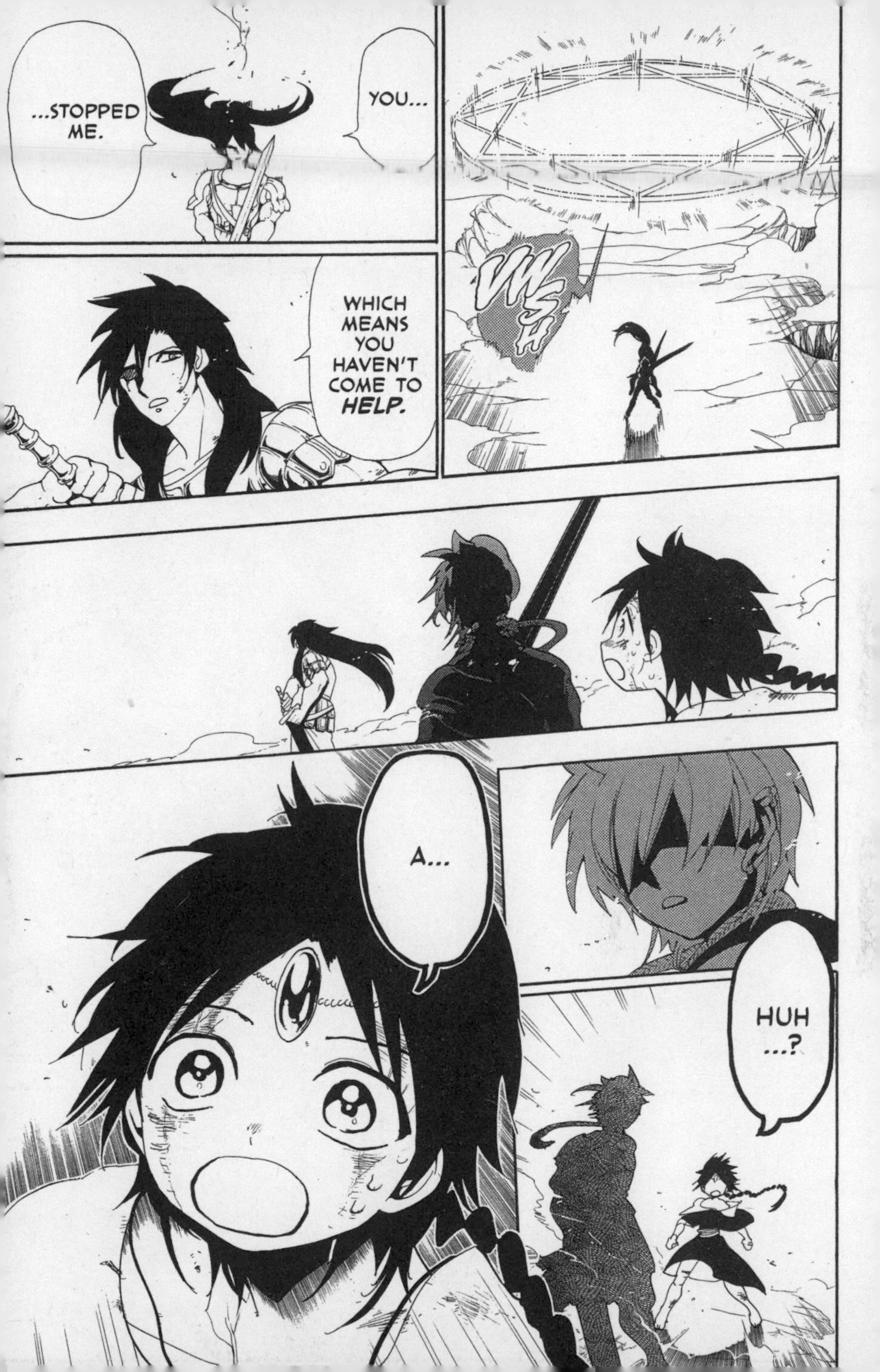
VWSH
YOU...
...STOPPED ME.
WHICH MEANS YOU HAVEN'T COME TO *HELP.*
HUH ...?
A...

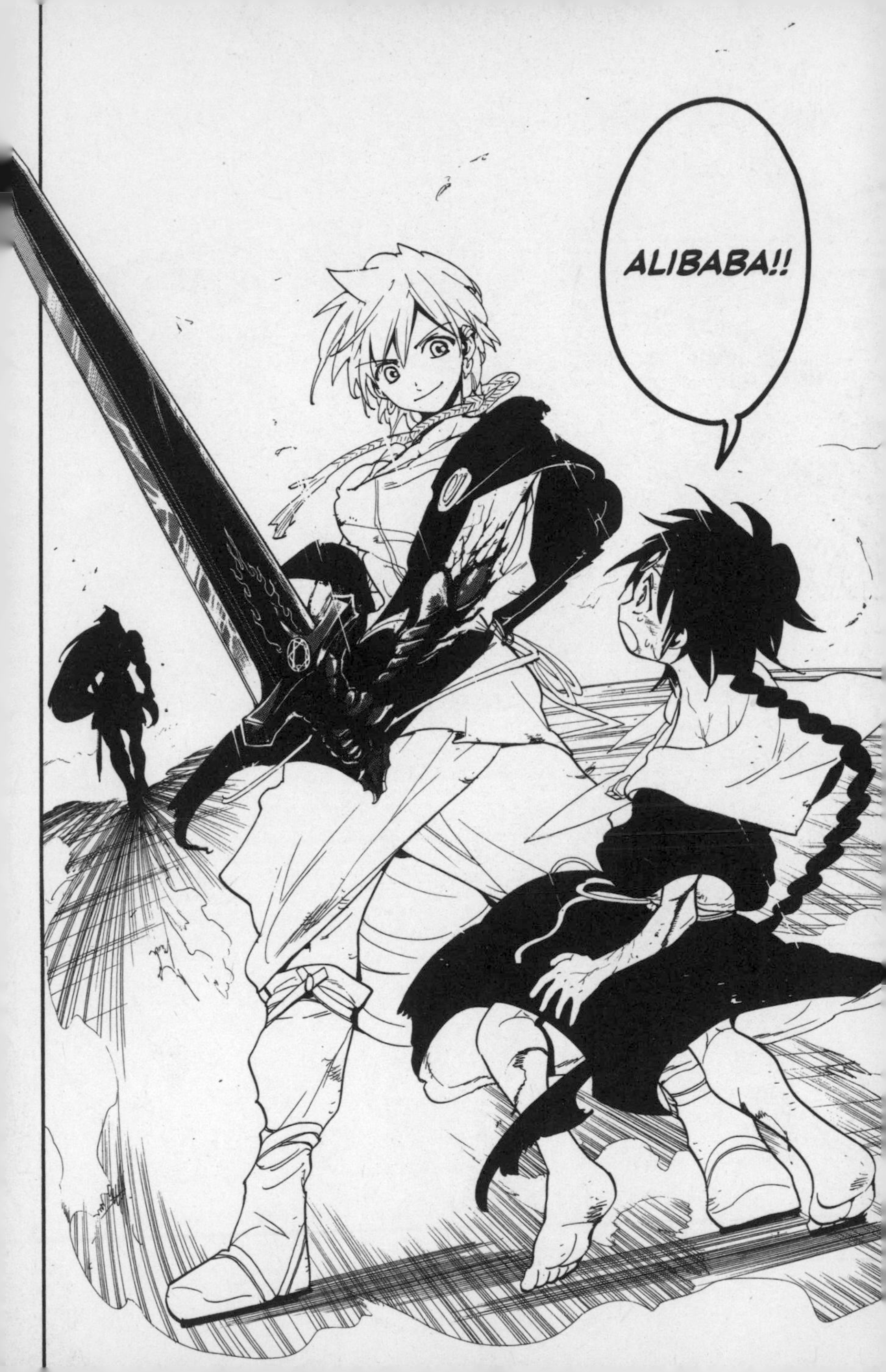
ALIBABA!!

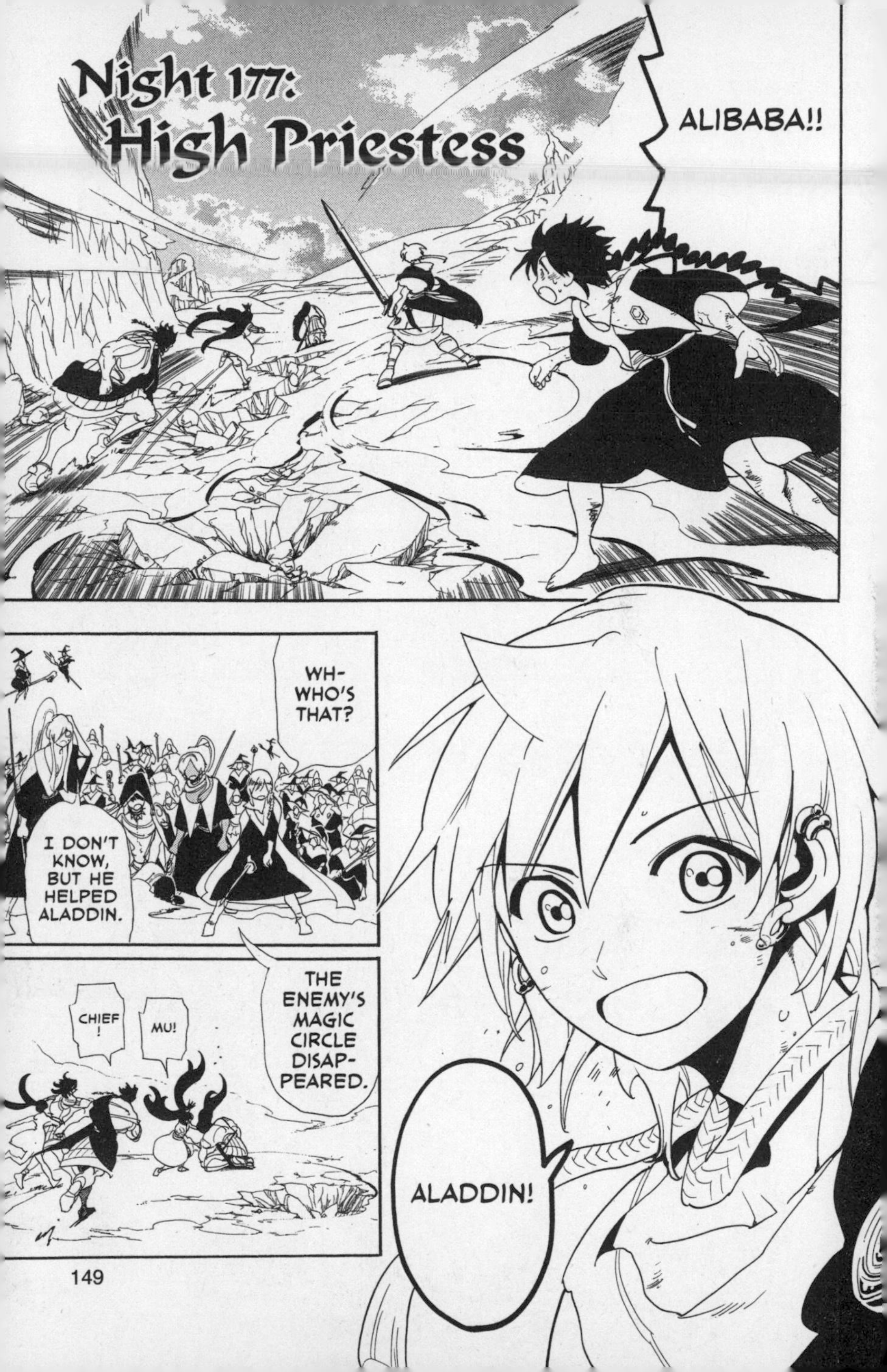
Night 177: High Priestess
ALIBABA!!
ALADDIN!
WH-WHO'S THAT?
I DON'T KNOW, BUT HE HELPED ALADDIN.
THE ENEMY'S MAGIC CIRCLE DISAP-PEARED.
MU!
CHIEF!

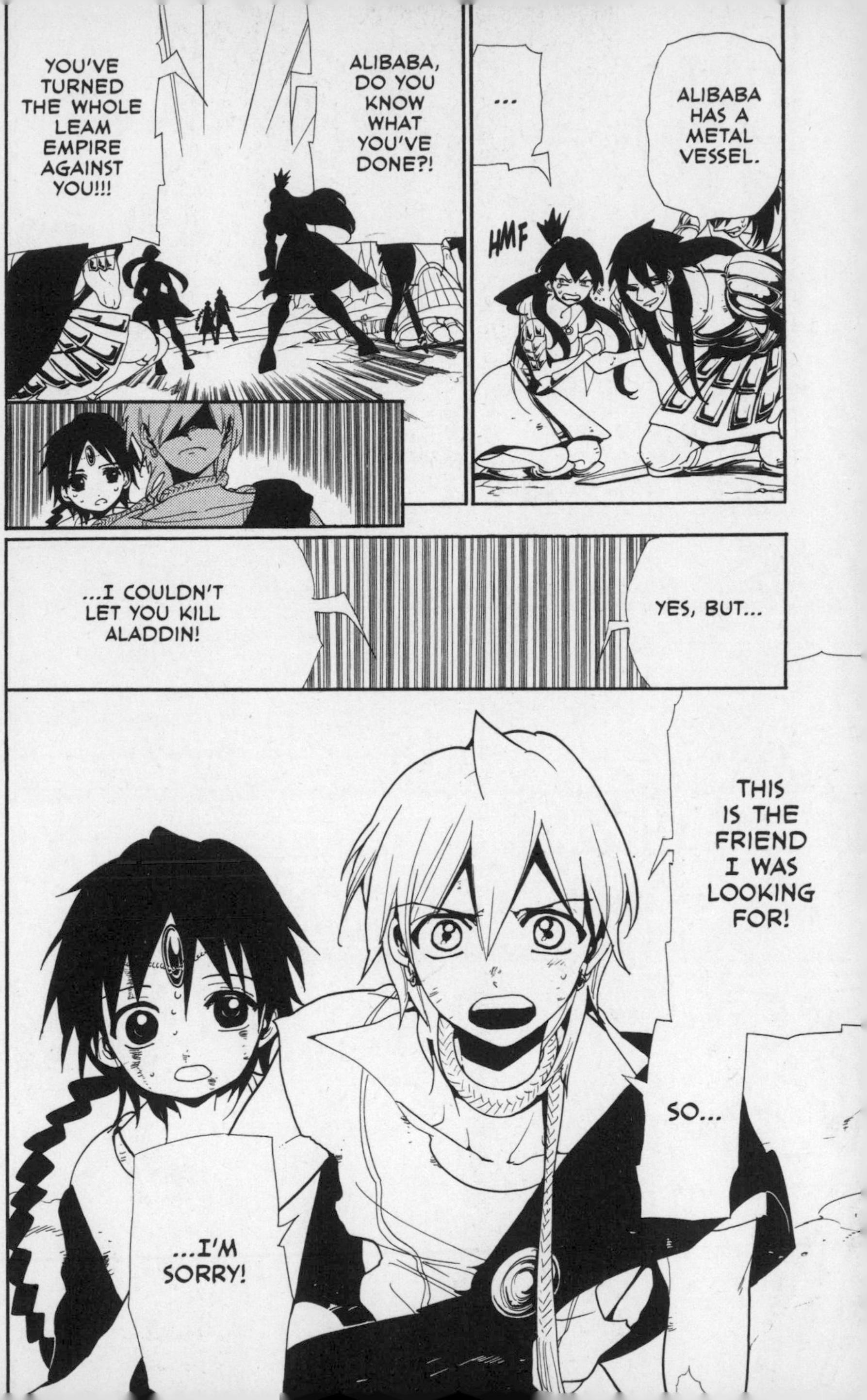
ALIBABA HAS A METAL VESSEL.
...
HMF
ALIBABA, DO YOU KNOW WHAT YOU'VE DONE?!
YOU'VE TURNED THE WHOLE LEAM EMPIRE AGAINST YOU!!!
YES, BUT...
...I COULDN'T LET YOU KILL ALADDIN!
THIS IS THE FRIEND I WAS LOOKING FOR!
SO...
...I'M SORRY!

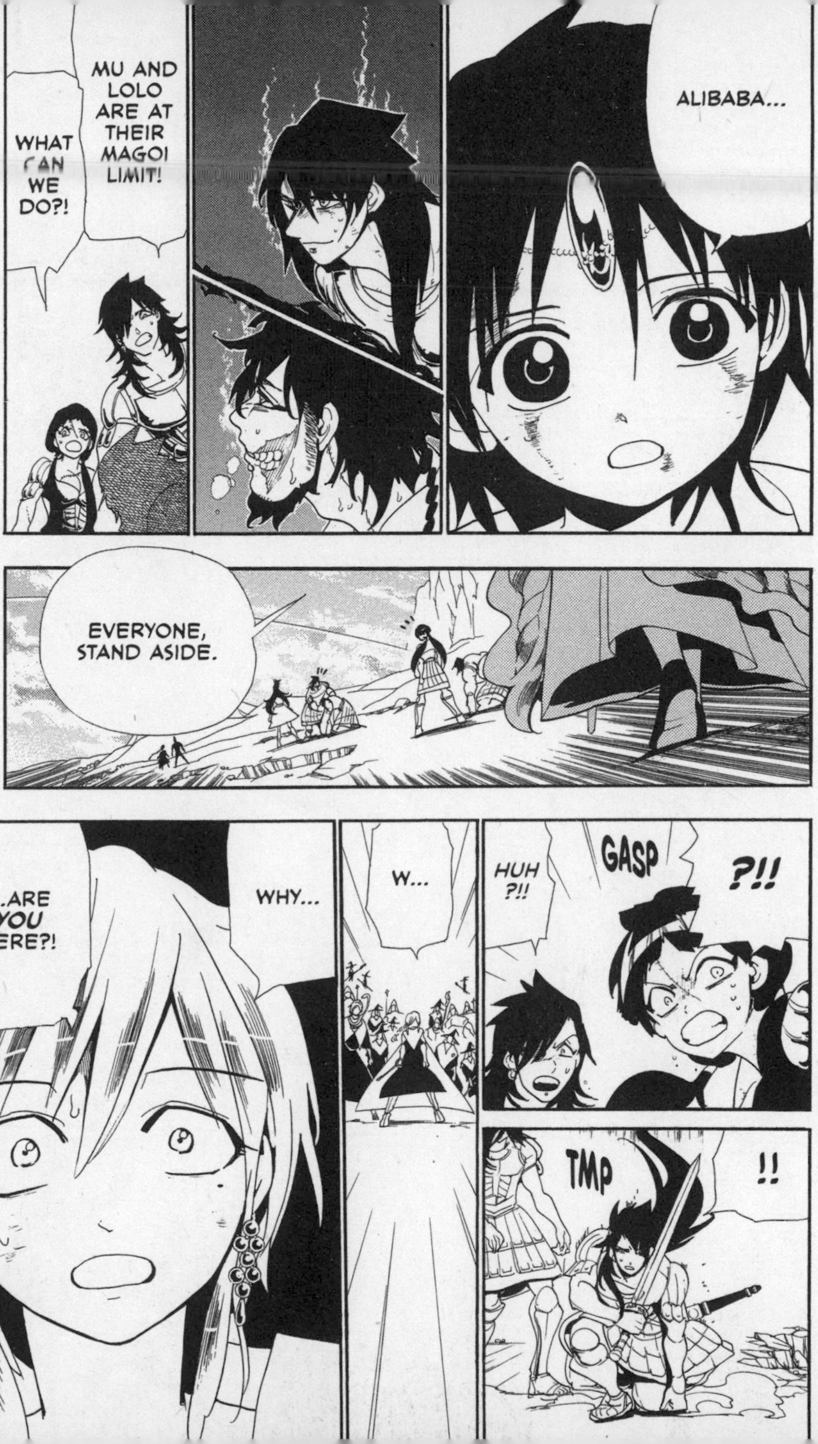
ALIBABA...
MU AND LOLO ARE AT THEIR MAGOI LIMIT!
WHAT CAN WE DO?!
EVERYONE, STAND ASIDE.
GASP
?!!
HUH ?!!
TMP
!!
W...
WHY...
...ARE *YOU* HERE?!

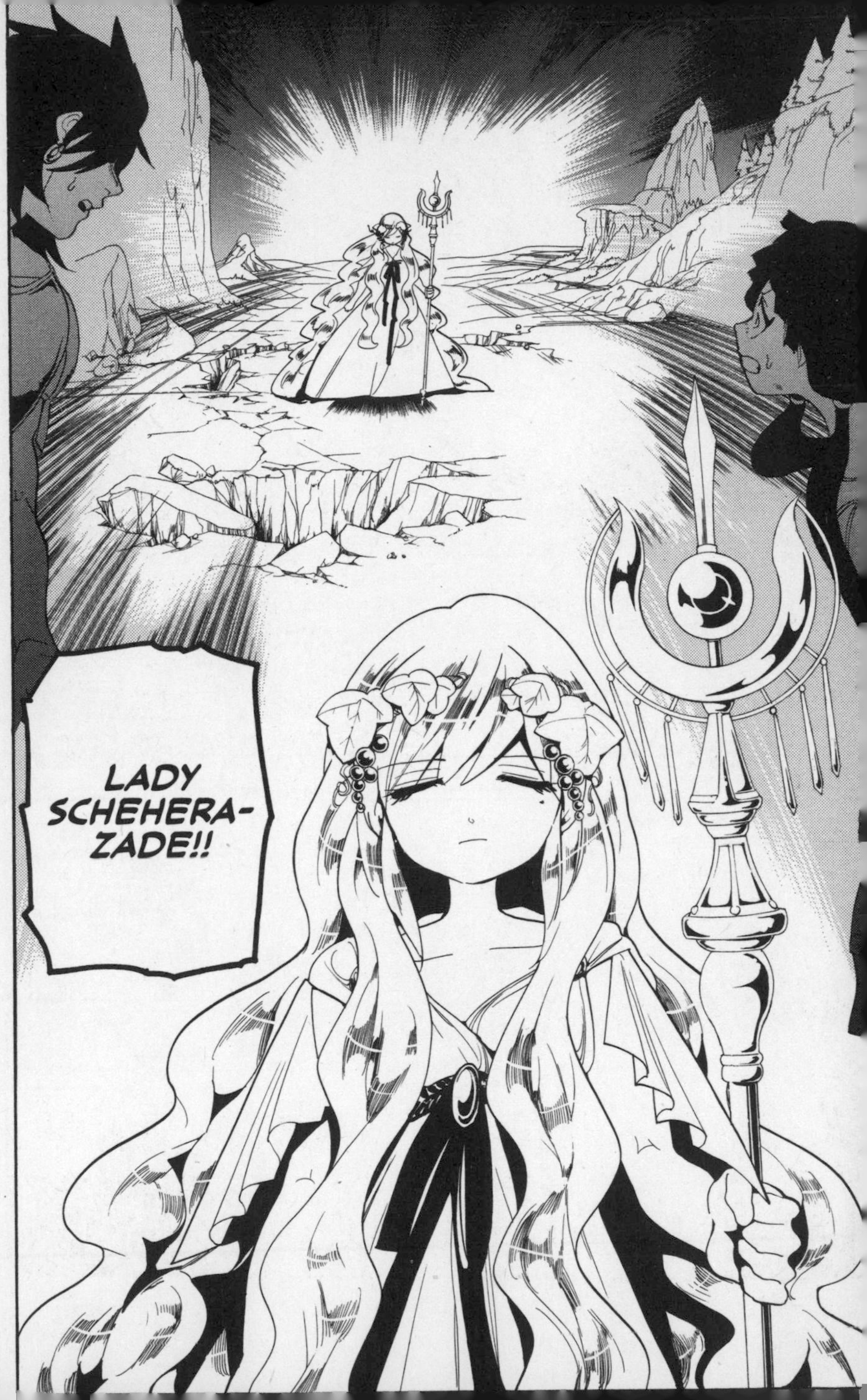
LADY SCHEHERA-ZADE!!

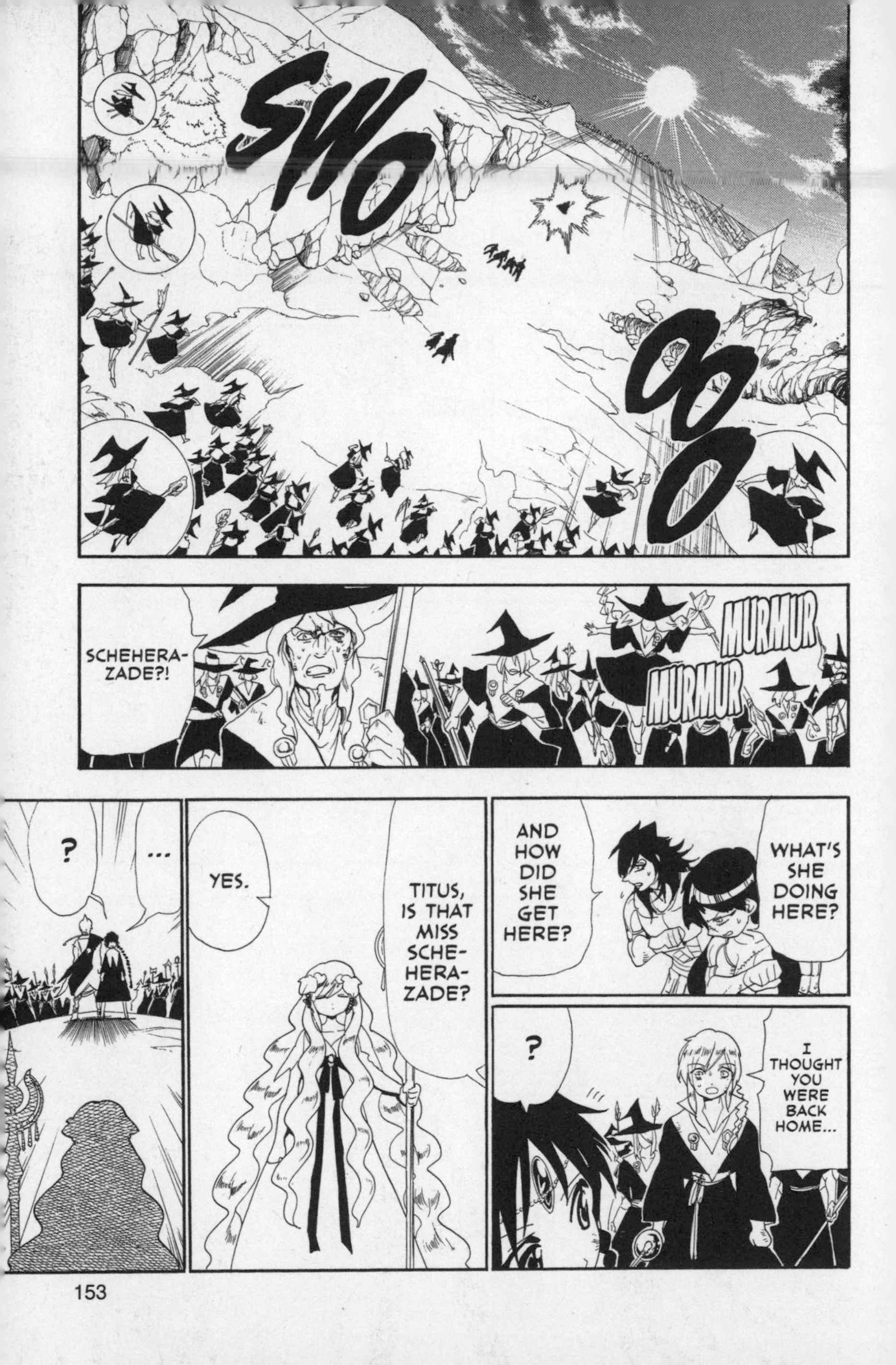
SWOOOO
MURMUR
MURMUR
SCHEHERA-ZADE?!
WHAT'S SHE DOING HERE?
AND HOW DID SHE GET HERE?
I THOUGHT YOU WERE BACK HOME...
?
TITUS, IS THAT MISS SCHE-HERA-ZADE?
YES.
...
?

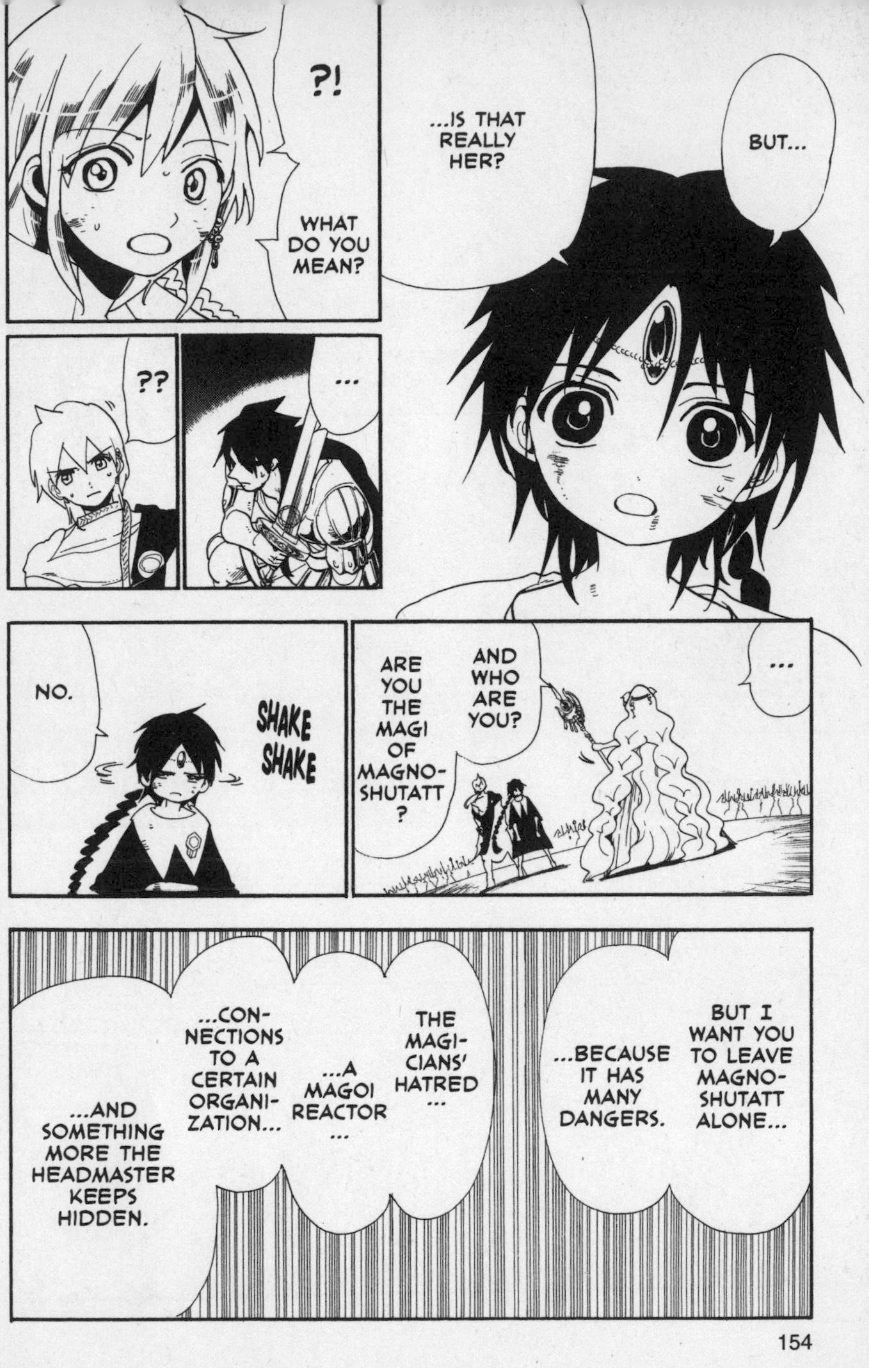
BUT...
...IS THAT REALLY HER?
?!
WHAT DO YOU MEAN?
...
??
...
AND WHO ARE YOU?
ARE YOU THE MAGI OF MAGNOSHUTATT?
NO.
SHAKE SHAKE
BUT I WANT YOU TO LEAVE MAGNOSHUTATT ALONE...
...BECAUSE IT HAS MANY DANGERS.
THE MAGICIANS' HATRED...
...A MAGOI REACTOR...
...CONNECTIONS TO A CERTAIN ORGANIZATION...
...AND SOMETHING MORE THE HEADMASTER KEEPS HIDDEN.

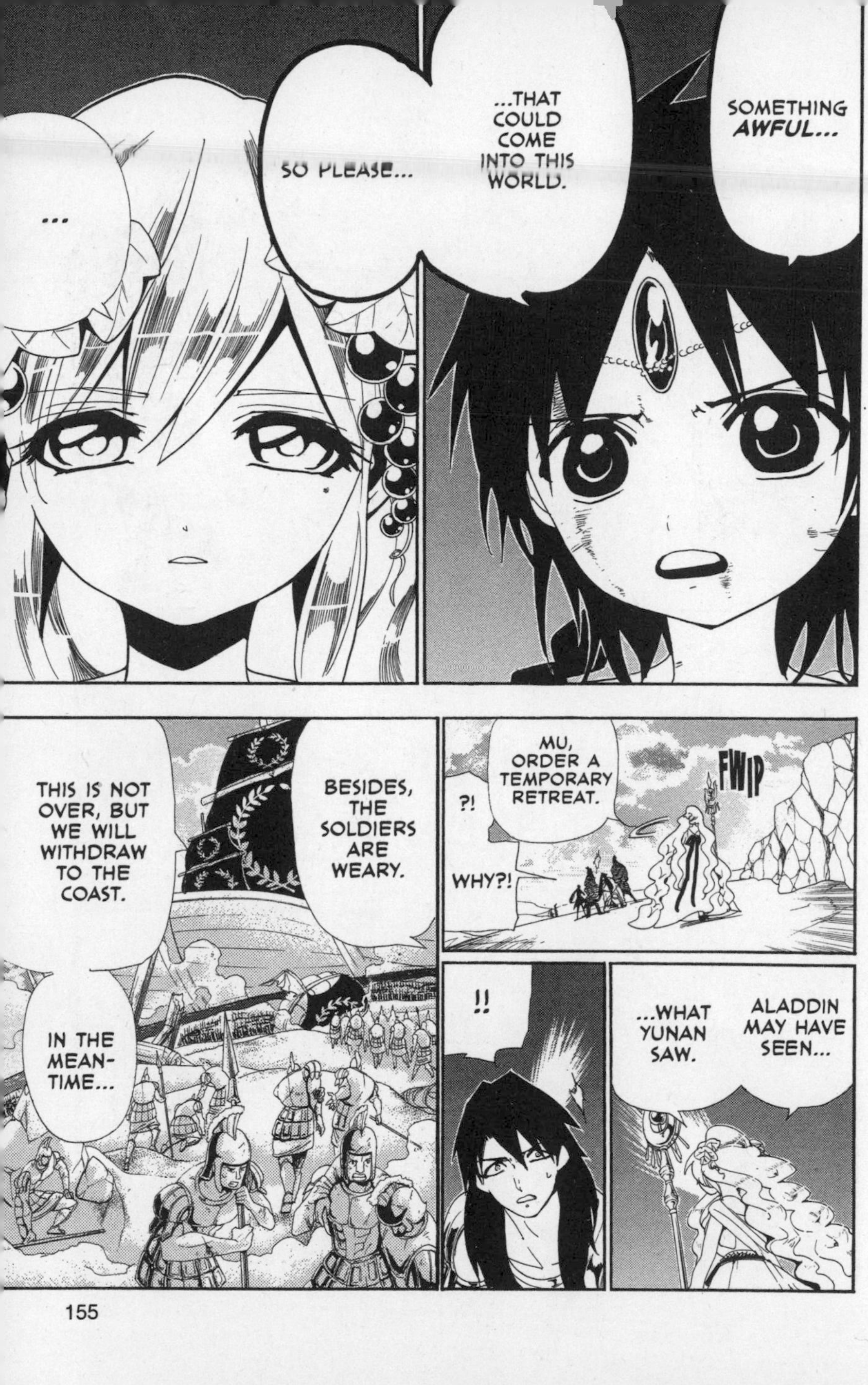
SOMETHING *AWFUL...*
...THAT COULD COME INTO THIS WORLD.
SO PLEASE...
...
MU, ORDER A TEMPORARY RETREAT.
FWIP
?!
WHY?!
ALADDIN MAY HAVE SEEN...
...WHAT YUNAN SAW.
!!
BESIDES, THE SOLDIERS ARE WEARY.
THIS IS NOT OVER, BUT WE WILL WITHDRAW TO THE COAST.
IN THE MEAN-TIME...

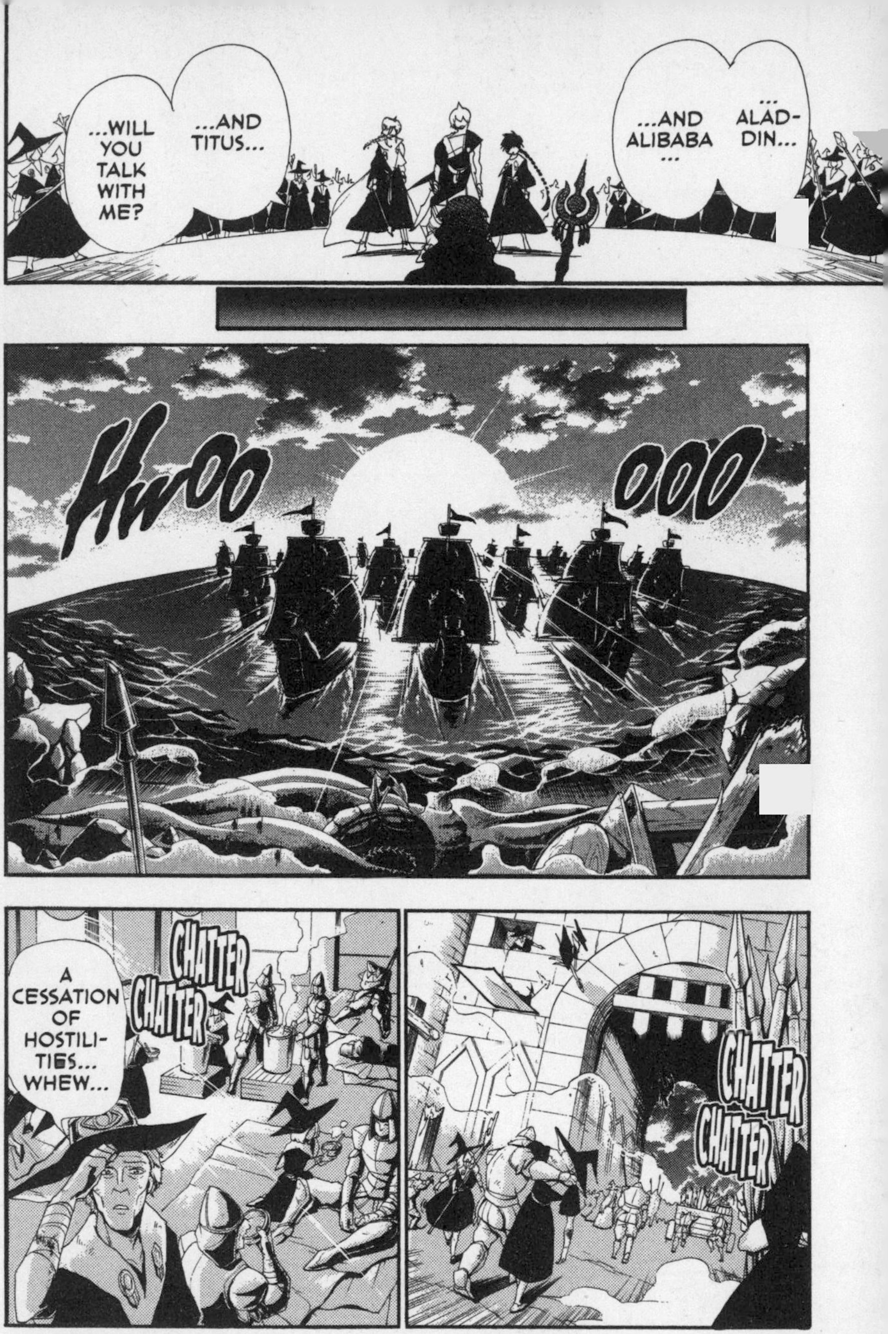
... ALAD-DIN...
...AND ALIBABA ...
...AND TITUS...
...WILL YOU TALK WITH ME?
HWOO OOO
CHATTER CHATTER
CHATTER CHATTER
A CESSATION OF HOSTILI-TIES... WHEW...

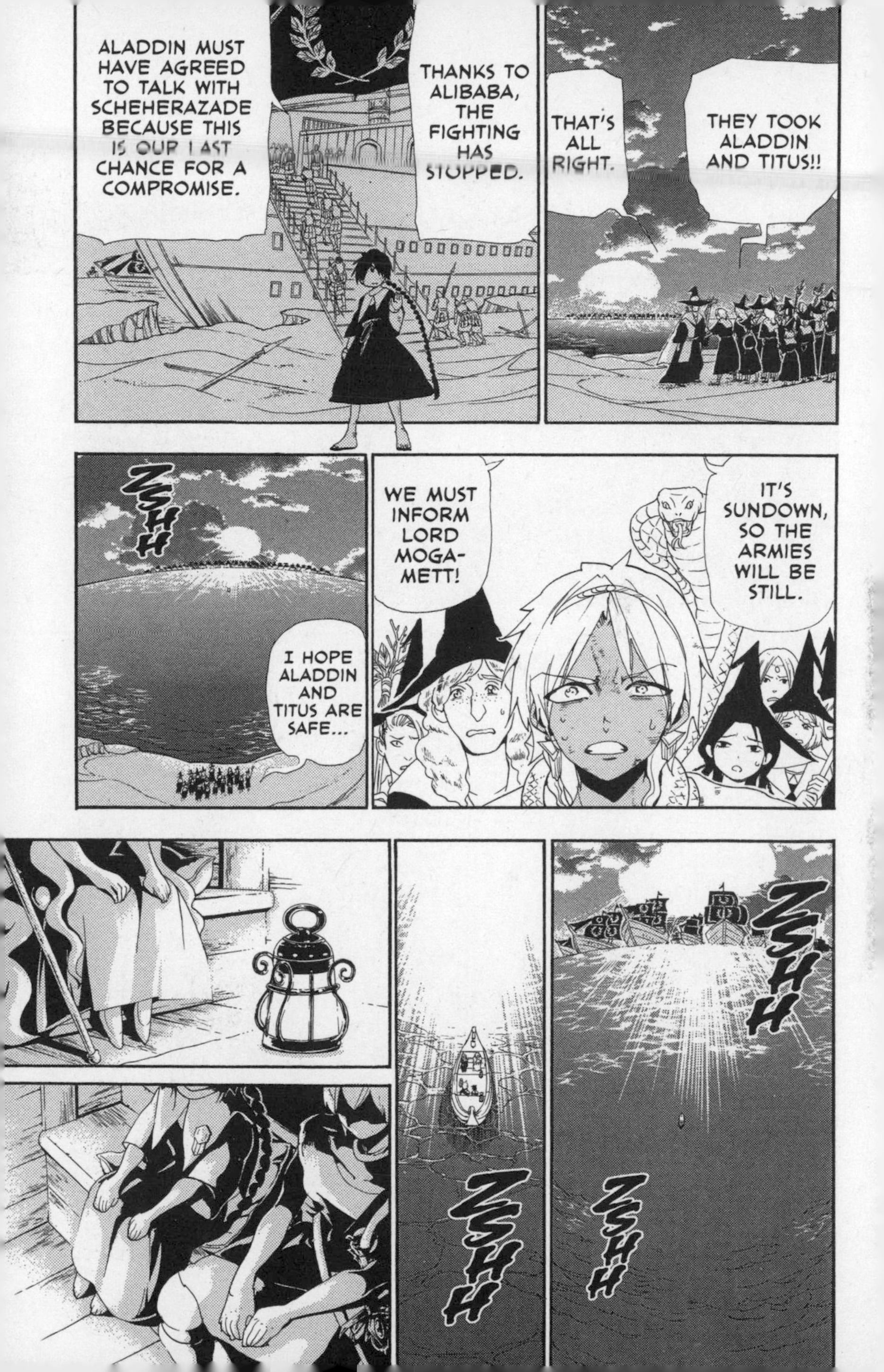
THEY TOOK ALADDIN AND TITUS!!
THAT'S ALL RIGHT.
THANKS TO ALIBABA, THE FIGHTING HAS STOPPED.
ALADDIN MUST HAVE AGREED TO TALK WITH SCHEHERAZADE BECAUSE THIS IS OUR LAST CHANCE FOR A COMPROMISE.
IT'S SUNDOWN, SO THE ARMIES WILL BE STILL.
WE MUST INFORM LORD MOGA-METT!
ZSHH
I HOPE ALADDIN AND TITUS ARE SAFE...
ZSHH
ZSHH
ZSHH

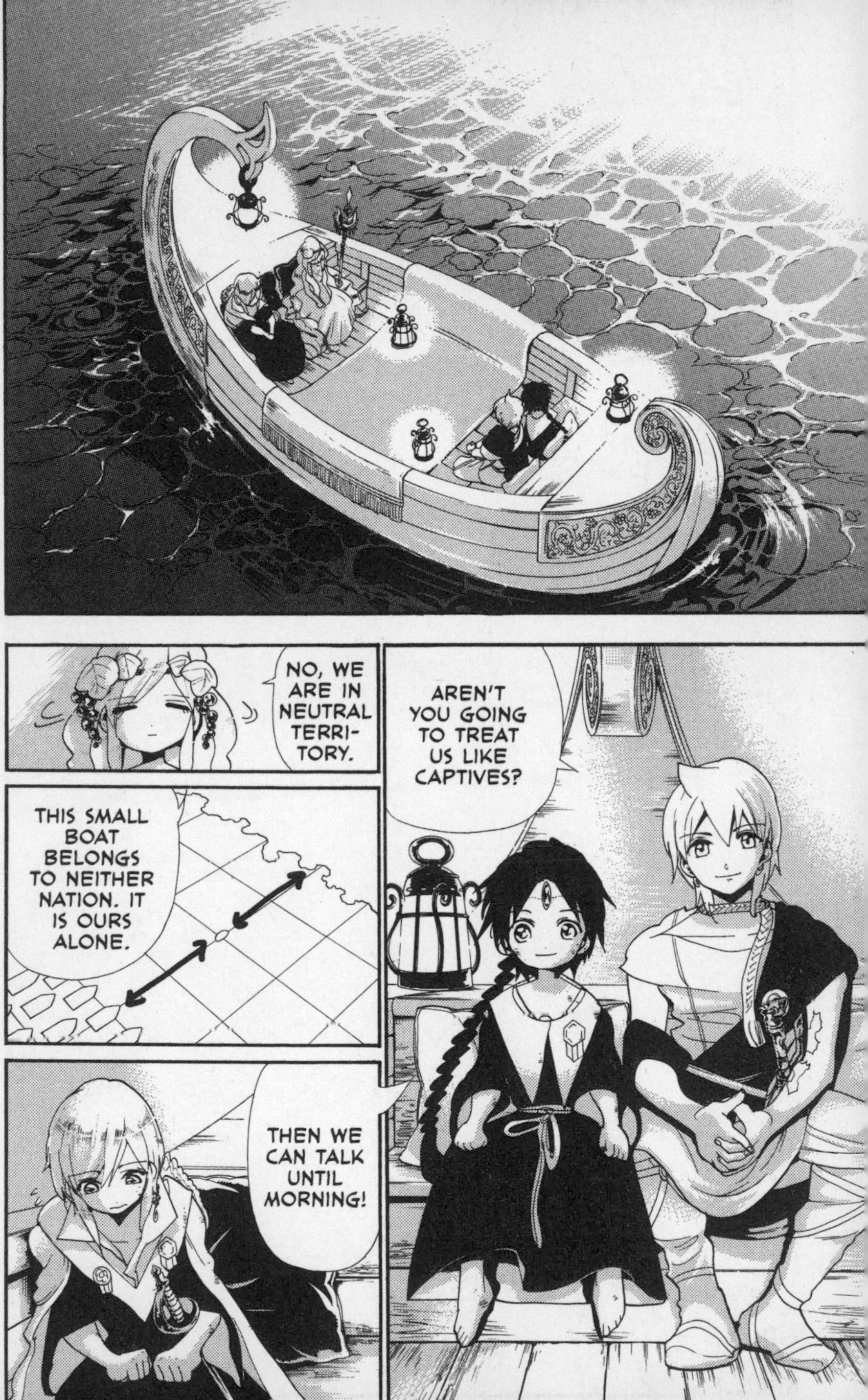
AREN'T YOU GOING TO TREAT US LIKE CAPTIVES?
NO, WE ARE IN NEUTRAL TERRITORY.
THIS SMALL BOAT BELONGS TO NEITHER NATION. IT IS OURS ALONE.
THEN WE CAN TALK UNTIL MORNING!

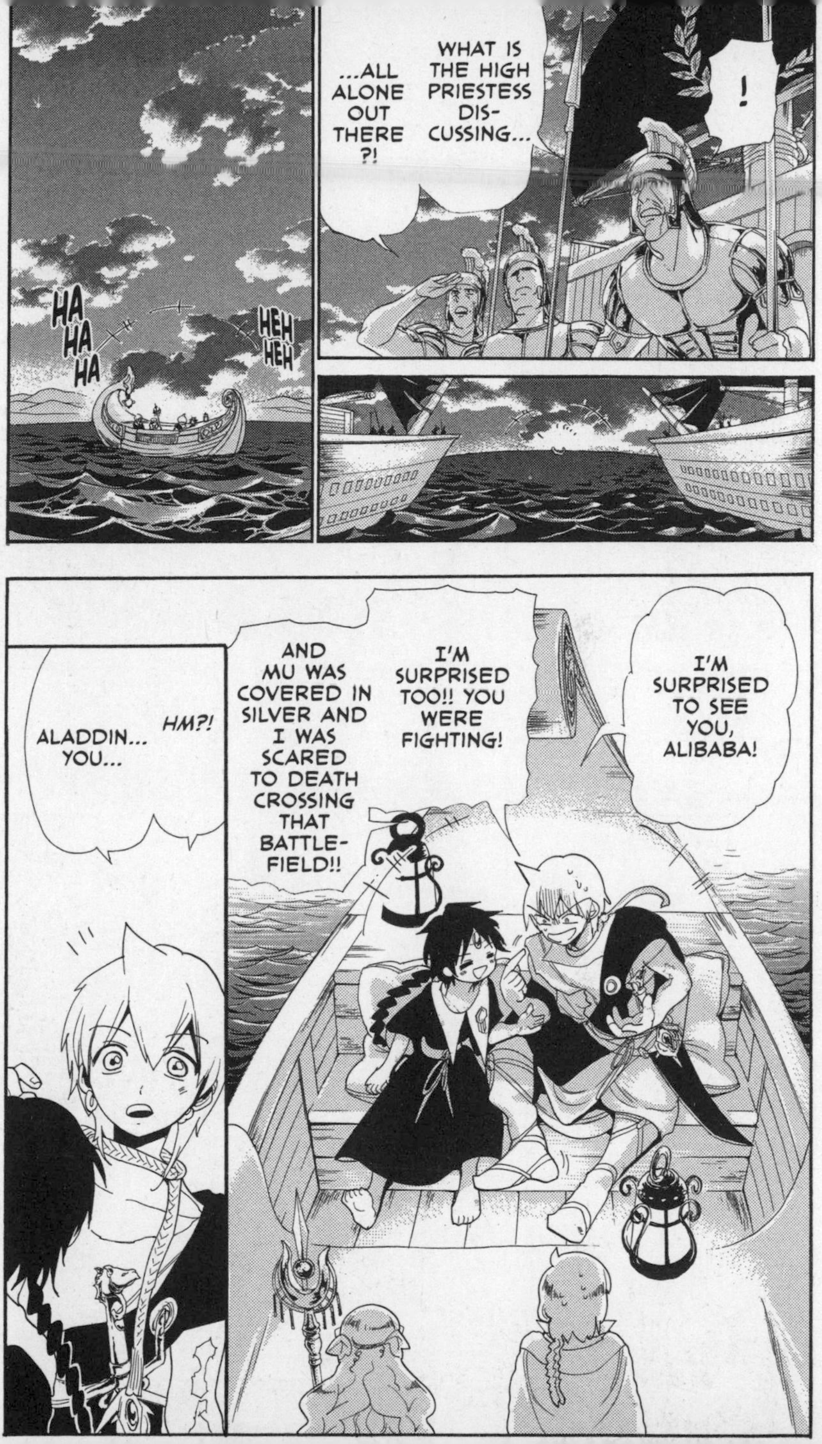
!
WHAT IS THE HIGH PRIESTESS DIS-CUSSING...
...ALL ALONE OUT THERE?!
HEH HEH
HA HA HA
I'M SURPRISED TO SEE YOU, ALIBABA!
I'M SURPRISED TOO!! YOU WERE FIGHTING!
AND MU WAS COVERED IN SILVER AND I WAS SCARED TO DEATH CROSSING THAT BATTLE-FIELD!!
HM?!
ALADDIN... YOU...

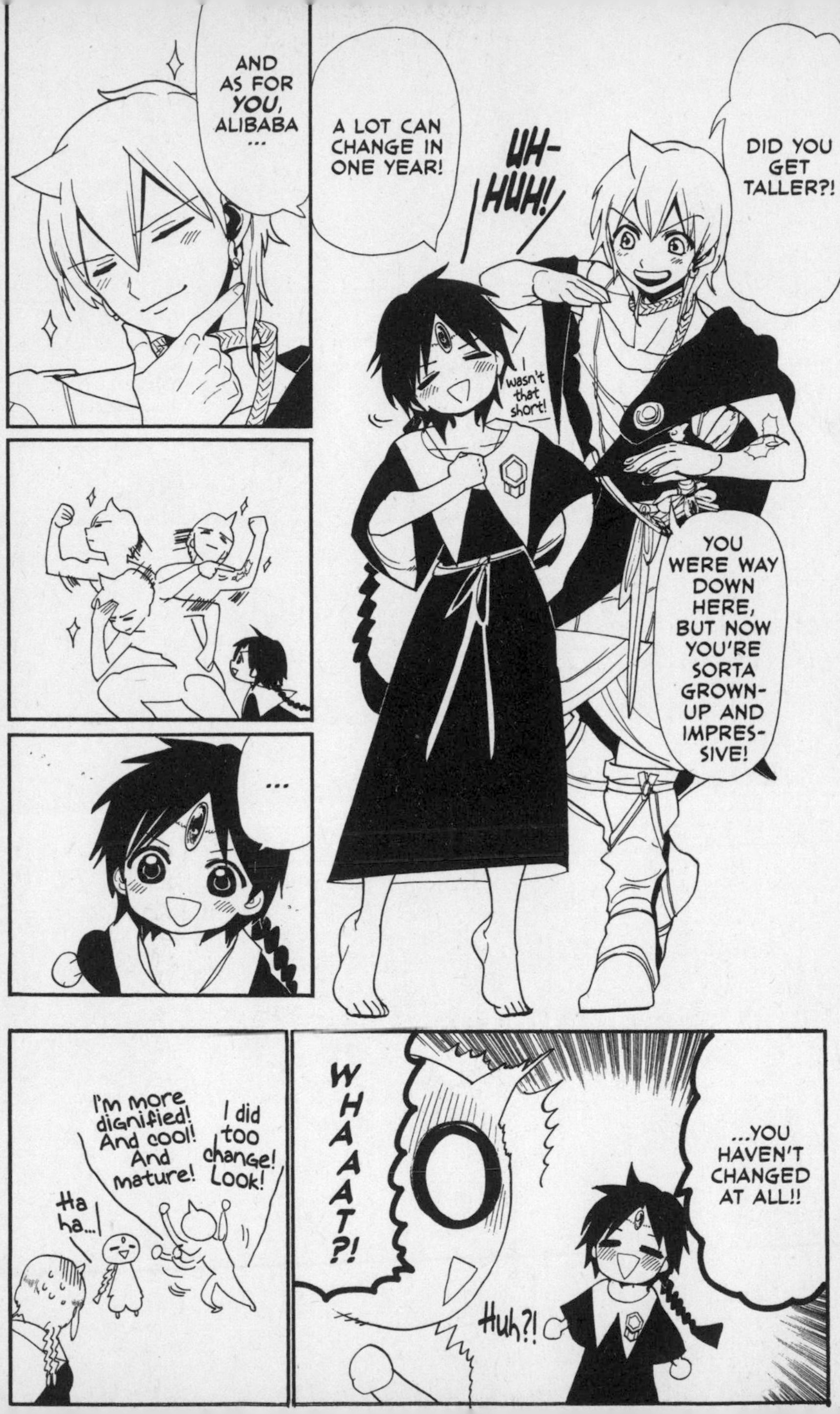
DID YOU GET TALLER?!
UH-HUH!
A LOT CAN CHANGE IN ONE YEAR!
I wasn't that short!
YOU WERE WAY DOWN HERE, BUT NOW YOU'RE SORTA GROWN-UP AND IMPRES-SIVE!
AND AS FOR *YOU*, ALIBABA...
...
...YOU HAVEN'T CHANGED AT ALL!!
WHAAAT?!
Huh?!
I did too change! Look!
I'm more dignified! And cool! And mature!
Ha ha...

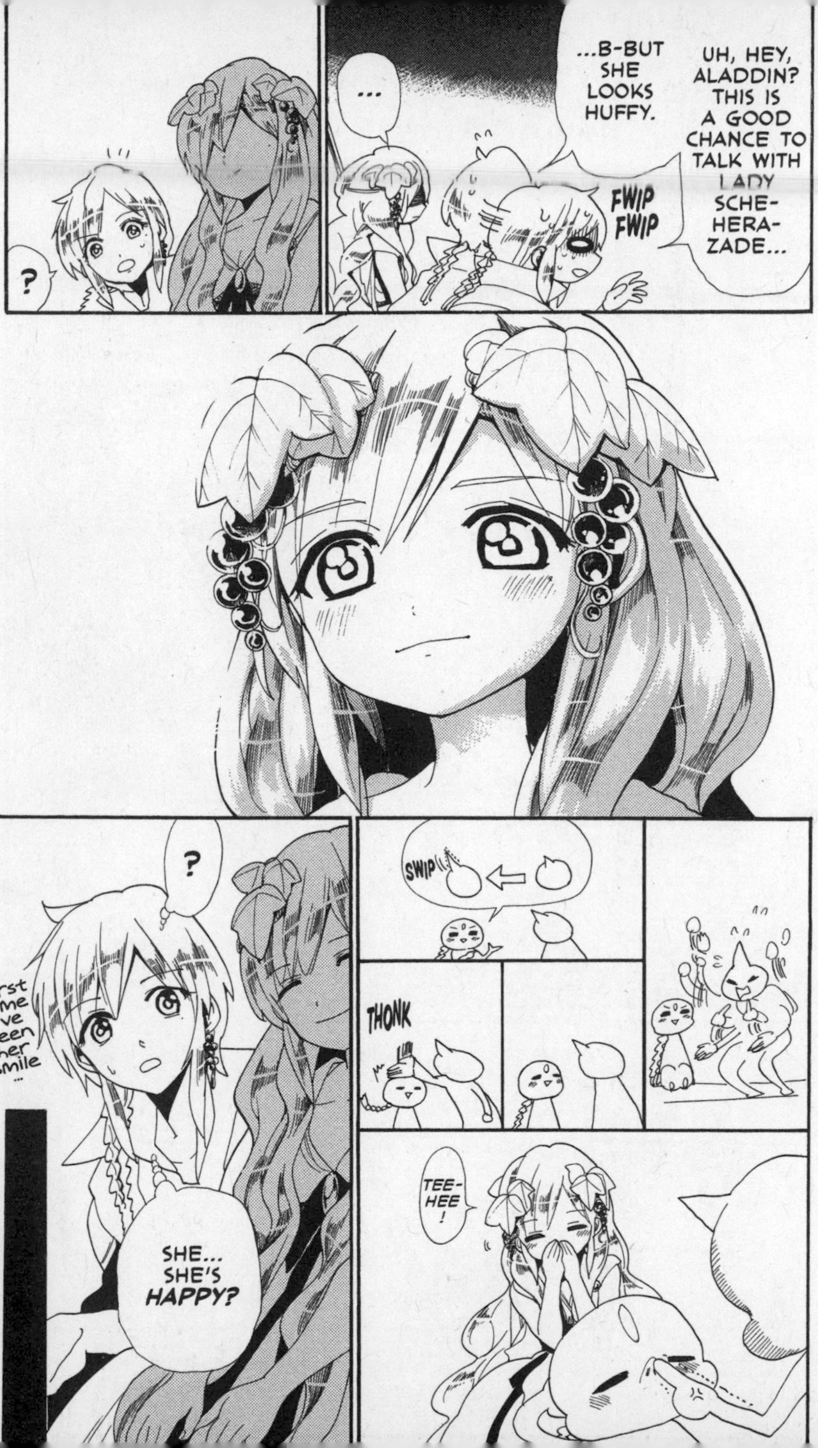
UH, HEY, ALADDIN? THIS IS A GOOD CHANCE TO TALK WITH LADY SCHE-HERA-ZADE...
...B-BUT SHE LOOKS HUFFY.
FWIP FWIP
...
?
SWIP
THONK
TEE-HEE!
?
First time I've seen her smile...
SHE... SHE'S HAPPY?

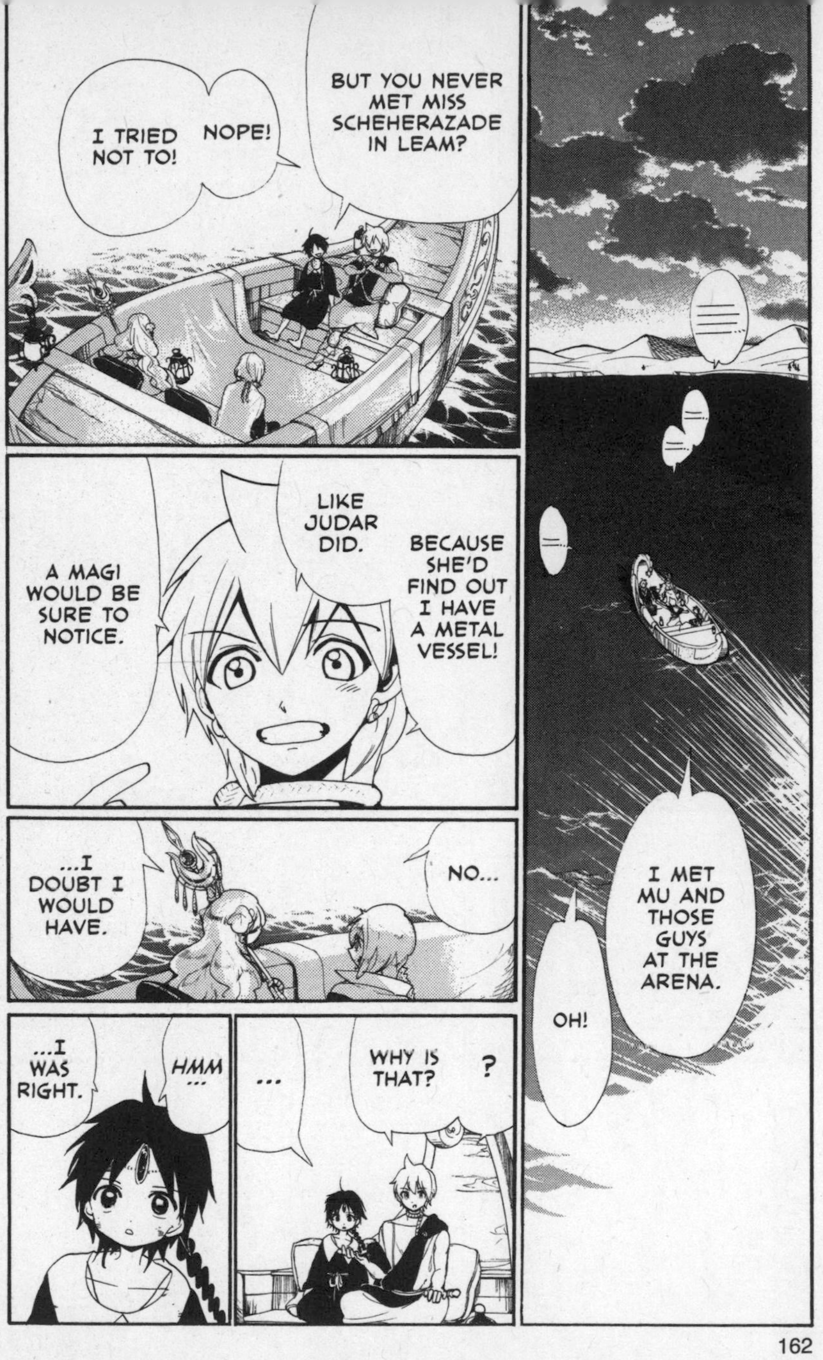
I MET MU AND THOSE GUYS AT THE ARENA.
OH!
BUT YOU NEVER MET MISS SCHEHERAZADE IN LEAM?
NOPE!
I TRIED NOT TO!
BECAUSE SHE'D FIND OUT I HAVE A METAL VESSEL!
LIKE JUDAR DID.
A MAGI WOULD BE SURE TO NOTICE.
NO...
...I DOUBT I WOULD HAVE.
?
WHY IS THAT?
...
HMM...
...I WAS RIGHT.

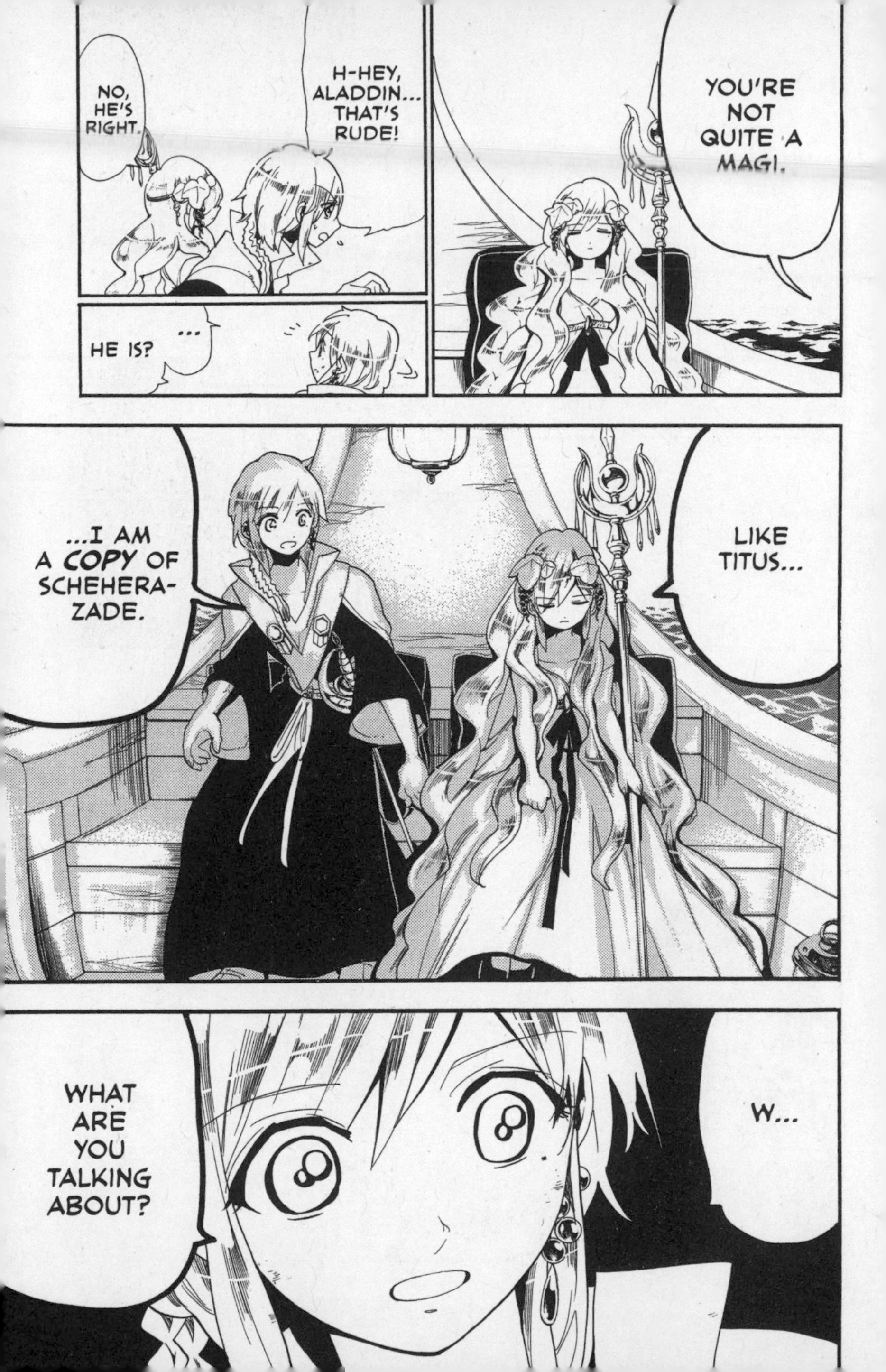
YOU'RE NOT QUITE A MAGI.
H-HEY, ALADDIN... THAT'S RUDE!
NO, HE'S RIGHT.
...
HE IS?
LIKE TITUS...
...I AM A COPY OF SCHEHERA-ZADE.
W...
WHAT ARE YOU TALKING ABOUT?

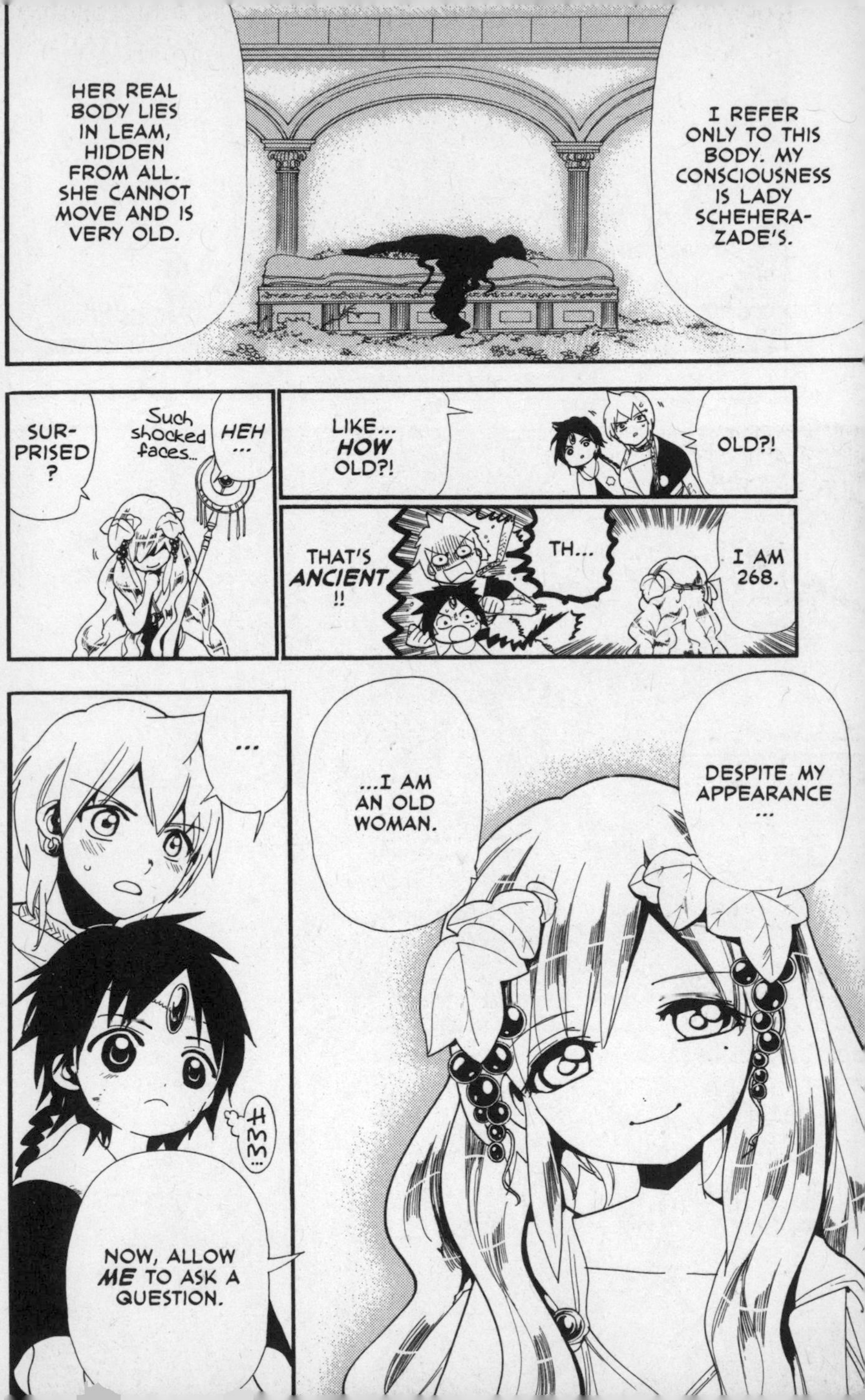
I REFER ONLY TO THIS BODY. MY CONSCIOUSNESS IS LADY SCHEHERAZADE'S.
HER REAL BODY LIES IN LEAM, HIDDEN FROM ALL. SHE CANNOT MOVE AND IS VERY OLD.
OLD?!
LIKE... *HOW* OLD?!
I AM 268.
TH...
THAT'S *ANCIENT*!!
HEH...
Such shocked faces...
SURPRISED?
DESPITE MY APPEARANCE...
...I AM AN OLD WOMAN.
...
NOW, ALLOW *ME* TO ASK A QUESTION.

WHAT IS MATAL MOGAMETT HIDING? WHAT IS HE ATTEMPTING TO ACCOMPLISH?

TELL ME...

SOB
SOB
SOB
SOB

ACADEMY CITY, MAGNO-SHUTATT

...

WE LOST 161 LEVEL 2 MAGICIANS AND 89 LEVEL 1 MAGICIANS. IT'S A TRAGEDY!

SOB
SOB
SOB

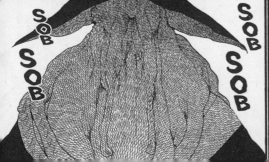

SOB
SOB
SOB
SOB

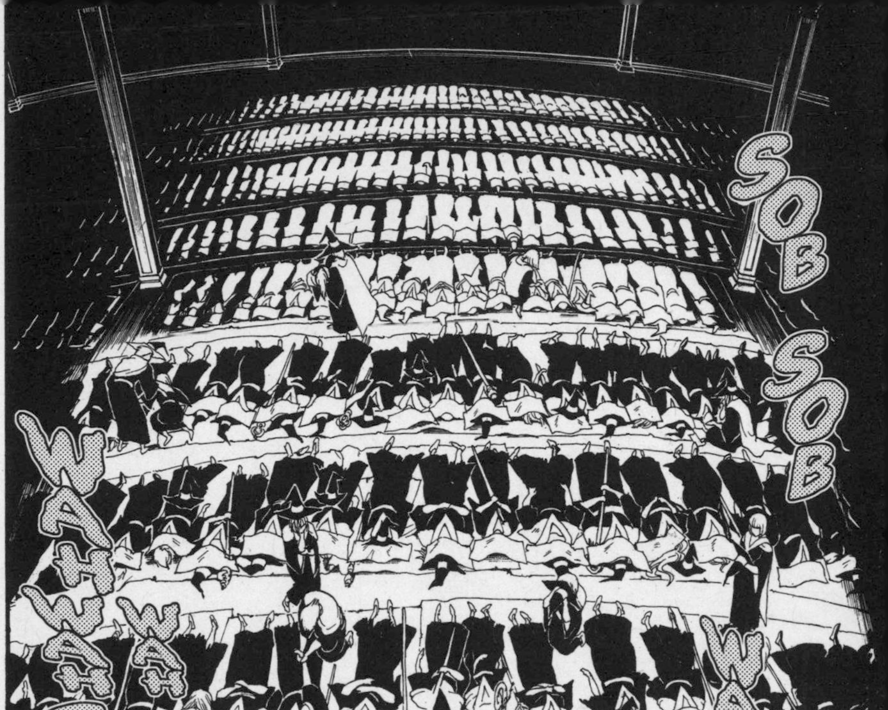
SOB
SOB
WAH
WAH
WAHWAH
SOB

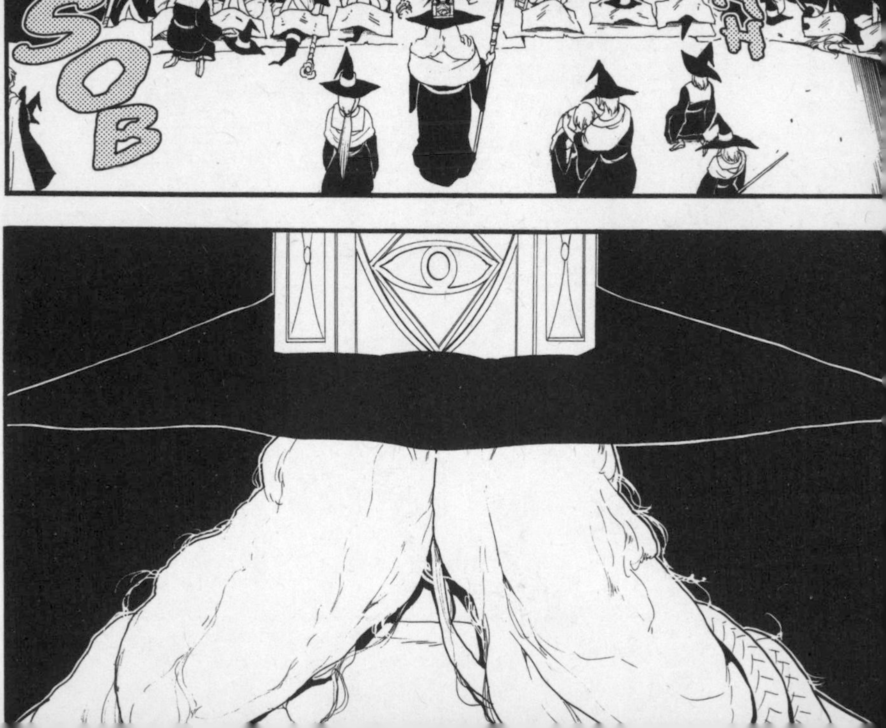

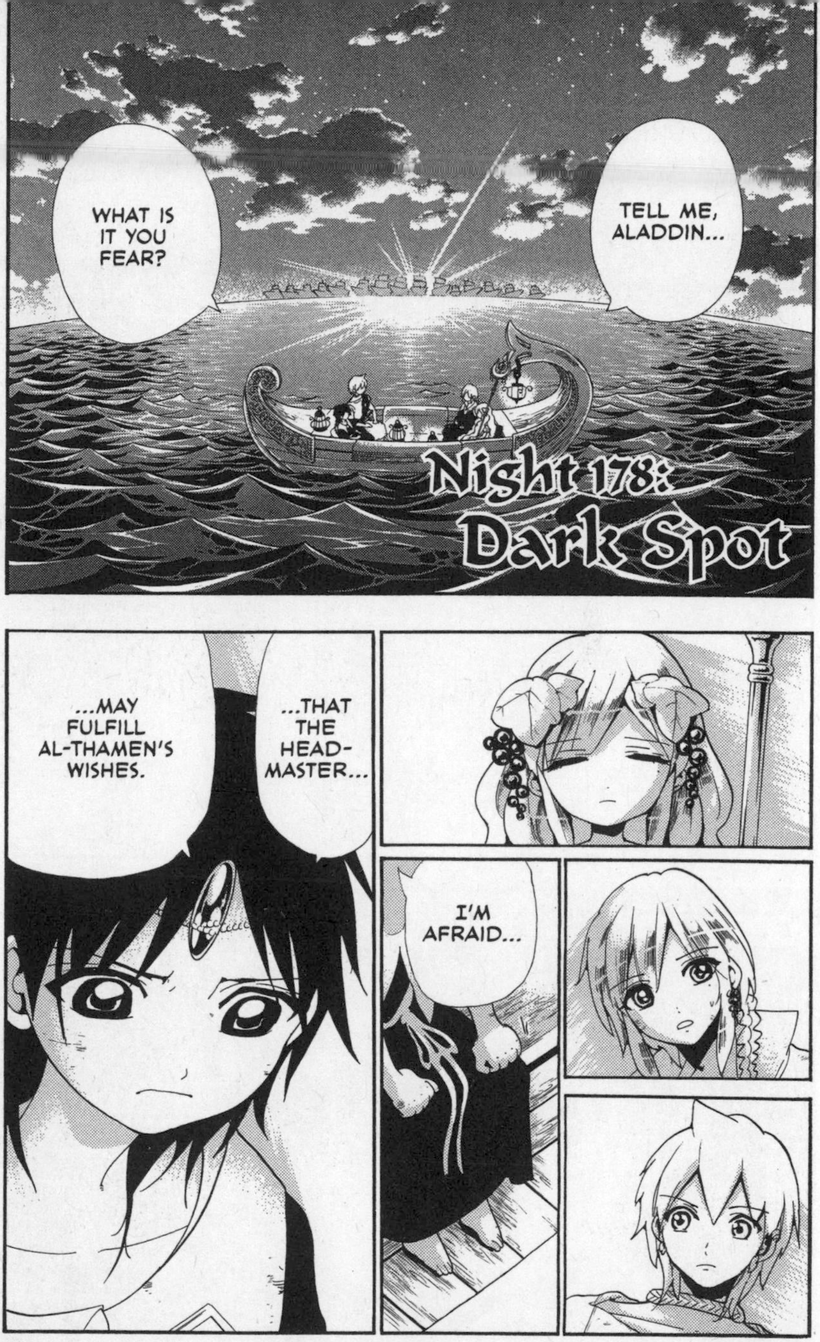
TELL ME, ALADDIN...
WHAT IS IT YOU FEAR?
Night 178: Dark Spot
I'M AFRAID...
...THAT THE HEAD-MASTER...
...MAY FULFILL AL-THAMEN'S WISHES.

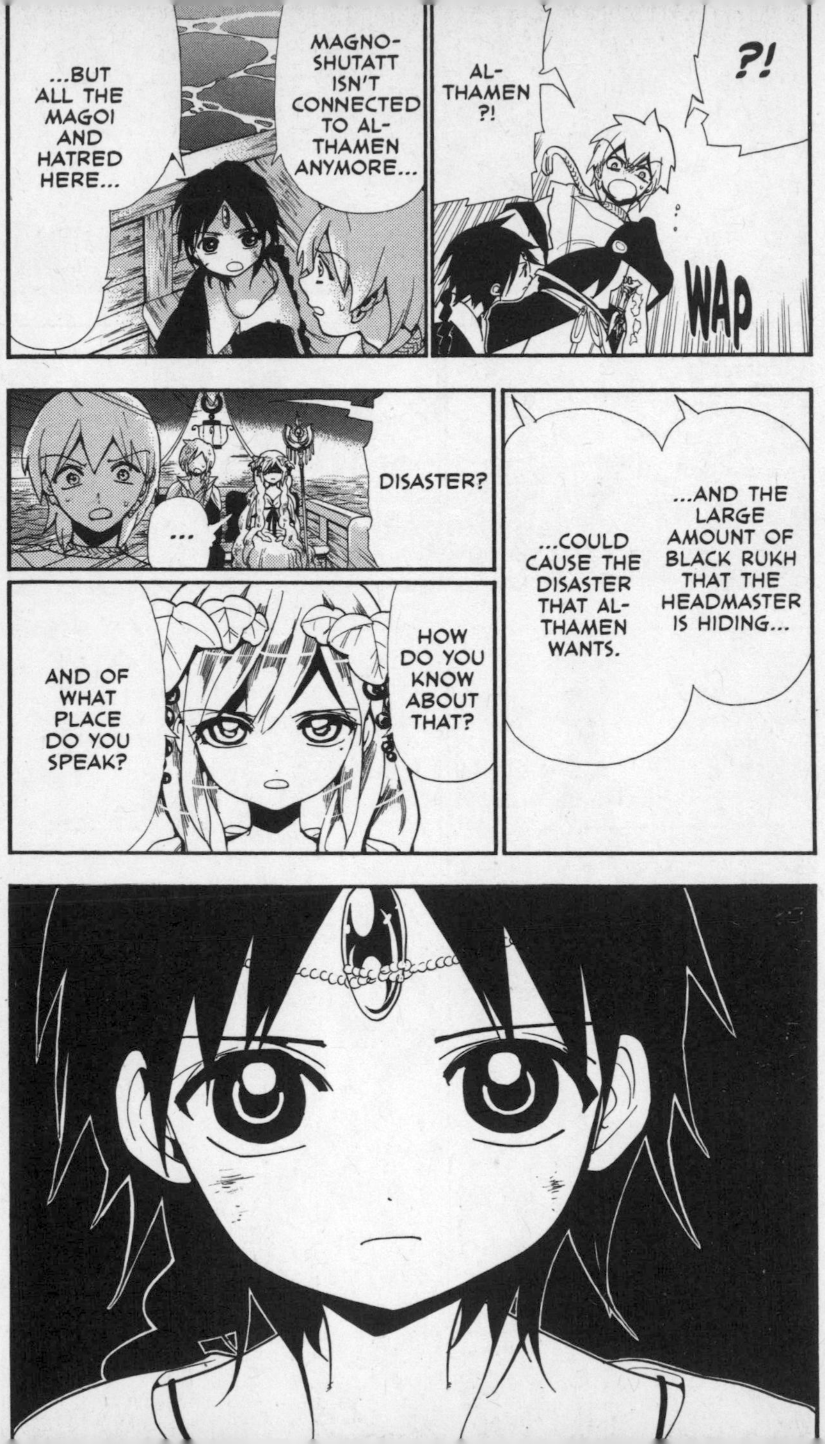
?!
AL-THAMEN ?!
WAP
MAGNO-SHUTATT ISN'T CONNECTED TO AL-THAMEN ANYMORE...
...BUT ALL THE MAGOI AND HATRED HERE...
...AND THE LARGE AMOUNT OF BLACK RUKH THAT THE HEADMASTER IS HIDING...
...COULD CAUSE THE DISASTER THAT AL-THAMEN WANTS.
DISASTER?
...
HOW DO YOU KNOW ABOUT THAT?
AND OF WHAT PLACE DO YOU SPEAK?

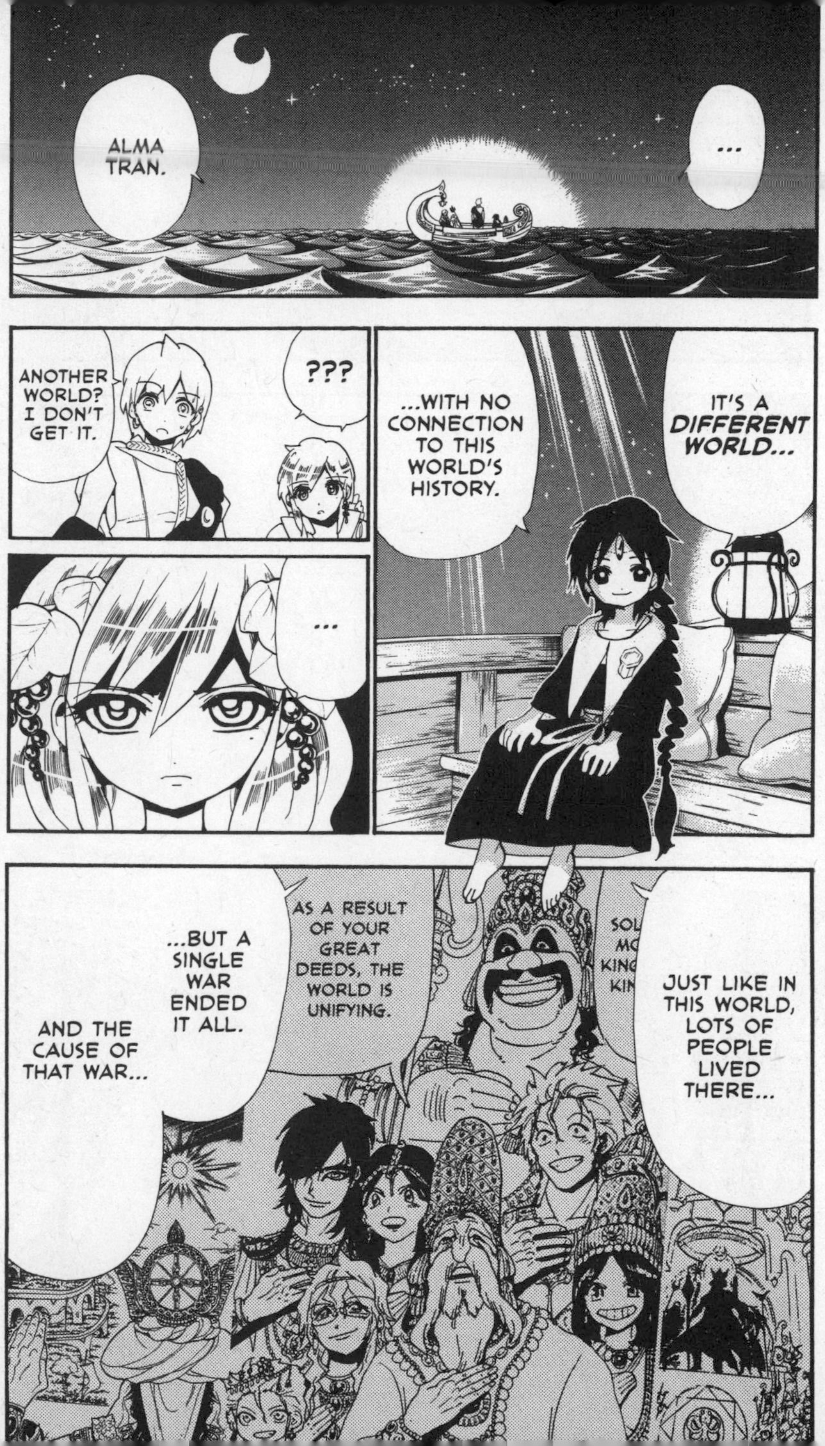
...
ALMA TRAN.
IT'S A *DIFFERENT WORLD...*
...WITH NO CONNECTION TO THIS WORLD'S HISTORY.
???
ANOTHER WORLD? I DON'T GET IT.
...
JUST LIKE IN THIS WORLD, LOTS OF PEOPLE LIVED THERE...
AS A RESULT OF YOUR GREAT DEEDS, THE WORLD IS UNIFYING.
...BUT A SINGLE WAR ENDED IT ALL.
AND THE CAUSE OF THAT WAR...

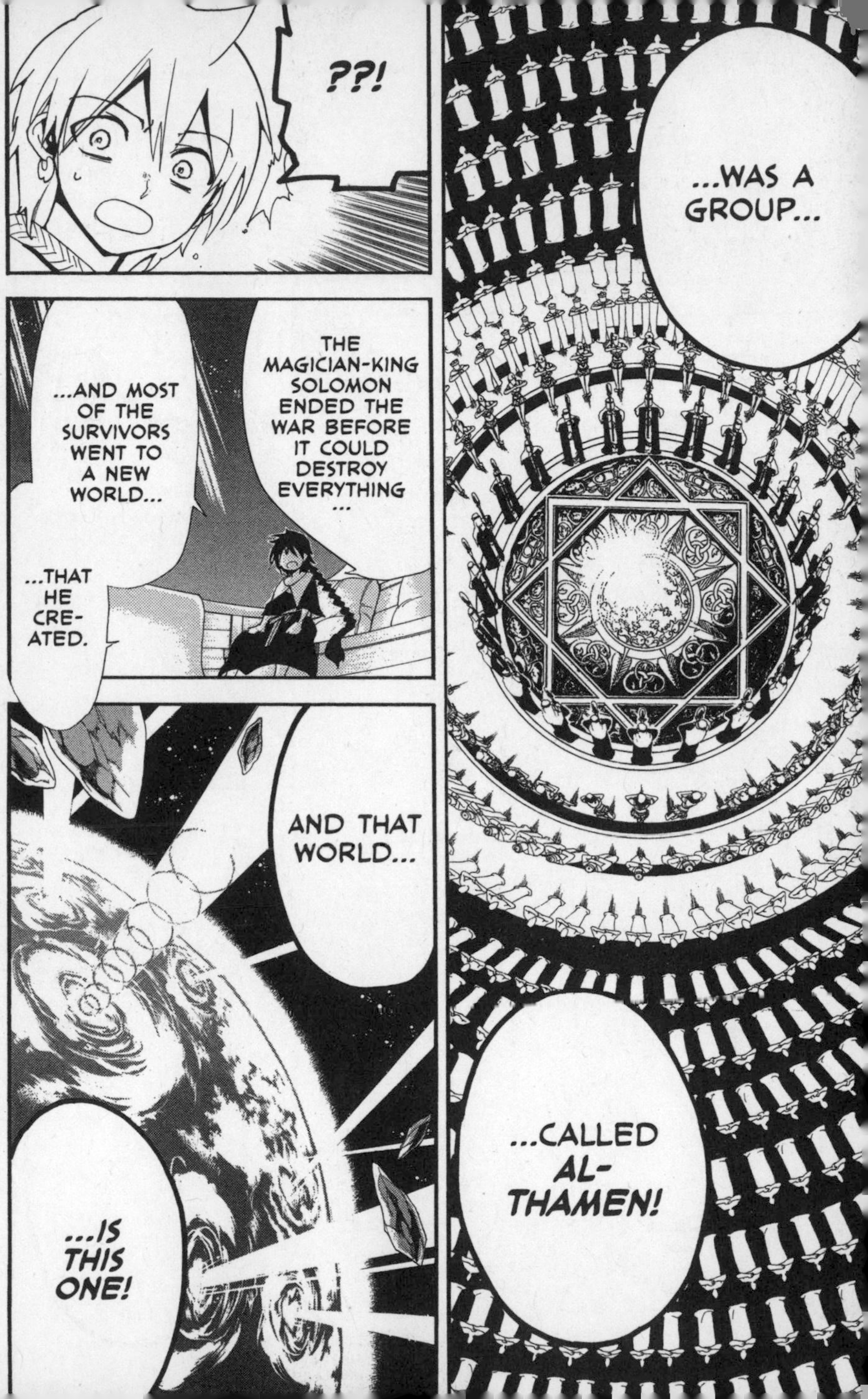
...WAS A GROUP...
...CALLED AL-THAMEN!
??!
THE MAGICIAN-KING SOLOMON ENDED THE WAR BEFORE IT COULD DESTROY EVERYTHING...
...AND MOST OF THE SURVIVORS WENT TO A NEW WORLD...
...THAT HE CREATED.
AND THAT WORLD...
...IS THIS ONE!

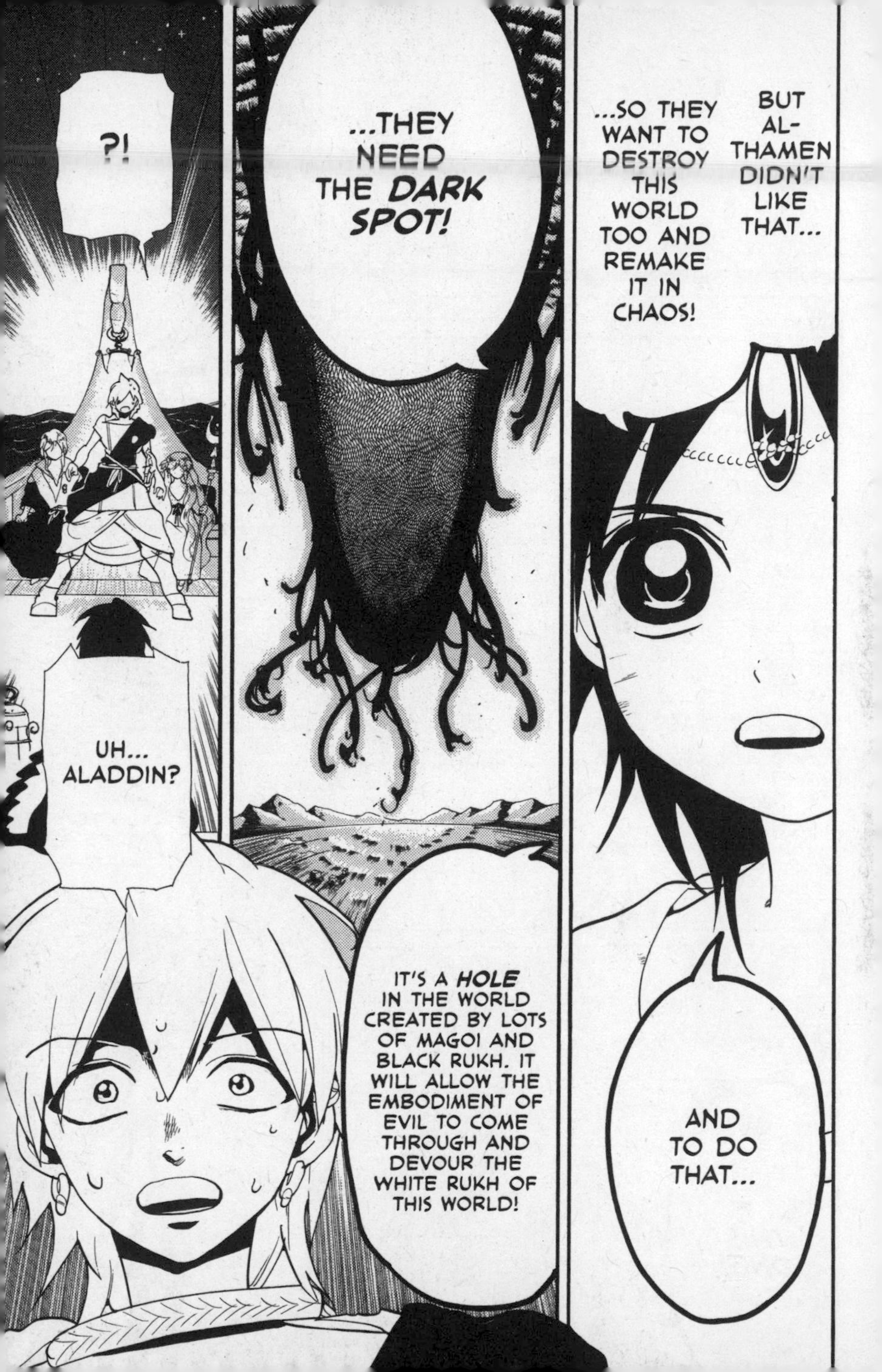
BUT AL-THAMEN DIDN'T LIKE THAT...
...SO THEY WANT TO DESTROY THIS WORLD TOO AND REMAKE IT IN CHAOS!
AND TO DO THAT...
...THEY NEED THE *DARK SPOT!*
?!
UH... ALADDIN?
IT'S A *HOLE* IN THE WORLD CREATED BY LOTS OF MAGOI AND BLACK RUKH. IT WILL ALLOW THE EMBODIMENT OF EVIL TO COME THROUGH AND DEVOUR THE WHITE RUKH OF THIS WORLD!

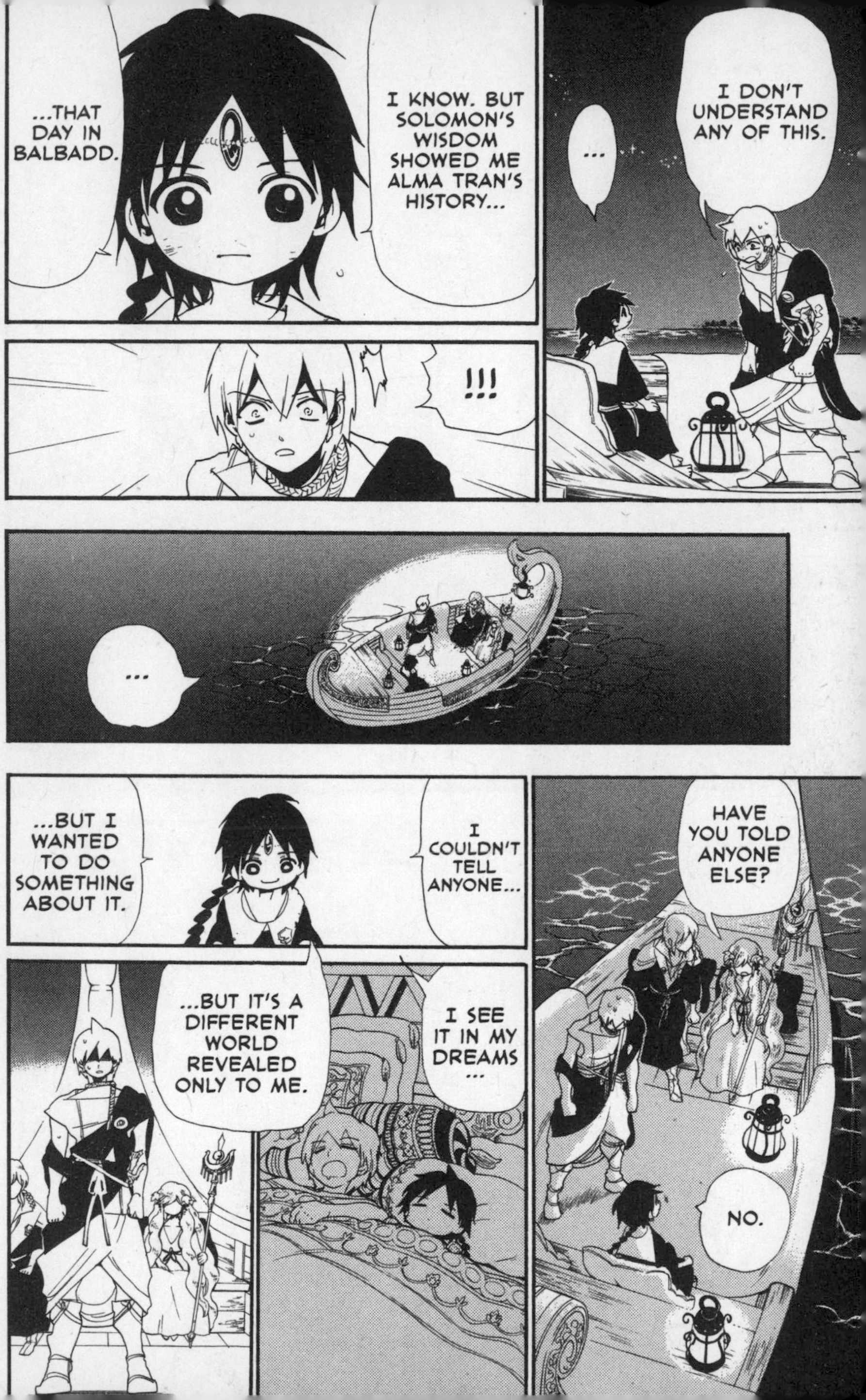
I DON'T UNDERSTAND ANY OF THIS.
...
I KNOW. BUT SOLOMON'S WISDOM SHOWED ME ALMA TRAN'S HISTORY...
...THAT DAY IN BALBADD.
!!!
...
HAVE YOU TOLD ANYONE ELSE?
NO.
I COULDN'T TELL ANYONE...
...BUT I WANTED TO DO SOMETHING ABOUT IT.
I SEE IT IN MY DREAMS...
...BUT IT'S A DIFFERENT WORLD REVEALED ONLY TO ME.

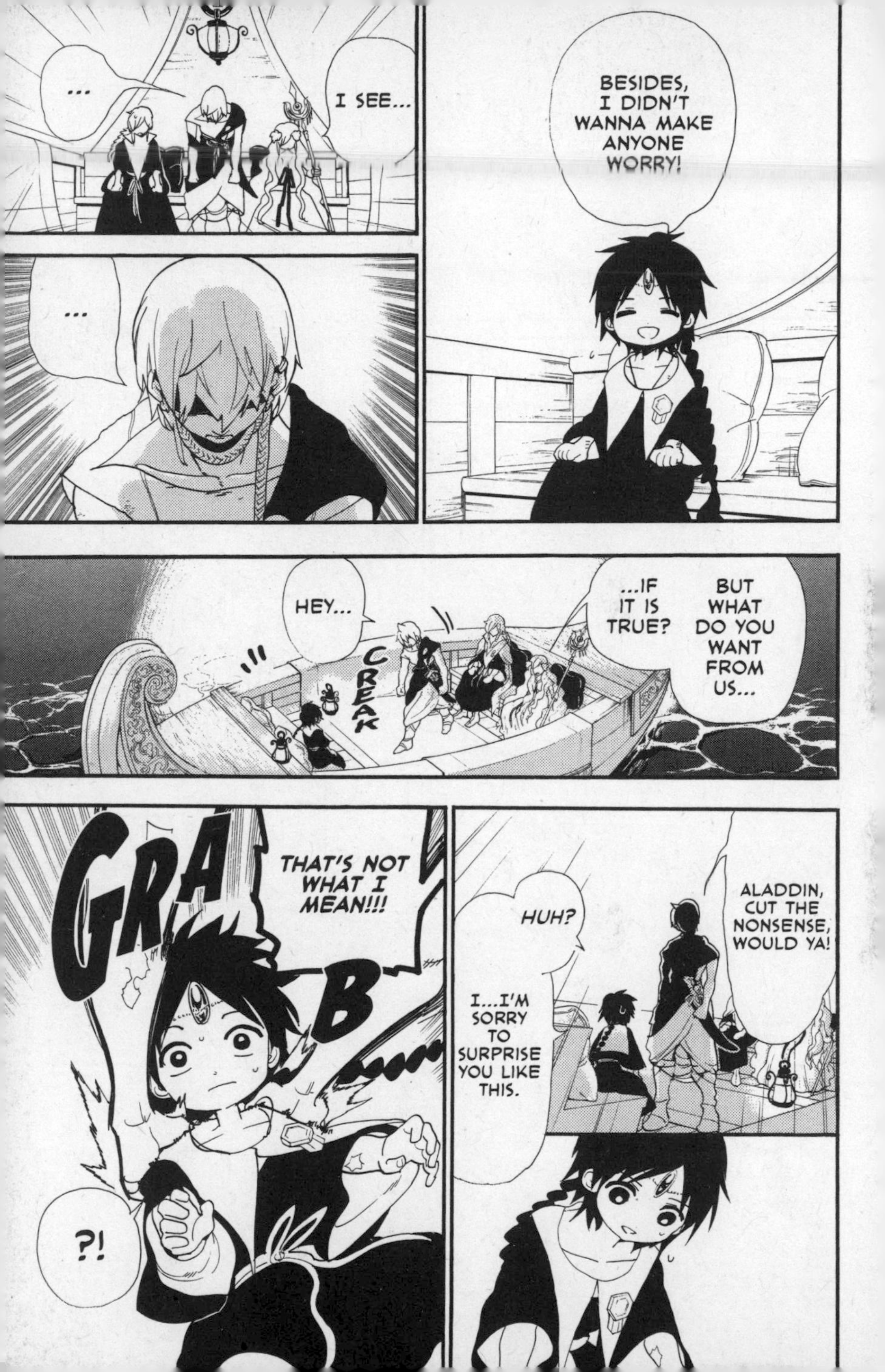
BESIDES, I DIDN'T WANNA MAKE ANYONE WORRY!
I SEE...
...
...
BUT WHAT DO YOU WANT FROM US...
...IF IT IS TRUE?
HEY...
CREAK
ALADDIN, CUT THE NONSENSE, WOULD YA!
HUH?
I...I'M SORRY TO SURPRISE YOU LIKE THIS.
GRAB
THAT'S NOT WHAT I MEAN!!!
?!

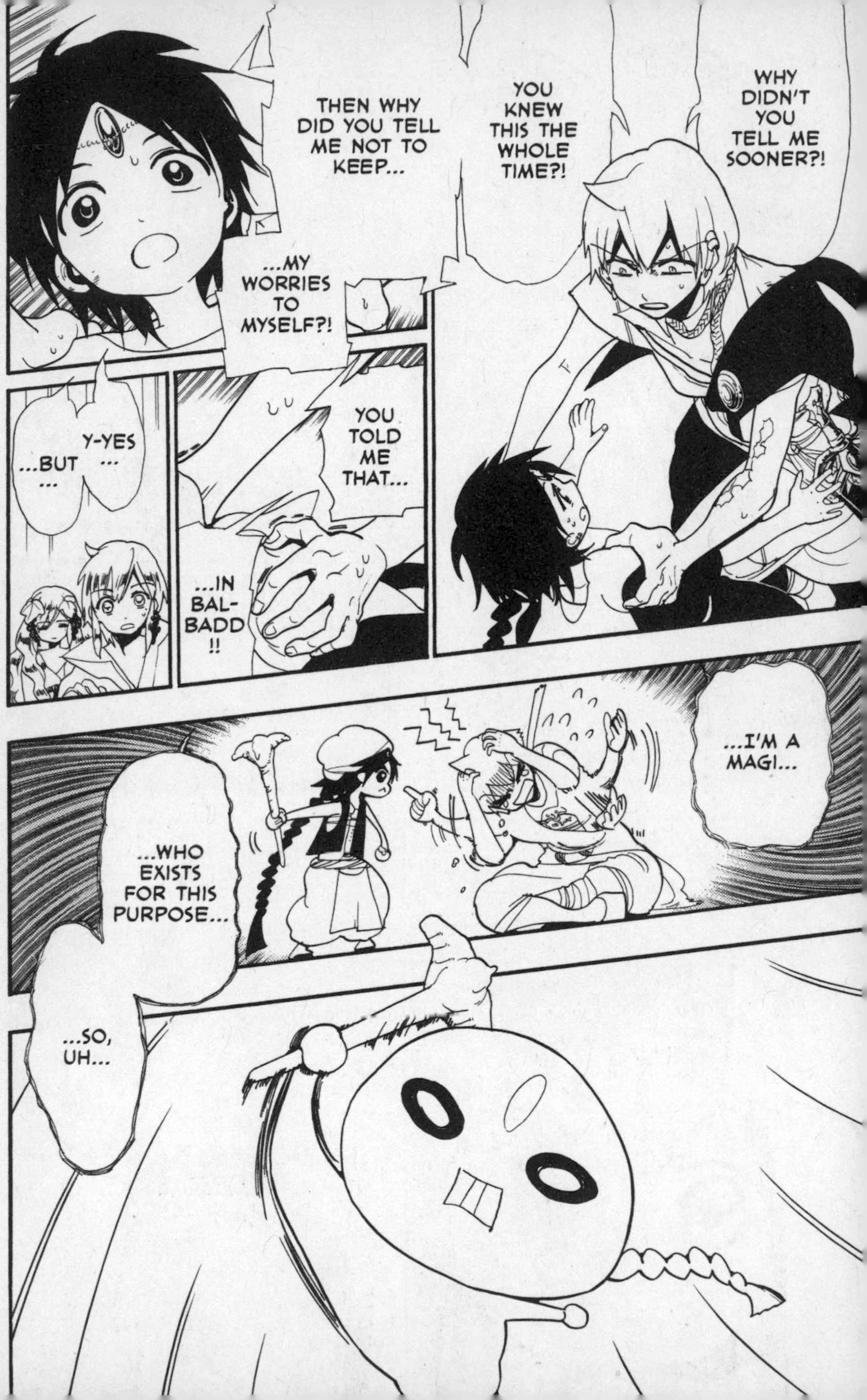
WHY DIDN'T YOU TELL ME SOONER?!
YOU KNEW THIS THE WHOLE TIME?!
THEN WHY DID YOU TELL ME NOT TO KEEP...
...MY WORRIES TO MYSELF?!
YOU TOLD ME THAT...
...IN BAL-BADD!!
Y-YES...
...BUT...
...I'M A MAGI...
...WHO EXISTS FOR THIS PURPOSE...
...SO, UH...

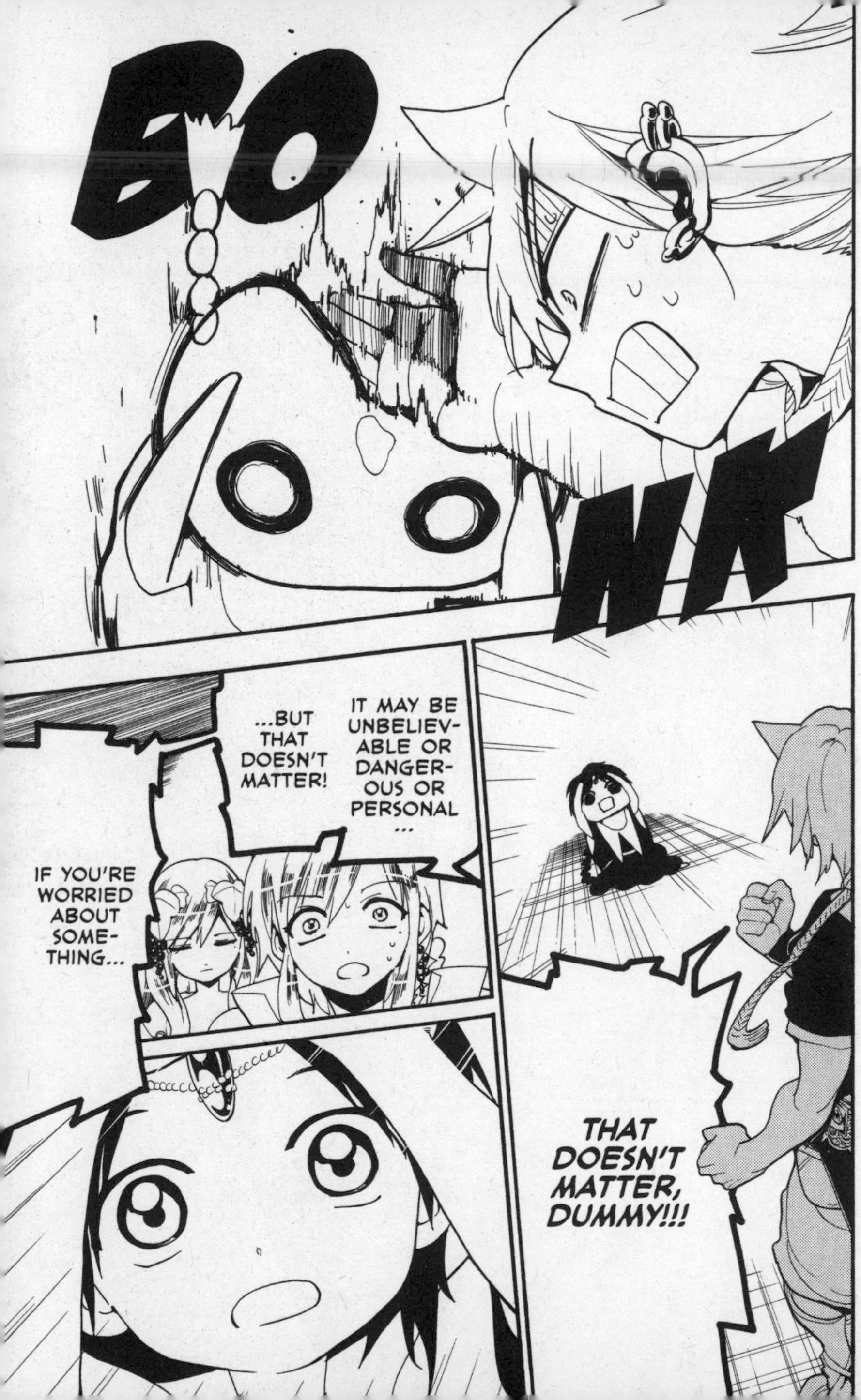
BO NK
THAT DOESN'T MATTER, DUMMY!!!
IT MAY BE UNBELIEVABLE OR DANGEROUS OR PERSONAL...
...BUT THAT DOESN'T MATTER!
IF YOU'RE WORRIED ABOUT SOMETHING...

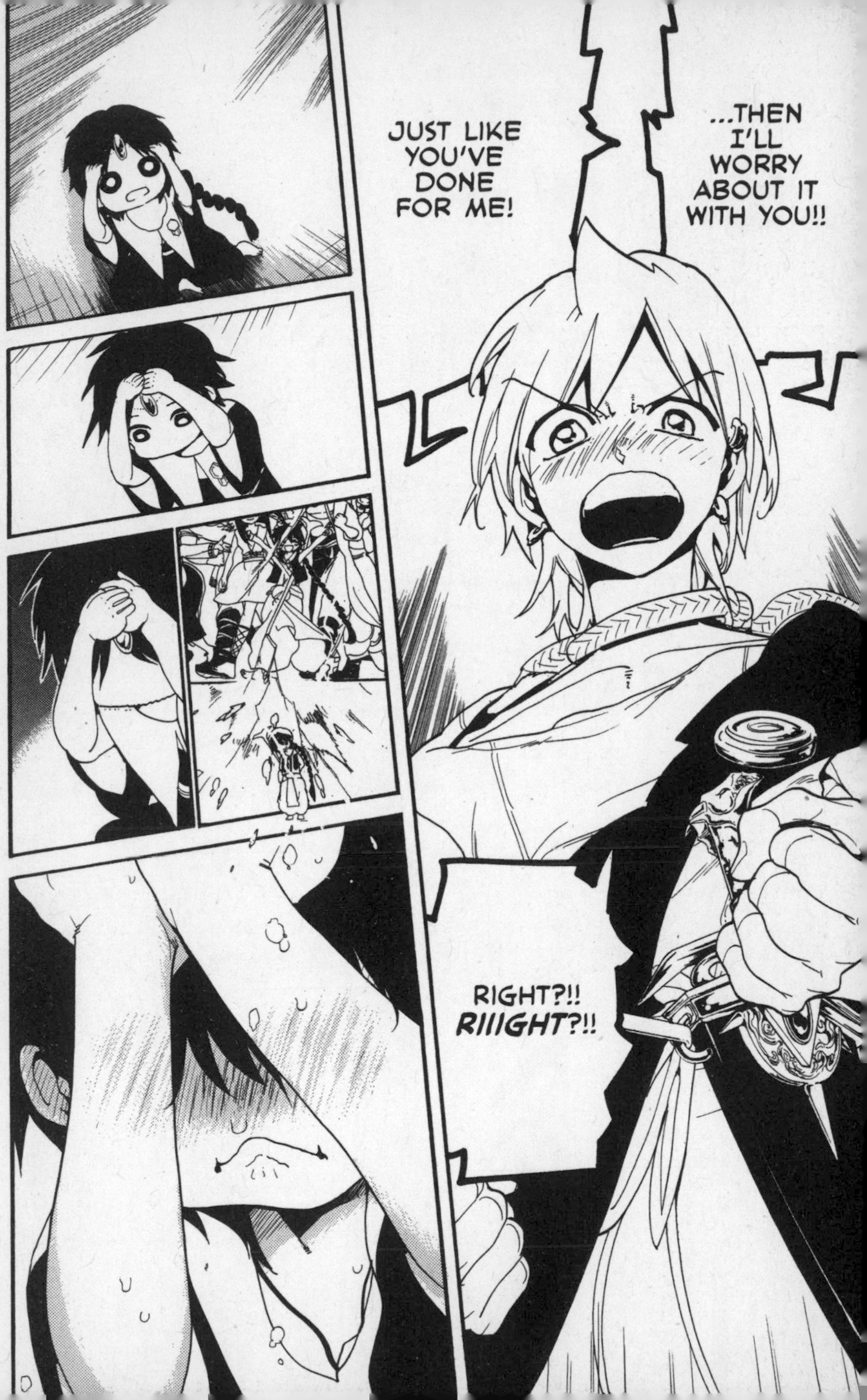
...THEN I'LL WORRY ABOUT IT WITH YOU!!
JUST LIKE YOU'VE DONE FOR ME!
RIGHT?!! *RIIIGHT?!!*

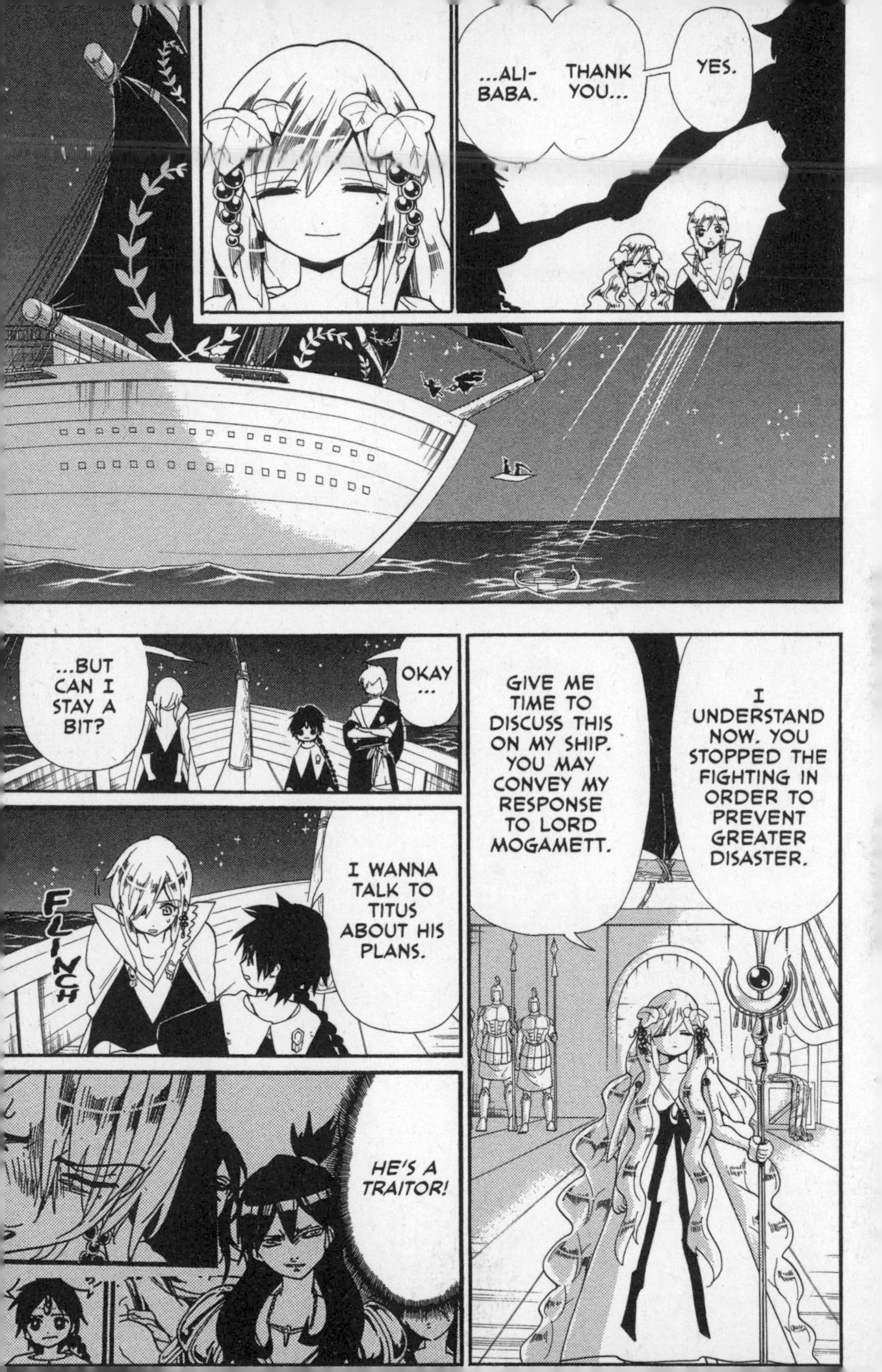

YES.
THANK YOU...
...ALI-BABA.
I UNDERSTAND NOW. YOU STOPPED THE FIGHTING IN ORDER TO PREVENT GREATER DISASTER.
GIVE ME TIME TO DISCUSS THIS ON MY SHIP. YOU MAY CONVEY MY RESPONSE TO LORD MOGAMETT.
OKAY...
...BUT CAN I STAY A BIT?
I WANNA TALK TO TITUS ABOUT HIS PLANS.
FLINCH
HE'S A TRAITOR!

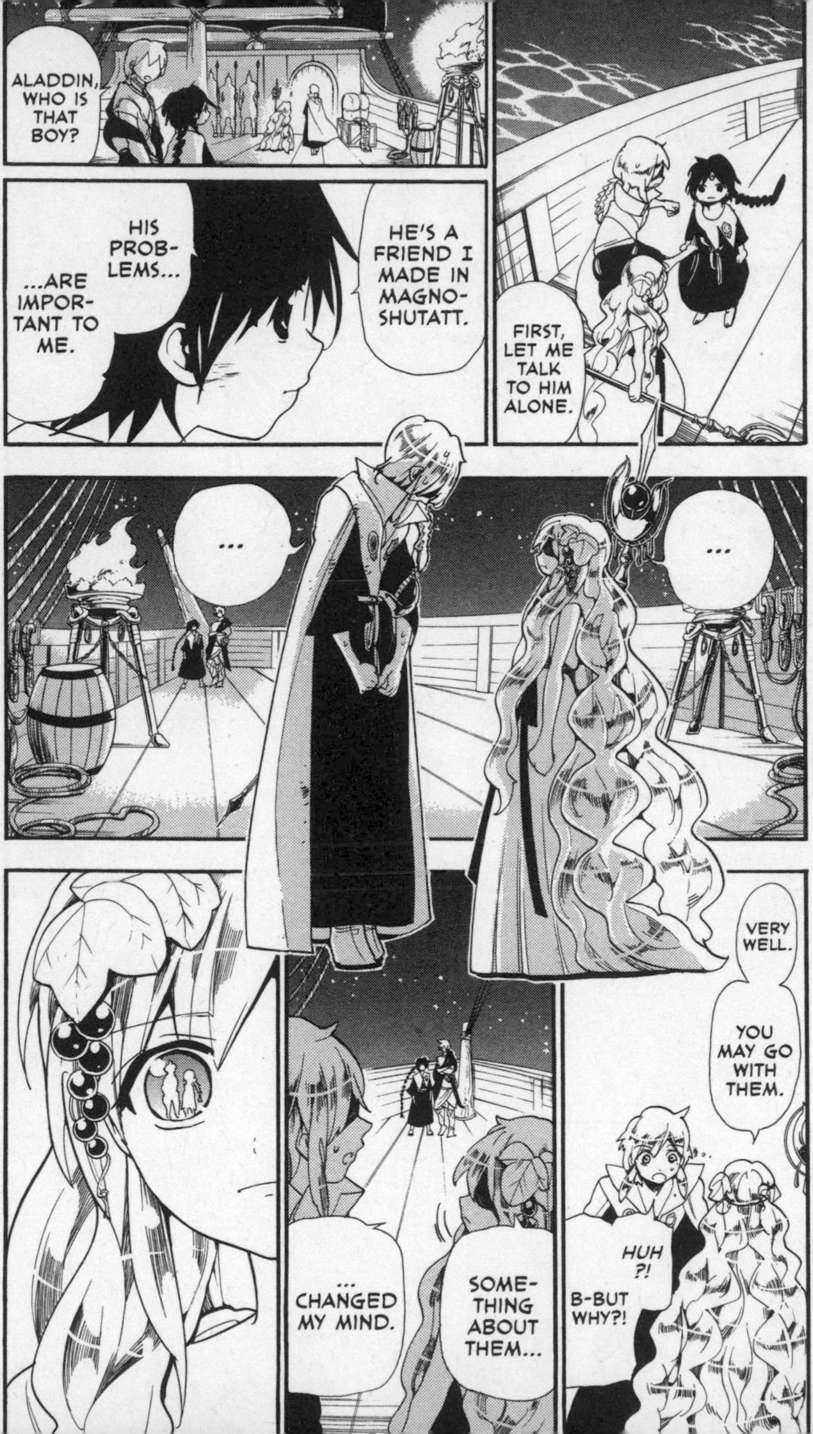
FIRST, LET ME TALK TO HIM ALONE.
ALADDIN, WHO IS THAT BOY?
HE'S A FRIEND I MADE IN MAGNO-SHUTATT.
HIS PROB-LEMS...
...ARE IMPOR-TANT TO ME.
...
...
VERY WELL.
YOU MAY GO WITH THEM.
HUH?!
B-BUT WHY?!
SOME-THING ABOUT THEM...
... CHANGED MY MIND.

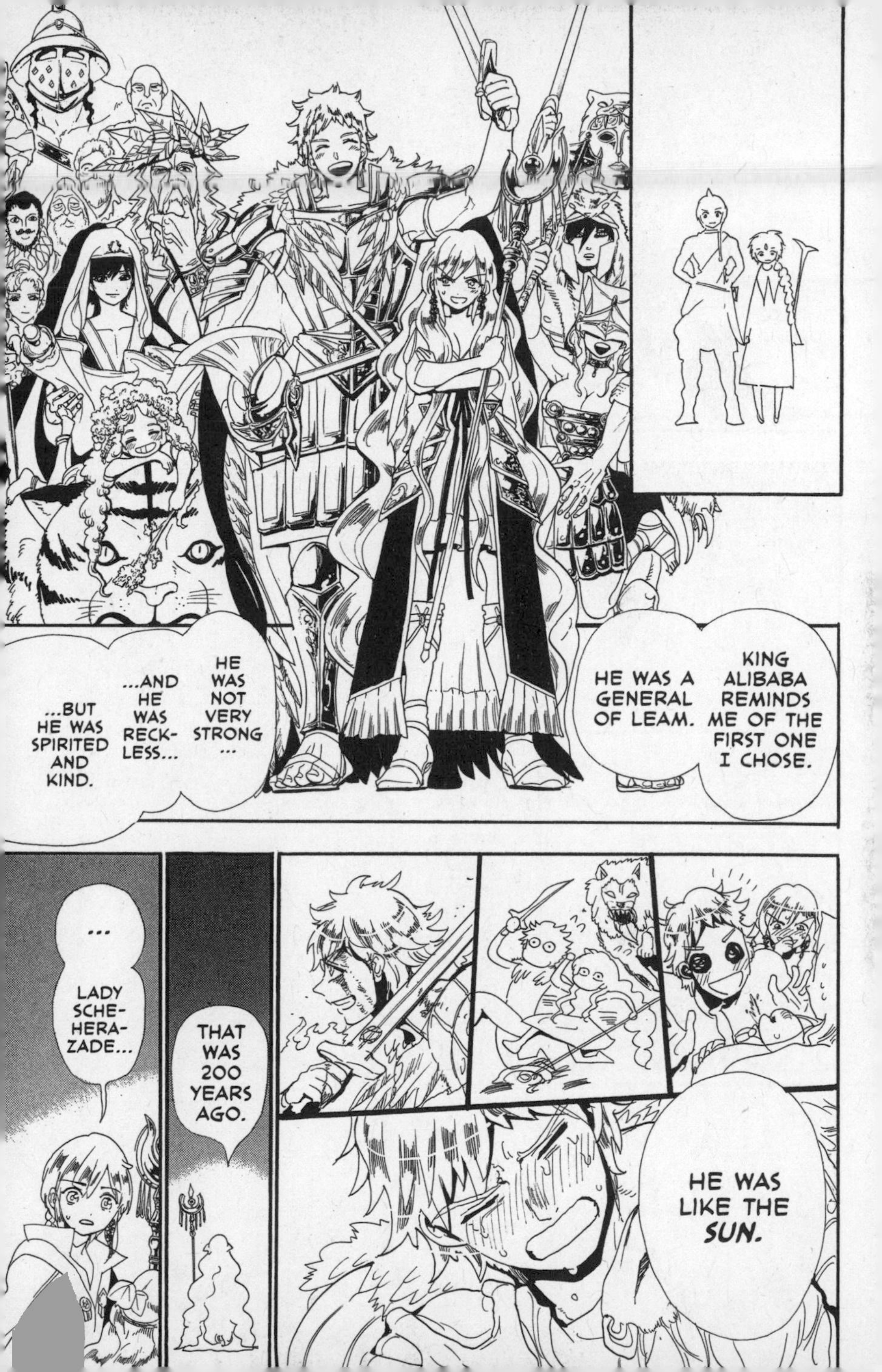
KING ALIBABA REMINDS ME OF THE FIRST ONE I CHOSE.
HE WAS A GENERAL OF LEAM.
HE WAS NOT VERY STRONG ...
...AND HE WAS RECKLESS...
...BUT HE WAS SPIRITED AND KIND.
HE WAS LIKE THE *SUN.*
THAT WAS 200 YEARS AGO.
...
LADY SCHEHERAZADE...

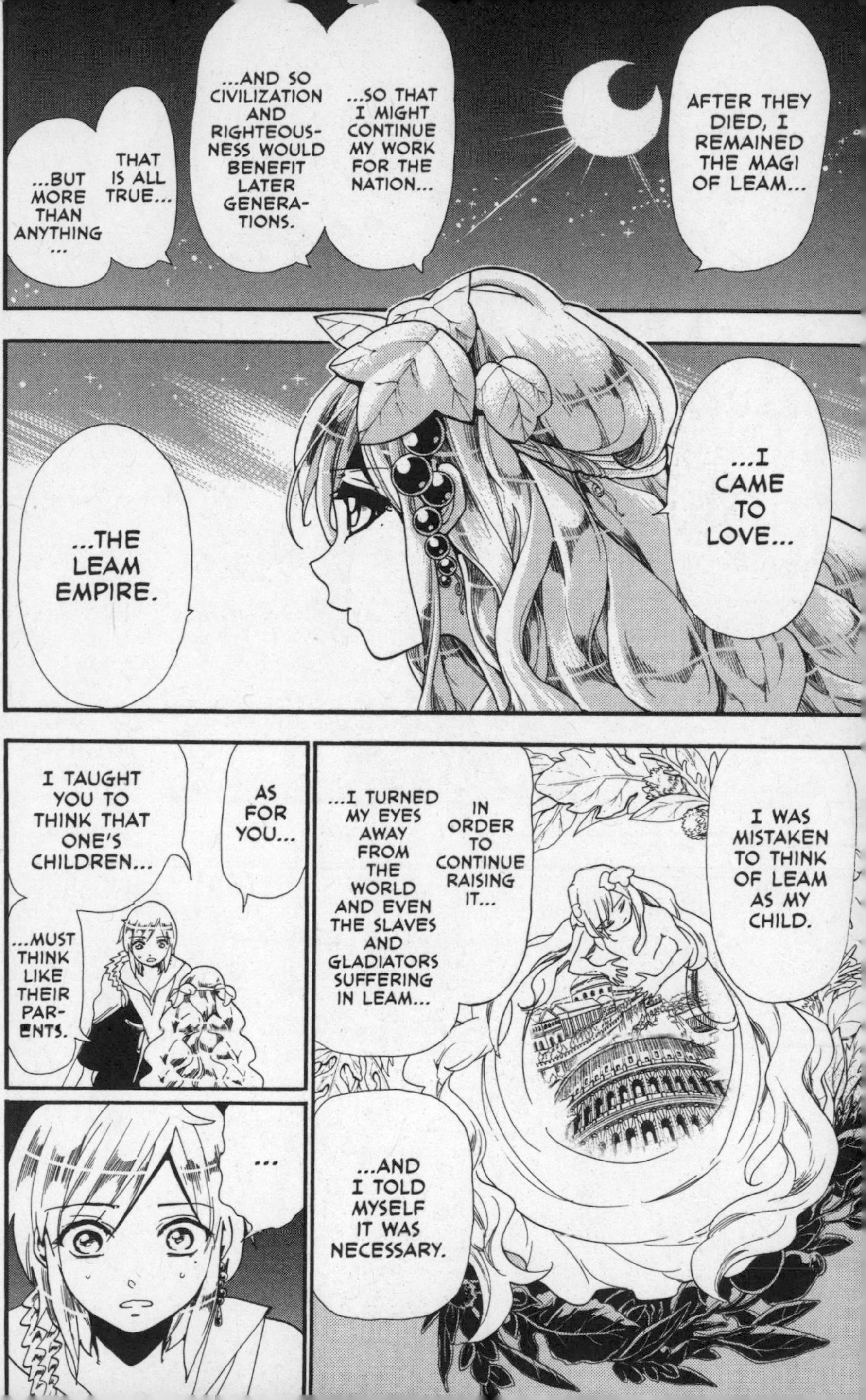
AFTER THEY DIED, I REMAINED THE MAGI OF LEAM...
...SO THAT I MIGHT CONTINUE MY WORK FOR THE NATION...
...AND SO CIVILIZATION AND RIGHTEOUSNESS WOULD BENEFIT LATER GENERATIONS.
THAT IS ALL TRUE...
...BUT MORE THAN ANYTHING...
...I CAME TO LOVE...
...THE LEAM EMPIRE.
I WAS MISTAKEN TO THINK OF LEAM AS MY CHILD.
IN ORDER TO CONTINUE RAISING IT...
...I TURNED MY EYES AWAY FROM THE WORLD AND EVEN THE SLAVES AND GLADIATORS SUFFERING IN LEAM...
...AND I TOLD MYSELF IT WAS NECESSARY.
AS FOR YOU...
I TAUGHT YOU TO THINK THAT ONE'S CHILDREN...
...MUST THINK LIKE THEIR PARENTS.
...

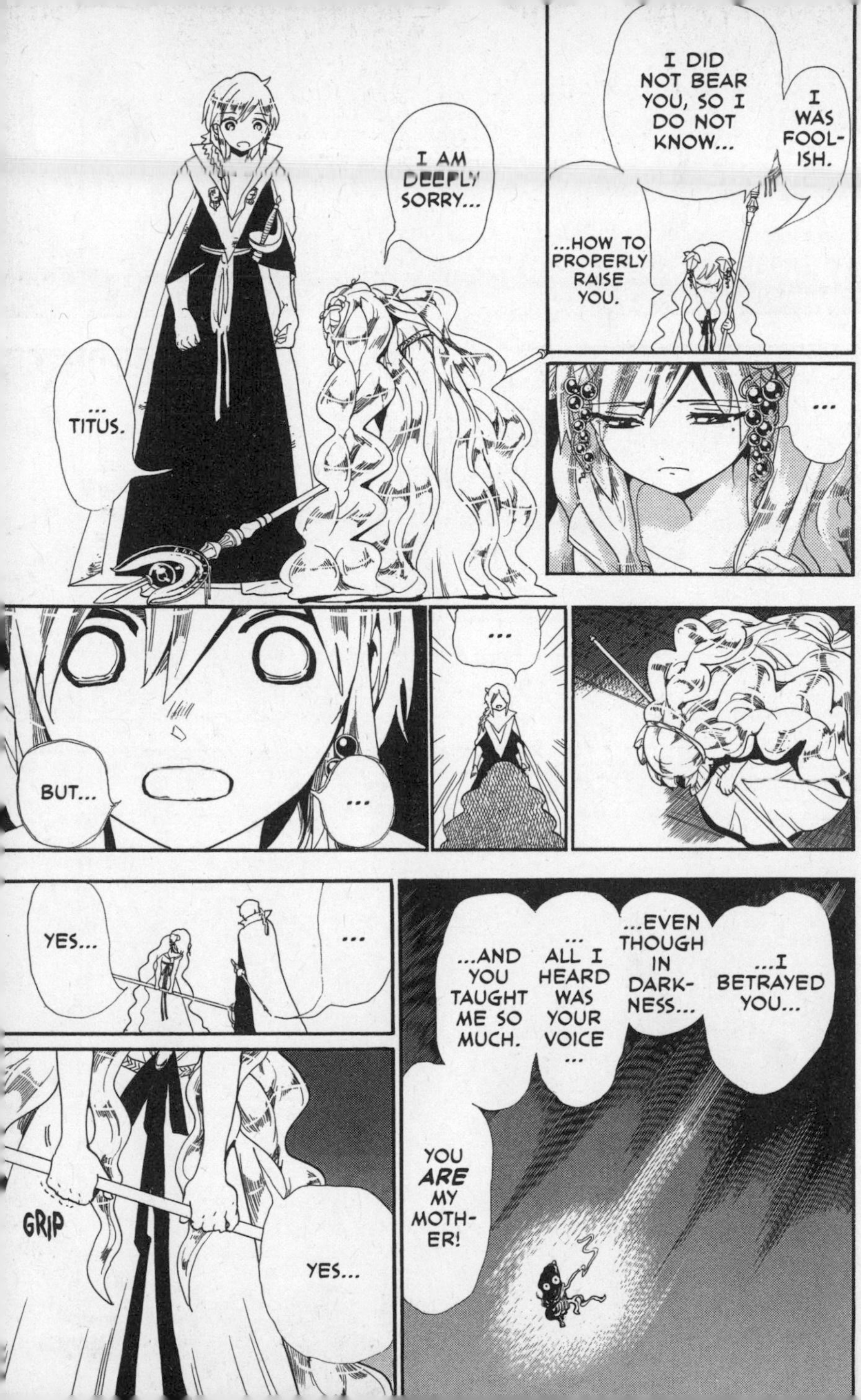
I WAS FOOL-ISH.
I DID NOT BEAR YOU, SO I DO NOT KNOW...
...HOW TO PROPERLY RAISE YOU.
...
I AM DEEPLY SORRY...
... TITUS.
...
...
BUT...
...I BETRAYED YOU...
...EVEN THOUGH IN DARK-NESS...
... ALL I HEARD WAS YOUR VOICE ...
...AND YOU TAUGHT ME SO MUCH.
YOU *ARE* MY MOTH-ER!
...
YES...
YES...
GRIP

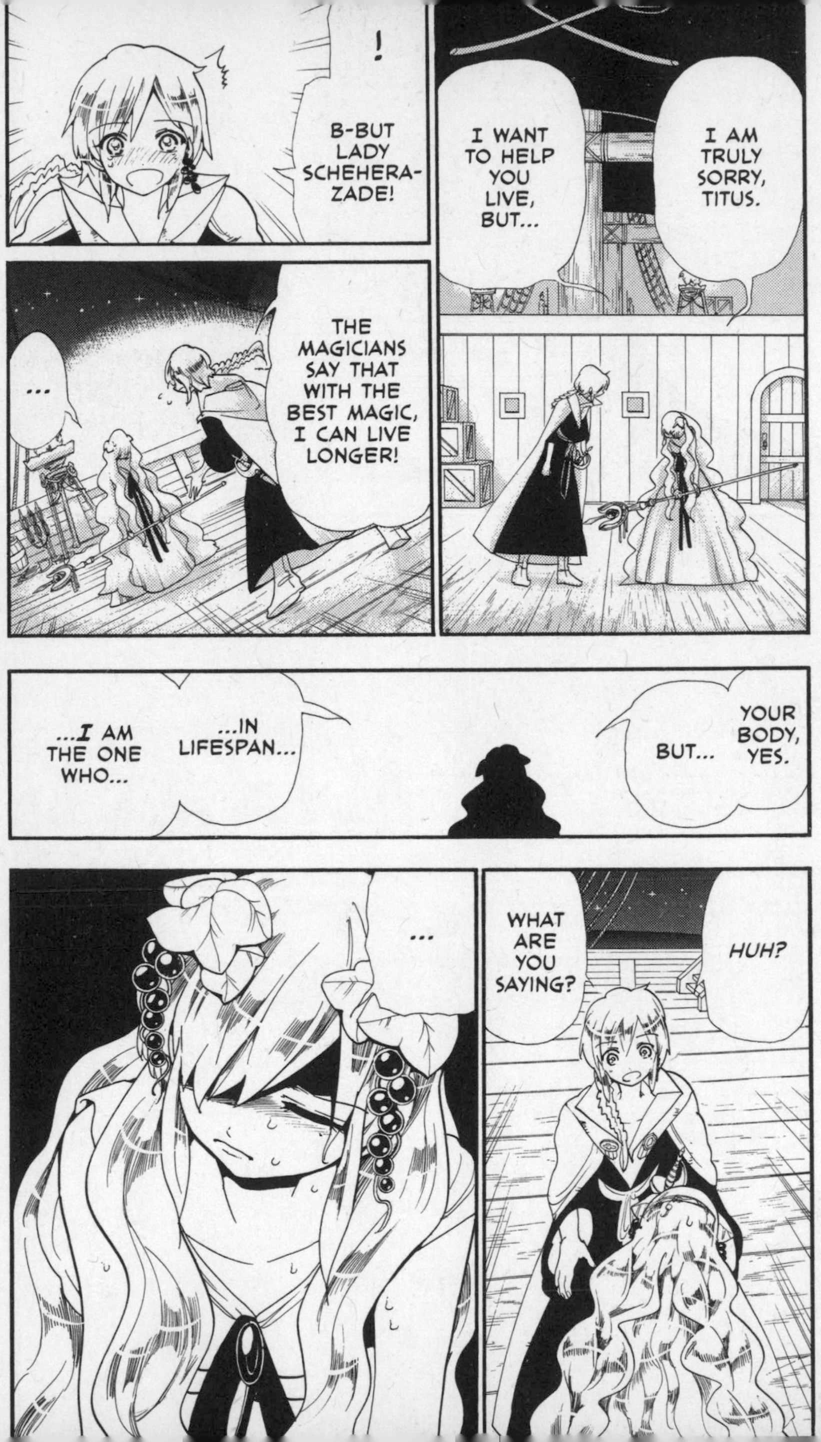
I AM TRULY SORRY, TITUS.
I WANT TO HELP YOU LIVE, BUT...
!
B-BUT LADY SCHEHERAZADE!
THE MAGICIANS SAY THAT WITH THE BEST MAGIC, I CAN LIVE LONGER!
...
YOUR BODY, YES.
BUT...
...IN LIFESPAN...
...*I* AM THE ONE WHO...
HUH?
WHAT ARE YOU SAYING?
...

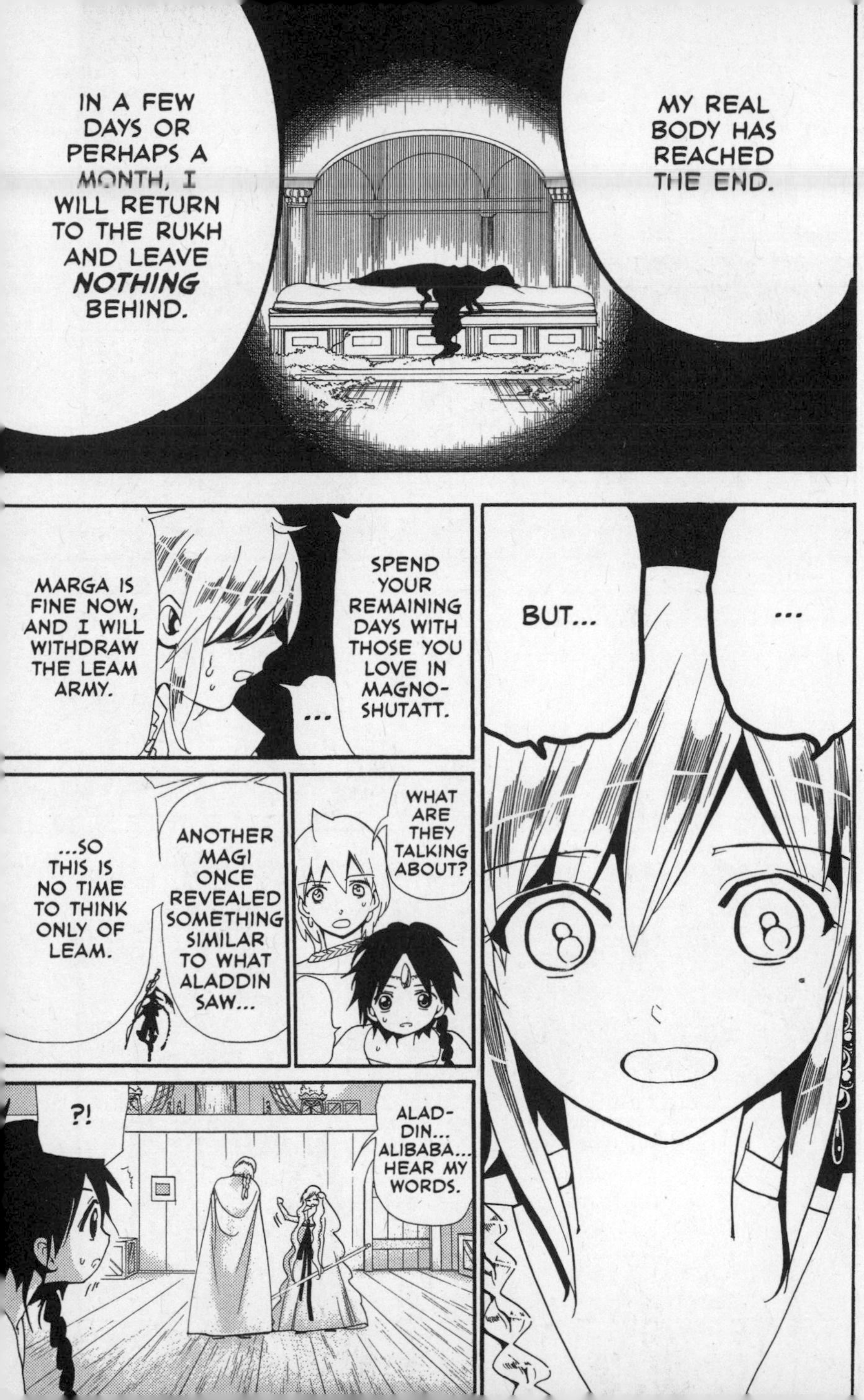
MY REAL BODY HAS REACHED THE END.
IN A FEW DAYS OR PERHAPS A MONTH, I WILL RETURN TO THE RUKH AND LEAVE *NOTHING* BEHIND.
...
BUT...
SPEND YOUR REMAINING DAYS WITH THOSE YOU LOVE IN MAGNO-SHUTATT.
...
MARGA IS FINE NOW, AND I WILL WITHDRAW THE LEAM ARMY.
WHAT ARE THEY TALKING ABOUT?
ANOTHER MAGI ONCE REVEALED SOMETHING SIMILAR TO WHAT ALADDIN SAW...
...SO THIS IS NO TIME TO THINK ONLY OF LEAM.
ALAD-DIN... ALIBABA... HEAR MY WORDS.
?!

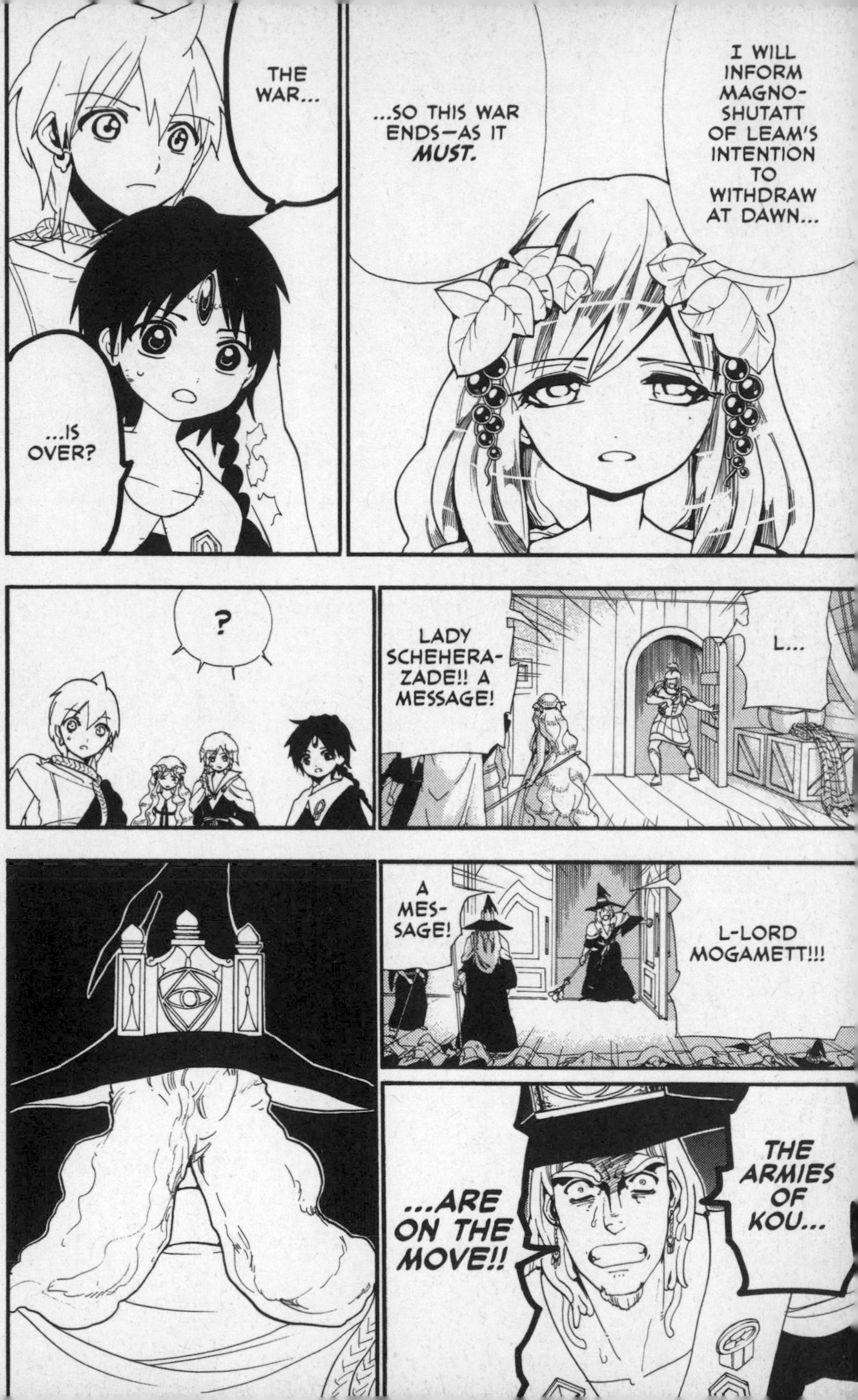
I WILL INFORM MAGNO-SHUTATT OF LEAM'S INTENTION TO WITHDRAW AT DAWN...
...SO THIS WAR ENDS—AS IT MUST.
THE WAR...
...IS OVER?
L...
LADY SCHEHERA-ZADE!! A MESSAGE!
?
L-LORD MOGAMETT!!!
A MES-SAGE!
THE ARMIES OF KOU...
...ARE ON THE MOVE!!

MAGI
The labyrinth of magic
18

Staff

Story & Art

Shinobu Ohtaka

Regular Assistants

Hiro Maizima

Yurika Isozaki

Tomo Niiya

Yuiko Akiyama

Megi

Aya Umoto

Editor
Kazuaki Ishibashi

Sales & Promotion
Shinichirou Todaka

Atsushi Chiku

Designer
Yasuo Shimura + Bay Bridge Studio

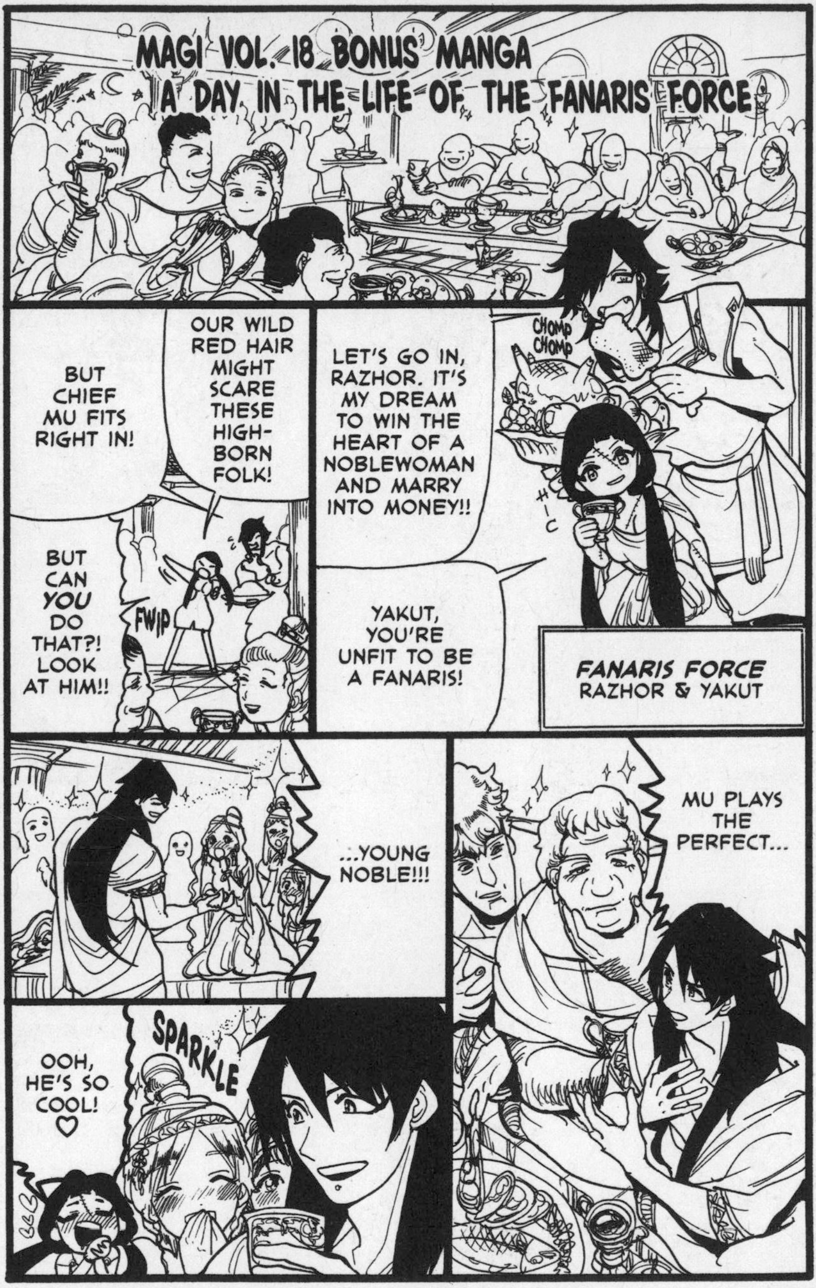
MAGI VOL. 18 BONUS MANGA
A DAY IN THE LIFE OF THE FANARIS FORCE
CHOMP CHOMP
HIC
FANARIS FORCE
RAZHOR & YAKUT
LET'S GO IN, RAZHOR. IT'S MY DREAM TO WIN THE HEART OF A NOBLEWOMAN AND MARRY INTO MONEY!!
YAKUT, YOU'RE UNFIT TO BE A FANARIS!
OUR WILD RED HAIR MIGHT SCARE THESE HIGH-BORN FOLK!
BUT CHIEF MU FITS RIGHT IN!
FWIP
BUT CAN *YOU* DO THAT?! LOOK AT HIM!!
MU PLAYS THE PERFECT...
...YOUNG NOBLE!!!
SPARKLE
OOH, HE'S SO COOL! ♡

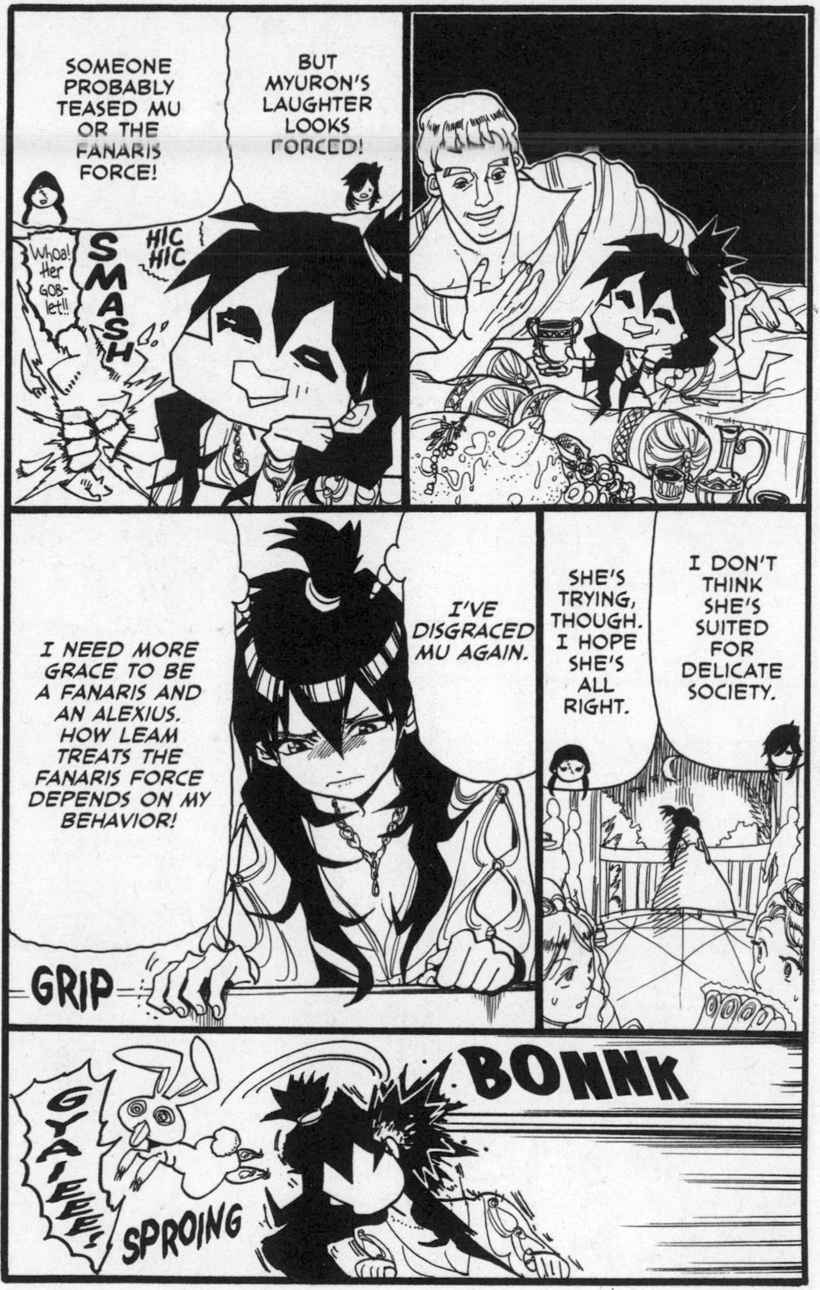
BUT MYURON'S LAUGHTER LOOKS FORCED!
SOMEONE PROBABLY TEASED MU OR THE FANARIS FORCE!
HIC HIC
SMASH
Whoa! Her GOB-let!!
I DON'T THINK SHE'S SUITED FOR DELICATE SOCIETY.
SHE'S TRYING, THOUGH. I HOPE SHE'S ALL RIGHT.
I'VE DISGRACED MU AGAIN.
I NEED MORE GRACE TO BE A FANARIS AND AN ALEXIUS. HOW LEAM TREATS THE FANARIS FORCE DEPENDS ON MY BEHAVIOR!
GRIP
BONNK
GYAIEEE!
SPROING

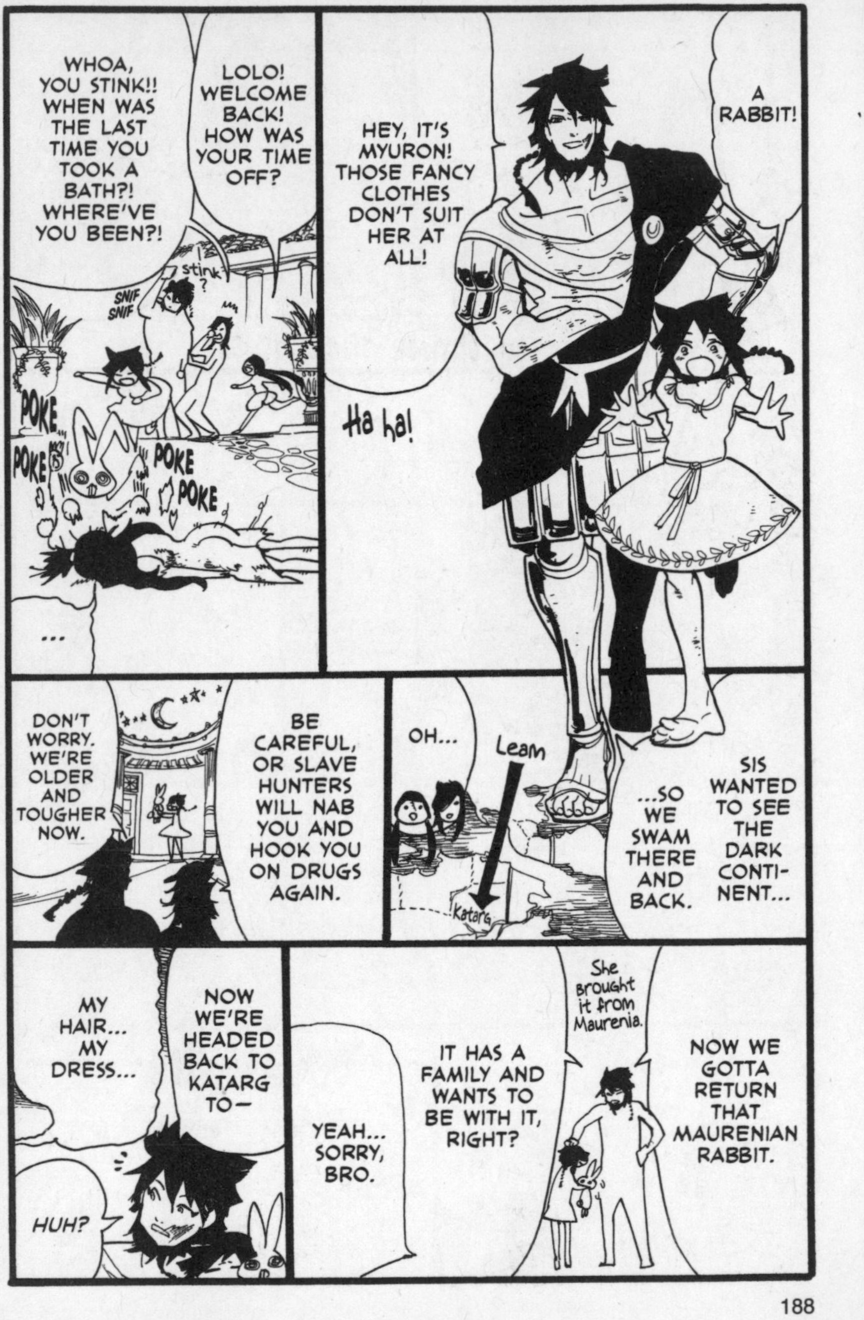
A RABBIT!
HEY, IT'S MYURON! THOSE FANCY CLOTHES DON'T SUIT HER AT ALL!
Ha ha!
LOLO! WELCOME BACK! HOW WAS YOUR TIME OFF?
WHOA, YOU STINK!! WHEN WAS THE LAST TIME YOU TOOK A BATH?! WHERE'VE YOU BEEN?!
stink?
SNIF SNIF
POKE POKE
POKE POKE
...
SIS WANTED TO SEE THE DARK CONTI-NENT...
...SO WE SWAM THERE AND BACK.
OH...
Leam
Katarg
BE CAREFUL, OR SLAVE HUNTERS WILL NAB YOU AND HOOK YOU ON DRUGS AGAIN.
DON'T WORRY. WE'RE OLDER AND TOUGHER NOW.
NOW WE GOTTA RETURN THAT MAURENIAN RABBIT.
She brought it from Maurenia.
IT HAS A FAMILY AND WANTS TO BE WITH IT, RIGHT?
YEAH... SORRY, BRO.
NOW WE'RE HEADED BACK TO KATARG TO—
MY HAIR... MY DRESS...
HUH?

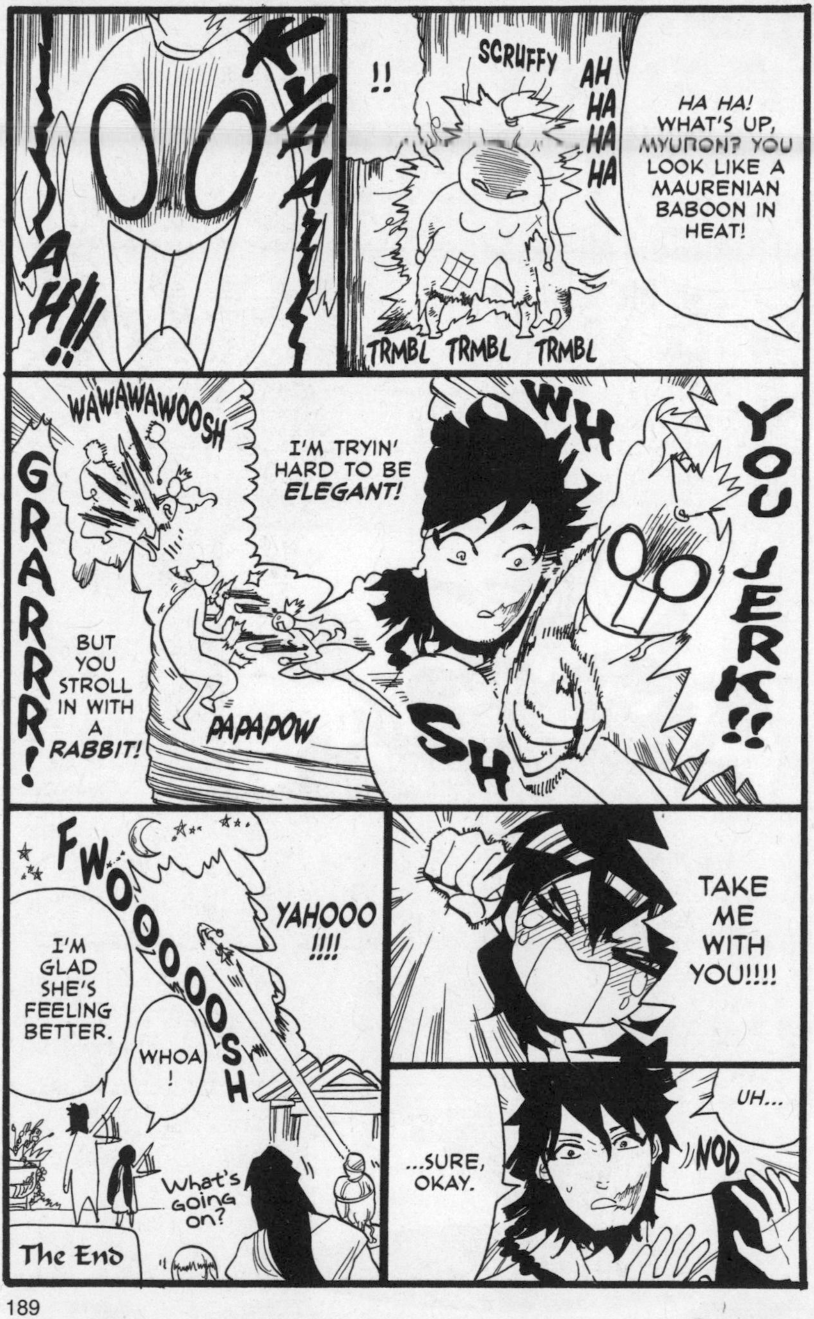
HA HA! WHAT'S UP, MYURON? YOU LOOK LIKE A MAURENIAN BABOON IN HEAT!
AH HA HA HA HA
SCRUFFY
!!
TRMBL TRMBL TRMBL
KYAAA
AH!!
YOU JERK!!
WH SH
I'M TRYIN' HARD TO BE ELEGANT!
BUT YOU STROLL IN WITH A RABBIT!
GRARRRR!
WAWAWAWOOSH
PAPAPOW
TAKE ME WITH YOU!!!!
UH...
NOD
...SURE, OKAY.
FWOOOOOOOSH
YAHOOO!!!!
I'M GLAD SHE'S FEELING BETTER.
WHOA!
What's going on?
The End

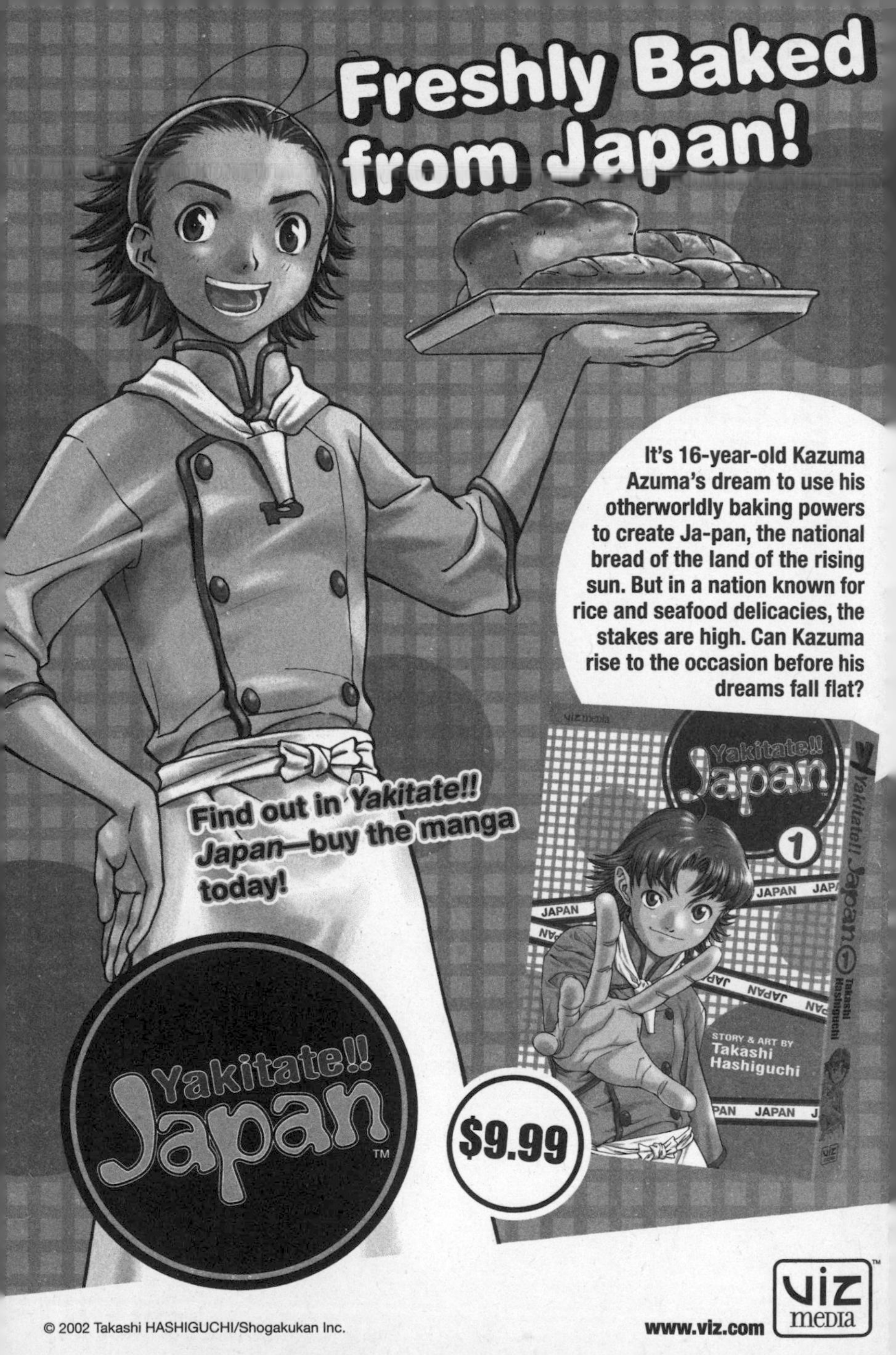
Freshly Baked from Japan!
It's 16-year-old Kazuma Azuma's dream to use his otherworldly baking powers to create Ja-pan, the national bread of the land of the rising sun. But in a nation known for rice and seafood delicacies, the stakes are high. Can Kazuma rise to the occasion before his dreams fall flat?
Find out in Yakitate!! Japan—buy the manga today!
Yakitate!! Japan™
$9.99
Yakitate!! Japan 1
STORY & ART BY Takashi Hashiguchi

You're reading the
WRONG WAY

MAGI reads from right to left, starting in the upper-right corner. Japanese is read from **right** to **left**, meaning that action, sound effects, and word-balloon order are completely reversed from English order.

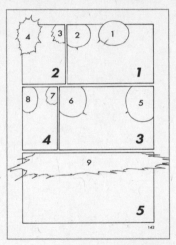